P9-DDP-468

The Reader's Digest Good Health Cookbooks

VEGETABLES AND DESSERTS

The Reader's Digest Good Health Cookbooks

VEGETABLES AND DESSERTS

THE READER'S DIGEST ASSOCIATION INC., PLEASANTVILLE, NEW YORK • MONTREAL

The Reader's Digest Good Health Cookbooks—VEGETABLES AND DESSERTS

The acknowledgements that appear on page 192 are hereby made a part of this copyright page.

Material in this book has previously appeared in *Creative Cooking* © 1977 The Reader's Digest Association, Inc. and *The Cookery Year* © 1973 The Reader's Digest Association Ltd.

First Edition 1986
Reprinted 1990

Library of Congress Catalog Card Number 85-62573

ISBN 0-89577-226-4

Printed in Scotland

Contents

How to use

The Good Health Cookbooks

Dieting need not be dreary. Whatever diet you may follow, you can still enjoy the classic dishes. Often, all you need are alternative ingredients that suit the recipe and suit the requirements of your diet. This book gives you the recipes for those classic dishes from *Creative Cooking*. It also gives you those vital alternatives. It has, in fact, several features unique in cookery books. In the special "Alternatives" column on each page, we identify how high each recipe is in salt, sugar, fat, cholesterol and fiber. We also give the calorie count. We check if it is gluten-free and wholefood. Then we suggest how you could adapt the recipe to any diet you, your family, or your guests might want to follow.

We do not lay down what diet you should follow. That is your decision. The book assumes that you yourself know what you want to do and tries to help you to do it by making suggestions (not commands), some or all of which you may want to follow. Perhaps you have been told to cut down drastically on salt; perhaps you have been thinking for some time that you should eat a little less sugar; perhaps you have a friend coming to a meal who cannot eat gluten or who is avoiding food high in cholesterol. You do not have to buy a new cookbook for each diet. You do not have to produce alternative meals for every guest. With these books, you can simply adapt the existing recipes to suit your needs.

You will find that we make use of a few conventions. This is mainly in order to avoid constant repetition. **The asterisk** (*) is used as follows:

1) Salt* indicates that this item may be omitted for those on a low-salt diet; the salt level of the recipe as given in the "Alternatives" column is calculated on the assumption that this salt has been omitted and that any ingredients that sometimes contain salt and sometimes don't (e.g. canned tomatoes) have been bought in their salt-free version.

2) Gluten-free* indicates that the recipe is free of gluten so long as gluten-free flour (or bread or breadcrumbs) is used where appropriate.

3) Wholefood* indicates that the recipe is wholefood if whole wheat flour (or bread or bread crumbs), brown rice and unrefined sugar are used where appropriate.

The levels of salt, **sugar**, **fat**, **cholesterol** and **fiber** for each recipe are denoted by symbols in the "Alternatives" column:

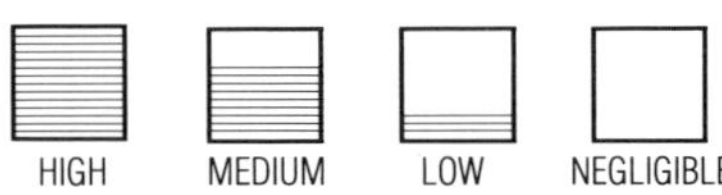

For definitions of what constitutes a high threshold level of any one of these, see under the appropriate diet on the following pages. Less than half this threshold level is considered low.

Calorie counts are given, firstly for the recipe as a whole and secondly as an indication of how many calories may be avoided as a result of following particular alternative suggestions.
Calories are automatically lost when either sugar or fat is significantly reduced. The calculations for calorie-loss can be no more than approximate, and occasionally are omitted, as so many factors can vary: the fat level of fish and meat at different times of the year, the exact amount of fat trimmed off a cut of meat, or the amount of sugar that will make a dish acceptably sweet to a particular palate.

Cooking hints on when it is appropriate or helpful to use a pressure cooker, slow cooker, food processor, freezer or microwave are indicated by a tick, together with any further information required. With a microwave it is always essential that you also consult the manufacturer's instructions, as cooking times vary from oven to oven.

With practice you should find that the technique and alternatives recommended in this book will work with recipes from other books. In this way it becomes simple to adapt recipes so that they are both healthy and delicious. That is how it ought to be.

The Diets

Low-salt diet

Sodium is acknowledged to be a contributory factor in hypertension (high blood pressure) and thus in coronary heart disease and strokes; it can also be involved in some kidney disorders.

By far the most concentrated source of sodium is common salt (sodium chloride), and many processed foods contain a lot of added salt.

Diets which are very severely restricted in sodium are on occasion prescribed, but we are not concerned with them here. A certain minimum of both sodium and chloride is essential to good health, and the majority of salt-conscious people will simply want to cut out excessive consumption.

While setting an exact figure is very difficult, as the total level of salt in a meal depends on the combination of foods eaten, a target of 5 grams a day (generally considered to be not excessive) can usually be reached by cutting down on cooking or table salt as well as on monosodium glutamate. Foods such as salted or cured pork products and most cheeses should be eaten only in small quantities. Then the sodium occurring naturally in meat and fish, even in sodium-rich shellfish, need not be avoided.

It is important to check the labels on cans. Some tomatoes, for instance, are canned with added salt, others not. Egg whites and dried fruit are also relatively high in sodium and should not be overindulged in.

Salt substitutes are available but we do not specify them: they do not taste like salt and anyone suffering from heart or kidney disease should not take them without medical approval.

Many of those wishing to cut down on salt will also want to combine this with cutting down on fat. Therefore, for example, although heavy cream contains much less sodium than light cream or milk does, we do not advocate replacing milk with heavy cream.

Salt is used to to mean both common salt (sodium chloride) and sodium in general. Where the level of salt in the recipe is given, this takes into account sodium occurring naturally in the ingredients; in the list of ingredients, salt refers, as usual, to the sodium chloride commonly used for seasoning.

The salt content of a recipe is taken to be high if it contains the equivalent of more than 2 egg whites or $1\frac{1}{4}$ cups of milk per person.

Low-sugar diet

Sugar is "empty calories:" it provides no nutrients, but concentrated calories for a very little weight of food.

Sugar is the first thing to go if you are on a calorie-controlled diet. It is also known to encourage tooth decay; and high consumption, especially of refined sugar, has been correlated with certain diseases.

Refined sugar is pure sucrose, the form of sugar which is the least desirable. Sugar occurs naturally in other forms – for example, fructose in fruit, lactose in milk, dextrose (glucose) and maltose. These do not always have the same harmful effect on the body as sucrose, and are not eaten in anything like the same sort of quantity.

A low-sugar diet, therefore, usually aims at cutting out as much refined sugar as possible. This can be done simply by using less of it and deliberately cultivating a less sweet tooth, or by replacing it to some extent with other forms of sugar. Honey, for instance (which is mainly fructose and glucose, with little sucrose) is sweeter than sugar so less of it is needed. In this way you can cut down on both sucrose and the total quantity of sugar. Molasses, although a form of sucrose, has a very strong taste and again a teaspoon of it can sometimes be used instead of a tablespoon or more of sugar.

In this book, when the level of sugar in a recipe is indicated, it takes into account both the general level of sugar, including all its various forms – sucrose, fructose, glucose etc. – as well as any added sugar specified in the recipe. In the list of ingredients, sugar refers to the added sugar which is virtually pure sucrose. The suggestions for decreasing the sugar content of a recipe almost always refer to sucrose.

We are not concerned here with sugar substitutes nor with special diabetic sweeteners and jams. We do not aim to preserve an ultra-sweet taste. What we aim to do is to cut down the amount of refined sugar and to make more use of fruit and of small quantities of honey and molasses. The results will be definitely less sweet but still delicious.

The sugar content of a recipe is taken to be high if it contains the equivalent of more than 1 tablespoon of sugar per person.

Low-fat and low-cholesterol diets

One of the most common reasons for eating less fat and cholesterol is that there appears to be an undisputed link between the presence of cholesterol in the blood and liability to heart attacks.

Populations who eat less fat have lower levels of heart disease, although their consumption of oil may be high, as in many Mediterranean countries. The exact link has not yet been established, and it appears that other foods, for example garlic, onions and polyunsaturated fat, as well as fiber, have the ability to lower blood cholesterol. However, more and more people are coming to the conclusion that cutting down on fats, especially saturated fats, cannot do them any harm. Certainly it will help calorie control: fat contains twice as many calories per ounce as protein or carbohydrate.

Whether you want to lose weight or reduce the risk of a heart attack, low-fat and low-cholesterol diets are similar in many ways. Both encourage cutting down on the saturated fats which contain cholesterol.

Saturated fats are usually of animal origin but not always: coconuts, for example, have a saturated fat content of 83%. Unsaturated fats are mainly of vegetable origin and are further divided into monounsaturated and polyunsaturated fats. (These terms refer to the way in which their molecules are chemically bonded.) They are generally liquid at room temperature.

Monounsaturated fats (the most usual example is olive oil, which is 73% monounsaturated fat) have no effect on the level of cholesterol in the blood. Polyunsaturated fats can in fact, as stated above, actually lower the blood cholesterol level. There are a few foods which are very high in cholesterol relative to their fat content, notably shellfish, fish roes, and variety meats such as liver, kidney, brains and sweetbreads.

Those on a low-fat diet will want to cut down on all fats and oils. Those aiming at a low-cholesterol intake will want to eliminate as far as possible all saturated fats and will be cautious about shellfish and variety meats. This book shows you how to do either or both of these.

However the book does not purport to give a diet which actually lowers blood cholesterol. For instance, in the recipes olive oil is often specified. Those on such a diet will replace olive oil with safflower, soy or sunflower oils. Nor does this book attempt to give a fat-free diet. Such a diet should only be attempted under medical supervision, and even then it is bound to have a minimal fat content. Some fat is necessary in our diet, particularly linoleic acid, an essential fatty acid, which cannot be manufactured by the body: it is found in oils, particularly safflower oil.

Some particular foods that will be found useful in both low-fat and low-cholesterol diets are:

- skim milk, both liquid and dried
- low-fat cheese, particularly cottage cheese and low-fat curd cheese, such as quark or fromage blanc
- low-fat imitation sour cream (5–10% fat as opposed to 18% in dairy sour cream)

For low-cholesterol diets:

- safflower, soy, sunflower and walnut oils
- (for frying over high heat): corn or peanut oils. It is, however, better to avoid frying over high heat as far as possible, since this changes the composition of the oils into something resembling saturated fat
- soft margarines with a high percentage of polyunsaturated oils (all margarines labeled "all vegetable" are virtually cholesterol-free)

The fat and cholesterol content of eggs is found only in the yolks, but in many cases yolks can be decreased or omitted, sometimes with a proportionate increase in the number of whites used.

The fat content of a recipe is taken to be high if it contains the equivalent of more than any 2 of the following per person:

1 tablespoon heavy cream or oil
½ tablespoon butter, lard, suet or margarine
1 egg yolk
½ ounce ham, bacon, pork or cheese

The above applies also to the cholesterol content of a recipe, except that unsaturated oils are freely allowed, and over ½ an egg yolk is considered to be high.

Fiber

The importance of fiber in the diet is now widely recognized, and many people pursue a high-fiber diet.

Since one of the best and easiest ways of increasing fiber intake is to eat a slice or two of whole wheat bread with your meal, the recipes themselves have not (except in one or two cases) been modified to include more fiber. The original versions of the recipes are already based on fresh ingredients, including vegetables, fruit and nuts (most of which are high in fiber), and wholefood adaptations are available for almost all the recipes, thus helping to increase the fiber level.

Gluten-free diet

As celiac sufferers are being identified more and more frequently, so the need for a gluten-free diet for them and for other gluten-sensitive patients is becoming widely recognized.

A gluten-free diet involves complete exclusion of gluten (a protein, found mainly in wheat but also, in a different form and to a lesser extent, in rye, barley and oats). Commercial gluten-free flour is available and can be used successfully for bread, and some pastry and cakes; if it is difficult to find or expensive to buy just for one recipe, there are other flours, many of which are familiar to those on wholefood diets, which are gluten-free. Chick pea flour, brown rice flour, cornstarch, potato starch and soy flour are perhaps the best known.

All labels on cans and jars must be carefully read, as wheat flour is a common ingredient not just in the obvious breads, cookies, cakes, pastries and many cereals, but in packet soups, baking powder, sausages, bouillon cubes, bottled sauces and baked beans as well as in some brands of mustard, ground white pepper, curry powder and cheap chocolate.

Gluten-free grains include rice, maize, millet and buckwheat. Cornstarch, chick pea flour and split pea flour are all suitable for making white sauces. For soufflés, cornstarch and potato starch (the latter is denser than wheat flour and half the amount given in the recipe is usually enough) can be used. Any of these will do for coating food which is to be fried. Millet flakes make a good gluten-free alternative to a breadcrumb coating.

As a gluten-free diet is often low in fiber, it is advisable to eat plenty of brown rice, other whole grains and potatoes. Pectin (available dried from specialist suppliers) can be used as a binding agent in doughs and batters; grated fresh apple can also sometimes be used.

Intolerance of gluten is often associated with an inability to digest fats, so that a low-fat diet may also need to be followed.

Wholefood diet

Since the recipes in this book are based firmly on fresh seasonal produce, they need little alteration to be acceptable to lovers of wholefood.

The main items to avoid are refined flour and sugar. Whole wheat flour and bread, and brown rice or sugar, can be used instead as desired. When buying brown sugar, look for the name of the country of origin on the packet. If this is not given, the sugar may be white sugar that has been colored brown with caramel.

In the case of sugar, it may also be necessary to follow any suggestion given for reducing the total, as a high level of even the comparatively unrefined brown sugar is not usually considered wholefood. Anything other than this will be covered in the Alternatives column. Where quantities or proportions are affected, as for instance in baking, this will also be covered.

Vegetarian diet

Many of the recipes in the section on Vegetables, Rice and Pasta in this book are suitable as they stand for vegetarians. It has been thought worthwhile to suggest adaptations for the remaining recipes in this section so that they too can be cooked for vegetarians.

CHILLED CARROT SOUP

It is well worth trying this soup of Mexican origin. It can be served hot, but the subtle flavor is more pronounced if the soup is chilled.

PREPARATION TIME: *20 min*
COOKING TIME: *45 min*
CHILLING TIME: *1 hour*
INGREDIENTS *(for 6):*
1¼ pounds carrots
1 onion
3–4 cloves garlic
1 potato
2 tablespoons butter
5 cups beef stock
Salt and black pepper*
GARNISH:
Finely chopped parsley

Peel and thinly slice the onion; peel and crush the garlic. Melt the butter in a heavy-based pan, and cook the onion and garlic gently over low heat. Keep the pan covered with a lid until the onion is soft and transparent but not colored. Meanwhile, top, tail and scrape the carrots, and then chop them roughly; peel and chop the potato. Add these to the onion and continue cooking, covered, for about 8 minutes. Bring the beef stock to the boil and pour it over the vegetables. Bring the contents of the pan to simmering point and maintain this over lowest possible heat for about 30 minutes.

Remove the soup from the heat and allow to cool slightly before liquidizing it until smooth. Alternatively, rub the soup through a fine sieve into a bowl. Chill the soup in the refrigerator for at least 1 hour.

Serve the soup in individual bowls, sprinkled with the finely chopped parsley.

LEBANESE CUCUMBER SOUP

There are many variations of this popular Middle Eastern soup. It can only be served cold, but is refreshing in hot weather and looks tempting with a few pink shrimp floating on top.

PREPARATION TIME: *15 min*
CHILLING TIME: *about 1 hour*
INGREDIENTS *(for 4–6):*
1 large or 2 small cucumbers
1¼ cups light cream
¾ cup plain yogurt
1 clove garlic
2 tablespoons tarragon vinegar
Salt and black pepper*
2 tablespoons finely chopped mint
GARNISH:
1 tablespoon finely chopped cocktail gherkins
Sprigs of mint
18 shrimp (optional)

Wash and dry the cucumber. Do not peel it, but grate it coarsely into a bowl. Stir in the cream and the yogurt. Peel and crush the garlic, and add to the cucumber, together with the vinegar. Season to taste with salt and freshly ground pepper. Stir in the chopped mint. Chill the soup in a refrigerator for at least 1 hour.

Serve the pale green soup in individual bowls.

For a summery look, garnish each bowl with chopped gherkins or a sprig of fresh mint. On special occasions, float a few shelled shrimp on top of the soup instead of the green garnish.

CRÈME VICHYSSOISE

Despite its French name, this soup was created by the chef of a New York hotel in 1910 and has since become universally famous. It is always served chilled.

PREPARATION TIME: *30 min*
COOKING TIME: *35–40 min*
CHILLING TIME: *3 hours*
INGREDIENTS *(for 6):*
2 pounds leeks
1 pound potatoes
¼ cup butter
1 stalk celery
2½ cups chicken stock
2½ cups milk
Salt and black pepper*
Freshly grated nutmeg
1¼ cups heavy cream
GARNISH:
Grated carrot

Trim the roots and coarse outer leaves from the leeks and wash them thoroughly in cold water. Slice the leeks diagonally into ¼ in pieces. Peel and coarsely dice the potatoes. Melt the butter in a large sauté pan and add the leeks and potatoes. Cook the vegetables over moderate heat for 7 minutes, stirring continuously. Add the scrubbed and coarsely chopped celery to the pan. Pour over the stock and milk, and bring the soup to the boil. Season with salt, freshly ground pepper and nutmeg. Simmer the soup for 25 minutes or until the vegetables are tender.

Allow the soup to cool slightly before liquidizing it or rubbing it through a sieve. Correct seasoning and stir in the cream.

Chill the soup in the refrigerator for 2–3 hours. Serve in individual bowls.

CHILLED CARROT SOUP

GLUTEN-FREE WHOLEFOOD
TOTAL CALORIES: ABOUT 425

This is a very healthy soup, using potato rather than cream as a thickening agent. The **fat** can be reduced even further by using only half the amount of butter, and the **cholesterol** eliminated by using oil instead. (Calories lost: up to 93.)
For a **vegetarian** soup, replace the beef stock with vegetable stock, mixed if you like with a little milk (skim milk can be used). (Calories lost: up to 25.)

Pressure cooker: ✓
Freezing: ✓ up to 2 months.
Microwave: ✓

LEBANESE CUCUMBER SOUP

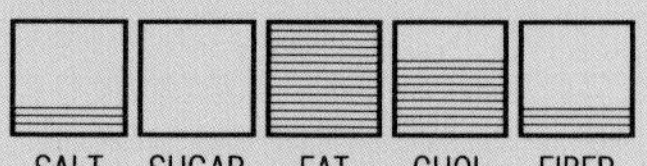

GLUTEN-FREE WHOLEFOOD
TOTAL CALORIES: ABOUT 840

To reduce the **fat** level to low, replace the cream completely with more yogurt: this would be traditional in Lebanon. For very low **cholesterol** use yogurt as above instead of cream, and omit the shrimp. (Calories lost: up to 539.)
For a **vegetarian** soup, omit the shrimp and garnish with extra mint (or coriander).

Food processor: ✓ to grate the cucumber.

CRÈME VICHYSSOISE

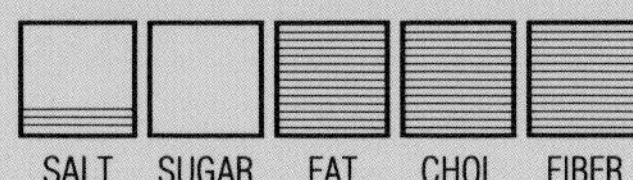

GLUTEN-FREE WHOLEFOOD
TOTAL CALORIES: ABOUT 2795

To reduce the **fat** and **cholesterol** levels to low, replace the butter with 1 tablespoon oil, the cream with half the quantity of low-fat yogurt or buttermilk, and the milk with skim milk. (Calories lost: up to 1680.)
This soup is **vegetarian** if water or vegetable stock is used instead of chicken stock.

Pressure cooker: √

Freezing: √ up to 2 months.

Microwave: √

GAZPACHO ANDALUZ

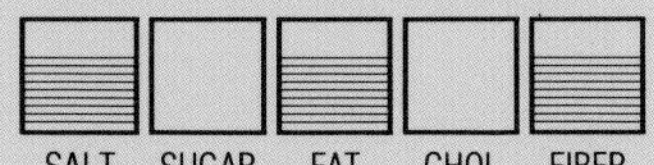

GLUTEN-FREE* WHOLEFOOD* VEGETARIAN
TOTAL CALORIES: ABOUT 2090

To reduce the **salt** content to low, look for unsalted tomato juice, and use unsalted bread. Check the canned pimientos are unsalted, or use fresh sweet peppers. Use only a few black olives, or avoid them entirely if you are aiming for a very low salt intake.
The **fat** level can be reduced to low simply by using half the amount of oil, omitting the mayonnaise and using toast instead of croûtons. (Calories lost: up to 890.)
Cooked brown rice could be used instead of **gluten-free** bread, as the soup is liquidized.

Food processor: √ to chop the tomatoes.

GAZPACHO ANDALUZ

On a hot summer day, a chilled soup is particularly welcome. This Andalusian salad soup is also decorative, served with several crisp, colorful garnishes. In Spain, ice cubes are added to each soup bowl before serving.

PREPARATION TIME: *35 min*
CHILLING TIME: *1–2 hours*
INGREDIENTS *(for 6):*
1½ pounds tomatoes
4 large, ½ in thick slices stale bread
2 large cloves garlic
4 teaspoons herb or red wine vinegar
3–4 tablespoons olive oil
2 cups tomato juice
2 canned pimientos
1 large Spanish onion
1 small cucumber
Salt and black pepper*
2 tablespoons mayonnaise (optional)
2 cups iced water
GARNISH:
1 small cucumber
2 small sweet peppers
4 large tomatoes
Bread croûtons (page 165)
Black olives
Raw onion rings, sliced hard-cooked eggs (optional)

Skin the tomatoes (page 160), remove the seeds and chop the flesh finely. Cut the crusts off the bread and crumble it into a large bowl. Peel and crush the garlic into the bowl. Stir in the vinegar and gradually add as much olive oil as the crumbs will absorb. Stir in the tomato flesh and juice and mix thoroughly. Chop the pimientos finely; peel and grate the onion and cucumber and stir all three into the tomato mixture. Season to taste with salt and freshly ground pepper. Put the mixture into a liquidizer until smooth, or rub it through a fine sieve.

The soup should be perfectly smooth – it can be made more creamy by adding mayonnaise (page 167). Dilute the soup with iced water until it has the consistency of thin cream. Adjust seasoning and put the soup in the refrigerator to chill.

The garnishes are traditionally served in separate small bowls, and the contents stirred into the soup until it is nearly solid. Peel and dice the cucumber, chop the prepared peppers and the skinned tomatoes. Fry the bread croûtons, and peel and thinly slice the onion. Small pitted black olives can also be served.

CHILLED WATERCRESS SOUP

Watercress is most often used as a garnish or in salads. It also makes a good basis for a smooth-textured chilled soup.

PREPARATION TIME: *20 min*
COOKING TIME: *45 min*
CHILLING TIME: *2 hours*
INGREDIENTS *(for 6–8):*
2 bunches watercress
¾ pound potatoes
1 onion
5 cups beef stock or bouillon
3 tablespoons butter
1 bay leaf
1 clove garlic (optional)
Salt and black pepper*
3 tablespoons heavy cream
GARNISH:
Grated nutmeg (optional)

Wash the watercress thoroughly in cold water and discard any tough stalks and yellow leaves. Peel and thickly slice the potatoes and the onion. Put the potatoes, onion, watercress, stock, butter, bay leaf and peeled garlic (if used) in a large saucepan. Season with salt and pepper.

Bring the soup to the boil, cover the pan with a lid and simmer until the potatoes and onion are quite soft. Remove the bay leaf and rub the soup through a coarse sieve. Alternatively, let the soup cool a little before liquidizing it.

Return the smooth soup to the pan, stir in the cream and heat the soup through without boiling. Pour into individual bowls and leave to cool before chilling.

Just before serving, sprinkle a little freshly grated nutmeg over the soup.

Serve with toast.

FARMHOUSE SOUP

This French vegetable soup makes a substantial meal on its own. Select vegetables according to availability and choice – the quantities in the recipe are merely a guide. Peas, green beans and watercress may be added when the soup comes to the boil.

PREPARATION TIME: *30 min*
COOKING TIME: *1 hour*
INGREDIENTS *(for 6):*
2–3 carrots
1–2 turnips
2–3 parsnips
1–2 leeks
½ small head of celery
1 large onion
2 ounces mushrooms
2 slices bacon
½ pound tomatoes
1 tablespoon butter
1 tablespoon flour
½ cup milk
4 cups white stock
Salt and black pepper*
Lemon juice
Mixed herbs
GARNISH:
1 tablespoon chopped mint or parsley
Bread croûtons (page 165)

Wash and peel the carrots, turnips and parsnips; dice them finely. Remove the roots and outer coarse leaves from the leeks, wash them thoroughly under cold running water and chop roughly. Scrub the celery and slice the sticks finely; peel and roughly chop the onion. Trim and slice the mushrooms finely. Dice the bacon. Skin and roughly chop the tomatoes (page 160).

Melt the butter in a large heavy-based pan and fry the

CHILLED WATERCRESS SOUP

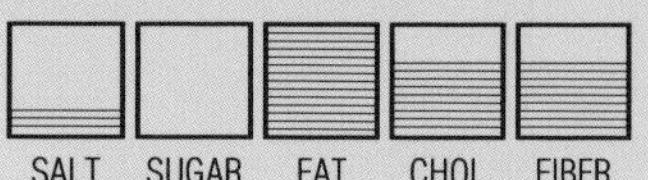

SALT SUGAR FAT CHOL FIBER

GLUTEN-FREE WHOLEFOOD
TOTAL CALORIES: ABOUT 895

To reduce **fat** and **cholesterol** levels to low, replace the butter with vegetable margarine or simply reduce it to 1½ tablespoons. Replace the cream with low-fat yogurt or cultured buttermilk. (Calories lost: up to 326.)
This soup is **vegetarian** if vegetable stock is used.

Pressure cooker: ☑
Freezing: ☑ up to 2 months.
Microwave: ☑

FARMHOUSE SOUP

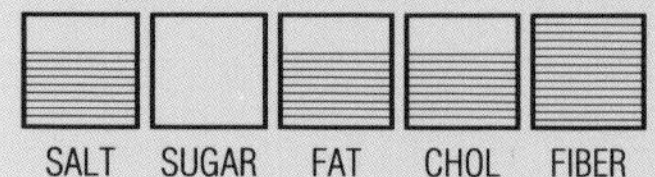

SALT SUGAR FAT CHOL FIBER

GLUTEN-FREE* WHOLEFOOD*
TOTAL CALORIES: ABOUT 1485

If the bacon is halved the level of salt will be low, assuming unsalted butter is used.
To reduce the **fat** and **cholesterol** levels to low, omit the bacon and soften the vegetables in 1 tablespoon of oil, adding a little stock and covering tightly. Use skim milk, and toast or cubes of firm tofu instead of croûtons. (Calories lost: up to 695.)
This soup is **vegetarian** if the bacon is omitted and water or vegetable stock used.

Pressure cooker: ☑
Freezing: ☑ up to 2 months.
Microwave: ☑

FRENCH TURNIP SOUP

GLUTEN-FREE* WHOLEFOOD* VEGETARIAN
TOTAL CALORIES: ABOUT 1500

To reduce the **fat** and **cholesterol** levels to low, soften the vegetables in 1 tablespoon oil, omitting the butter. To thicken the soup, instead of combining egg yolks and heavy cream, add 1–2 tablespoons split red lentils while simmering. (Calories lost: up to 715.)
Omitting the flour and adding lentils will add **fiber** as well as being automatically **gluten-free** and **wholefood**.

Pressure cooker: √ up to the stage of adding the eggs.

Microwave: √

CREAMED PEA SOUP

GLUTEN-FREE* WHOLEFOOD*
TOTAL CALORIES: ABOUT 995

To reduce the **fat** and **cholesterol** levels to low, replace the cream with quark or low-fat yogurt and the croûtons with almonds, walnuts or tofu dice. (Calories lost: up to 480.)
1 tablespoon of potato starch makes a good **gluten-free** alternative to wheat flour; replace the croûtons as above. These alterations also make the soup **wholefood**.

Freezing: √ up to 2 months.

Microwave: √

bacon, onion, celery and mushrooms over moderate heat until soft, but not browned. Add the prepared carrots, turnips, parsnips and leeks and fry them lightly. Remove the pan from the heat and stir in enough flour to absorb the remaining fat. Gradually blend in the milk. Return the pan to the heat, stir in the hot stock and bring the soup to the boil, stirring continuously. Add the tomatoes, stir well and bring the soup to simmering point.

If necessary, thin the soup with water or more milk. Season to taste with salt, freshly ground pepper, lemon juice and a pinch of mixed herbs. Cover the pan with a lid and simmer the soup over very low heat, until the root vegetables are tender, after about 45 minutes.

Serve the soup hot, garnished with mint or parsley and crisp bread croûtons. Garlic bread or a separate bowl of grated cheese would make the soup even more substantial.

Any left-over soup can be sieved or liquidized and thinned to taste with milk or tomato juice. Before serving, stir a little cream into each bowl and garnish as before.

FRENCH TURNIP SOUP

The first white turnips of the season appear in spring. The French frequently use these tasty, inexpensive root vegetables for a creamy soup.

PREPARATION TIME: *20 min*
COOKING TIME: *45 min*
INGREDIENTS *(for 6–8):*
¾ pound turnips
½ pound potatoes
1 leek
1 onion
¼ cup butter
2 tablespoons flour
2 quarts vegetable stock
Salt and black pepper*
2 large egg yolks
3 tablespoons heavy cream
GARNISH:
Bread croûtons (page 165)

Peel and dice the turnips and potatoes and rinse them in cold water. Remove the roots and coarse outer leaves from the leek, cut in half and rinse thoroughly under cold running water to remove all traces of dirt. Chop the leek coarsely. Peel and roughly chop the onion.

Melt the butter in a large pan and add the vegetables; cover the pan with a lid and cook the vegetables over low heat for about 10 minutes, without browning them. Add the flour and cook for a few minutes, stirring continuously. Gradually blend in the stock and season to taste with salt and freshly ground pepper. Simmer the soup over low heat for about 30 minutes, or until the vegetables are cooked.

Let the soup cool a little before putting it in the liquidizer or rubbing it through a fine sieve. Re-heat the soup over low heat.

Beat the egg yolks with the cream in a small bowl, blend in a little of the hot soup and then stir it all back into the soup. Stir over low heat for a few minutes, without allowing the soup to boil. Correct seasoning if necessary.

Serve at once, with a separate bowl of bread croûtons.

CREAMED PEA SOUP

It is well worth using fresh young peas for this, even though it entails the effort of shelling them. The taste really does come through; frozen peas are not at all the same.

PREPARATION TIME: *10 min*
COOKING TIME: *20 min*
INGREDIENTS *(for 4):*
2½ cups shelled green peas
2 tablespoons unsalted butter
1 tablespoon flour
5 cups stock
2 tablespoons heavy cream
*Salt**
Bread croûtons (page 165)

Cook the shelled peas gently in salted water for 10–15 minutes or until tender. Some people like to add a teaspoon of sugar and a squeeze of lemon juice to keep the bright color. Drain them as soon as they are cooked and rub them through a fine sieve or purée them in a liquidizer.

Make a smooth roux (page 166) from the butter and flour, and blend in the stock. Bring the mixture to the boil, add the pea purée and simmer for 10 minutes.

Strain this soup, add the cream and season with salt. Heat the soup through and serve it garnished with bread croûtons.

MINESTRONE

This soup, of Italian origin and with numerous regional variations, is substantial enough to serve as a meal on its own. For the first course of a meal, increase the amount of stock or use less vegetables.

PREPARATION TIME: *15 min*
COOKING TIME: *30–35 min*
INGREDIENTS *(for 4):*
1–2 carrots
1–2 stalks celery
1 onion
1 small turnip
1 potato
2 tablespoons unsalted butter or olive oil
1 clove garlic
1 quart ham or beef stock
2 large tomatoes
1 small leek
1 teacup shredded green cabbage or Brussels sprouts
⅔ cup rice or macaroni
Salt and black pepper*
GARNISH:
½–¾ cup grated Parmesan cheese

Peel or scrape the carrot, wash the celery and chop both finely. Peel and finely chop the onion, turnip and potato. Heat the butter or oil in a large, heavy-based pan and add the prepared vegetables, together with the peeled and crushed garlic. Sauté the vegetables for a few minutes until they begin to soften, then add the hot stock. Cover the pan with a lid and simmer the soup over low heat for 15 minutes or until the vegetables are almost tender.

Skin the tomatoes (page 160); cut them in half, remove all seeds and chop up the tomato flesh. Trim the roots and coarse outer leaves from the leek, wash thoroughly under cold running water, then shred it finely. Add the tomatoes, the leek and washed shredded cabbage or sprouts to the pan; bring the soup back to the boil. Add the rice or macaroni.

Simmer the soup over low heat – without the lid – for a further 10–15 minutes. Season the soup to taste with salt and freshly ground pepper and serve a bowl of grated Parmesan cheese separately.

BORSHCH

There are numerous variations of this famous Russian soup, but beets and sour cream are traditional in every borshch, whether it is served hot or cold.

PREPARATION TIME: *25 min*
COOKING TIME: *1 hour 20 min*
INGREDIENTS *(for 6):*
1 pound uncooked beets
1 onion
1 leek
1 carrot
1 turnip
1 large potato
1 stalk celery
5 cups strong beef, chicken or duck stock
1 bay leaf
1 tablespoon chopped parsley
Salt and black pepper*
1 tablespoon tomato paste
1 teaspoon sugar
1 tablespoon lemon juice
¾ cup sour cream
GARNISH:
3 tablespoons chopped mint or chives

Peel the beets, set aside about one-quarter and dice the remainder finely. Peel and thinly slice the onion; trim the roots and coarse outer leaves from the leek, wash it thoroughly under cold running water and chop it finely. Wash and peel the carrot and turnip, and shred into very thin strips. Wash, peel and dice the potato. Scrub the celery and chop it finely.

Put the prepared vegetables in a large pan with the stock, bay leaf, parsley, and a good seasoning of salt and freshly ground pepper. Cover the pan with a lid and simmer the soup for 30 minutes. Mix together the tomato paste, sugar and lemon juice in a small bowl and add to the soup. Continue cooking the soup over low heat for a further 30 minutes or until the root vegetables are tender.

Ten minutes before serving, grate the reserved beets and add to the soup. Thin with a little more stock if necessary. Stir 4 or 5 tablespoons of the soup into the sour cream and gradually stir this mixture back into the soup. Heat the soup through without boiling and serve at once, sprinkled with chopped mint or chives.

To serve the borshch cold – borshch givrée – chill the soup (it can be puréed if preferred) thoroughly before adding the sour cream. Before serving, add a little more lemon juice. Pour the soup into individual bowls, each containing an ice cube, and top with a swirl of sour cream. Finely chopped scallions, hard-cooked egg and grated cucumber can also be sprinkled on the top as a garnish, to give a decorative and appetizing effect.

MINESTRONE

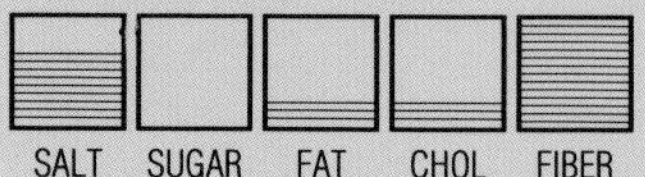

WHOLEFOOD*
TOTAL CALORIES: ABOUT 800

For a low **salt** level, use unsalted beef stock and not ham stock (avoid bouillon cubes), and only 2–3 tablespoons Parmesan. (Calories lost: up to 216.)
The **fiber** level will depend on the size of vegetables chosen. It will be higher if whole wheat pasta is used.
For a **wholefood** soup, use either whole wheat pasta or brown rice; rice is traditional in minestrone.
For a **gluten-free** soup, replace the pasta with dried navy beans which have been cooked in the stock. These are also traditional in minestrone.
For a **vegetarian** soup replace the meat stock with water or vegetable stock.

Freezing: ✓ up to 2 months.
Microwave: ✓

BORSHCH

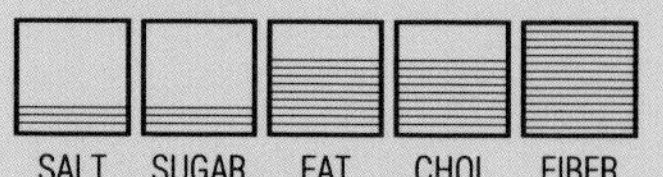

GLUTEN-FREE WHOLEFOOD*
TOTAL CALORIES: ABOUT 755

The low **salt** level assumes the stock is unsalted.
The **fat** and **cholesterol** levels can be reduced by replacing the sour cream with the same amount of quark or thick low-fat sour cream or yogurt.
Make sure the stock is not fatty. (Calories lost: up to 243.)

Use vegetable stock for a **vegetarian** soup.

Freezing: ☑ up to 2 months.
Microwave: ☑

FRENCH ONION SOUP

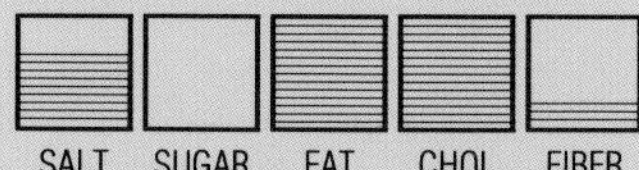

GLUTEN-FREE* WHOLEFOOD*
TOTAL CALORIES: ABOUT 1365

The **salt** level can be reduced to low by halving the amount of cheese used, and making sure the stock is unsalted. For very low salt, use unsalted bread. The **fat** and **cholesterol** levels can be reduced to low by cooking the onions in 2 teaspoons butter and 2 teaspoons oil, instead of the butter given, and again by using less cheese, say half, or substituting cottage cheese. (Calories lost: up to 600.)
Use water or vegetable stock for a **vegetarian** version.

Pressure cooker: ☑ (without the topping).

Freezing: ☑ up to 3 months without the topping.

Microwave: ☑

FRENCH ONION SOUP

Although Les Halles in Paris no longer exists, onion soup is permanently associated with that famous market. The porters kept out the cold by drinking vast mugs of this traditional soup.

PREPARATION TIME: *20 min*
COOKING TIME: *1 hour*
INGREDIENTS *(for 4):*
1 pound onions
4–6 tablespoons unsalted butter
5 cups chicken or beef stock
*½ teaspoon salt**
2 tablespoons flour
4 slices French bread, ½ in thick
1 cup grated Gruyère cheese

Peel and thinly slice the onions. Melt 2 tablespoons of the butter in a large saucepan and add the onions. Cover with a lid and cook over low heat for about 15 minutes, until the onions are soft and transparent. Remove the lid and continue frying the onions, stirring occasionally, until they are golden brown. Stir in the stock and salt. Replace the lid and simmer the soup for 30 minutes. In a small basin, mix the flour with ½ cup of water until thoroughly blended. Add to the soup and stir until it comes back to the boil. Simmer for 2–3 minutes until the soup has thickened, then draw the pan off the heat.

Meanwhile, butter both sides of each slice of French bread; sprinkle half the cheese over the bread. Bake the bread, on a baking sheet, in a pre-heated oven, at 350°F (180°C, mark 4) until the bread is crisp and the cheese has melted. Arrange the bread in individual bowls and pour over the hot onion soup.

Serve the remaining grated cheese in a separate bowl.

LETTUCE SOUP

A surplus of home-grown lettuce, or those not quite crisp enough for a salad, can be used for an economical soup. The pale green, light-textured soup is ideal on a chilly summer or autumnal day.

PREPARATION TIME: *10 min*
COOKING TIME: *15 min*
INGREDIENTS *(for 4–6):*
1 head Boston lettuce
*Salt**
1 small onion
3 tablespoons butter
2 cups chicken stock
Black pepper, sugar, grated nutmeg
2 cups milk
1–2 egg yolks
2 tablespoons light cream
GARNISH:
Bread croûtons (page 165)

Wash the lettuce leaves thoroughly and blanch them for 5 minutes in boiling salted water. Drain and rinse under cold running water. Chop the leaves; peel and finely chop the onion.

Melt the butter in a saucepan and fry the onion in it for 5 minutes, until soft. Add the lettuce shreds, setting a few aside. Pour the stock over the onions and lettuce and bring the soup to the boil. Season to taste with salt, freshly ground pepper, sugar and nutmeg.

Allow the soup to cool slightly before liquidizing it or rubbing it through a sieve. Add the milk to the soup and reheat gently; simmer for 5 minutes.

Lightly beat together the egg yolks and cream. Spoon a little of the hot, but not boiling, soup into this and blend thoroughly. Pour the egg mixture into the soup and simmer gently until the soup thickens. On no account should it reach boiling point, or the eggs will curdle.

Just before serving, add the rest of the lettuce shreds. Ladle the soup into plates and serve with a bowl of crisp bread croûtons, or toast.

ELIZA ACTON'S APPLE SOUP

In 1845, Eliza Acton published her *Modern Cookery*, the first important English cookery book. It included this recipe for a tart apple soup. Miss Acton gives Burgundy as the place of origin, but a similar soup was known in medieval Britain.

PREPARATION TIME: *10 min*
COOKING TIME: *30 min*
INGREDIENTS *(for 6):*
¾ pound cooking apples
5 cups beef or mutton stock
½ teaspoon ground ginger
Salt and black pepper*
4 rounded tablespoons long grain rice

Remove all fat from the surface of the prepared cool stock (page 163). Wash the apples and chop them roughly, without removing peel or core. Bring the stock to the boil in a large pan, add the apples and cover the pan with a lid. Simmer the soup over low heat until the apples are tender.

Pour the soup through a sieve, rubbing through as much of the fruit pulp as possible. Stir in the ginger and season with salt and ground pepper. Re-heat the soup and remove any scum.

While the soup is cooking, boil the rice in plenty of salted water. Drain thoroughly through a sieve and keep the rice warm.

Spoon the soup into bowls, and serve the rice separately.

LETTUCE SOUP

GLUTEN-FREE* WHOLEFOOD*
TOTAL CALORIES: ABOUT 1165

To reduce the **fat** and **cholesterol** levels to low, soften the onion and lettuce in 2 teaspoons oil, omitting the remaining butter. Use skim milk, and to keep the cholesterol level to low, replace the yolks with 1 whole egg beaten into low-fat sour cream or quark. (Calories lost: up to 571.)
Using sliced almonds instead of croûtons will make the soup **gluten-free**. Substitute vegetable stock for the chicken stock to make it **vegetarian**.

Freezing: ☑ up to 2 months.
Microwave: ☑

ELIZA ACTON'S APPLE SOUP

GLUTEN-FREE WHOLEFOOD*
TOTAL CALORIES: ABOUT 470

This recipe needs no changes to make it fit healthy eating guidelines, provided the stock is well skimmed of fat. To raise the **fiber** level a little and make the soup **wholefood**, use brown rice, cooked for 45 minutes in 2¼ times its volume of water. You can use vegetable stock for a **vegetarian** soup.

Freezing: ☑ up to 2 months (without the rice).
Microwave: ☑

TOMATO SOUP

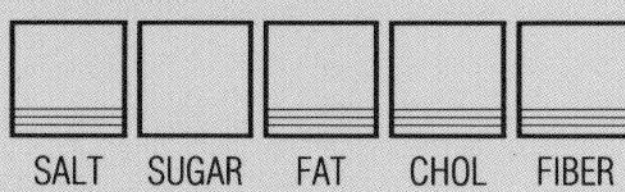

GLUTEN-FREE WHOLEFOOD*
TOTAL CALORIES: ABOUT 590

This soup needs no changes to suit healthy eating guidelines.

Freezing: √ up to 2 months.
Microwave: √

MEXICAN HOT POT SOUP

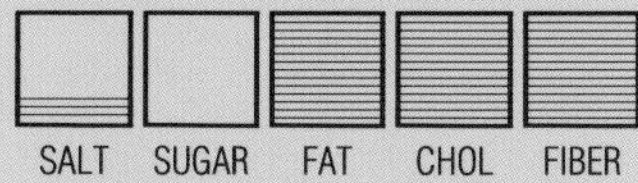

GLUTEN-FREE WHOLEFOOD
TOTAL CALORIES: ABOUT 1420

The **salt** level is low assuming that unsalted butter is used, and the tomatoes, kidney beans and chick peas bought are unsalted, or fresh tomatoes and dried beans are used.
The **fat** and **cholesterol** levels can be reduced to low by using 1 tablespoon of oil, in place of bacon fat or butter, to soften the onion, or by preparing this stage the other way around: even very lean ground beef will provide enough fat to brown itself, if heated gently in a heavy-based pan, to which the onion can then be added. Instead of garlic bread, include garlic in the dish, and serve with unbuttered rolls. (Calories lost: up to 235.)

Freezing: √ up to 2 weeks.
Microwave: √

TOMATO SOUP

This is a very simple, basic method of making soup, and one which brings out to the full the true taste of the tomatoes. Try to find really ripe and sweet ones, preferably beefsteak tomatoes.

Short grain (or round grain) rice, such as the Italian Arborio rice, is probably the best for this kind of soup, but if there is none to hand, long grain rice can quite well be used.

PREPARATION TIME: *25 min*
COOKING TIME: *30 min*
INGREDIENTS *(for 6):*
1 pound ripe tomatoes
1 onion
2 tablespoons butter
Salt and black pepper*
½ cup rice
5 cups white stock
Bouquet garni (page 183)

Peel and finely chop the onion. Skin the tomatoes (page 164), cut them in half and remove the seeds with a teaspoon. Chop the tomato flesh roughly. Melt the butter in a large heavy-based pan and cook the onion over low heat until transparent. Add the tomato flesh, and season with salt and pepper. Blend in the rice and stock, and add the bouquet garni. Bring the soup to boiling point and cover the pan with a lid. Reduce the heat and simmer the soup for 15–20 minutes, or until the rice is tender. Remove the bouquet garni.

Rub the purée through a sieve – a liquidizer will not get rid of any remaining tomato seeds. Re-heat the soup and adjust seasoning.

MEXICAN HOT POT SOUP

This is the kind of winter soup which is a meal in itself. The ingredients include red kidney beans and chick peas. Dried beans should be soaked overnight.

PREPARATION TIME: *10 min*
COOKING TIME: *45 min*
INGREDIENTS *(for 4):*
1 large onion
1 sweet green or red pepper
¼ cup bacon fat or butter
½ pound ground beef
16-ounce can tomatoes
16-ounce can or ⅔ cup dried red kidney beans
8-ounce can or ⅓ cup dried chick peas (garbanzos)
2 cups stock or bouillon
½ teaspoon chili powder
*Salt**
GARNISH:
Lettuce

Peel and finely chop the onion, cut off the stalk base of the pepper, remove the seeds and chop the pepper finely. Melt the fat in a large heavy-based pan, and fry the onion until it begins to color. Add the meat and continue frying over medium heat until it is well browned.

Add the tomatoes with their juice, the drained or soaked beans, chick peas and chopped pepper. Stir in the stock or bouillon, mixing thoroughly. Season to taste with chili powder and a little salt. Cover the pan, and simmer the soup for 30 minutes. Allow to cool; put through a liquidizer or rub it through a sieve.

Re-heat the thick soup before serving. Garnish with finely shredded lettuce and serve with hot garlic bread: cut a crusty loaf into thick slices and spread each with garlic butter. Put the slices back to the original loaf form, wrap it in foil and heat in the oven for about 10 minutes, at 350°F (180°C, mark 4).

APPLE AND NUT SALAD

Sour cream is a refreshing, less fatty dressing than mayonnaise. It is here combined with fruits, nuts and vegetables in a crisp salad to serve with cold meat.

PREPARATION TIME: *30 min*
INGREDIENTS *(for 4–5):*
4 crisp eating apples
1 tablespoon lemon juice
¾ cup roughly chopped walnuts
¾ cup sour cream
¼ head white cabbage
3 stalks celery
12 large radishes
⅓ cup raisins
Salt and black pepper*

Wash and core the apples and chop them into rough chunks. Put them in a bowl and sprinkle the lemon juice over them to prevent the apples going brown. Set aside one-third of the walnuts for garnish. Pour the sour cream into a bowl and stir in the apples and remaining walnuts.

Remove any damaged and coarse outer leaves from the cabbage, wash it and cut out the thick center stalk. Shred it finely, first one way then the other. Scrub and thinly slice the celery. Remove leaves and roots from the radishes and slice them evenly. Cut the raisins in half.

Stir all these ingredients into the sour cream and season to taste with salt and freshly ground pepper. Spoon the salad into a serving dish and garnish with the remaining walnuts.

SALADE NIÇOISE

There are numerous versions of this Provençal hors-d'oeuvre, but all have in common the basic ingredients of lettuce, eggs, anchovy fillets, black olives and tomatoes.

PREPARATION TIME: *25 min*
INGREDIENTS *(for 6):*
2 eggs
½ pound green beans
¾ pound firm tomatoes
½ onion
1 lettuce heart
½ green pepper
½ cup garlic-flavored French dressing (page 167)
7-ounce can of tuna fish
Small can anchovy fillets
½ cup small black olives

Hard-cook the eggs for 8–10 minutes, then plunge them into cold water. Shell and quarter them, and set aside to cool. Top and tail the green beans, wash them and cook in boiling salted water for 5–8 minutes; drain and set aside to cool.

Skin the tomatoes (page 160) and cut into quarters. Peel and thinly slice the onion, break it into individual rings. Wash and dry the lettuce. Clean the pepper, cut out the core and seeds, and slice it thinly.

Put half the French dressing in a shallow bowl and toss the shredded lettuce and beans in it. Drain and flake the tuna fish and arrange it, with the drained anchovy fillets, olives, green pepper and onion rings, on top of the lettuce and beans. Surround with the quartered tomatoes and hard-cooked eggs. Sprinkle over the remaining dressing and serve the salad immediately.

ARTICHOKES WITH MUSHROOMS

Artichoke bottoms with garlic dressing make an unusual side salad for cold meats and poultry. Alternatively, serve the artichokes as a first course.

PREPARATION TIME: *25 min*
COOKING TIME: *45–60 min*
INGREDIENTS *(for 6):*
6 large globe artichokes
12 large mushrooms
6 tablespoons olive oil
6 tablespoons white wine vinegar
1 clove garlic
Salt and black pepper*

Trim off the stems and rinse the artichokes thoroughly under cold running water. Put them in a large saucepan of boiling water, cover with a lid and boil until a leaf pulls away easily. Remove the artichokes, then drain them upside-down and leave to cool completely.

Wash and trim the mushrooms; cut them into slices, discarding the stalks. Pour the oil into a small bowl, add the vinegar and peeled and crushed garlic; season to taste with salt and freshly ground pepper.

Pull off and discard all the leaves and the fine filaments around the base of the artichokes. Set the artichoke bottoms on individual serving plates, and arrange the mushroom slices on top; pour over garlic dressing.

APPLE AND NUT SALAD

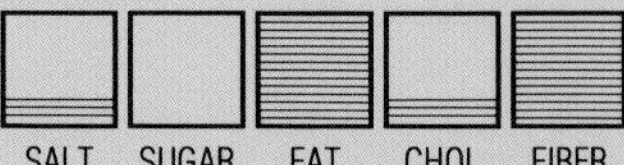

GLUTEN-FREE WHOLEFOOD VEGETARIAN
TOTAL CALORIES: ABOUT 1045

Walnuts are roughly half oil; to limit the **fat** content of the salad to low, use only ½ cup, and replace the sour cream with low-fat yogurt. This will give a very low **cholesterol** content too. (Calories lost: up to 374.)

Food processor: ✓ for chopping.

SALADE NIÇOISE

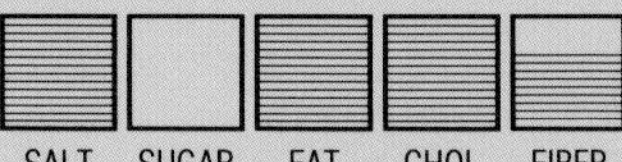

GLUTEN-FREE WHOLEFOOD
TOTAL CALORIES: ABOUT 2255

Tuna fish, anchovies and olives are all very high in **salt** when preserved. To limit this amount, replace the anchovies with cubes of boiled potato, and use only ¼ cup olives. However, the level will still be fairly high unless you substitute fresh fish for the canned tuna, lightly poaching or steaming it.
To reduce the **fat** level, choose tuna canned in brine rather than oil (or again, use fresh fish), and olives kept in brine rather than in oil. Make a French dressing with only 2 tablespoons oil, using a well-flavored olive or walnut oil to give the small amount maximum impact. For a low **cholesterol** dish, use only 1 egg. (Calories lost: up to 1555.)

ARTICHOKES WITH MUSHROOMS

SALT SUGAR FAT CHOL FIBER

GLUTEN-FREE WHOLEFOOD VEGETARIAN
TOTAL CALORIES: ABOUT 930

To reduce the **fat** level to low, use only 3–4 tablespoons oil and the same of vinegar or lemon juice. This simply means the dish has less dressing. If wished, a dollop of quark or low-fat sour cream can be placed on top of each portion. An alternative dressing can be made using tahini (sesame seed paste). Mix 3 tablespoons with the same amount of water until smooth. Blend in 3 tablespoons oil and add lemon juice, garlic and seasonings to taste. (Calories lost: up to 270.)

FRESH ASPARAGUS

The asparagus season lasts only a few weeks. It has such a good, subtle flavor that the best way to serve it is the simplest, as here.

PREPARATION TIME: *10 min*
COOKING TIME: *20–30 min*
INGREDIENTS *(for 4):*
2 pounds asparagus
$\frac{3}{4}$–1 cup butter or 6 tablespoons olive oil and 2 tablespoons white wine vinegar
Salt and black pepper*

Wash the asparagus carefully and lightly scrape the lower parts of the stems, away from the delicate tips. Young fresh asparagus needs no further preparation, but if the stems are woody towards the base, trim off the wood, keeping the stems at a uniform length.

Tie the asparagus in bundles of 10–12, using soft tape so as not to damage the stems. Bring a large pan of lightly salted water to the boil. Place the bundles of asparagus upright in it, with the tips above the water. Time of cooking varies according to the age, size and length of the asparagus, but as a general rule asparagus is cooked when the tips are soft to the touch.

Untie the asparagus and drain carefully without breaking the tips. Serve the asparagus on individual plates, either warm with melted butter or cold with a French dressing (page 167), served separately. Asparagus is traditionally eaten with the fingers. Dip the tips in the butter or dressing and leave any woody parts of the stems. Finger bowls, with luke-warm water and a slice of lemon, are required.

FRESH ASPARAGUS

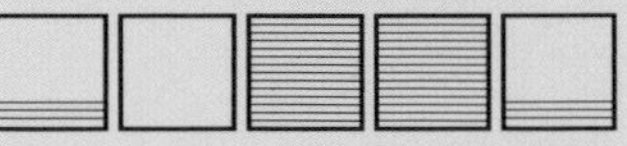

GLUTEN-FREE WHOLEFOOD VEGETARIAN
TOTAL CALORIES: ABOUT 1745

The high **fat** and **cholesterol** levels assume that butter is used. If French dressing is used instead, the fat content is only half that of butter. The amount can be reduced to medium or low by mixing 1 tablespoon olive oil with 4 tablespoons of low-fat sour cream. Or less oil can be used, reducing the vinegar in proportion. If oil and vinegar are used, the cholesterol is nil. (Calories lost: up to 1369.)

Freezing: ☑ up to 1 year.

AVOCADO, PEAR AND NUT SALAD

GLUTEN-FREE WHOLEFOOD* VEGETARIAN
TOTAL CALORIES: ABOUT 1580

The **salt** content can be reduced to low by using mustard rather than Worcestershire sauce, and unsalted nuts.
Avocados have a very high oil level. However, their rich texture makes it simple to replace the cream with low-fat yogurt or quark, so the **fat** level can be cut to medium, and the **cholesterol** to very low. The nuts also have a high oil level, about 50%; so use half the amount, toasting before chopping as this gives a more pervasive flavor. (Calories lost: up to 452.)
This is **gluten-free** if the mustard used contains no gluten. Check the label.

AVOCADO AND CITRUS SALAD

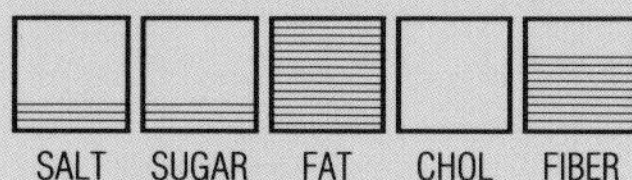

SALT SUGAR FAT CHOL FIBER

GLUTEN-FREE WHOLEFOOD* VEGETARIAN
TOTAL CALORIES: ABOUT 1000

The high **fat** level comes from the oil in the avocado, and cannot be avoided except by reducing the proportion of avocado to other ingredients. This can be done without making the salad too citrus-dominated by adding about 6 ounces cubed melon or ripe pear to the mixture, in place of each avocado you choose to omit. (Calories lost: up to 241.)

GUACAMOLE

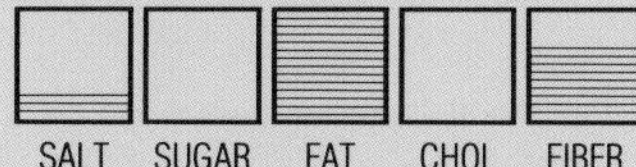

SALT SUGAR FAT CHOL FIBER

GLUTEN-FREE WHOLEFOOD VEGETARIAN
TOTAL CALORIES: ABOUT 980

Avocados are naturally about 20% oil on average, although the amount can vary between 11% and 39% according to season. This means that 3 ounces avocado provides about 1 tablespoon oil, making a high **fat** dish. The only way to reduce the amount, apart from serving smaller portions, is to omit the added oil and replace up to half the avocado with sieved cottage cheese or ricotta. (Calories lost: up to 457.) One way of serving smaller helpings is to use the dip to stuff a baked potato.

Food processor: √

Freezing: √ up to 2 months.

AVOCADO, PEAR AND NUT SALAD

Avocado and pears discolor quickly when peeled. For this salad it is essential to mix the dressing first and sprinkle the diced pears generously with lemon juice before blending them quickly into the dressing.

PREPARATION TIME: *15 min*
CHILLING TIME: *1 hour*
INGREDIENTS *(for 6)*:
3 avocados
1 cup sour cream
2 teaspoons tarragon vinegar
Salt and black pepper*
Dijon-style mustard or Worcestershire sauce
Sugar
Juice of a lemon
1 large or 2 small pears
3 tablespoons salted almonds or peanuts
GARNISH:
Chopped chives

Put the sour cream in a mixing bowl and stir in the vinegar. Season to taste with salt, freshly ground pepper, mustard or Worcestershire sauce and a little sugar. Mix thoroughly.

Cut the avocados in half, remove the seeds and carefully scoop out the flesh. Leave a narrow inner lining of flesh on the avocado shells and set them aside. Cut the flesh into dice and put them in a bowl. Sprinkle with lemon juice. Peel, core and dice the pears, add to the avocado and sprinkle with the remaining lemon juice.

Chop the salted almonds roughly and set a little aside for garnishing. Mix the remainder with the avocado and pears. Pour over the dressing and blend thoroughly. Pile the salad into the avocado shells and wrap each half in foil. Chill for 1 hour.

Just before serving, unwrap the avocado shells, arrange them on small plates and garnish with the chopped almonds and chives.

AVOCADO AND CITRUS SALAD

Slightly overripe avocados mixed with citrus fruit provide a tangy appetizer. Alternatively, serve the salad with cold ham, chicken or shellfish.

PREPARATION TIME: *30 min*
INGREDIENTS *(for 4–6)*:
3 large avocados
Juice of a small lemon
1 large grapefruit
1 large orange
Sugar (optional)
GARNISH:
Orange segments
Mint

Peel the avocados. Cut them into quarters and remove the seeds; cut the flesh into thin sections and pour the lemon juice over them. Cut a slice from top and bottom of the grapefruit and orange so that they stand flat on a board. Cut downwards, in narrow strips, through peel and pith and remove. With a sharp knife, cut between the flesh and segment skins; put the flesh into a large bowl and squeeze the segment skins over the fruit so that no juice is wasted.

Carefully blend the avocado and lemon juice with the citrus fruits; sweeten to taste if necessary. Spoon the mixture into individual serving dishes and garnish with skinned orange segments and sprigs of mint.

GUACAMOLE

This is a Mexican hors-d'oeuvre or dip of avocados. Very ripe avocados, suitable for mashing, are often sold cheaply.

PREPARATION TIME: *10 min*
CHILLING TIME: *30 min*
INGREDIENTS *(for 6)*:
3 ripe avocados
½ small grated onion
2 crushed cloves garlic
1 tablespoon lemon juice
1 tablespoon olive oil
Salt and black pepper*
Cayenne pepper
¼ teaspoon Worcestershire sauce
Tabasco sauce

Cut the avocados in half and remove the seeds. Mash the avocado flesh with the onion and garlic until smooth. Blend in the lemon juice and oil; season to taste with salt, freshly ground pepper, cayenne and the sauces. Chill for 30 minutes.

Serve on individual plates on lettuce leaves, or in serving glasses. Mixed raw vegetables, such as celery sticks, or slices of carrot, green pepper and radish, could be used for the dip.

TOMATO ICE

The Italians invented the water ice or sherbet, which is an iced and sweetened juice or extract. This adaptation of a sherbet makes a refreshing appetizer.

PREPARATION TIME: *10 min*
COOKING TIME: *25 min*
FREEZING TIME: *4 hours*
INGREDIENTS *(for 6):*
3 pounds ripe tomatoes
1 small onion
2 teaspoons marjoram
1 tablespoon tomato paste
Juice of a lemon
Sugar to taste
GARNISH:
Mint, lemon or cucumber

Wash, wipe and roughly chop the tomatoes. Peel and roughly chop the onion. Put the tomatoes, onion and marjoram in a large saucepan. Bring to the boil, cover with a lid and simmer over low heat for 25 minutes or until the tomatoes are soft. Stir occasionally to prevent the tomatoes sticking to the pan. Rub the mixture through a sieve into a large bowl, and stir in the tomato paste, lemon juice and sugar. Leave the mixture to cool. Spoon it into a plastic freezer container, cover with a lid and freeze for at least 4 hours or overnight.

Turn the mixture out when frozen solid, crush with a rolling pin and pile the tomato crystals into individual serving glasses. Garnish with sprigs of mint, lemon or cucumber slices.

TOMATOES WITH HORSERADISH MAYONNAISE

For this dish choose large firm tomatoes of equal size. Serve them on their own, chilled, as an appetizer. They also make a good picnic dish, and can be served as a side dish with cold meat or broiled steaks and chops.

PREPARATION TIME: *20 min*
CHILLING TIME: *2 hours*
INGREDIENTS *(for 4–6):*
8 firm tomatoes
½ cup mayonnaise (page 167)
*Salt**
½ cup heavy cream
Lemon juice
2 rounded tablespoons fresh grated horseradish
GARNISH:
Chopped chives, chervil, basil or parsley

First prepare the mayonnaise and set it aside. Skin the tomatoes (page 160), and slice off the tops with a serrated knife. Carefully scoop out the seeds and juice with a teaspoon, without breaking the flesh. Sprinkle the inside of the tomato cups with salt, stand them upside down on a plate to drain, and chill them in the coldest part of the refrigerator for 2 hours.

Lightly whip the cream and mix it into the mayonnaise; add lemon juice to taste and stir in the grated horseradish (the tomato caps may also be chopped and stirred into the mayonnaise). Chill on the bottom shelf of the refrigerator for about 1 hour.

Just before serving, spoon the horseradish mayonnaise evenly into tomato cups and sprinkle with chopped herbs.

TOMATO ICE

SALT SUGAR FAT CHOL FIBER

GLUTEN-FREE WHOLEFOOD* VEGETARIAN
TOTAL CALORIES: ABOUT 240

This recipe needs no changes to fit healthy eating guidelines, apart from limiting the **sugar** used to flavor, and if possible, using unsalted tomato paste.

Food processor: ✓

Freezing: ✓ up to 6 months.

Microwave: ✓ for the tomatoes.

TOMATOES WITH HORSERADISH MAYONNAISE

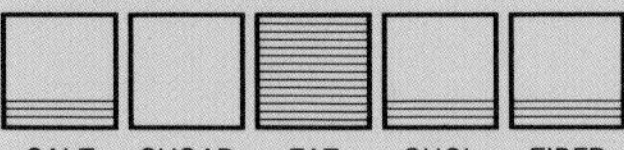

SALT SUGAR FAT CHOL FIBER

GLUTEN-FREE WHOLEFOOD VEGETARIAN
TOTAL CALORIES: ABOUT 2170

The high **fat** level can be reduced to low by replacing the mayonnaise with a low-fat style of dressing, now easy to buy, and the cream with low-fat sour cream, yogurt or cultured buttermilk, giving an even lower **cholesterol** count as well. A mixture of sieved cottage cheese (or ricotta) and low-fat sour cream could replace the mayonnaise and cream altogether. (Calories lost: up to 1562.)

HONEYDEW CUPS

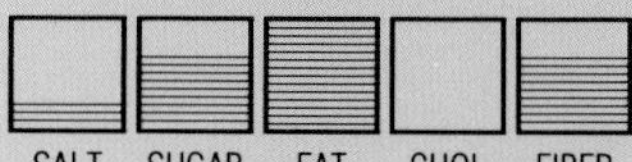

SALT SUGAR FAT CHOL FIBER

GLUTEN-FREE WHOLEFOOD* VEGETARIAN
TOTAL CALORIES: ABOUT 1170

To reduce the **fat** level to low, use only 2 tablespoons oil, and one of lemon juice or vinegar. Make up the volume of dressing with quark, low-fat yogurt, or 2 tablespoons tahini (sesame seed paste) blended to a smooth purée with 2 tablespoons water. (Calories lost: up to 520.)

MELON AND HAM GONDOLAS

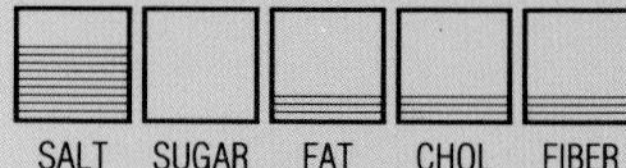

SALT SUGAR FAT CHOL FIBER

GLUTEN-FREE WHOLEFOOD
TOTAL CALORIES: ABOUT 200

This kind of ham is extremely salty: even a small slice will provide around 200 mg sodium, or 500 mg salt, about 10% of a desirable daily maximum.
The **fat** and **cholesterol** levels are low simply because the portions of ham are small, say under ½ ounce a slice. However, this assumes that the fatty edge of the ham is not eaten.
A leaner alternative, and one which keeps to the Italian theme, is thin slices of *bresaola*, from the mountains of Northern Italy. This is beef cured by being air-dried, rather in the same way as Parma ham. It also goes well with melon, either honeydew or cantaloupe. (Calories lost: up to 30.)

HONEYDEW CUPS

A well-chilled melon salad is a good choice before a rich main course. For a special occasion, choose three small melons, and serve the salad in the scooped-out melon halves.

PREPARATION TIME: *40 min*
CHILLING TIME: *1 hour*
INGREDIENTS *(for 6):*
1 large honeydew or cantaloupe melon
1 cucumber
Salt and black pepper*
6 tomatoes
DRESSING:
1–2 tablespoons sugar
3 tablespoons lemon juice or tarragon vinegar
6 tablespoons salad oil
GARNISH:
2 teaspoons each chopped mint, chives, and chervil or parsley

Peel the cucumber and cut it into ½ in dice; sprinkle with salt and leave to stand for 30 minutes. Cut the melon in half across and remove the seeds. Carefully scoop out the flesh in small balls, or cut it into small wedges. Skin the tomatoes (page 160), cut them in half and remove cores and seeds. Chop the tomato flesh roughly.

Mix the ingredients for the dressing, adding the oil last of all. Rinse the cucumber in cold water and pat dry on absorbent kitchen paper towels.

Put the melon, tomato and cucumber in a large bowl, pour over the dressing and mix well. Chill the salad in the refrigerator for 1 hour, stirring occasionally.

Serve the salad in individual glass bowls and sprinkle with the mixed chopped herbs.

MELON AND HAM GONDOLAS

Sweet ripe melon combines perfectly with raw ham, such as Parma ham, or with the Westphalian variety from Germany. This dish is traditional in Italy, but is now popular also throughout the world.

PREPARATION TIME: *12 min*
INGREDIENTS *(for 6):*
½ large ripe honeydew melon
6 wafer-thin slices raw ham
Juice of a lemon
Black pepper
GARNISH:
Lemon wedges

Chill the melon thoroughly. Cut it into six long slices, scoop out the seeds and cut the skin away. Put one piece of melon on each slice of ham and wrap the ham neatly over the melon. Sprinkle with lemon juice and freshly ground pepper.

Serve the melon gondolas garnished with wedges of lemon.

LEEKS VINAIGRETTE

In place of the inevitable green salad of lettuce and cucumber try this cold leek salad as a side dish with any type of meat.

PREPARATION TIME: *15 min*
COOKING TIME: *30 min*
INGREDIENTS *(for 4):*
8 small leeks
1 bay leaf
Salt and black pepper*
1 teaspoon sugar
2 tablespoons wine vinegar
¼ teaspoon Dijon-style mustard
3–4 tablespoons olive oil
1 tablespoon freshly chopped parsley
GARNISH:
2 hard-cooked eggs

Remove the coarse outer leaves from the leeks; trim off the roots and cut away the green tops, leaving about 4 in of white stem on each leek. Slice the leeks in half lengthwise, open them carefully and wash well under cold running water to remove all traces of grit.

Tie the halved leeks in four bundles, put them in a pan of boiling salted water and add the bay leaf. Bring back to the boil, then lower the heat to simmering point. Cover the pan with a lid and cook the leeks for 30 minutes or until tender. Lift them carefully from the water and leave to drain and cool.

Arrange the cold leeks in a serving dish and prepare the dressing: put salt and freshly ground pepper in a mixing bowl, add the sugar, vinegar and mustard. Blend thoroughly before adding the oil, mixing well. Taste for sharpness, adding more vinegar if necessary. Stir in the chopped parsley, and spoon the dressing over the leeks. Leave to marinate until ready to serve.

Garnish the leeks with slices of hard-cooked eggs.

FRIED LEEKS

This dish is an excellent appetizer and is probably best served lukewarm. It can also be served hot with any broiled or roast meat, or as a side dish or salad with cold ham and chicken.

PREPARATION TIME: *10 min*
COOKING TIME: *25 min*
INGREDIENTS *(for 4–6):*
2 pounds leeks
4 tomatoes
6 tablespoons olive oil
2 cloves garlic
1 bay leaf
*Salt**
Juice of ½ lemon
Black pepper

Cut away the roots and any damaged green leaves from the leeks, slice them in half lengthwise and wash under cold running water to remove all traces of grit. Cut into 1 in slices. Skin the tomatoes (page 160). Heat half the oil in a large frying pan and add the leeks. Peel the garlic and crush over the leeks, then add the bay leaf. Season to taste with salt and freshly ground pepper.

Cover the pan with a lid and cook over low heat for 20 minutes. Chop the tomatoes, add them to the pan with the rest of the oil and cook for a further 5 minutes. Remove the bay leaf.

Spoon the leeks into a serving dish and sprinkle the lemon juice over.

LEEKS À LA NIÇOISE

French vegetable dishes or salads prepared *à la niçoise* imply the addition of tomatoes and usually a garlic flavoring. This dish can be served hot with broiled fish, meat or chicken or cold as an hors-d'oeuvre.

PREPARATION TIME: *15 min*
COOKING TIME: *20 min*
INGREDIENTS *(for 4):*
2 pounds young leeks
½ pound tomatoes
3–4 tablespoons olive oil
*Salt**
1 large clove garlic
1 tablespoon fresh chopped parsley
Lemon juice
Black pepper

Cut the roots and most of the green tops off the leeks, so they are of even length. Rinse them thoroughly under cold running water and dry them on absorbent paper towels.

Skin the tomatoes (page 160) and chop them roughly.

Heat the oil in a flameproof casserole over medium heat and put in the leeks side by side. Fry until lightly colored underneath, then turn them over and season with salt and freshly ground pepper. Cover the casserole with a lid, and cook the leeks over gentle heat for 10 minutes or until the thick white part is tender. Lift out the leeks and keep them warm.

Add the tomatoes, crushed garlic and parsley to the casserole and cook briskly for 2 or 3 minutes, stirring continuously. Adjust seasoning and sharpen to taste with lemon juice. Put the leeks back into the sauce and serve hot or cold.

LEEKS VINAIGRETTE

SALT SUGAR FAT CHOL FIBER

GLUTEN-FREE WHOLEFOOD VEGETARIAN
TOTAL CALORIES: ABOUT 925

To give a low **fat** and **cholesterol** content, use only 2 tablespoons best quality oil, plus 3 tablespoons thick low-fat yogurt. Replace the egg garnish with thin slices of sweet red pepper, ground coriander seed or some coarsely grated carrot. (Calories lost: up to 410.)

Microwave: ✓ for the leeks.

FRIED LEEKS

SALT SUGAR FAT CHOL FIBER

GLUTEN-FREE WHOLEFOOD VEGETARIAN
TOTAL CALORIES: ABOUT 1120

To reduce the high **fat** level, use only 1 tablespoon of oil in the leek pan, and add a few tablespoons of stock before covering and cooking. This method of half-frying, half-steaming gives a delicious result. The mushrooms can be added without any extra oil. (Calories lost: up to 675.)
The fiber level assumes that you use most of the leeks: the green parts, provided they are not damaged, need not be discarded.

Freezing: ✓ up to 3 months. Once frozen it is best reheated and eaten hot rather than served as a salad.
Microwave: ✓ for the leeks.

LEEKS À LA NIÇOISE

SALT SUGAR FAT CHOL FIBER

GLUTEN-FREE WHOLEFOOD VEGETARIAN
TOTAL CALORIES: ABOUT 855

To reduce the amount of **fat** to low, use only 1 tablespoon of oil, with 2–3 tablespoons of stock; cook the leeks by a mixture of frying and steaming, as in the notes on the previous recipe. (Calories lost: up to 405.) To make sure that the green parts do not get over-cooked while waiting for the thicker white parts to become tender, cut deep slits from the base 2 in up the leek in a cross, allowing the cooking heat to penetrate the base of the leek more easily.

Freezing: ✓ up to 3 months. Once frozen it is best reheated and served hot rather than as a salad.

Microwave: ✓ for the leeks.

ONIONS À LA GRECQUE

SALT SUGAR FAT CHOL FIBER

GLUTEN-FREE WHOLEFOOD* VEGETARIAN
TOTAL CALORIES: ABOUT 1455

The low **salt** level assumes that the tomato paste is unsalted, leaving only a small amount from the wine.
The amount of **sugar** added is generous; many people will be satisfied with only 1 tablespoon. (Calories lost: up to 157.)
To reduce the level of **fat** to low, use only 2 tablespoons best quality oil, preferably cold-pressed, which will give maximum flavor for quantity. (Calories lost: up to 405.)

ONIONS À LA GRECQUE

This classic French hors-d'oeuvre of baby onions provides an unusual first course. The baby onions should be served chilled.

PREPARATION TIME: *1 hour*
COOKING TIME: *40 min*
CHILLING TIME: *2 hours*
INGREDIENTS *(for 6):*
1½ pounds small onions
SAUCE:
2½ cups dry white wine
¼ cup sugar
5 tablespoons olive oil
8 juniper berries
Juice of a lemon
1 bay leaf
2-ounce can tomato paste
6 sprigs parsley
¼ teaspoon basil
*Salt**
Black pepper
GARNISH:
3 tablespoons chopped parsley

Bring a large saucepan, holding at least 2 quarts of water, to the boil.

Cut the tops and bottoms from the onions and drop them into the boiling water for 1 minute. Drain the onions in a colander; cool slightly before peeling the onions.

Put all the sauce ingredients, with 1¼ cups of water, into a heavy-based pan; season this sauce to taste with salt and freshly ground pepper before adding the peeled onions.

Bring to the boil and simmer over low heat for 20 minutes or until the onions are tender, but not disintegrating. Remove the onions; mark the level of the sauce and boil briskly for about 15 minutes or until it has reduced to three-quarters.

Strain the sauce through a sieve over the onions; leave to cool and chill for a few hours in the refrigerator.

Serve the onions, in the sauce, in soup plates and garnish the dish with the finely chopped parsley.

GREEN BEANS MIMOSA

A green salad need not be composed of the ubiquitous lettuce and cucumber – crisp cooked beans make a refreshing change.

PREPARATION TIME: *10 min*
COOKING TIME: *3–4 min*
INGREDIENTS *(for 4–6):*
1 pound young green beans
*Salt**
6 tablespoons olive oil
2 tablespoons lemon juice
GARNISH:
1 large hard-cooked egg

Top, tail and wash the beans, leaving them whole. Cook them in salted water for 3–4 minutes – they should stay crisp. Drain the beans and arrange them in a round shallow serving dish, radiating from the center.

Pour the olive oil, mixed with the lemon juice, over the still-warm beans. Add more salt if necessary, and set the beans aside to cool.

Separate the white and yolk of the hard-cooked egg. Chop the white finely and rub the yolk through a coarse sieve.

Before serving, decorate the beans. Arrange the egg white in the center of the dish and scatter the yolk among the beans to resemble mimosa.

ONION QUICHE

The recipe for this rich creamy quiche comes from Alsace in France. Serve it hot or cold, cut into wedges, as a first course. It can also be served with a green salad as a main course for a light lunch.

PREPARATION TIME: *45 min*
COOKING TIME: *40 min*
INGREDIENTS *(for 4–6):*
1 pound onions
¼ cup unsalted butter
1 bay leaf
Salt and pepper*
¾ quantity standard pastry (page 171)
2 large eggs
Grated nutmeg
½ cup heavy cream
½ cup milk

Peel the onions and slice them thinly. Melt the butter in a frying pan and add the onions and bay leaf. Season with salt and pepper and cover the onions closely with a piece of buttered wax paper. Cover the pan with a tight-fitting lid and cook the onions over low heat for 30 minutes or until they are soft and golden. Shake the pan occasionally to prevent them sticking.

Prepare the pie pastry and roll it out, ¼in thick, on a lightly floured surface. Line an 8–9 in wide flan ring, standing on a baking sheet, with the pastry. Trim the edge and prick the pastry base with a fork. Beat the eggs lightly in a large bowl and season with salt, pepper and nutmeg. Stir in the cream and milk. Drain the onions in a colander, remove the bay leaf and spread the onions over the pastry case. Strain the egg mixture

GREEN BEANS MIMOSA

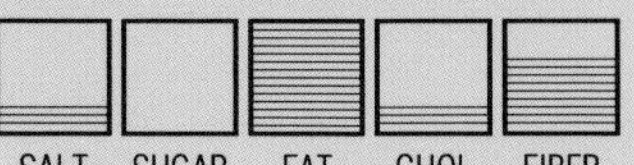

SALT SUGAR FAT CHOL FIBER

GLUTEN-FREE WHOLEFOOD VEGETARIAN
TOTAL CALORIES: ABOUT 935

To reduce the **fat** level to low, use only 2 tablespoons best quality oil, to give maximum flavor, and add 4 tablespoons low-fat yogurt or quark to the mixture. This will change the appearance of the dish, giving a thicker, less transparent coating to the beans, but is attractive in its own way. If preferred, put the dressing in the center of the beans, covering with the egg white, and only toss together when serving. (Calories lost: up to 575.)

ONION QUICHE

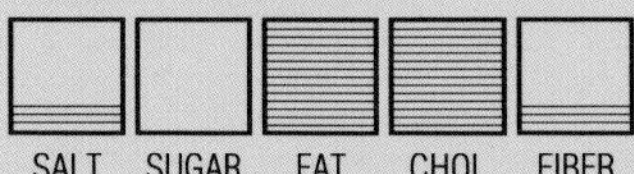

SALT SUGAR FAT CHOL FIBER

GLUTEN-FREE* WHOLEFOOD* VEGETARIAN
TOTAL CALORIES: ABOUT 2625

To reduce the **fat** level, use a different pastry base, such as yeast dough or a biscuit dough made with 2 cups self-rising flour, ¼ cup butter and ¾ cup skim milk. Cook the onions in only 1 tablespoon butter, or replace this with soft margarine or oil, adding a few spoonfuls of stock to prevent them drying out.
For the filling, make a thick white sauce by pouring 1¼ cups very hot skim milk onto a tablespoon of cornstarch that has been mixed to a paste with a very little milk. Return this mixture to the saucepan and stir over gentle heat until it boils. Remove the pan from the heat and stir in one whole

beaten egg. Season to taste and continue with the recipe. These changes give a low fat and **cholesterol** content. (Calories lost: up to 1018.)
This dish can be cooked without pastry in a casserole, and served with a decorative edge of mashed piped potato to make it **gluten-free.**

Freezing: ✓ up to 3 months.

CORN ON THE COB

GLUTEN-FREE WHOLEFOOD VEGETARIAN
TOTAL CALORIES: ABOUT 1950

Reducing the **fat** and **cholesterol** means finding a satisfactory replacement for the butter dressing. You can simply brush the corn with melted butter, using about 1 teaspooon per ear, then sprinkle generously with pepper (giving low fat and cholesterol), or place the cooked corn under a hot broiler for a minute on either side to bring out the flavor, then serve without any dressing. (Calories lost: up to 1155.)

BEET WITH ORANGE

GLUTEN-FREE WHOLEFOOD VEGETARIAN
TOTAL CALORIES: ABOUT 480

This recipe needs no changes to suit healthy eating guidelines. For an even more acceptably **wholefood** dish, use the no-added-sugar marmalade available from health food stores.

through a sieve over the onions.

Bake the quiche in the center of an oven pre-heated to 400°F (200°C, mark 6) for 40 minutes. When cooked, the pastry should be golden and the filling set; it will sink slightly as the quiche cools.

CORN ON THE COB

Corn is a favorite vegetable in America and is gaining popularity in Europe. Corn on the cob should be creamy in color and with soft tender kernels. Serve as an accompanying vegetable, or separately as an appetizer.

PREPARATION TIME: *10 min*
CHILLING TIME: *1 hour*
COOKING TIME: *5 min*
INGREDIENTS *(for 4):*
4 ears of corn
½–¾ cup butter
Salt and black pepper*
2 teaspoons sugar

Pepper butter, to be served with the corn, should be made well in advance so that it can be chilled. Stir the butter until smooth and season highly with freshly ground pepper and extra salt to taste. Shape the butter into an oblong roll and wrap it in foil or wax paper. Chill in the refrigerator.

Remove the leaves and silky tassels from the corn and put the ears, with the sugar, in a shallow pan holding just enough boiling water to cover them. Keep the water on the boil and cook the corn for just 5 minutes. Drain.

Serve the corn at once, with the butter cut in ¼ in thick slices on a separate plate. Insert special corn holders, small skewers or strong toothpicks at either end of each ear by which to hold it, and provide napkins.

BEET WITH ORANGE

In this salad, cooked beet is combined with orange marmalade, fine-shred or sweet. The two flavors blend surprisingly well and suit any strong game, goose or duck.

PREPARATION TIME: *5 min*
COOKING TIME: *10 min*
INGREDIENTS *(for 4):*
1 pound cooked beets
2 tablespoons unsalted butter
1 heaping tablespoon marmalade
Juice of half orange
GARNISH:
Slice of orange

Skin and cut the cooked beets into dice. Measure the butter, marmalade and orange juice into a saucepan, heat until the butter melts, then add the beets. Simmer gently, stirring occasionally, for about 10 minutes, until the liquid has evaporated and the beets are evenly glazed.

Spoon the beets into a hot serving dish. Cut towards the center of a thin orange slice, twist the two halves in opposite directions and place it on the beets as a garnish.

RATATOUILLE

This Provençal dish, in which all the vegetables complement each other, can be served as soon as cooked but is even better if left overnight for the flavors to develop. It makes an excellent appetizer and is good both hot and cold.

PREPARATION TIME: *30 min*
COOKING TIME: *50 min*
INGREDIENTS *(for 6–8):*
2 large zucchini
2 large eggplants
5 large tomatoes
1 large green pepper
1 small sweet red pepper
1 large onion
2 cloves garlic
6 tablespoons olive oil
Salt and black pepper*

Cut the stalks off the zucchini and eggplants. Wash well and cut them crosswise into ¼in thick slices. Put them in a colander, cover with a plate and weight this down; leave for 1 hour to press out excessive moisture. Skin the tomatoes (page 160) and chop them roughly. Wash the peppers, remove the white inner ribs and all seeds, and dice the flesh. Peel and coarsely chop the onion and garlic.

Heat the oil in a large frying pan and fry the onion and garlic for 5 minutes over low heat until transparent. Add the peppers, cook for a further 10 minutes, then add the remaining ingredients and season to taste with salt and freshly ground pepper. Cover the pan with a lid and cook the mixture over low heat for 35 minutes, stirring from time to time. Correct seasoning.

CHICORY AND ORANGE SALAD

A slightly sharp, refreshing salad which goes well with most kinds of game, cold meats or stuffed joints. Either endive or chicory can be used: both have the slightly bitter taste that combines well with orange. The red chicory of Treviso, *radicchio rosso*, makes a vivid color contrast with the orange. Grapefruit can also be used: the pink variety is very sweet and adds yet another touch of color.

PREPARATION TIME: *20 min*
INGREDIENTS *(for 6):*
1 head of chicory (flat or curled) or 4 heads of Belgian endive
3 oranges
French dressing (page 167)

Remove any brown outer leaves from the endive or chicory and the root ends from the endive. Wash and drain thoroughly, then cut the endive or chicory into thin slices, crosswise. Peel the oranges with a sharp knife, removing all the white pith with the peel. Slice the oranges thinly in cross-section and remove the seeds. If the oranges are large, cut each slice in two.

Mix the endive or chicory and the orange slices in a serving bowl, and pour over the French dressing (made with orange juice instead of vinegar). Toss and serve.

CUCUMBER IN SOUR CREAM

This unusual salad, in a refreshing summery dressing, goes well with both hot and cold meats. It is especially suitable with roast beef, veal or chicken.

PREPARATION TIME: *15–20 min*
CHILLING TIME: *2 hours*
INGREDIENTS *(for 4–6):*
1 large or 2 small cucumbers
1 tablespoon flour
½ teaspoon each of salt, sugar and dry mustard*
2 tablespoons tarragon or white wine vinegar
2 egg yolks
4 tablespoons olive oil
¾ cup sour cream
2 tablespoons finely chopped chives

Put the flour, salt, sugar and mustard in a small, heavy-based pan with 1 tablespoon of water. Cook over low heat, stirring until the ingredients are thoroughly blended. Gradually add the vinegar and 2 tablespoons of water. Continue cooking until the mixture has thickened to a smooth sauce. Bring this quickly to the boil, then simmer for 2–3 minutes.

Remove the pan from the heat and beat the egg yolks into the sauce, one at a time. Add the oil, a few drops at a time. Chill in the refrigerator.

About an hour before serving, stir the sour cream and the chopped chives into the sauce. Return it to the refrigerator.

Wash and peel the cucumber (remove the seeds if necessary) and cut it into ½in cubes. Just before serving, stir the cucumber into the sour cream.

RATATOUILLE

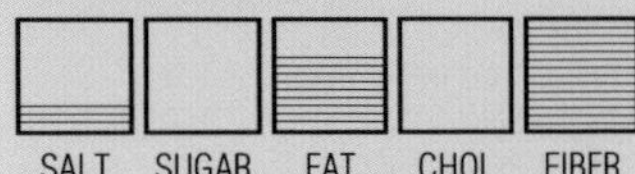

GLUTEN-FREE WHOLEFOOD VEGETARIAN
TOTAL CALORIES: ABOUT 985

To give a low **fat** level, use only 2 tablespoons olive oil, of best quality, to soften the onions and garlic, adding a few tablespoons of stock and covering the pan with a lid to prevent the vegetables becoming dry. (Calories lost: up to 540.)

Freezing: ☑ up to 9 months.
Microwave: ☑

CHICORY AND ORANGE SALAD

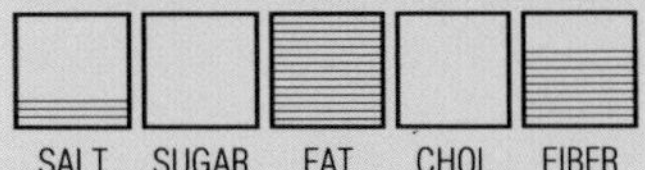

GLUTEN-FREE WHOLEFOOD VEGETARIAN
TOTAL CALORIES: ABOUT 1245

To reduce the **fat** level to low, use only 3 tablespoons of French dressing (i.e. 2 of oil and 1 of orange juice), replacing the remaining oil with low-fat yogurt, or, for a slightly higher fat content, low-fat sour cream. (Calories lost: up to 774.)

CUCUMBER IN SOUR CREAM

GLUTEN-FREE* WHOLEFOOD* VEGETARIAN
TOTAL CALORIES: ABOUT 1140

To reduce the **fat** and **cholesterol** levels to low,

replace the dressing as follows. Mix 2 heaping tablespoons powdered skim milk with $1\frac{1}{4}$ cups water. Put in a liquidizer with 1 tablespoon oil, 1 small egg and 2 tablespoons tarragon or white wine vinegar. Blend slowly. Gradually add 2 teaspoons flour and 1 teaspoon mustard and season to taste with salt, pepper, and sugar. Continue blending until quite smooth. Pour into a saucepan and bring to boiling point, stirring continuously. Simmer gently for 3–4 minutes. Leave to cool and stir in $\frac{1}{2}$ cup low-fat sour cream or yogurt 1 hour before serving. (Calories lost: up to 731.)

LETTUCE, CHEESE AND FRUIT PLATTER

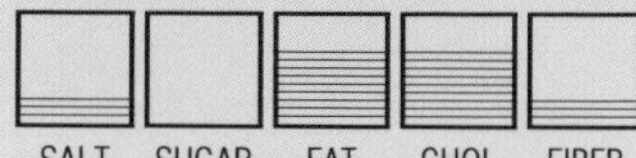

SALT SUGAR FAT CHOL FIBER

GLUTEN-FREE WHOLEFOOD VEGETARIAN
TOTAL CALORIES: ABOUT 1775

It is assumed that you have used fresh pineapple or rings canned in juice with no added **sugar**.
If only 2 tablespoons of French dressing are used, the dish will be low **fat** (apart from the walnuts, which could be halved in amount), and free from **cholesterol**.
Alternatively, a dressing of low-fat yogurt mixed half and half with lemon juice and apple juice is very good. (Calories lost: up to 1054.)

LETTUCE, CHEESE AND FRUIT PLATTER

A salad of cheese and fruit makes a light and nourishing lunch on its own. Choose seasonal fruit such as oranges and pineapple, or sliced bananas, first tossed in lemon juice.

PREPARATION TIME: *10 min*
INGREDIENTS *(for 4):*
1 small head of lettuce
Bunch watercress
2 oranges
4 pineapple rings
1 cup cottage cheese
French dressing or mayonnaise (page 167)
GARNISH:
$\frac{1}{2}$ cup coarsely chopped walnuts

Separate the leaves of the lettuce and cut off any coarse stems and damaged leaves; wash the leaves and dry them thoroughly on a clean cloth. Remove the lower coarse stems of the watercress, and wash the leaves. Cut a slice from the top and base of each orange before removing peel and all white pith; slice the oranges thinly across.

Arrange the lettuce in the center of a platter with the orange slices and pineapple rings around the edge. Arrange the cottage cheese on the fruit and garnish with sprigs of watercress.

Sprinkle the walnuts over the cheese. Mayonnaise or a good French dressing may be served separately, with crusty bread and/or crispbread and butter.

SAVORY CUCUMBER

Cucumber rarely appears cooked, but in this French recipe, stuffed cucumbers are served hot as a savory snack.

PREPARATION TIME: *10 min*
COOKING TIME: *50 min*
INGREDIENTS *(for 6):*
3 cucumbers
¾ cup long grain rice
1 large onion
9 tablespoons butter
½ pound mushrooms
4 lean slices bacon
Salt and black pepper*
3 eggs
GARNISH:
Chopped parsley

Wash, but do not peel, the cucumbers. Cut each in half crosswise, then cut each half in two lengthwise. Scrape out the seeds with the point of a teaspoon and discard. Cook the cucumbers for 10 minutes in boiling, lightly salted water; drain through a colander and keep warm.

Cook the rice in a large pan of boiling salted water for 25–30 minutes. While the rice is cooking, peel and chop the onion, and cook over gentle heat in ¼ cup of the butter until translucent, but not brown.

Trim and thinly slice the mushrooms; add to the onions. Cut the bacon into narrow strips; add to the mixture in the pan and season with salt and freshly ground pepper. When the rice is cooked, drain in a sieve and rinse under cold running water. Stir it into the onion mixture, adding ¼ cup of butter. Cook over low heat, stirring occasionally, for 5–10 minutes.

Lightly beat the eggs and season with salt and pepper. Cook two or three small omelettes in the remaining butter. Roll the omelettes up and cut them into strips about ½ in wide. Add these to the rice mixture.

To serve, arrange the cucumber 'boats' on a hot dish and spoon the rice mixture over them. Sprinkle with chopped parsley.

CUCUMBER WITH SHRIMP AND MUSHROOMS

Cucumber is usually served raw in salads or sandwiches, but it loses nothing of its flavor or freshness by being cooked. This quick little hors-d'oeuvre has something of the delicate taste of Chinese food.

PREPARATION TIME: *15 min*
COOKING TIME: *15 min*
INGREDIENTS *(for 4):*
1 large or 2 small cucumbers
Salt and black pepper*
¼ pound button mushrooms
3 tablespoons butter
1 teaspoon flour
5 tablespoons chicken stock
5 tablespoons light cream
Soy sauce (optional)
¼ pound peeled cooked shrimp
GARNISH:
Finely chopped chives, basil or dill
Cucumber twists

Wash the cucumber, but do not peel it. Cut it into ½ in dice and cook for 3–4 minutes in boiling, lightly salted water. Rinse the cucumber in cold water and drain thoroughly in a colander. Trim the mushrooms and cut them into ¼ in thick slices.

Melt the butter in a small pan and cook the mushrooms for 2–3 minutes or until lightly browned. Add the diced cucumber and simmer, covered with a lid, for 2–3 minutes over low heat. Sprinkle in the flour and blend thoroughly; gradually add the stock and cream, stirring the mixture until smooth. Bring gently to the boil and season to taste with salt, freshly ground pepper and a few drops of soy sauce. Simmer for

SAVORY CUCUMBER

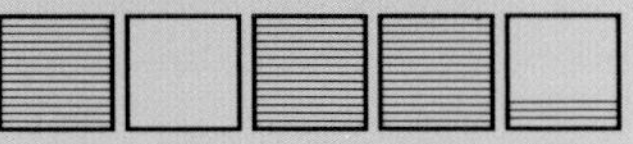

GLUTEN-FREE WHOLEFOOD*
TOTAL CALORIES: ABOUT 2490

The high **salt** level comes mainly from the bacon, if the butter used is unsalted. It can be reduced to low by replacing the bacon with diced sweet peppers. This will make the dish **vegetarian** and also reduce the **fat** and **cholesterol**, while maintaining the color of the dish. For low fat, instead of cooking the vegetables in butter, use 1 tablespoon of oil. Mushrooms produce liquid of their own. For a low cholesterol count, use only 1 egg. For more fiber, use brown rice, cooking in 2¼ times its volume of water so the water is all absorbed after 40–50 minutes of simmering: this retains in the rice vitamins and minerals that, using the other method, are transferred to the water and thrown away. (Calories lost: up to 970.)

Microwave: ☑

CUCUMBER WITH SHRIMP AND MUSHROOMS

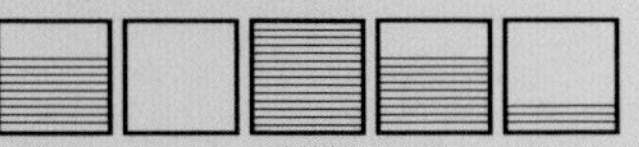

GLUTEN-FREE* WHOLEFOOD*
TOTAL CALORIES: ABOUT 670

Do not use more than the few drops of soy sauce specified or the **salt** level will be high. Shrimp are naturally fairly high in salt, although not compared to foods such as smoked fish. If wished, reduce the amount

used, possibly replacing some with monkfish cubes, as this fish has a lobster-like texture. It also has much less **cholesterol** than shrimp have.
The **fat** can be reduced to low by cooking the mushrooms in a pan lightly brushed with oil, omitting the butter, and replacing the cream with low-fat sour cream or creamy milk. If this is done, and monkfish now used instead of half the shrimp, the cholesterol will also be low. (Calories lost: up to 276.)

PEARS IN TARRAGON CREAM

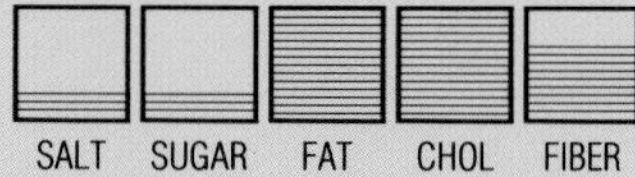

SALT SUGAR FAT CHOL FIBER

GLUTEN-FREE WHOLEFOOD* VEGETARIAN
TOTAL CALORIES: ABOUT 1570

For a low **fat** and **cholesterol** level, replace the cream with quark or low-fat sour cream. (Calories lost: up to 1020.)

WALDORF SALAD

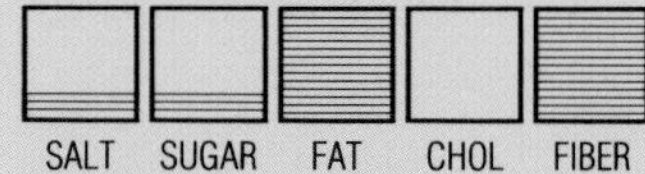

SALT SUGAR FAT CHOL FIBER

GLUTEN-FREE WHOLEFOOD* VEGETARIAN
TOTAL CALORIES: ABOUT 1880

Walnuts are roughly half oil, with a particularly high level of linoleic acid – an essential nutrient. However, if wished, halve the amount used. This will give a low **fat** dish if you also replace the mayonnaise with a mixture of quark with seasoning as suggested; low fat yogurt could also be used half and half with low-fat sour cream. (Calories lost: up to 1436.)

another 2–3 minutes, then stir in the shrimp and heat through.

Spoon into a warmed serving dish or individual deep scallop shells. Sprinkle with the herbs and decorate with thin twists of cucumber. Serve the cucumber mixture immediately, with thinly sliced brown bread and butter, or crisp toast fingers.

PEARS IN TARRAGON CREAM

For this simple first course, choose firm, but ripe, squat pears. They are served with a classic French tarragon cream.

PREPARATION TIME: *10 min*
CHILLING TIME: *1 hour*
INGREDIENTS *(for 6):*
6 pears
1¼ cups heavy cream
2 tablespoons tarragon vinegar
Sugar
Salt and black pepper*

Chill the pears in the refrigerator. Beat the cream and vinegar together until thick, but not too stiff. Season to taste with sugar, salt and freshly ground pepper. Peel and halve the pears and scoop out the center cores with a teaspoon.

Serve the pears, rounded side up, on individual small plates and with the tarragon cream spooned over them.

WALDORF SALAD

This salad was created at the Waldorf-Astoria Hotel in New York. The tart combination of apple and celery is an excellent counter-balance to rich meats.

PREPARATION TIME: *20 min*
STANDING TIME: *30 min*
INGREDIENTS *(for 6):*
1 pound tart red eating apples
2 tablespoons lemon juice
1 teaspoon sugar
½ cup mayonnaise (page 167)
½ head celery
½ cup chopped walnuts
1 head of lettuce

Wash and core the apples, slice one apple finely and dice the remainder. Dip the apple slices in a dressing of lemon juice, sugar and 1 tablespoon of the mayonnaise. Set aside. Toss the diced apple in the dressing and let it stand for 30 minutes.

Scrub and chop the celery. Add the celery and walnuts to the diced apple, with the rest of the mayonnaise, and mix thoroughly. Line a serving bowl with the cleaned and chilled lettuce leaves, pile the salad into the center and garnish with the apple.

FASOULIA

In Greece, this regional dish of white beans is usually served as a vegetable course on its own. It can accompany any kind of meat and is particularly good with lamb. Preparations should begin 12 hours in advance.

PREPARATION TIME: *8 min*
COOKING TIME: *3¼ hours*
INGREDIENTS *(for 4):*
1⅓ cups dried navy beans
1 large onion
½ cup olive oil
2 cloves garlic
1 bay leaf
½ teaspoon powdered thyme
1 tablespoon tomato paste
Juice of a lemon
Salt and black pepper*
GARNISH:
Coarsely chopped parsley

Soak the navy beans in plenty of cold water for 12 hours. The following day, peel and coarsely chop the onion; fry it in the olive oil in a deep sauté pan until it takes color. Drain the beans and add to the onion, together with the peeled and crushed garlic, the bay leaf, thyme and tomato paste. Cook over a moderate heat for 10 minutes, then add boiling water to cover the beans by about 1 in. Continue cooking, covered, at a gentle simmer for about 3 hours or until the beans are quite tender, but not mushy. Add the lemon juice and season to taste. Allow the beans to cool in the liquid which should have the consistency of a thick sauce.

Serve the cold beans in their liquid garnished with parsley.

NAPOLEON'S BEAN SALAD

In exile on St Helena, Napoleon was still emperor at his own table. This salad of white beans is said to have been a favorite of his and was served every day at lunchtime. The beans should be soaked for at least 8 hours before they are cooked.

PREPARATION TIME: *10 min*
COOKING TIME: *2–3 hours*
CHILLING TIME: *1 hour*
INGREDIENTS *(for 6):*
1⅓ cups dried navy beans
1 onion
1 carrot
Bouquet garni (page 183)
Salt and black pepper*
½ cup finely chopped parsley, chervil, tarragon, chives or scallions
5 tablespoons olive oil
1 tablespoon tarragon vinegar
1 rounded teaspoon Dijon-style mustard
½ teaspoon sugar

Soak the beans in a bowl of water for 8 hours or overnight. Drain the beans and put them in a large pan or casserole. Peel and quarter the onion and carrot, and add them, with the bouquet garni and plenty of black pepper, to the beans. Pour over enough water to cover the beans by ½ in. Put a lid on the pan and cook in the center of a pre-heated oven, at 275°–300°F (140°–160°C, mark 1–2) for 3 hours, or on top of the stove at simmering point, for 2 hours. If necessary, top up with water during cooking so that the beans do not dry out.

Season the cooked beans to taste with salt and cook for another 5 minutes. Drain the beans in a colander, remove the onion, carrot and bouquet garni, and put the beans in a large serving bowl. Add the chopped herbs, oil, vinegar, mustard and sugar to the beans. Stir to blend the ingredients thoroughly and leave to chill in the refrigerator for about 1 hour.

LETTUCE AND CELERY SALAD

Most rich meat dishes, especially those with sweet stuffings, are better accompanied by a side salad than by a vegetable dish.

PREPARATION TIME: *10 min*
INGREDIENTS *(for 4–6):*
4 heads of lettuces
4 celery stalks
DRESSING:
1 teaspoon Dijon-style mustard
*½ teaspoon salt**
1 teaspoon sugar
½ cup light cream
½ cup olive oil
3 tablespoons tarragon vinegar
GARNISH:
Celery leaves

Strip the outer leaves off the lettuce and cut each head into four. Trim off roots and coarse leaves from the celery, scrub and chop the sticks coarsely. Place these ingredients in a serving bowl.

To make the dressing, blend the mustard, salt and sugar in a mixing bowl; stir in the cream. Beat in the olive oil, drop by drop, and when all the oil is absorbed, gradually beat in the vinegar until the dressing has the consistency of thick cream. Pour the dressing over the celery and lettuce, toss and serve garnished with a few celery leaves.

FASOULIA

SALT SUGAR FAT CHOL FIBER

GLUTEN-FREE WHOLEFOOD VEGETARIAN
TOTAL CALORIES: ABOUT 2000

Boil navy beans rapidly for 10 minutes before covering them and continuing the cooking. This ensures that any poisonous chemicals are destroyed.
Reduce the **fat** level to low by cooking the onion in a pan lightly brushed with oil. Keep the pan covered so that the onion cooks by a mixture of frying and steaming. If wished, add a little more good-quality oil at the end to give the characteristic Mediterranean flavor. (Calories lost: up to 1079.)

NAPOLEON'S BEAN SALAD

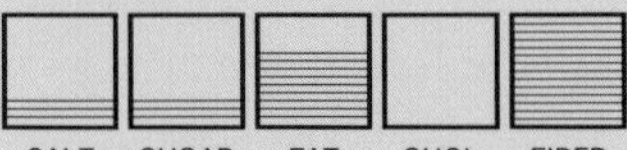

SALT SUGAR FAT CHOL FIBER

GLUTEN-FREE WHOLEFOOD* VEGETARIAN
TOTAL CALORIES: ABOUT 1325

Boil navy beans rapidly for 10 minutes before covering them and continuing the cooking. This ensures that any poisonous chemicals are destroyed.
For a low **fat** dish, reduce the amount of oil to 2 tablespoons. (Calories lost: up to 405.)

Pressure cooker: ✓ for the beans.

LETTUCE AND CELERY SALAD

SALT SUGAR FAT CHOL FIBER

GLUTEN-FREE* WHOLEFOOD* VEGETARIAN
TOTAL CALORIES: ABOUT 1800

For a low **fat** dish, the dressing can be changed to use only 1 tablespoon oil, with ½ cup low-fat yogurt, cultured buttermilk or a mixture of either of these with low-fat sour cream. (Calories lost: up to 1474.) Check that the mustard is **gluten-free**.

SPINACH RAMEKINS

This unusual appetizer is a creamy pâté of spinach, sardines and eggs. Serve it with grissini (Italian bread sticks) or toast.

PREPARATION TIME: *10–15 min*
CHILLING TIME: *½–1 hour*
INGREDIENTS *(for 4):*
1 pound fresh bulk spinach
1 onion
½ teaspoon dried tarragon
1–2 tablespoons finely chopped parsley
1 hard-cooked egg
4 canned sardines
2 tablespoons heavy cream
Salt and black pepper*
GARNISH:
1 hard-cooked egg
4 anchovy fillets

Pull the spinach leaves off the stalks and wash in several changes of cold water to remove all traces of soil. Peel and finely chop the onion. Put the wet spinach in a large saucepan with the onion, tarragon and parsley; cover with a lid. Cook over low heat for 7–10 minutes, or until softened, then drain thoroughly.

Chop one hard-cooked egg and the sardines and blend with the spinach. Rub the mixture through a coarse sieve, or liquidize it to a purée. Stir in the cream and season to taste with salt and freshly ground pepper. Spoon the creamed spinach into individual ramekins or small serving dishes and chill in a refrigerator until set.

For the garnish, separate the white and yolk of the hard-cooked egg; chop the white finely and sieve the yolk. Decorate each ramekin with alternate rows of white and yolk. Split the anchovy fillets in half and lay them on top in a criss-cross pattern.

PEPPER, ANCHOVY AND TOMATO SALAD

This unusual and tasty salad goes perfectly with broiled veal chops and with most chicken dishes. It can also be served on its own as a light beginning to a substantial meal.

PREPARATION TIME: *35 min*
CHILLING TIME: *30 min*
INGREDIENTS *(for 4):*
2 large sweet red peppers
3 large tomatoes
2 small cans anchovy fillets
1 small clove garlic
3–4 tablespoons olive oil
Juice of half lemon
Salt and black pepper*

Put the peppers under a hot broiler, turning them frequently until the skins are charred and black all over. The black outer skin then rubs off easily under cold running water. Remove the stalk ends and seeds from the peppers and cut out any white pith. Cut the flesh into wide strips with scissors. Skin the tomatoes (page 160), cut them into slices and remove the seeds. Drain the anchovy fillets and rinse them in cold water to remove excess oil and salt; ease them carefully apart.

Arrange the pepper strips on a flat serving dish with the sliced tomatoes, and lay the anchovy fillets on top in a lattice pattern.

Peel and crush the garlic and mix with the oil. Pour this dressing over the salad and sprinkle with lemon juice, salt and very little freshly ground pepper. Chill for at least 30 minutes before serving.

SPINACH RAMEKINS

GLUTEN-FREE WHOLEFOOD
TOTAL CALORIES: ABOUT 600

The high level of **salt** comes from the anchovy fillets plus the canned sardines. To reduce the level to low, omit the anchovies (garnish with strips of sweet pepper instead) and use only 2 sardines.
The **fat** and **cholesterol** can be reduced to moderate, despite the natural oils of sardines, by the following steps: drain sardines canned in oil thoroughly, replace the cream with quark or low-fat sour cream, and omit the egg used for garnish, replacing with egg white only or with finely diced sweet red pepper. (Calories lost: up to 177.)

Food Processor: √
Freezing: √ up to 3 months.
Microwave: √

PEPPER, ANCHOVY AND TOMATO SALAD

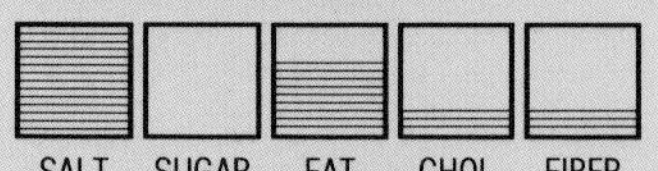

GLUTEN-FREE WHOLEFOOD
TOTAL CALORIES: ABOUT 750

Anchovies are saturated in **salt**, even after rinsing in water. For a low salt level, replace the anchovies with 6 ounces monkfish, lightly poached in stock for 6–8 minutes, then cut into cubes or strips.
To reduce **fat** level to low, simply use only 1 or 1½ tablespoons oil, adding some low-fat yogurt if more bulk is wanted for the dressing. (Calories lost: up to 405.)

PEPERONATA

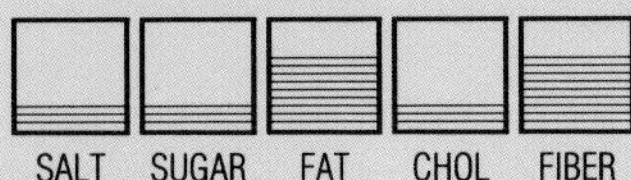
SALT SUGAR FAT CHOL FIBER

GLUTEN-FREE WHOLEFOOD* VEGETARIAN
TOTAL CALORIES: ABOUT 650

To reduce the **fat** level to low, cook the onion and peppers in only 2 teaspoons butter or the same amount of oil, covering the pan so that the juice from the vegetables moistens the dish without evaporating. (Calories lost: up to 381.)

Freezing: ✓ up to 3 months.
Microwave: ✓

CELERIAC SALAD WITH PARMA HAM

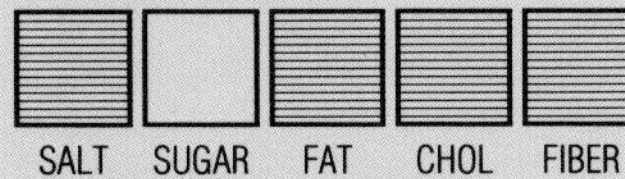
SALT SUGAR FAT CHOL FIBER

GLUTEN-FREE WHOLEFOOD
TOTAL CALORIES: ABOUT 865

The **salt** comes almost entirely from the ham, and even halving the amount will still leave the level high. If wished, serve very small portions, say 1 ounce per person (still moderately high) and complete the salad with slices of apple tossed in orange juice, or cubes of melon.
If the fat from the ham is not eaten, most of the **fat** comes from the mayonnaise, which is 80% oil. To avoid this, replace it with quark or low-fat sour cream, thinning with a little lemon juice if necessary. The fat level will then be low but the **cholesterol** level still remains high, due to the ham. (Calories lost: up to 429.)

PEPERONATA

This spicy casserole of sweet peppers and tomatoes is of Italian origin. It is served hot with broiled meat and fish, or cold as a side salad or appetizer.

PREPARATION TIME: *10 min*
COOKING TIME: *30–35 min*
INGREDIENTS *(for 4):*
4 large sweet red or green peppers
1 onion
8 large tomatoes
1 clove garlic
Salt and black pepper*
2 tablespoons unsalted butter
2 tablespoons olive oil
2 teaspoons sugar (optional)

Peel and finely chop the onion. Remove the stalks and wash the peppers; cut them in half lengthwise and remove the inner ribs and the seeds. Cut the peppers into narrow strips. Skin the tomatoes (page 160) and chop them coarsely. Peel the garlic and mash it to a paste with a little salt.

Heat the butter and oil in a heavy-based pan; add the onion and peppers. Cover the pan with a lid and fry the vegetables gently until soft, but not brown. Add the tomatoes and garlic and season to taste with freshly ground pepper and sugar. Put the lid back on the pan and continue cooking over very low heat, stirring occasionally, for 25–30 minutes. The mixture should now be soft, and the juices from the tomatoes should have evaporated. Correct seasoning if necessary.

Spoon the mixture into a serving dish and serve hot or cold.

CELERIAC SALAD WITH PARMA HAM

The large celery root – or celeriac – is becoming a popular vegetable here. It can also be served raw in a salad, with Parma ham or thinly sliced salami.

PREPARATION TIME: *10–15 min*
COOKING TIME: *2–3 min*
INGREDIENTS *(for 4):*
1 large celeriac
2–3 rounded tablespoons mayonnaise (page 167)
¼ teaspoon Dijon-style mustard
12 slices Parma ham

Peel the celeriac. Cut it into narrow slices and then into matchstick-thin pieces. Add to a pan of boiling salted water and blanch for 2–3 minutes; drain in a colander and allow to cool. Blend together the mayonnaise and mustard and toss the celeriac in this dressing.

Arrange the Parma ham on individual plates, allowing three thin slices per person. Divide the salad between the portions.

TOMATO SALAD

Tomatoes can make a refreshing beginning to a meal, or they can be served as a side dish with cold meats.

PREPARATION TIME: *20 min*
CHILLING TIME: *1 hour*
INGREDIENTS *(for 6):*
12 tomatoes
2 teaspoons sugar
Salt and black pepper*
4 tablespoons olive or corn oil
4 teaspoons white wine vinegar
1 tablespoon chopped chives or tarragon

Skin and thinly slice the tomatoes (page 160) and place them in a shallow serving dish. Sprinkle over the sugar, and season to taste with salt and freshly ground pepper.

Mix the oil and vinegar together, and sprinkle over the tomatoes. Add chopped chives or tarragon and leave the salad to chill in the refrigerator for at least 1 hour before serving. Turn the tomato slices once or twice.

MUSHROOM SALAD

Mushrooms should be used as soon as possible after purchase. They tend to go limp and brown when stored in the refrigerator.

PREPARATION TIME: *15 min*
STANDING TIME: *1 hour*
INGREDIENTS *(for 4–6):*
1 pound large mushrooms
Salt and black pepper*
2 teaspoons Worcestershire sauce
1 tablespoon soy sauce

Wash and trim the mushrooms, and slice them as thinly as possible into a deep serving dish. Season to taste with salt and freshly ground pepper, and sprinkle over the Worcestershire and soy sauces. Mix the salad well and set aside for about 1 hour, turning the mushroom slices from time to time in the dressing.

The mushrooms will have made quite a lot of juice by the time they are ready for serving; this is an essential part of the dressing and should not be drained off.

ZUCCHINI AND CHIVES SALAD

Zucchini are very popular as a cooked vegetable. They are also suitable for a fresh chilled salad to serve with cold meat and poultry.

PREPARATION TIME: *10 min*
COOKING TIME: *5 min*
CHILLING TIME: *1 hour*
INGREDIENTS *(for 4):*
$\frac{3}{4}$ pound zucchini
1 tablespoon olive or corn oil
Juice of half lemon
Salt and black pepper*
1 heaping tablespoon chopped chives.

Wash the zucchini thoroughly and top and tail them. Bring a large pan of lightly salted water to the boil, drop in the zucchini and boil for 5 minutes to soften them slightly and reduce the bitterness of the skin. Drain the zucchini immediately in a colander and rinse in cold water.

Cut the drained zucchini crosswise into $\frac{1}{2}$ in thick slices and put them in a shallow serving dish. Make a dressing from the oil and lemon juice, season with salt and freshly ground pepper and pour over the zucchini. Add the chopped chives and blend thoroughly before chilling the salad.

SALAD ELONA

This unusual salad of cucumber and strawberries is an ideal side dish to serve with cold chicken and turkey, or with delicately flavored fish such as salmon and sole.

PREPARATION TIME: *15 min*
CHILLING TIME: *1 hour*
INGREDIENTS *(for 4–6):*
1 small cucumber
12 large strawberries
Salt and black pepper*
1–2 tablespoons dry white wine or white wine vinegar

Peel the cucumber and slice it thinly. Wash and hull the strawberries, drain them in a colander and then cut them into thin, even slices. Arrange the slices in a decorative pattern in a shallow serving dish – an outer circle of cucumber, slightly overlapped by a circle of strawberry, then more cucumber, finishing with a center of strawberry slices. Season lightly with salt and freshly ground pepper. Sprinkle the wine or vinegar over the salad and chill in the refrigerator before serving.

TOMATO SALAD

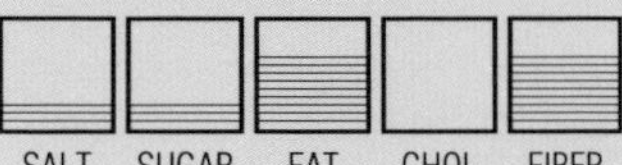

SALT SUGAR FAT CHOL FIBER

GLUTEN-FREE WHOLEFOOD* VEGETARIAN
TOTAL CALORIES: ABOUT 665

To reduce the **fat** level to low, use only 1–2 tablespoons good quality oil for flavor, mixed with the same amount of low-fat yogurt, sour cream or quark. (Calories lost: up to 250.)

MUSHROOM SALAD

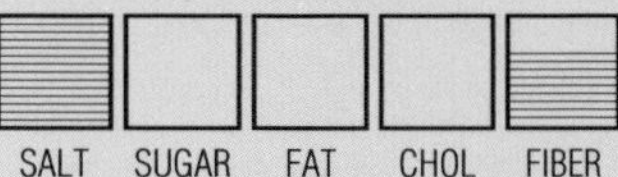

SALT SUGAR FAT CHOL FIBER

GLUTEN-FREE WHOLEFOOD VEGETARIAN
TOTAL CALORIES: ABOUT 70

To reduce the **salt** level to low, replace the soy sauce with 2–3 tablespoons of lemon juice, adding a very little honey to it first if you like to reduce the tartness.
For a **gluten-free** dressing, make sure the soy sauce contains no gluten. Many makes do, but the Japanese equivalent, tamari, should not contain any wheat derivatives. Alternatively, replace the soy sauce as suggested above.

ZUCCHINI AND CHIVES SALAD

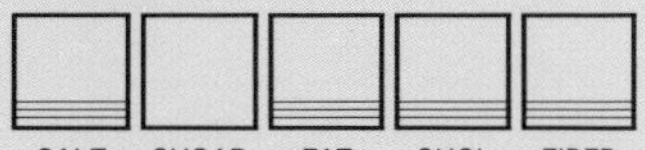

GLUTEN-FREE WHOLEFOOD VEGETARIAN
TOTAL CALORIES: ABOUT 185

The **salt** level is low assuming that you have not salted the water for cooking the zucchini. This recipe needs no changes to fit healthy eating guidelines. However, the zucchini may retain more nutrients and flavor if steamed or cooked in ½ in stock or water, tightly covered, rather than being boiled.

SALAD ELONA

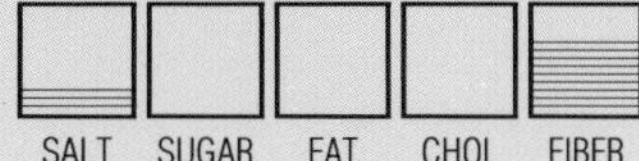

GLUTEN-FREE WHOLEFOOD VEGETARIAN
TOTAL CALORIES: ABOUT 100

This dish needs no changes at all to fit healthy eating guidelines. Strawberries, like other soft fruit, are higher in fiber than many salad vegetables.

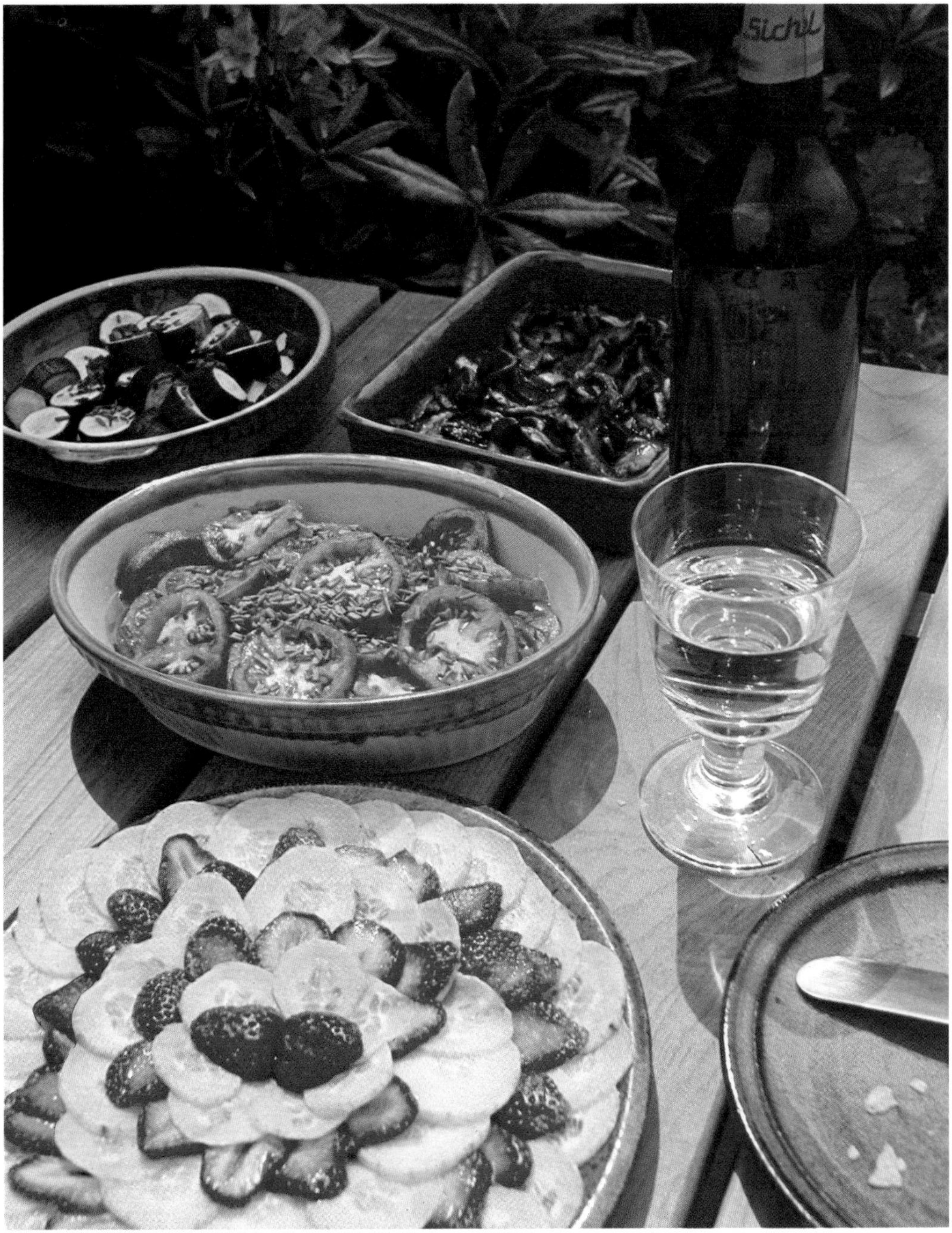

IMAM BAYILDI

This Turkish dish takes its name from the Imam, or Muslim holy man. He is said to have swooned with pleasure – or from overeating – after being served this eggplant dish.

PREPARATION TIME: *30 min*
COOKING TIME: *40 min*
INGREDIENTS *(for 6):*
3 large eggplants
Salt and black pepper*
Olive oil
3 large onions
¾ pound tomatoes
1 clove garlic
½ teaspoon ground cinnamon
1 teaspoon sugar
1 tablespoon chopped parsley
1 heaping tablespoon finely chopped pine nuts (optional)

Cut the stalk ends from the eggplants, wipe them and put them in a large saucepan. Add boiling water and cover with a lid; cook the eggplants for 10 minutes. Drain the eggplants, plunge them into cold water and leave for 5 minutes. Cut them in half lengthwise and scoop out most of the flesh, leaving a ½ in thick shell. Set aside the scooped-out flesh. Arrange the shells in a buttered ovenproof dish and sprinkle them with a little salt and freshly ground pepper. Pour 4 teaspoons of olive oil in each shell and cook the eggplants, uncovered, in the center of an oven pre-heated to 350°F (180°C, mark 4) for 30 minutes.

While the eggplant shells are cooking, peel and finely chop the onions; skin the tomatoes (page 160) and chop them. Peel and crush the garlic. Heat two tablespoons of oil in a frying pan, add the onions and garlic and fry gently for 5 minutes, then add the tomatoes, cinnamon, sugar and parsley; season to taste with salt and pepper. Continue simmering this mixture until the liquid has reduced by half, after about 20 minutes. Chop the eggplant flesh and add to the frying pan, with the chopped pine nuts (if used), and cook for a further 10 minutes.

Remove the eggplant shells from the oven, stuff them with the tomato mixture and serve hot or cold, on its own, or with roast and broiled meat.

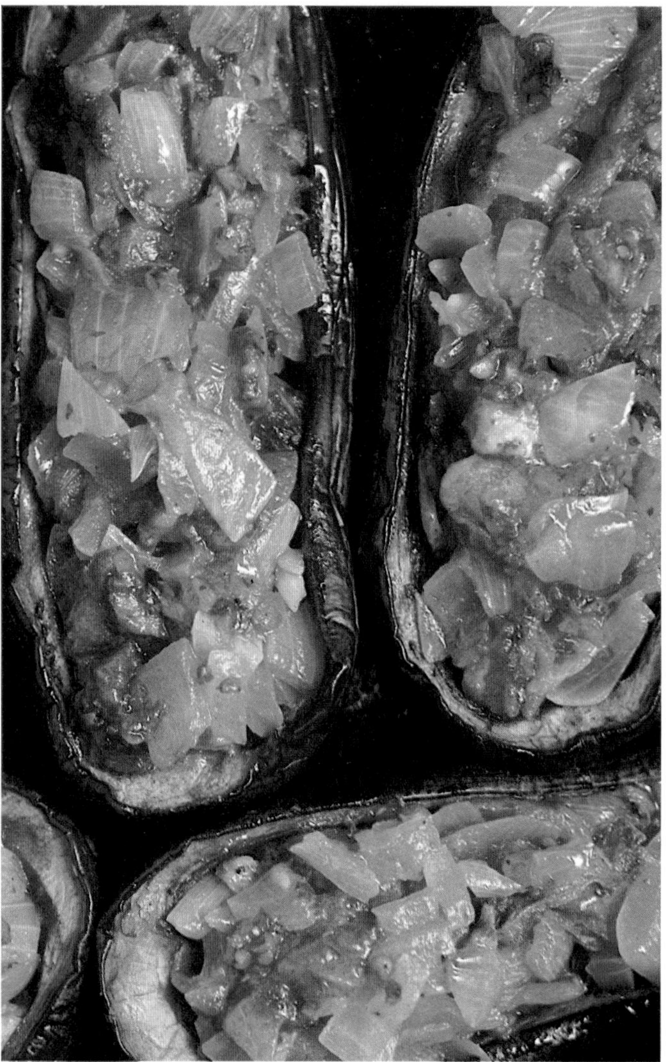

IMAM BAYILDI

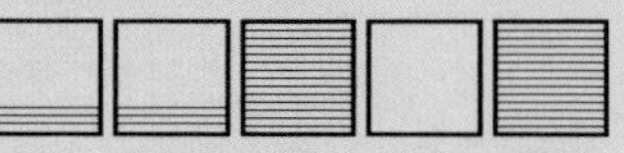

SALT SUGAR FAT CHOL FIBER

GLUTEN-FREE WHOLEFOOD* VEGETARIAN
TOTAL CALORIES: ABOUT 850

To reduce the **fat** content to low, omit the olive oil added to each shell. Cook the onions and garlic in a heavy-based pan brushed lightly with oil. (Calories lost: up to 404.)

Freezing: ✓ up to 2 months.

EGGPLANT WITH HAM

SALT SUGAR FAT CHOL FIBER

GLUTEN-FREE WHOLEFOOD
TOTAL CALORIES: ABOUT 2715

The high **salt** level is due to the ham. If only half the amount is used, the level will be moderate. To reduce the overall **fat** to low, choose lean ham, and do not fry the eggplant shells. Brush them lightly with oil and broil on either side for about 4–6 minutes or until tender. Cook the eggplant flesh in a pan lightly brushed with oil, using the same method for the ham. Make the sauce without adding extra fat, although a teaspoonful or two of butter added to the pan at this stage could be allowed. Use skim milk. Do not dot the dish with butter, but cover it with foil for a few minutes to keep moist before uncovering to brown. This gives low fat and, if half the quantity of ham is used, fairly low **cholesterol**. (Calories lost: up to 1545.)

Freezing: ✓ up to 1 month.

BRAISED CELERY

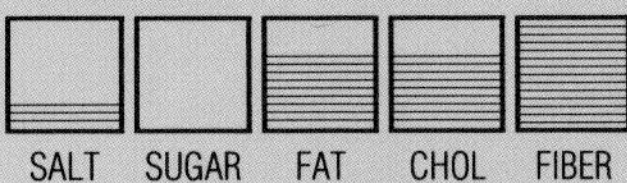

GLUTEN-FREE* WHOLEFOOD*
TOTAL CALORIES: ABOUT 550

To give a low **fat** and **cholesterol** content, add no more than 1 teaspoon of butter per person in the form of beurre manié. Alternatively, replace this thickening method with 2 teaspoons of arrowroot, blended to a smooth paste with a little cold water, then blended into the mixture for the last few minutes of cooking. (Calories lost: up to 253.) This also makes the recipe **gluten-free**. For a **vegetarian** dish, substitute water or vegetable stock for the chicken stock.

Freezing: √ up to 6 months.

Microwave: √

BAKED CABBAGE

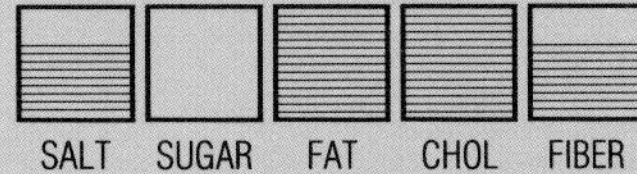

GLUTEN-FREE* WHOLEFOOD* VEGETARIAN
TOTAL CALORIES: ABOUT 1490

For a low **salt** level, use unsalted nuts and only ½ cup cheese.
For low **fat** and **cholesterol** levels, make the sauce by the blending method (page 166), omitting the butter. Use skim milk and only half the amount of peanuts and cheese. (Calories lost: up to 763.)
Gluten-free rice flour can be used to make the sauce.

Freezing: √ up to 2 months.

Microwave: √

EGGPLANT WITH HAM

For this hot lunch or supper dish, the eggplants are filled with a ham stuffing.

PREPARATION TIME: *25 min*
COOKING TIME: *20 min*
INGREDIENTS *(for 4):*
4 eggplants
6 ounces cooked ham, in ¼ in thick slices
½ cup olive oil
¼ cup unsalted butter
2 teaspoons flour
1¼ cups milk
Salt and black pepper*
Juice of half lemon
1–1⅓ cups dry breadcrumbs

Remove the stalk ends from the eggplants and wipe them with a damp cloth. Cut each eggplant in half lengthwise with a sharp knife, and carefully scoop out the flesh without breaking the skin. Finely dice the eggplant flesh and the ham.

Heat the oil in a heavy-based pan over moderate heat and fry the eggplant shells until brown, turning them over with a spatula. Remove and drain on crumpled kitchen paper towels. Cook the diced eggplant flesh in the oil in the pan and, when softened and lightly browned, remove from the pan and drain. Melt half the butter in another pan and cook the ham until brown.

Sprinkle the flour into the pan in which the eggplant was cooked and blend until the oil is absorbed. Gradually add enough milk to make a thick white sauce (page 166), stirring all the time. Mix in the cooked ham and eggplant; add lemon juice and season to taste.

Spoon this mixture into the eggplant shells and set them in a buttered baking dish. Sprinkle breadcrumbs over the stuffing and dot with the remaining butter. Bake near the top of the oven, pre-heated to 400°F (200°C, mark 6), until brown. Serve at once.

BRAISED CELERY

This can be made ahead of time: if you do this, cook it for only 30 minutes and reheat gently when needed for about 10 minutes.

PREPARATION TIME: *20 min*
COOKING TIME: *40 min*
INGREDIENTS *(for 12):*
6 heads of celery
1 Spanish onion
6 small carrots
1¼ cups chicken stock
Salt and black pepper*
Beurre manié (page 166)
Parsley

Peel the onion, scrape the carrots, and slice them thinly. Trim the roots off the celery and remove any damaged stalks; scrub thoroughly, then cut each stalk in half lengthwise, and remove the green leafy tops. Blanch the celery for 10 minutes in boiling water, drain carefully in a colander, and put in a large fireproof dish. Cover with the thinly sliced onion and carrots; pour over the stock and season to taste.

Cover the pan with a lid or foil and simmer the celery over low heat, until tender, after about 40 minutes. About 5 minutes before the end of cooking time, add pieces of beurre manié to thicken the stock as desired. Serve the celery sprinkled with finely chopped parsley.

BAKED CABBAGE

Firm white winter cabbage is one of the least expensive vegetables. Baked in a cheese sauce, it goes well with sausages and bacon.

PREPARATION TIME: *30 min*
COOKING TIME: *15 min*
INGREDIENTS *(for 6):*
1½ pound head of white cabbage
3 tablespoons butter
3 tablespoons flour
1 cup milk
Salt and black pepper*
Ground mace or nutmeg
½ cup chopped salted peanuts
½–1 cup grated Cheddar cheese

Discard any damaged outer leaves and cut the cabbage into quarters. Cut out the center stalk and shred the cabbage finely.

Heat ½ in of water in a large heavy-based saucepan and add 1 teaspoon of salt. Put in the washed cabbage, a handful at a time, seasoning each layer with freshly ground black pepper.

Cover the pan with a lid and cook over low heat for about 10 minutes, or until the cabbage is cooked, but still crisp.

Meanwhile, make a thick white sauce (page 166). Season to taste.

Butter an ovenproof dish lightly and arrange a layer of cabbage over the bottom. Cover with some of the sauce and sprinkle with nuts and cheese. Fill the dish with layers of cabbage, sauce, nuts and cheese, finishing with cheese. Bake in the center of an oven pre-heated to 425°F (220°C, mark 7) for 15 minutes, or until the cheese is golden brown.

Serve the cabbage at once.

BROCCOLI WITH POULETTE SAUCE

In this recipe, broccoli is served with a classic French vegetable sauce whose creamy-white color contrasts well with the dark green vegetable.

PREPARATION TIME: *10 min*
COOKING TIME: *30 min*
INGREDIENTS *(for 4–6):*
2 pounds broccoli
Salt and black pepper*
¼ cup butter
1 tablespoon flour
1 egg yolk
Juice of half lemon
2 tablespoons heavy cream

Trim the tough stalk and any leaves off the broccoli head or heads. Wash thoroughly in cold water. Put the broccoli in a large pan of boiling salted water. Cover the pan with a lid and simmer over low heat for about 15 minutes or until just tender. Lift the broccoli carefully into a colander to drain; cover it with a dry cloth to keep it warm and set the liquid aside.

Melt the butter in a small saucepan, then take the pan off the heat. Stir in the flour to make a roux (page 166), and gradually blend in 1¼ cups of the broccoli liquid. Bring this sauce to the boil over low heat and simmer for about 10 minutes. Beat the egg yolk with 2 teaspoons of lemon juice and 2 tablespoons of the hot sauce. Remove the sauce from the heat and blend in the egg mixture.

Stir in the cream. Keep the sauce warm, but do not allow it to boil or the egg and cream will curdle. Season to taste with salt, freshly ground pepper and more lemon juice. Put the broccoli in a warm deep serving dish and pour over the sauce.

BAKED CAULIFLOWER CHEESE

In this dish the strong, smooth flavor of Gruyère cheese contrasts well with crisp cauliflower. The more usual Cheddar, perhaps mixed with a little Parmesan, can replace it but is less subtle. The Gruyère is particularly good in this rich, egg-based sauce, much more of a party piece than the usual béchamel. It can be served with broiled or roasted meats.

PREPARATION TIME: *20 min*
COOKING TIME: *50 min*
INGREDIENTS *(for 6):*
1 large cauliflower
1 onion
¼ cup unsalted butter
1½ cups fresh breadcrumbs
1¼ cups milk
½ cup grated Gruyère cheese
Salt and black pepper*
Ground nutmeg
5 beaten eggs

Cut away the coarse outer leaves from the cauliflower and break off the florets. Bring a large pan of lightly salted water to the boil. Add the florets, cover the pan with a lid, and boil gently for 5–8 minutes. Drain.

Meanwhile, finely chop the onion. Melt half the butter and fry the onion for 10 minutes. Butter the inside of a 2-quart baking dish and line it with ½ cup of breadcrumbs.

In a saucepan, bring the milk to the boil and add the Gruyère and the remaining butter. Season to taste with salt, pepper and a little nutmeg. Stir in the remaining breadcrumbs and the fried onion. Remove from the heat and blend in the beaten eggs. Fold the

BROCCOLI WITH POULETTE SAUCE

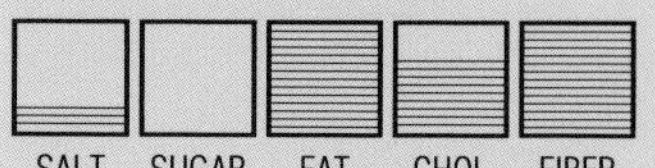

GLUTEN-FREE* WHOLEFOOD* VEGETARIAN
TOTAL CALORIES: ABOUT 830

To reduce the **fat** and **cholesterol** levels to low, make the sauce with only 2 tablespoons of butter and half the flour. Mix the remaining flour to a smooth paste with a very little cold water, and add to the roux after you have worked in some of the liquid. Replace the heavy cream with light cream, sour cream or quark. (Calories lost: up to 286.)

Microwave: ✓ for the broccoli.

BAKED CAULIFLOWER CHEESE

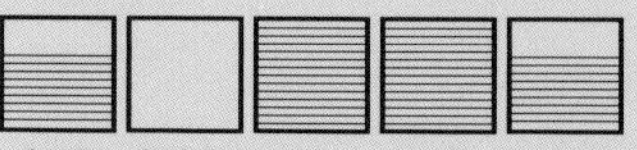

GLUTEN-FREE* WHOLEFOOD* VEGETARIAN
TOTAL CALORIES: ABOUT 1360

The **salt** comes mainly from the breadcrumbs and cheese, so the only way of significantly reducing it is to use less cheese and breadcrumbs made from bread with little or no added salt. The **fat** level can be reduced to medium by frying the onion in a pan lightly brushed with oil, omitting the butter. Keep the pan covered, but if the onion gets dry, add a spoonful or two of stock or water. Use skim milk, and only 3 eggs. (Calories lost: up to 511.) **Cholesterol** content will also be medium.

Microwave: ✓ for the cauliflower.

CAULIFLOWER WITH ALMONDS

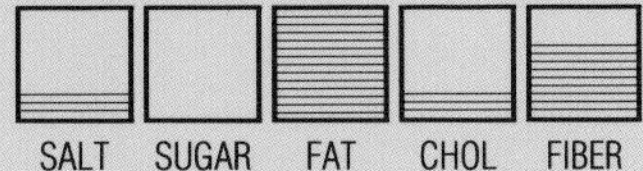

GLUTEN-FREE WHOLEFOOD VEGETARIAN
TOTAL CALORIES: ABOUT 780

To reduce the **fat** level to low, and eliminate **cholesterol**, toast the almonds on a baking sheet lightly brushed with oil under a medium broiler, omitting the butter. (Calories lost: up to 285.)
The **salt** level is low assuming that the cauliflower is cooked without salt, and that unsalted butter is used.

Microwave: ☑ for the cauliflower.

CAULIFLOWER POLONAISE

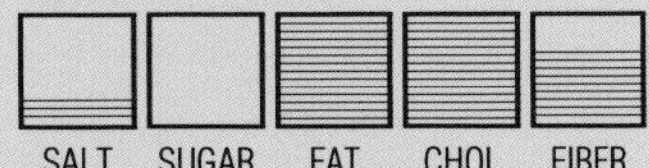

GLUTEN-FREE* WHOLEFOOD* VEGETARIAN
TOTAL CALORIES: ABOUT 800

The low **salt** level assumes that you cook the cauliflower in unsalted water, use unsalted butter and, if possible, low-salt bread for the crumbs. If you cannot find low-salt bread, the salt level will be low to medium, given that eggs also provide some sodium.
If wished, use only 1 egg. This will reduce the **fat** and **cholesterol** levels to low if you also use only half the amount of butter to crisp the crumbs. (Calories lost: up to 275.)

Microwave: ☑ for the cauliflower.

cauliflower into the sauce and spoon the mixture into the baking dish.

Bake on the lower shelf of an oven pre-heated to 325°F (170°C, mark 3) for 50 minutes or until firm.

CAULIFLOWER WITH ALMONDS

Crisp toasted almonds complement the delicate flavor and texture of lightly cooked cauliflower, making this an ideal accompaniment for a fish or meat dish in a rich sauce.

PREPARATION TIME: *10 min*
COOKING TIME: *12 min*
INGREDIENTS *(for 4):*
1 large cauliflower
*Salt**
¼ cup clarified butter (page 182)
½ cup sliced almonds

Dissolve two tablespoons of salt in a large bowl of cold water. Cut away the coarse outer leaves from the cauliflower and break the individual florets from the central stem, leaving a short stalk on each. Drop the florets in the salted water, together with the inner pale green leaves.

Bring a large pan of salted water to the boil; cook the drained cauliflower, covered, over low heat for 5–8 minutes. Drain through a colander.

Meanwhile, fry the almonds in the clarified butter over low heat until deep brown. Put the cauliflower in a dish and spoon over the almonds and butter.

CAULIFLOWER POLONAISE

Plainly cooked cauliflower is an excellent accompaniment to meat or poultry served in a rich sauce. The attractive garnish makes the dish particularly appetizing.

PREPARATION TIME: *15 min*
COOKING TIME: *20 min*
INGREDIENTS *(for 4–6):*
1 cauliflower
¼ cup butter
2 hard-cooked eggs
⅔ cup dried breadcrumbs
2 tablespoons chopped parsley
Salt and black pepper*
Lemon juice

Cut off the tough outer leaves and thick stalk base of the cauliflower. Wash thoroughly. Cook the cauliflower whole in boiling salted water for 10–15 minutes or until just tender. Drain in a colander and cover with a dry cloth to keep warm.

Meanwhile, shell the eggs, remove the yolks and rub them through a sieve; chop the whites finely with a stainless steel knife. Melt the butter in a small pan and fry the breadcrumbs until crisp. Remove the pan from the heat, stir in the parsley and season with salt, freshly ground pepper and lemon juice.

Place the cauliflower in a warm serving dish, sprinkle with the toasted breadcrumbs, and garnish with the egg yolks and whites in an attractive pattern.

TURKISH FRIED CARROTS

In Turkey, cold or warm yogurt is often used to dress vegetables and salads. Early or mature carrots are equally suitable for this dish, which goes well with lamb.

PREPARATION TIME: *15 min*
COOKING TIME: *20 min*
INGREDIENTS *(for 4)*:
1 pound carrots
Salt and black pepper*
1 tablespoon seasoned flour (p. 184)
2 tablespoons olive oil
$1\frac{1}{4}$ cups plain yogurt
GARNISH:
1 tablespoon chopped mint or 1 teaspoon caraway seeds

Peel or scrape the carrots and wash them. Cut them across into $\frac{1}{4}$ in thick slices. Bring a pan of salted water to the boil and cook the carrots for about 10 minutes or until nearly tender. Drain in a colander, then spread the carrots on paper towels so as to dry thoroughly.

Toss the carrots in seasoned flour, shaking off any surplus. Heat the oil in a heavy-based pan and fry the carrots over moderate heat until golden brown. Season to taste with salt and freshly ground pepper. Put the yogurt in a separate pan over low heat, and let it warm through. Do not let it reach boiling point or it will curdle.

Spoon the carrots into a hot serving dish, pour over the yogurt, and sprinkle with mint or caraway seeds.

CARROTS PAYSANNE

In cookery, *paysanne* refers to vegetables cooked in butter and used to garnish meat and poultry. Young carrots make a good accompaniment to broiled meat.

PREPARATION TIME: *15 min*
COOKING TIME: *30 min*
INGREDIENTS *(for 4–6)*:
1 pound small carrots
1 large onion
2 slices lean bacon
5 tablespoons unsalted butter
$\frac{1}{2}$–$1\frac{1}{4}$ cups chicken stock or water
1 teaspoon sugar
4 tablespoons heavy cream
*Salt**
GARNISH:
Finely chopped parsley

Trim the tops and roots from the carrots, scrape them and wash thoroughly. Blanch the carrots for 5 minutes in boiling salted water, then drain in a colander.

Peel and thinly slice the onion. Dice the bacon. Melt the butter in a wide shallow pan over low heat, and cook the onion and bacon until just soft and beginning to color.

Add the carrots to the bacon and onion, and pour over enough stock or water to barely cover the vegetables. Cover the pan with a lid and cook over moderate heat until the carrots are tender. Lift out the carrots and keep them hot.

Boil the liquid over high heat until it has reduced to a few tablespoons. Add the sugar and cream, and season to taste with salt. Simmer the liquid, uncovered, until the sauce has thickened slightly.

Pour the cream sauce over the carrots and sprinkle with parsley.

TURKISH FRIED CARROTS

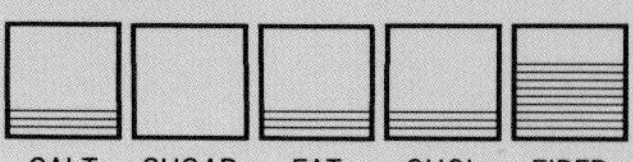

SALT SUGAR FAT CHOL FIBER

GLUTEN-FREE* WHOLEFOOD* VEGETARIAN
TOTAL CALORIES: ABOUT 580

Microwave: ☑ for the carrots.

CARROTS PAYSANNE

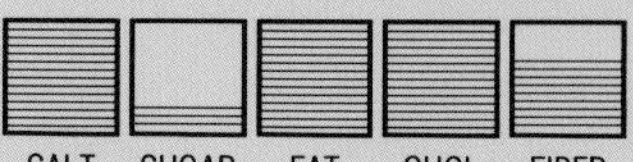

SALT SUGAR FAT CHOL FIBER

GLUTEN-FREE WHOLEFOOD
TOTAL CALORIES: ABOUT 1120

The high **salt** level comes almost entirely from the bacon. To reduce it to low, use only 1 slice of bacon.
If, as well, the butter is omitted and the onion is cooked in a heavy pan brushed lightly with oil together with the bacon, and the heavy cream replaced with sour cream or low-fat yogurt, the dish will have a low fat and **cholesterol** level. (Calories lost: up to 745.)

GLAZED CARROTS

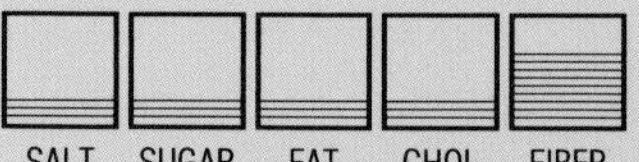

SALT SUGAR FAT CHOL FIBER

GLUTEN-FREE WHOLEFOOD VEGETARIAN
TOTAL CALORIES: ABOUT 310

To avoid raising the **salt** level, do not sprinkle the carrots with salt before serving. If wished, add a generous amount of extra parsley and pepper instead.

Microwave: ☑

RAGOÛT OF LETTUCE AND PEAS

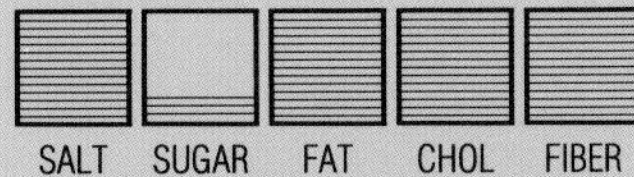

GLUTEN-FREE* WHOLEFOOD*
TOTAL CALORIES: ABOUT 1900

The **salt** level is high because of the ham. To reduce the level to low, use not more than 2 ounces. If wished, some more onions can be added to the dish to restore the bulk.
The high **fat** level comes mainly from the butter, if lean ham is used, and from the fried bread garnish. For low fat, toss the vegetables in only 2 tablespoons butter, or a mixture of butter and oil. Garnish the dish with scallion, cut in long slivers, or with poached whole mushrooms. If only 2 ounces of ham is used the cholesterol will also be low. (Calories lost: up to 880.)
This will also make the dish **gluten-free**.

Microwave: ✓

PEAS AND SCALLIONS

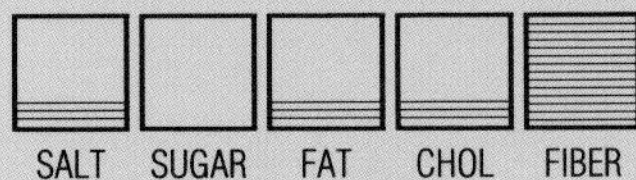

GLUTEN-FREE* WHOLEFOOD*
TOTAL CALORIES: ABOUT 1075

For a **gluten-free** dish, make the beurre manié with cornstarch, rice, buckwheat or other gluten-free flour.
For a **vegetarian** dish, use water or vegetable stock instead of chicken stock.

Microwave: ✓

GLAZED CARROTS

The full flavor of tender carrots is retained by cooking them in a buttery glaze. They are suitable for serving with thick meat casseroles, and with roast lamb and pork as well as with broiled chops.

PREPARATION TIME: *10 min*
COOKING TIME: *20–25 min*
INGREDIENTS *(for 4):*
1 pound young carrots
2 tablespoons unsalted butter
Salt and black pepper*
1 teaspoon sugar
1 heaping teaspoon chopped parsley

Scrub and scrape the carrots and cut them into slices about ¼ in thick. Melt the butter in a saucepan, add the carrot slices and season with the freshly ground pepper and the sugar. Add sufficient cold water to just cover the carrots. Bring to the boil, cover the pan with a lid and simmer gently for 15–20 minutes or until the carrots are tender.

Remove the lid; increase the heat and cook the carrots until the liquid has evaporated and only the butter remains – do not allow the carrots to brown. Draw the pan off the heat; add the parsley and toss with the carrots in the butter glaze. Sprinkle with salt and turn the carrots into a hot serving dish.

RAGOÛT OF LETTUCE AND PEAS

Peas that are no longer quite young are the main components of this French vegetable stew. It makes a filling dish on its own, but can also be served with roast meat and poultry.

PREPARATION TIME: *25 min*
COOKING TIME: *45 min*
INGREDIENTS *(for 4):*
2 large heads Boston lettuce
2 pounds fresh peas
12–16 large scallions
6 ounces lean cooked ham
6 tablespoons butter
Salt and black pepper*
1–2 sugar cubes
GARNISH:
Fried bread triangles

Shell the peas, setting aside about a dozen of the smaller pods. Remove the coarse outer leaves from the lettuce, and cut the heads into quarters lengthwise; wash and drain thoroughly. Trim the roots and stems from the scallions. Cut the ham into ½ in cubes.

Melt 5 tablespoons of the butter in a large, heavy-based pan over moderate heat. Put the lettuce, peas, pea pods and scallions into the pan and coat them carefully in the butter. Season to taste with salt and freshly ground pepper. Add the ham and 3 tablespoons of hot water; cover the pan with a tight fitting lid.

Cook over very low heat for 35–45 minutes depending on the age of the peas; they should be tender but not mushy when cooked. Shake the pan from time to time to prevent sticking.

Before serving, remove the pea pods and stir in the sugar cubes and remaining butter.

Serve the ragoût hot, garnished with triangles of fried bread.

PEAS AND SCALLIONS

It is a happy coincidence that scallions and young garden peas both appear at the same time in early summer. They make an excellent combination with roast lamb or chicken.

PREPARATION TIME: *15–20 min*
COOKING TIME: *20–30 min*
INGREDIENTS *(for 4–6):*
2½ pounds fresh green peas
10–12 scallions
1¼ cups chicken stock
Beurre manié (page 166)
Salt and black pepper*

Shell the peas. Trim the roots and outer leaves from the scallions; wash them and cut the stems off the scallions, leaving about 1 in of green on each bulb. Put the scallions in a pan with the stock and bring slowly to simmering point. Cook gently until they begin to soften, then add the peas and continue to cook over low heat until the peas are tender, after about 20 minutes.

When the peas are just cooked, crumble in the beurre manié and stir carefully, so that the peas do not break up, until the stock has thickened to a sauce. Season to taste with salt and freshly ground pepper. Serve hot.

WESTPHALIAN BEANS AND PEARS

A blending of sweet and sharp flavors is characteristic of German cooking. This recipe for green beans makes a good vegetable dish with broiled or roast pork and ham.

PREPARATION TIME: *15 min*
COOKING TIME: *30 min*
INGREDIENTS *(for 4–6):*
1 pound green beans
4 large pears
2 cups stock or bouillon
Lemon rind
4 slices bacon
2 tablespoons brown sugar
1 tablespoon tarragon vinegar

Peel the pears and cut them in half lengthwise. Remove the cores and cut each half across into three or four pieces. Bring the stock to the boil, and drop in a thin piece of lemon rind, together with the pears. Simmer, uncovered, over low heat for 10 minutes.

Meanwhile, top and tail the beans (remove the strings as well if necessary). Wash the beans and add them to the pears. Continue cooking over low heat.

Cut the bacon, crosswise, into ½ in wide strips. Fry the bacon strips, with no additional fat, in a pan over low heat, until the fat runs and the bacon becomes crisp. Remove the bacon from the pan with a slotted spoon and keep it warm. Stir the sugar into the fat in the frying pan, blend in the vinegar and 2 tablespoons pear and bean liquid. Mix thoroughly, then add to the pan with the pears and beans. Simmer, uncovered, until the liquid has reduced to a syrupy sauce and the beans are tender. Remove the piece of lemon rind.

Spoon the beans, pears and liquid into a hot serving dish and sprinkle with the bacon.

GREEN BEANS, TUSCANY STYLE

This spicy Italian method of cooking beans is a useful way of preparing green beans towards the end of their season. They go well with roast or broiled meat and poultry.

PREPARATION TIME: *10 min*
COOKING TIME: *15 min*
INGREDIENTS *(for 4):*
1 pound green beans
¼ cup butter
1 tablespoon olive oil
2 teaspoons chopped fresh sage or 1 tablespoon chopped fresh parsley
1 large clove garlic
*Salt**
1 tablespoon grated Parmesan cheese
Black pepper

Wash, top, tail and string the beans. Cut them into 2 in chunks. Cook the beans in boiling salted water over low heat until just tender. Drain the beans thoroughly and cover them with a cloth to keep them warm.

Heat the butter and oil over moderate heat; stir in half the sage or parsley and the peeled and crushed garlic. Fry for 1 minute, then add the beans. Season to taste with salt and freshly ground pepper and stir over low heat for 5 minutes.

Mix in the Parmesan cheese, and serve the beans at once, sprinkled with herbs.

ZUCCHINI AU GRATIN

The subtle flavor and light consistency of zucchini make them an excellent accompaniment to delicately flavored fish, chicken or veal dishes.

PREPARATION TIME: *5 min*
COOKING TIME: *25–30 min*
INGREDIENTS *(for 4):*
6 zucchini
¼ cup unsalted butter
*Salt**
⅓ cup grated Cheddar or Brick cheese
4 tablespoons heavy cream (optional)
Black pepper

Wipe the zucchini with a clean damp cloth; do not peel them, but cut off the stalk ends. Slice each one in half lengthwise with a sharp knife.

Melt the butter in a shallow, flameproof dish and fry the zucchini, cut side downwards, until light golden. Turn the zucchini over, season them with salt and freshly ground pepper and sprinkle the grated cheese over them.

Cover the dish with a lid or foil and bake in the center of a preheated oven at 375°F (190°C, mark 5), for 20 minutes.

Heat the cream in a small pan over moderate heat. Do not let it reach boiling point, and pour it over the zucchini just before serving.

WESTPHALIAN BEANS AND PEARS

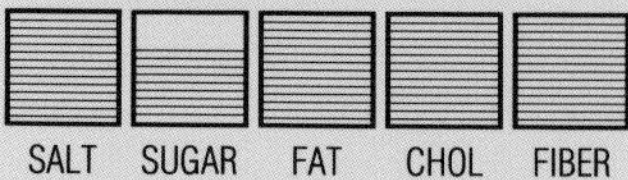

SALT SUGAR FAT CHOL FIBER

GLUTEN-FREE WHOLEFOOD
TOTAL CALORIES: ABOUT 660

Most of the **salt** comes from the bacon. To reduce it, substitute the same amount of ham, giving a medium level if serving 4 people, low if serving 6.
If wished, the amount of **sugar** can be reduced. Add half the amount, and check the flavor.
Substituting ham also makes the dish low in **fat** and **cholesterol**, provided the stock is not fatty. Heat the ham in a heavy pan lightly brushed with oil, as it will not produce enough fat, if lean, to lubricate itself. (Calories lost: up to 59.)

Microwave: ✓ for the beans and the pears.

GREEN BEANS, TUSCANY STYLE

SALT SUGAR FAT CHOL FIBER

GLUTEN-FREE WHOLEFOOD VEGETARIAN
TOTAL CALORIES: ABOUT 650

The low **salt** level assumes that the butter is unsalted.
To reduce the **fat** level to low, use only 2 teaspoons butter and 1 of oil. To eliminate **cholesterol** from the dish, apart from a tiny amount from the cheese, substitute vegetable margarine for the butter. (Calories lost: up to 390.)

Microwave: ✓ for cooking the beans.

ZUCCHINI AU GRATIN

SALT SUGAR FAT CHOL FIBER

GLUTEN-FREE WHOLEFOOD VEGETARIAN
TOTAL CALORIES: ABOUT 865

This type of cheese is less salty than some, and the amount used is not large enough to give a high level of **salt**.
The **fat** level can be cut to low and **cholesterol** to moderate by cooking the zucchini in a heavy pan brushed lightly with oil, omitting the remaining fat. The cream can be replaced with low-fat sour cream or yogurt into which 1 teaspoon cornstarch has been smoothly blended. (Calories lost: up to 463.)

Microwave: ✓

ZUCCHINI IN HOLLANDAISE SAUCE

SALT SUGAR FAT CHOL FIBER

GLUTEN-FREE* WHOLEFOOD*
TOTAL CALORIES: ABOUT 2030

Hollandaise sauce is naturally extremely high in both **fat** and **cholesterol**. To achieve a low fat dish, therefore, involves using another dressing, such as a cheese sauce made by the blending method (see page 166) using skim milk and sharp Cheddar or Parmesan. In this way a small amount of cheese, with its high fat and considerable salt level, will give enough flavor. (Calories lost: up to 1559.)

Microwave: ✓ for baking the zucchini.

ZUCCHINI IN HOLLANDAISE SAUCE

The delicate flavor of young zucchini is best preserved when served with melted butter or a simple sauce.

PREPARATION TIME: *30 min*
COOKING TIME: *30 min*
INGREDIENTS *(for 6)*:
1 pound zucchini
2 tablespoons unsalted butter
Salt and black pepper*
Juice of half lemon
SAUCE:
¾ cup plus 2 tablespoons unsalted butter
3 egg yolks
1–2 tablespoons lemon juice
1 tablespoon water or dry white wine
*Salt**
3 tablespoons grated Parmesan cheese
Black pepper

Wash the zucchini and trim off the stalks; blanch in boiling water for 1–2 minutes. Drain, wipe dry and cut the zucchini in half lengthwise. With a pointed teaspoon, take out a shallow groove in each half.

Arrange the zucchini, cut side up, in a large, shallow, lightly buttered flameproof dish. Sprinkle with salt, freshly ground pepper and the lemon juice. Cut the remaining butter into small pieces over the zucchini. Cover the dish tightly. Bake in the center of a pre-heated oven at 350°F (180°C, mark 4) for 25 minutes.

Meanwhile, cut ¾ cup of the butter into small pieces and let it melt slowly in a small, heavy-based pan over low heat. As soon as the butter has melted, remove the pan from the heat, and pour the butter into a jug. Put the 3 egg yolks into the same pan and beat thoroughly with a wire whisk. Add 1 tablespoon of lemon juice and 1 of water (or wine), with a good pinch of salt; beat again. Add 1 tablespoons of cold butter to the egg yolk mixture and put the pan over low heat on a flame-tamer. Cook, whisking steadily, until the egg yolks are creamy and beginning to thicken enough to coat the wires of the whisk. Remove the pan from the heat and beat in the remaining butter.

Add the melted butter to the egg mixture, drop by drop, whisking continuously. As the mixture thickens, the butter may be added more rapidly. When the sauce has the consistency of thick cream, season to taste with salt, pepper and lemon juice. If the sauce is too thick, it can be thinned with about a tablespoon of water or light cream. Finally, stir in 2 tablespoons of grated Parmesan cheese.

Spoon the sauce into the grooves of the cooked zucchini, and sprinkle with the remaining cheese. Put the dish under a hot broiler until the cheese is lightly browned. Serve at once. They are especially good with roast chicken or lean roast meat.

STUFFED SQUASH RINGS

Large zucchini or other summer squash, stuffed and baked, make a good lunch or supper dish on their own.

PREPARATION TIME: *25 min*
COOKING TIME: *45 min*
INGREDIENTS *(for 2–4):*
1 short thick summer squash (about 2 pounds)
6 tablespoons butter
2 ounces mushrooms
¼ pound lean cooked ham
2 teaspoons chopped parsley
¼ teaspoon dried summer savory
*Salt**
1–2 tablespoons fresh breadcrumbs
Black pepper

Wash the squash and wipe it dry; cut it into rings 1½–2 in thick. Remove the peel unless the squash is very young and tender. Spoon out the seeds. Butter a large ovenproof dish thoroughly and arrange the squash rings in this in a single layer.

Trim the mushrooms and chop them roughly. Dice the ham. Heat 2 tablespoons of the butter in a pan and lightly fry the mushrooms and ham for 2–3 minutes. Add the parsley and savory, and season to taste with salt and freshly ground pepper. Stir in enough breadcrumbs to bind the stuffing.

Lightly sprinkle the squash rings with salt and pepper before filling them with the stuffing. Dot with the remaining butter and cover the dish tightly with foil so that the squash will cook in its own steam. Bake in the center of a pre-heated oven at 375°F (190°C, mark 5) for 45 minutes or until the rings are tender.

Serve the squash rings straight from the dish, with a hot cheese or tomato sauce.

SQUASH CASSEROLE

Summer squash has such a high water content that it loses most of its flavor if steamed or cooked in water. But firmness and taste is preserved by cooking squash in butter in a casserole. It goes well with broiled meat and fish.

PREPARATION TIME: *10 min*
COOKING TIME: *30 min*
INGREDIENTS *(for 4–6):*
1 summer squash (about 2 pounds)
3 tablespoons butter
2 tablespoons mixed fresh herbs – tarragon, mint, parsley and chives
Salt and black pepper*

Cut the squash into 1 in thick slices; peel and cut them into rough chunks, discarding the seeds. Butter an ovenproof dish thoroughly. Add the squash with the remaining butter cut into small pieces and sprinkle with the fresh, finely chopped herbs. Season with salt and freshly ground pepper.

Cover the dish with a lid or foil and bake in the center of a pre-heated oven at 350°F (180°C, mark 4) until just tender, after about 30 minutes. Be careful not to overcook. Serve the squash at once, straight from the dish.

STUFFED SQUASH RINGS

GLUTEN-FREE* WHOLEFOOD*
TOTAL CALORIES: ABOUT 890

For a low **salt** level, use only 1 ounce of ham and compensate by using ½ cup pine nuts.
For low **fat** and **cholesterol** omit the butter and brush both the dish for the squash and the pan for cooking the mushrooms very lightly with oil. (Calories lost: up to 420.)
Other possible substitutes for some or all of the ham: up to ½ ounce dried mushrooms, soaked for half an hour before using, or finely chopped Florence fennel.
Both these are low in salt and fat, and fennel is high in **fiber**.

Freezing: ☑ up to 6 months.
Microwave: ☑

SQUASH CASSEROLE

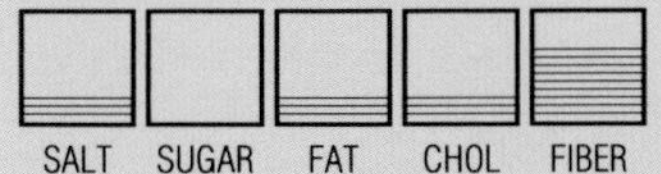

GLUTEN-FREE WHOLEFOOD VEGETARIAN
TOTAL CALORIES: ABOUT 440

The low **salt** level assumes that the butter is unsalted or only slightly salted.
If wished, the amount of butter can be reduced by up to half, giving very low **fat** and **cholesterol**. (Calories lost: up to 148.)

Freezing: ☑ up to 6 months.
Microwave: ☑

BRAISED ENDIVE

GLUTEN-FREE WHOLEFOOD
TOTAL CALORIES: ABOUT 240

This recipe needs no changes to suit healthy eating guidelines, although some people will prefer to avoid all **cholesterol** by replacing the butter with vegetable margarine or oil. For a **vegetarian** dish, use vegetable stock.

Freezing: ✓ up to 2 months.
Microwave: ✓

CHAMPIGNONS À LA CRÈME

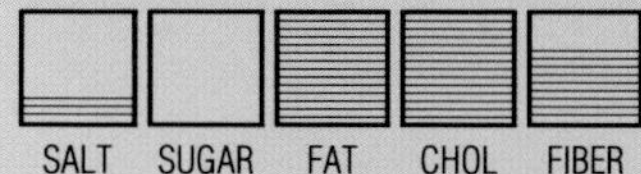

GLUTEN-FREE* WHOLEFOOD* VEGETARIAN
TOTAL CALORIES: ABOUT 1155

To reduce the **fat** and **cholesterol** content to low is very difficult without abandoning the character of the recipe. To reduce to medium, cook the mushrooms in 1 teaspoon butter mixed with 1 teaspoon of oil, brushed over a heavy-bottomed pan, and replace the cream with sour cream. For a version lower in fat, use low-fat sour cream, which has less than a quarter of the fat of heavy cream, but still enough to give a medium fat content in this quantity. Do not boil the sauce if making these substitutions. (Calories lost: up to 640.)

Freezing: ✓ up to 3 months.

BRAISED ENDIVE

The sharp, clean taste of endive goes particularly well with roast pork, goose or duck.

PREPARATION TIME: *15 min*
COOKING TIME: *35 min*
INGREDIENTS *(for 4):*
4 heads of Belgian endive
1 small onion
2 tablespoons unsalted butter
Salt and black pepper*
½ cup chicken or beef stock
GARNISH:
Chopped parsley

Wash the endive, trim off the root ends and cut each head in half lengthwise. Scoop out the small pieces of tough core at the base of each heart.

Peel and finely chop the onion. Melt the butter in a flameproof casserole over low heat and fry the onion in the butter until soft and transparent, but not browned. Add the endive, fry until golden on both sides, then season to taste with salt and freshly ground pepper.

Remove the dish from the heat. Pour the stock over the endive, cover the dish closely with a lid or foil and cook in the center of an oven pre-heated to 350°F (180°C, mark 4) for 35 minutes.

Serve the braised endive straight from the dish, sprinkled with finely chopped parsley.

CHAMPIGNONS À LA CRÈME

For this dish of mushrooms in cream sauce, choose small firm mushrooms which will not break up during cooking. Serve them with broiled meat or chicken, or on buttered toast as a quick snack.

PREPARATION TIME: *10 min*
COOKING TIME: *7 min*
INGREDIENTS *(for 4):*
1 pound button mushrooms
¼ cup unsalted butter
Salt and black pepper*
Dried mixed herbs
2 teaspoons flour
½ cup heavy cream
1 rounded tablespoon chopped parsley
Juice of half lemon

Perfect button mushrooms need only to be rinsed in cold water, drained and patted dry on absorbent paper towels. Trim the stalks level with the caps. Melt the butter in a pan and fry the mushrooms for 1–2 minutes, tossing to coat them evenly with the butter. Season to taste with salt, freshly ground pepper and the mixed herbs. Cook for a few more minutes to draw out the juices of the mushrooms.

Sprinkle the flour into the pan and stir thoroughly with a wooden spoon until well blended. Gradually stir in all the cream; bring the sauce to the boil, stirring continuously until it has thickened. Allow to simmer over low heat for 1–2 minutes, then add the parsley and lemon juice and serve immediately.

ROASTED ONIONS

The sweet flavor of large Spanish onions is particularly enhanced by roasting them whole. Serve as an accompaniment to meat dishes, or cook alongside baked potatoes as part of a vegetarian meal.

PREPARATION TIME: *5 min*
COOKING TIME: *2½–3 hours*
INGREDIENTS *(for 6):*
6 large Spanish onions
4–6 tablespoons butter
*Coarse salt**
GARNISH:
Parsley sprigs

Line a deep roasting pan with foil to prevent the sugar contained in the onions from sticking to the pan. Cut the roots from the unpeeled, washed onions, and stand them upright in the pan. Bake in the center of the oven, pre-heated to 350°F (180°C, mark 4), for 2½ hours or until the onions are tender when tested with a skewer.

Remove the pan from the oven, carefully peel off the onion skins, and set the onions on a hot serving dish. Open the tops slightly with a pointed knife blade and push a pat of butter into each. Sprinkle the onions with salt, and top each with a small sprig of parsley.

BROWN TOM

The name of this dish describes a casserole of fresh tomatoes with a crumble of bacon and brown breadcrumbs. Serve it on its own, or with broiled sausages for lunch or supper.

PREPARATION TIME: *20 min*
COOKING TIME: *30–35 min*
INGREDIENTS *(for 4):*
1 pound tomatoes
1 large onion
2 slices lean bacon
4 large slices whole wheat bread
1 tablespoon chopped parsley
1½ teaspoons chopped fresh basil
3 tablespoons butter
Salt and black pepper*
Sugar

Peel and roughly chop the onion; cut the bacon into pieces. Put the onion and bacon through the fine blade of the grinder. Remove the crust and crumble the bread into the bacon and onion mixture. Now add the herbs. Skin and thinly slice the tomatoes (page 160).

Put a layer of the bacon and crumb mixture in the bottom of a buttered, shallow fireproof dish. Cover this with a layer of tomatoes and season with salt, freshly ground pepper and a little sugar. Repeat these layers until all the ingredients are used up, finishing with a layer of bacon crumbs.

Dot with the remaining butter and bake near the top of the oven at 400°F (200°C, mark 6) for 30–35 minutes or until brown and bubbling. Serve at once.

TOMATOES WITH GREEN PEAS

Large firm tomatoes are ideal for stuffing, and may be served with broiled or roast meats. They can also be served as a hot first course, allowing one tomato per person. The stuffing used in the recipe for squash rings on page 46 can also be used – in fact both stuffings are interchangeable.

PREPARATION TIME: *20 min*
COOKING TIME: *15 min*
INGREDIENTS *(for 6):*
6 large firm tomatoes
1 small onion
3 tablespoons butter
1 cup cooked peas
2 teaspoons chopped fresh mint
Salt and black pepper*
1 egg yolk
GARNISH:
Black olives

Remove the leaf bases, and wash and dry the tomatoes thoroughly. Slice off the top of each with a sharp, serrated knife, and carefully take out the core and seeds with a pointed teaspoon. Turn the tomatoes upside-down to drain thoroughly while making the stuffing.

Peel and finely chop the onion. Melt 2 tablespoons of the butter in a small, heavy-based pan and cook the onion over moderate heat until soft, but not colored. Add the cooked peas and chopped mint to the onion. Cook the mixture for 3 minutes, stirring all the time. Allow the mixture to cool slightly, then rub it through a coarse sieve or liquidize it to a purée.

Return the purée to the pan and season to taste with salt and freshly ground pepper. Beat the

ROASTED ONIONS

GLUTEN-FREE WHOLEFOOD VEGETARIAN
TOTAL CALORIES: ABOUT 730

To reduce the **fat** and **cholesterol** level to low, simply replace the pat of butter inserted in each cooked onion with a spoonful of sour cream, quark or thick low-fat yogurt. (Calories lost: up to 495.)

BROWN TOM

GLUTEN-FREE* WHOLEFOOD*
TOTAL CALORIES: ABOUT 915

Most of the **salt** comes from the bacon, with some from the bread. To reduce the level to low, use only 1 slice of bacon and unsalted breadcrumbs. This will also reduce the level of **fat** and **cholesterol**, which can be further reduced to low by greasing the baking dish sparingly with oil or vegetable margarine, and omitting dots of fat on top of the dish. If concerned about the dish drying out during baking, cover with foil for first 20 minutes. (Calories lost: up to 268.)

Freezing: ✓ up to 2 months.

TOMATOES WITH GREEN PEAS

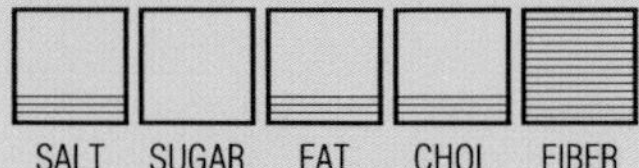

SALT SUGAR FAT CHOL FIBER

GLUTEN-FREE WHOLEFOOD VEGETARIAN
TOTAL CALORIES: ABOUT 520

Those on a **cholesterol**-lowering regime can replace the butter with vegetable margarine or oil, or use a half-and-half mixture, and omit the egg yolk, thickening the vegetable mixture by gentle simmering or by adding a teaspoonful of arrowroot made into a smooth paste with a little water. (Calories lost: up to 65.) Otherwise, this recipe suits healthy eating guidelines.

Microwave: √

LEEKS IN YOGURT SAUCE

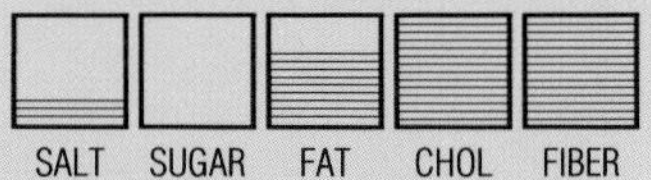

SALT SUGAR FAT CHOL FIBER

GLUTEN-FREE WHOLEFOOD VEGETARIAN
TOTAL CALORIES: ABOUT 580

The **fat** and **cholesterol** content can be low if the yogurt used is low-fat, and if the number of egg yolks is reduced, using 1 whole egg and 1 teaspoon of arrowroot mixed to a smooth paste with cold water instead. (Calories lost: up to 105.)

egg yolk lightly, then add it to the peas and onions. Stir over low heat until the mixture thickens. Remove from the heat and set the stuffing aside to cool and stiffen.

Season the inside of the drained tomatoes with salt and pepper and spoon in the prepared stuffing. Replace the tomato lids and secure each with a wooden toothpick.

Arrange the tomatoes in a well-buttered ovenproof dish and cover tightly with foil. Bake in an oven pre-heated to 375°F (190°C, mark 5) for 15 minutes or until the tomatoes are just tender, but still retaining their shape.

Serve the tomatoes hot, garnished with an olive on top of each toothpick.

LEEKS IN YOGURT SAUCE

The first young leeks come on the market in late summer. They can be served cold with chicken or fish.

PREPARATION TIME: *15 min*
COOKING TIME: *30 min*
INGREDIENTS *(for 4–6):*
8 slender leeks
Juice of a large lemon
½ teaspoon salt
12 black peppercorns
12 fennel seeds
6 coriander seeds
6 sprigs parsley
2 shallots
SAUCE:
1 cup plain yogurt
3 egg yolks
2 teaspoons lemon juice
Salt and black pepper*
Dijon-style mustard
GARNISH:
Fresh chopped parsley

Prepare a broth from 2 cups of water, the lemon juice, spices, herbs and peeled and sliced shallots. Bring to the boil and cook for 10 minutes.

Meanwhile, trim the leeks, slit them halfway down from the top and wash them thoroughly under cold running water.

Put the leeks in a frying pan, wide enough to take them in one layer; pour the strained broth over them. Cover the pan with a lid and simmer the leeks gently for 10–15 minutes, until soft. Leave them to cool in the liquid.

For the sauce, beat the yogurt, egg yolks and lemon juice together in a bowl, and place it over a pan of gently simmering water. Cook the sauce, stirring frequently, until it has thickened, after about 15 minutes. Season with salt, pepper and mustard, and set aside.

Before serving, drain the leeks thoroughly and cut each into two or three diagonal pieces. Arrange them in a serving dish, spoon the yogurt sauce over the leeks and sprinkle with parsley.

PARSNIPS MOLLY PARKIN

This vegetable casserole is an unusual combination of parsnips, tomatoes, cheese and cream. It goes well with plain roast lamb and pork.

PREPARATION TIME: *40 min*
COOKING TIME: *40 min*
INGREDIENTS *(for 6):*
2 pounds parsnips
1 pound tomatoes
5 tablespoons oil
6 tablespoons butter
3 tablespoons brown sugar
Salt and black pepper*
$1\frac{1}{2}$ cups grated Gruyère cheese
$1\frac{1}{4}$ cups light or heavy cream
4 rounded tablespoons fresh breadcrumbs

Peel the parsnips, cut away and discard any hard central cores. Slice the parsnips thinly. Skin the tomatoes (page 160), remove the seeds and cut the flesh into slices. Heat the oil in a pan and lightly fry the parsnips for 4 minutes.

Grease a large casserole dish with half the butter, and place a layer of parsnips in the bottom. Sprinkle with a little sugar, salt and freshly ground pepper and add a little cream, before covering with a layer of tomatoes. Spread a little more cream and cheese over the tomatoes and repeat these layers until all the ingredients are used up, finishing off with cream and cheese. Top with the breadcrumbs and dot with the remaining butter.

Cook the parsnip casserole for 40 minutes in the center of an oven pre-heated to 325°F (170°C, mark 3). Serve straight from the casserole.

GARLIC POTATOES

Mashed or creamed potatoes are given additional flavor by garlic. The bitterness is reduced if the garlic is boiled for a few minutes first.

PREPARATION TIME: *20 min*
COOKING TIME: *2 hours*
INGREDIENTS *(for 6):*
3 pounds potatoes
5 cloves garlic
$\frac{1}{2}$ cup unsalted butter
2 tablespoons flour
$1\frac{1}{4}$ cups milk
*1 teaspoon salt**
Black pepper
3 tablespoons heavy cream
3 heaping tablespoons finely chopped parsley

Wash and dry the potatoes, prick them with a fork, and bake for $1\frac{1}{2}$ hours or until tender on the center shelf of an oven pre-heated to 400°F (200°C, mark 6).

Put the garlic in a small pan, cover with water; boil for 2 minutes, then drain and peel. Melt half the butter in a heavy-based saucepan and add the garlic. Cover the pan, and cook the garlic gently for 10 minutes or until tender. Remove the garlic. Stir the flour into the butter in the pan and cook over low heat for 2 minutes. Gradually blend in the boiling milk, stirring constantly until the sauce is smooth and thick. Add the salt, a few twists of pepper and the garlic. Boil for 2 minutes.

Liquidize the sauce or rub it through a sieve, then return it to the pan and heat through. Set aside.

Scoop the flesh from the baked potatoes, rub it through a sieve and beat in the remaining butter,

PARSNIPS MOLLY PARKIN

SALT SUGAR FAT CHOL FIBER

GLUTEN-FREE* WHOLEFOOD* VEGETARIAN
TOTAL CALORIES: ABOUT 4000

The high **salt** content of the cheese can only be reduced by using less cheese, say half, giving a low/medium salt total.
The **sugar** content can be reduced to low by adding only 1 tablespoon.
The very high **fat** content can be reduced to low by using only 2 tablespoons butter (or vegetable margarine or a mixture) to grease and dot the dish; half the cheese; only 2 teaspoons of oil with a few spoonfuls of stock or water to brown the parsnips; and low-fat sour cream mixed with low-fat yogurt, or yogurt alone, to layer. (Calories lost: up to 2495.)

Freezing: ☑ up to 2 months.

GARLIC POTATOES

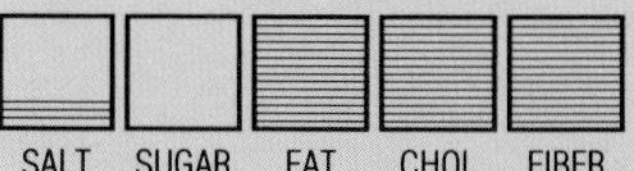

SALT SUGAR FAT CHOL FIBER

GLUTEN-FREE* WHOLEFOOD* VEGETARIAN
TOTAL CALORIES: ABOUT 2400

The **fat** and **cholesterol** levels can be reduced to low by using only 2 tablespoons butter to cook the garlic and make the sauce; and replacing the butter and cream beaten into the potatoes and garlic sauce with quark or low-fat sour cream. (Calories lost: up to 708.)

Microwave: ☑ for the initial cooking of the potatoes.

LIMOGES POTATO PIE

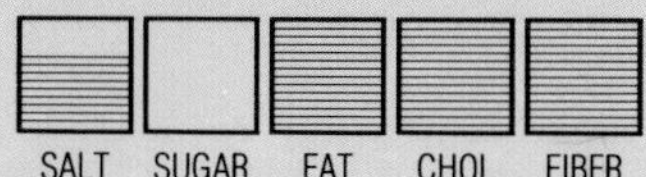

VEGETARIAN
TOTAL CALORIES: ABOUT 3430

For a low **salt** level, use pastry prepared without salt.
The **fat** level is raised considerably by the puff pastry. To reduce this, use a yeast pastry, or a cobbler topping such as the biscuit dough on page 26.
Within the pie, the fat and **cholesterol** levels can be reduced to low by omitting the dots of butter and replacing the cream with low-fat yogurt. (Calories lost: up to 1241.)
Gluten-free puff pastry is not successful, but you could use instead a low-fat pastry.
Puff pastry is also difficult to make well with whole wheat flour, so for a **wholefood** dish, a topping as suggested above is preferable.

Freezing: ✓ up to 3 months.

CELERIAC AND POTATO PURÉE

GLUTEN-FREE WHOLEFOOD VEGETARIAN
TOTAL CALORIES: ABOUT 1050

For low **fat** and **cholesterol** replace the butter and cream with the same amount of quark or low-fat sour cream, with 2 teaspoons of butter for flavor if wished. (Calories lost: up to 406.)

Freezing: ✓ up to 3 months.

Microwave: ✓ for the celeriac.

a little at a time. Season to taste with salt and pepper. Stir the cream into the garlic purée, then beat the mixture into the potatoes. Stir in the parsley.

Heat the mashed potato through if necessary, pile it back into the potato skins and serve at once.

LIMOGES POTATO PIE

In spring the country around Limoges in France can be wet and cold. Consequently, the regional food tends to be warm and filling. This potato pie can be served as a supper dish on its own or as a first course.

PREPARATION TIME: *35 min*
COOKING TIME: *35 min*
INGREDIENTS *(for 6):*
1 pound prepared puff pastry
1½ pounds new potatoes
1 small onion
3–4 cloves garlic
Salt and black pepper*
Nutmeg
¼ cup butter
6 tablespoons light cream
6 tablespoons heavy cream
1 egg
Bunch of fresh parsley, chives and chervil

Roll out half the puff pastry on a lightly floured board and use to line a 10 in flan ring or shallow cake pan. Wash and scrape the potatoes. Slice them thinly, using a mandolin slicer or the cucumber blade on a grater, into a bowl of cold water to prevent them turning brown.

Bring a pan of lightly salted water to the boil, put in the sliced potatoes and cook for 2 minutes only, after the water has returned to the boil. Drain the potatoes thoroughly through a colander. Peel and finely chop the onion and garlic.

Put a layer of potato slices on top of the pastry base, sprinkle with the onion and garlic and season with a little salt, nutmeg and freshly ground pepper. Repeat these layers, seasoning each, until all the vegetables are used up, finishing with a layer of potato. Dot the vegetables with the butter, cut into small pieces. Mix the creams together and pour about half over the potatoes.

Roll out the remaining pastry and cover the pie, sealing the edges firmly. Make a small hole in the center of the pastry lid for the steam to escape. Beat the egg into the remaining cream and brush a little of this mixture over the pastry to glaze it while cooking. Score the pastry lightly into sections with a sharp knife – this makes it easier to cut the finished pie into portions.

Bake the pie near the top of a pre-heated oven at 450°F (230°C, mark 8) for 30 minutes. Protect the pastry with a piece of buttered paper if the pastry browns too quickly.

Chop the fresh herbs finely and blend them into the remaining egg and cream mixture. When the pie is cooked, pour the cream and egg mixture into the center hole using a small kitchen funnel. Do this slowly in case there is not room for all the cream. Return the pie to the oven for 5 minutes then serve at once.

CELERIAC AND POTATO PURÉE

Celeriac, or celery root, is a turnip-shaped, knobbly root vegetable that is gaining popularity here. It has a strong celery flavor, and the leaves can be used for flavoring soups and stews. As a purée, it is particularly good served with game.

PREPARATION TIME: *10 min*
COOKING TIME: *45 min*
INGREDIENTS *(for 4–6):*
1 pound celeriac
3 cups cooked mashed potatoes
3 tablespoons butter
3 tablespoons heavy cream
Salt and black pepper*

Scrub the celeriac thoroughly in cold water to remove all traces of dirt. Put it in a pan of boiling salted water and cook, unpeeled, for 35–40 minutes or until quite tender. Leave to cool slightly, then peel the celeriac and chop it finely. Purée it through a sieve, or in a food processor.

Blend the celeriac purée with the mashed potatoes, add the butter and cream, and season to taste with salt and freshly ground black pepper. Heat the purée through over low heat before serving.

NOISETTE POTATOES

Small golden balls of fried potatoes make an attractive garnish for steaks, chops or sautéed meat. They should be left to soak for a few hours to remove excess starch. The cooked potatoes can be tossed in dissolved meat juices and sprinkled with parsley. They are then known as *pommes de terre à la parisienne*.

PREPARATION TIME: *20 min*
COOKING TIME: *10 min*
INGREDIENTS *(for 6):*
2 pounds potatoes
3 tablespoons salt★
6 tablespoons unsalted butter

Peel the potatoes and leave them to soak for 2 hours in cold water in which 2 tablespoons salt have been dissolved. Drain and dry the potatoes. Using a ball scoop, take out small balls, about the size of walnuts, from the potatoes.

Bring a pan of water to the boil, add 1 tablespoon salt and cook the potato balls over low heat for 3 minutes. Drain through a colander and dry on a clean dish towel.

Melt the butter over gentle heat in a sauté pan. Toss the potatoes in the butter for about 5 minutes until golden and cooked through.

Using a slotted spoon, lift the potato balls into a warm serving dish, sprinkle with a little salt and serve.

SCALLOPED POTATOES

For this recipe, choose firm, waxy potatoes which will not break up during long, slow cooking. The potato gratin can be served with any type of broiled or roast meat, or it can be made into a main dish by adding ground ham or flaked cooked fish between the potato layers.

PREPARATION TIME: *15–20 min*
COOKING TIME: *1½ hours*
INGREDIENTS *(for 6):*
1½ pounds potatoes
1 onion
¼ cup butter
Salt★ and black pepper
1 cup grated Cheddar or Gruyère cheese
1 egg
1¼ cups milk

Peel and wash the potatoes, and cut them into thin slices. Peel and finely chop the onion. Use a little of the butter to grease a shallow, ovenproof dish. Arrange the potato slices in layers in the dish, sprinkling each layer with onion, cheese, salt and freshly ground pepper. Finish with a thick layer of cheese and dot with the remaining butter.

Beat the egg and milk together and pour this mixture carefully over the potatoes. Cover the dish with buttered wax paper or foil. Bake in the center of an oven preheated to 350°F (180°C, mark 4) for 1½ hours, or until the potatoes are tender, and the topping is golden. If cooked too quickly, the egg and milk will curdle.

NOISETTE POTATOES

SALT SUGAR FAT CHOL FIBER

GLUTEN-FREE WHOLEFOOD VEGETARIAN
TOTAL CALORIES: ABOUT 1340

To reduce the **salt** level to low, omit the soaking in salt water and choose the driest potatoes possible. This will also avoid the loss of vitamin C and some minerals from the potatoes to the water during soaking. Cook the potato balls in unsalted water.
For a low **fat** and **cholesterol** level, toss in 2 tablespoons butter or vegetable margarine or oil, before broiling under medium heat for several minutes until cooked through. (Calories lost: up to 370.)

SCALLOPED POTATOES

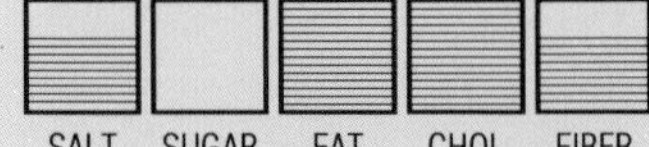

SALT SUGAR FAT CHOL FIBER

GLUTEN-FREE WHOLEFOOD VEGETARIAN
TOTAL CALORIES: ABOUT 1690

Most of the **salt** (assuming you are using unsalted butter) comes from the cheese, and the only way to reduce this is to use less cheese, say half the amount. Grate it finely and use the strongest flavored cheese available, so that a smaller amount gives maximum flavor. This will also help to reduce the high **fat** and **cholesterol** together with using only 1 tablespoon butter to grease and dot the dish, and skim milk. These changes will give a low fat and cholesterol level. (Calories lost: up to 595.)

GALETTE LYONNAISE

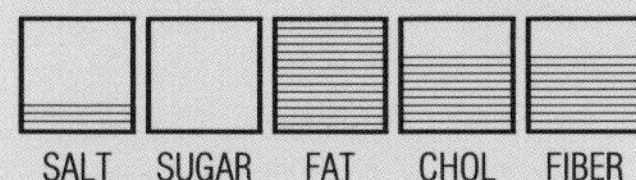

GLUTEN-FREE WHOLEFOOD VEGETARIAN
TOTAL CALORIES: ABOUT 1045

The low **salt** level assumes you are using unsalted butter.
To reduce the **fat** and **cholesterol** levels to low, cook the onions in 2 teaspoons butter and 2 of oil, omitting the remaining butter dotted on top. Reduce the amount of cholesterol further if wished by adding only the white of the egg, although 1 yolk between 4 is not a high cholesterol level. (Calories lost: up to 397.)

Freezing: ☑ up to 3 months.

SOUFFLÉ POTATOES

GLUTEN-FREE WHOLEFOOD VEGETARIAN
TOTAL CALORIES: ABOUT 1870

To reduce the **fat** and **cholesterol** levels to low, use only 2 egg yolks (but 3 whites), and replace the butter and cream beaten into potatoes with the same amount of low-fat sour cream or quark, or a mixture. This will actually produce a lighter soufflé, but as it will have less solidity, serving immediately becomes even more vital. (Calories lost: up to 751.)

Microwave: ☑ for the initial baking of the potatoes.

GALETTE LYONNAISE

This savory potato dish with its classic Lyonnaise flavoring of onion and cheese is excellent with both fish and meat. Extra cheese may be mixed with the potato in addition to the topping.

PREPARATION TIME: *35 min*
COOKING TIME: *25 min*
INGREDIENTS *(for 4):*
1 pound potatoes
½ pound onions
5 tablespoons butter
1 egg
Salt and black pepper*
Pinch nutmeg
2 tablespoons grated Cheddar, Gruyère or Parmesan cheese
GARNISH:
Parsley sprigs

Peel the potatoes, cut them into even pieces and boil them in lightly salted water. Rub the potatoes through a coarse sieve. Peel and finely chop the onions. Heat ¼ cup of butter and cook the onions over low heat until they are soft and golden. Stir the contents of the pan into the potatoes. Add the beaten egg and season to taste with salt, freshly ground pepper and nutmeg.

Spoon the potato mixture into a greased, shallow ovenproof dish; smooth the top, sprinkle over the grated cheese and dot with the remaining butter. Bake the potatoes in the center of a preheated oven, at 400°F (200°C, mark 6), for about 20 minutes or until golden brown on top.

Serve the potatoes straight from the dish, garnished with sprigs of parsley.

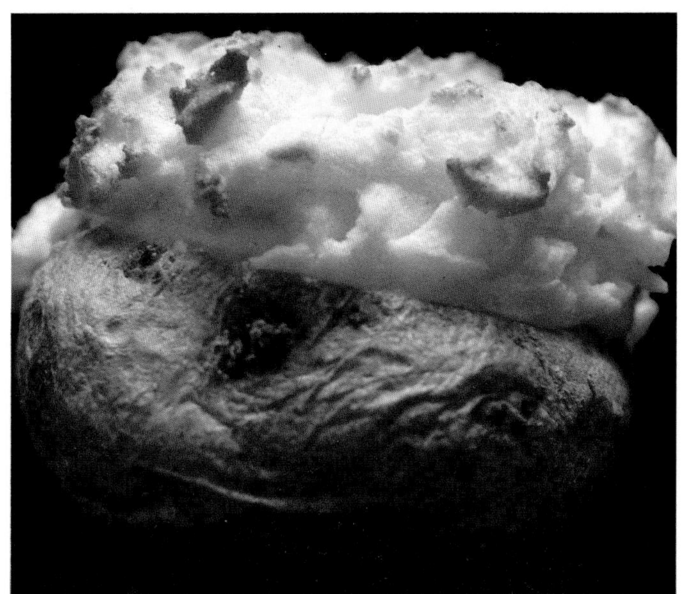

SOUFFLÉ POTATOES

With just a little extra trouble, plain baked potatoes can be transformed into light and fluffy individual soufflés. They are ideal with all meats, particularly so with steak.

PREPARATION TIME: *15 min*
COOKING TIME: *1¾ hours*
INGREDIENTS *(for 6):*
6 large potatoes
¼ cup unsalted melted butter
½ cup heavy cream
3 eggs
Salt and black pepper*

Wash and dry the potatoes, prick them lightly with a fork and bake for 1½ hours or until tender on the middle shelf of an oven preheated to 400°F (200°C, mark 6). Cut a lid lengthwise off the baked potatoes, scoop the flesh out into a bowl and mix in with it the melted butter and cream. Separate the eggs and stir the yolks into the potato mixture. Beat the egg whites with a little salt until stiff and fold into the potato mixture. Season to taste with freshly ground pepper.

Pile this soufflé mixture back into the hollow potato skins, return to the oven and bake at the same temperature for 15 minutes, or until the soufflés are well risen.

Serve immediately, before the soufflés have time to collapse and go flat.

CREAMED SPINACH

Young crisp spinach leaves should be cooked as soon as possible after buying or gathering them. This dish goes well with most roast meats, particularly with ham.

PREPARATION TIME: *10 min*
COOKING TIME: *10–15 min*
INGREDIENTS *(for 4):*
2 pounds bulk spinach
½ teaspoon salt★
2 tablespoons butter
¼ teaspoon grated nutmeg
6 tablespoons heavy cream

Remove the stalks and coarse midribs from the spinach and throw away any bruised leaves. Wash the spinach thoroughly in several changes of cold water to get rid of all sand and grit. Put the spinach in a large saucepan with only the water clinging to the leaves. Cook over low heat, shaking the pan, until the spinach has reduced in volume and made its own liquid. Add the salt and cover the pan with a lid.

Cook gently for 5–8 minutes, then drain the spinach thoroughly through a fine sieve, squeezing out as much liquid as possible with a potato masher.

Chop the spinach roughly on a board. Melt the butter in the saucepan, add the spinach and nutmeg and heat through before stirring in the cream. Spoon into a hot serving dish.

SPINACH ROLL

Late summer spinach or even the frozen variety is ideal for this Yugoslavian puff pastry dish. It will serve as a light meal on its own, or it can be part of a packed lunch or picnic.

PREPARATION TIME: *45 min*
COOKING TIME: *30 min*
INGREDIENTS *(for 4):*
2 pounds fresh bulk spinach
¾ pound prepared puff pastry
⅓ cup cottage cheese
3 eggs
¼ cup grated Parmesan cheese
Salt★ and black pepper
1 egg yolk

Roll the puff pastry out on a floured surface to a rectangle 12 in long by 8 in wide, and ¼ in thick. Lightly grease and flour a baking sheet.

Wash the spinach thoroughly, discarding any stalks and tough midribs. Put it, still wet, in a large saucepan. Cover with a lid and cook over low heat for 5–7 minutes, or until just tender. Drain the spinach thoroughly in a colander. Chop it finely, and drain again (do not squeeze it completely dry).

Rub the cottage cheese through a sieve to remove any lumps. Separate the eggs. Lightly beat the yolks and add them to the spinach in a mixing bowl. Blend in the cottage and the Parmesan cheeses and season with salt and freshly ground pepper. Beat the egg whites until stiff and fold into the mixture.

Moisten the edges of the pastry with cold water and spoon the spinach mixture down the center of the rectangle and to within 1 in of the shorter edges. Quickly

CREAMED SPINACH

GLUTEN-FREE WHOLEFOOD VEGETARIAN
TOTAL CALORIES: ABOUT 745

To reduce the level of **fat** and **cholesterol** to low, add only 1 tablespoon butter and 1 tablespoon of light cream to the spinach. (Calories lost: up to 414.)

Freezing: ☑ without cream up to 1 year; with cream up to 2 months.

Microwave: ☑

SPINACH ROLL

VEGETARIAN
TOTAL CALORIES: ABOUT 2170

The **salt** level comes mainly from the cheese. If wished, unsalted quark can be used in place of the cottage cheese, giving a low salt level. This assumes there is no salt added to the pastry. If you use bought puff pastry, the salt level will probably be quite high.
To reduce the **fat** and **cholesterol** levels to low, the puff pastry needs to be replaced with a lower-fat wrapping such as yeast or strudel dough, and 2 yolks should be omitted from the mixture. Use a little of the egg white only to glaze. (Calories lost: up to 430.)

Freezing: ☑ up to 3 months.

Microwave: ☑ for cooking the spinach.

PEPPERS WITH BEEF STUFFING

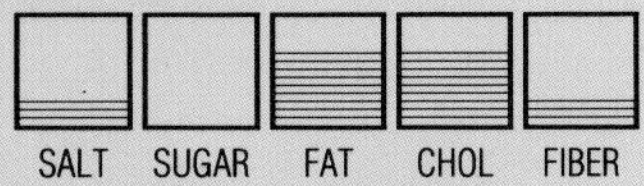

SALT SUGAR FAT CHOL FIBER

GLUTEN-FREE* WHOLEFOOD*
TOTAL CALORIES: ABOUT 950

To keep the **salt** level low, cook the peppers in unsalted water and use unsalted bread.
The **fat** level can be reduced by choosing very lean meat, ideally buying a lean piece and grinding at home. The amount of oil can also be reduced to half. If wished, the egg can be omitted to give a low **cholesterol** level. (Calories lost: up to 191.)

Freezing: √ up to 2 months.
Microwave: √

CHESTNUT AND POTATO PURÉE

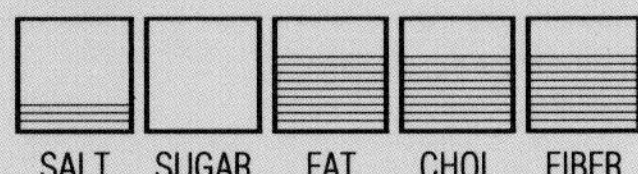

SALT SUGAR FAT CHOL FIBER

GLUTEN-FREE WHOLEFOOD
TOTAL CALORIES: ABOUT 1470

The low **salt** level depends on there being no salt in the stock.
To reduce the **fat** and **cholesterol** levels to low, replace the cream with quark or low-fat sour cream, and reduce the amount of butter added to 2 tablespoons. (Calories lost: up to 264.)
For a **vegetarian** dish, simmer the chestnuts in water or vegetable stock.

Freezing: √ up to 3 months.

fold the pastry over the spinach, close the edges tightly, and seal all three sides firmly with the lightly beaten egg yolk. Roll out the pastry trimmings and use to decorate the top of the roll. Brush with the remaining egg yolk to glaze the pastry.

Make two or three slits in the top of the pastry for the steam to escape. Carefully lift the pastry roll on to the baking sheet.

Bake in the center of a preheated oven, at 450°F (230°C, mark 8) for 20 minutes, then reduce the temperature to 350°F (180°C, mark 4) for another 10 minutes, or until the pastry is well risen and golden brown. Serve the roll, hot or cold, cut into thick slices.

PEPPERS WITH BEEF STUFFING

Large, squat peppers filled with a savory meat stuffing make a light lunch or supper dish on their own. They can also be included in cold buffet or picnic fare.

PREPARATION TIME: *20 min*
COOKING TIME: *30 min*
INGREDIENTS *(for 4):*
4 equal-sized sweet peppers
1 onion
1½ tablespoons olive oil
6–8 ounces ground beef or pork
1 thick slice bread
1 egg
Salt and black pepper*
Summer savory

Wash and dry the peppers. Use a sharp knife to cut off the stalk ends with a small circle of pepper attached to each. Set the stalks aside and remove the seeds and ribs carefully from the peppers without breaking the skins. Scald the peppers for 5 minutes in a pan of boiling, lightly salted water. Lift out the peppers and drain them, upside down.

Peel and finely chop the onion, and cook it until transparent in 1 tablespoon of the oil in a heavy-based pan. Add the beef, stirring continuously until it has browned and separated into grains. Remove the pan from the heat.

Remove the crust from the bread and soak it in the lightly beaten egg. Mash the bread and egg with a fork and stir it into the beef; season to taste with salt, freshly ground pepper and summer savory. Blend thoroughly until the stuffing is firm, but still moist.

Brush the bottom of an ovenproof dish with oil. Spoon the stuffing loosely into the peppers and place them upright in the dish. Brush the skins lightly with oil and put 2 or 3 tablespoons of water in the bottom of the dish. Cover it tightly with foil and a lid and bake in the center of a preheated oven, at 375°F (190°C, mark 5) for 30 minutes or until tender.

Arrange the peppers on a warmed serving dish and replace the stalk caps at an angle so that a little of the stuffing shows. Serve with hot crusty French bread and a tomato sauce (you can use the pizza topping given on pages 68–69) flavored with paprika and sour cream.

CHESTNUT AND POTATO PURÉE

Chestnuts are traditionally served as stuffing or as garnishes with game birds. This purée of potato and chestnuts is an excellent vegetable to serve with game, turkey or roast ham.

PREPARATION TIME: *20 min*
COOKING TIME: *30 min*
INGREDIENTS *(for 6–8):*
¾ pound fresh chestnuts or 8-ounce can chestnut purée
2½ cups stock or bouillon
3 cups mashed potatoes
*Salt**
¼ cup butter
4–5 tablespoons light cream
Ground nutmeg or black pepper
4 rounded tablespoons chopped celery heart

Make a small cut on the flat side of each chestnut and roast them on top of the stove in a chestnut pan or on a baking sheet near the top of a hot oven. After 5–10 minutes, the skins will crack. Peel the two layers of skin from the chestnuts while still warm.

Put the stock in a saucepan, add the peeled chestnuts and cover the pan with a lid. Bring to the boil, then simmer the chestnuts for 20 minutes or until tender. Drain the chestnuts and rub them through a coarse sieve.

Blend the chestnut purée with the mashed potato, stir in the butter and heat the mixture through over low heat. Blend in enough cream to give the purée a fluffy texture, and season with salt and ground nutmeg or pepper.

Blend in the chopped celery just before serving.

STUFFED GREEN PEPPERS

For this recipe, choose squat round peppers that will stand upright.

PREPARATION TIME: *20 min*
COOKING TIME: *50 min*
INGREDIENTS *(for 4):*
4 equal-sized sweet green peppers
½ cup long grain rice
1 small onion
2 ounces mushrooms
2 slices lean bacon
2 tablespoons unsalted butter
4–6 chicken livers
Salt and black pepper*
1 rounded teaspoon chopped parsley
1 small egg
¼–½ cup grated Parmesan cheese
1¼ cups tomato sauce (use the pizza topping given on pages 68–69)

Cut a circle around the base of each green pepper to remove the stem and seeds. Place the peppers in a basin and cover with boiling water. Allow to stand for 5 minutes, then drain thoroughly and set the peppers aside.

For the stuffing, first cook the rice in a large pan of boiling salted water. Simmer for 8–10 minutes or until the rice is tender; drain through a colander. Peel the onion, wash and trim the mushrooms and chop both finely. Dice the bacon. Melt the butter in a heavy-based pan and sauté the bacon, onion and mushrooms for a few minutes. Add the chicken livers whole and cook for a few minutes, then remove the livers and chop them into tiny pieces; return to the pan. Stir in the cooked rice, salt, pepper and parsley; remove the pan from the heat. Lightly beat the egg and use it to bind the rice and liver mixture.

Arrange the peppers, cut surface uppermost, in a buttered fireproof dish. Spoon the rice mixture into the peppers, and sprinkle them with half the grated cheese.

Spoon 2 tablespoons of cold water into the dish and set it above the center of an oven pre-heated to 350°F (180°C, mark 4); cook for 35–40 minutes.

Immediately before serving, sprinkle the peppers with the remaining cheese. Serve a bowl of hot tomato sauce separately.

STUFFED GREEN PEPPERS

SALT SUGAR FAT CHOL FIBER

GLUTEN-FREE WHOLEFOOD*
TOTAL CALORIES: ABOUT 1515

For low **salt** use only 1 slice bacon and half the Parmesan. This will also reduce the **fat** and **cholesterol**. To reduce the fat further, to low, cook the bacon, onion and mushrooms in a pan brushed with oil. For low cholesterol, replace the chicken livers with more mushrooms. (Calories lost: up to 250.)
Use brown rice for **wholefood** and to increase the **fiber** level. Cook it for about 40 minutes in 2¼ times its volume of water.

Freezing: ✓ up to 2 months.
Microwave: ✓

RICE SALAD WITH FLORENCE FENNEL

SALT SUGAR FAT CHOL FIBER

GLUTEN-FREE WHOLEFOOD*
TOTAL CALORIES: ABOUT 2910

For moderate **salt**, use half the olives and tuna. Half or all the weight of fish can be replaced by a fresh fish such as monkfish, lightly poached and cut into cubes.
The high **fat** level comes from the mayonnaise, which also contains cholesterol to add to that from the egg garnish. To reduce fat and **cholesterol** to low, dress the salad with a mixture of yogurt and lemon juice, with fresh herbs and only 1 tablespoon of best quality oil,

and use tuna canned in brine. In place of the eggs, the salad can be garnished with toasted sliced almonds, say 2 tablespoons, which will still provide a little fat, but no cholesterol. (Calories lost: up to 962.)

NASI GORENG

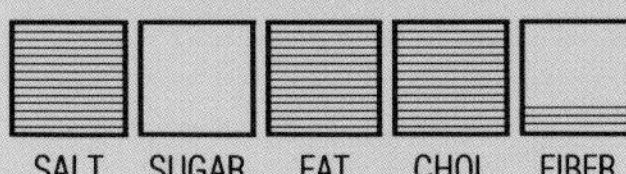

GLUTEN-FREE* WHOLEFOOD*
TOTAL CALORIES: ABOUT 3680

For low **salt** omit the soy sauce. For low **fat** use only 1 tablespoon of oil to cook the onion and meat, covering the mixture to prevent it drying out. Use only a light brushing of oil in which to cook the scallions and omelette.
For moderate **cholesterol** make half the amount of omelette. (Calories lost: up to 1653.)
Tamari, the Japanese soy sauce, is **gluten-free**.

Freezing: √ up to 1 month.

ALMOND RICE

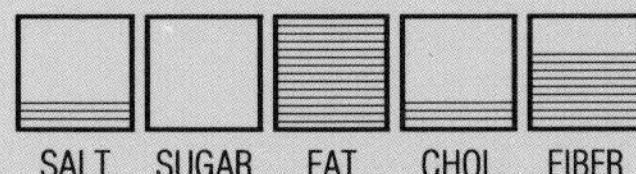

GLUTEN-FREE WHOLEFOOD*
TOTAL CALORIES: ABOUT 1200

For low **fat** use only 1 tablespoon butter and half the almonds. (Calories lost: up to 233.)
Reducing the almonds will make this a low **fiber** dish; using brown rice will make it high in fiber and **wholefood**. Brown rice requires about half as much stock again.

Freezing: √ up to 3 months.

RICE SALAD WITH FLORENCE FENNEL

The sweet aniseed flavor of bulbous Florence fennel blends well with rice and Pernod-flavored mayonnaise. The salad is usually served with cold meat or fish.

PREPARATION TIME: *30 min*
COOKING TIME: *20 min*
CHILLING TIME: *30 min*
INGREDIENTS: *(for 4–6):*
1 cup long grain rice
2 Florence fennel bulbs
7-ounce can tuna fish
1 cup black olives
½ cup mayonnaise (page 167)
1 tablespoon Pernod
GARNISH:
3 hard-cooked eggs
6 scallions

Bring a large pan of lightly salted water to the boil and cook the rice for 20 minutes. Rinse and drain the rice thoroughly in a sieve and set it aside to cool.

Trim the fennel, wash the bulbs in cold running water, then cut them into thin slices. Drain the oil from the tuna fish and break the flesh up with a fork. Mix the rice, fennel, tuna and olives together in a salad bowl. Stir the Pernod into the mayonnaise and fold this dressing into the salad.

Trim the scallions and cut them in half lengthwise. Shell and quarter the eggs. Garnish the salad with the onions and eggs and leave it to chill in the refrigerator for 30 minutes.

NASI GORENG

This Indonesian rice dish with omelette is an excellent way of using up cooked meat, poultry, fish, shellfish and vegetables.

PREPARATION TIME: *30 min*
COOKING TIME: *35 min*
INGREDIENTS *(for 6):*
1 cup long grain rice
2 ounces dried shrimp
¾ cup peanut oil
2 onions
1 clove garlic
1 fresh chili or ½ teaspoon chili powder
1 cup cooked diced meat
Salt and black pepper*
OMELETTE:
1–2 tablespoons butter or vegetable oil
3–4 scallions
1 tomato
Salt and chili powder*
3–4 tablespoons soy sauce
4 eggs
Cucumber slices

Peel and finely chop the onions and garlic and the scallions for the omelette. Finely shred the fresh chili; skin and chop the tomato. Boil and drain the rice. Spread it on a dish to cool and meanwhile soak the shrimp in cold water.

Heat the oil in a large pan and fry the onions until transparent. Add the garlic and chili and fry for 3 more minutes. Stir in the meat and cook for 2 minutes, before adding the rice and the drained shrimp. Continue frying, stirring frequently, until the rice turns pale golden. Season to taste. Put the rice mixture on a warm serving dish.

For the omelette, fry the scallions in the oil until soft. Add the tomato and cook for a further 2–3 minutes. Season with salt, chili powder and half the soy sauce. Cook for 3 minutes. Beat the eggs lightly and stir them into the pan, cover and cook the omelette, over low heat, until set. Remove from the pan, and shred the omelette finely.

Arrange the omelette over the rice, sprinkle with the remaining soy sauce and garnish with cucumber slices.

ALMOND RICE

Many rice dishes make good accompaniments to broiled poultry and ham.

PREPARATION TIME: *5 min*
COOKING TIME: *25 min*
INGREDIENTS *(for 4):*
1 cup long grain rice
1 onion
2 tablespoons unsalted butter
2 tablespoons raisins
2 cups chicken stock
*½ teaspoon salt**
½ cup toasted sliced almonds
GARNISH:
1 tablespoon chopped parsley

Peel and finely chop the onion. Melt the butter in a saucepan and add the onion; cover the pan with a lid and cook over low heat for about 5 minutes until the onion is soft. Add the rice and toss it with the onion and butter. Stir in the raisins and add the hot stock and the salt. Bring to the boil, lower the heat and cover the pan with a lid. Simmer the rice gently for 15–20 minutes or until it is tender.

When cooked, fluff the rice up with a fork, fold in the almonds and spoon it all into a hot serving dish. Sprinkle with parsley.

RISOTTO BIANCO

Rice is the staple food in northern Italy, as pasta is in the south. An Italian risotto is served quite plainly, with butter and cheese.

PREPARATION TIME: *10 min*
COOKING TIME: *20–25 min*
INGREDIENTS *(for 4–6):*
1 cup Italian rice
1 small onion
1 small clove garlic
6 tablespoons butter
2 teaspoons olive oil
$3\frac{1}{2}$–4 cups white stock
Salt and black pepper*
1 cup grated Parmesan cheese

Peel and finely chop the onion and garlic. Heat $\frac{1}{4}$ cup of the butter with the oil in a deep sauté pan and cook the onion and garlic until soft and just beginning to color. Add the rice to the pan. Cook over low heat, stirring continuously, until the rice is yellow and shiny.

Add a third of the hot stock to the rice; bring to the boil, stir, then cover the pan with a lid. Cook over moderate heat until all the liquid is absorbed, then gradually stir in the remaining stock. Cover the pan again, and simmer the rice, stirring occasionally, until all the stock has been absorbed, after about 15 minutes. The rice should then be creamy and firm. Watch the risotto carefully while cooking to see that it does not dry out.

Season the risotto to taste with salt and freshly ground pepper. Stir in the remaining butter and half the cheese. Spoon the risotto into a warm shallow dish, stir lightly with a fork, and sprinkle with the rest of the cheese.

RISOTTO ALLA MILANESE

There are several versions of Milanese rice, some being made with chicken broth, others with white wine or Marsala. The classic flavoring of saffron, however, is always included. The rice can be served as a course on its own, and is also the traditional accompaniment to *osso buco* (stewed shank of veal).

PREPARATION TIME: *20 min*
COOKING TIME: *20 min*
INGREDIENTS *(for 6):*
2 cups Italian or short grain rice
1 marrow bone
1 small onion
6 tablespoons unsalted butter
$\frac{1}{2}$ cup dry white wine
2 quarts beef stock
$\frac{1}{2}$ teaspoon powdered saffron
$\frac{3}{4}$ cup grated Parmesan cheese

Ask the butcher to chop the bone into several pieces, so that the marrow can be easily extracted with a skewer – it should yield about 2 ounces. Peel and finely chop the onion.

Melt half the butter in a large pan, add the marrow and onion and fry over moderate heat until transparent. Pour the wine over the onion and boil briskly until reduced by half. Add the rice and sauté, stirring continuously, until it begins to change color.

Stir the boiling stock, a cupful at a time, into the rice, until completely absorbed. Blend in all the stock and finally stir in the saffron. The rice should be tender after 15–20 minutes. If necessary, add a little hot water to prevent the rice drying out.

Stir the remaining butter and grated Parmesan cheese into the rice and serve at once.

ORANGE RICE

Savory rice, instead of potatoes, goes well with chicken or veal dishes in cream sauce. The rice can also be used cold as a base for a salad.

PREPARATION TIME: *10 min*
COOKING TIME: *30 min*
INGREDIENTS *(for 6):*
2 cups long grain rice
1 small onion
3 stalks celery
6 tablespoons unsalted butter
2 large oranges
Salt and black pepper*
2 sprigs thyme

Peel and finely chop the onion; wash the celery and cut into narrow slices. Melt the butter in a large, heavy-based pan and fry the onion and celery over low heat for about 5 minutes, until the onion is soft. Finely grate the rind from the oranges; squeeze the flesh and strain the juice. Add $3\frac{1}{2}$–4 cups of cold water to the pan, together with the orange rind and juice, a pinch of salt and the thyme. Bring this mixture to the boil.

Wash the rice and pour it into the orange mixture. Bring back to the boil and simmer, stirring occasionally, for about 25 minutes, until the rice is tender and the liquid absorbed.

Before serving, remove the thyme and season with freshly ground pepper.

RISOTTO BIANCO

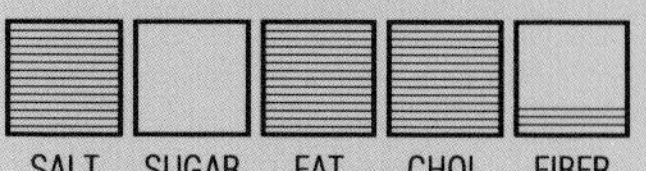

SALT SUGAR FAT CHOL FIBER

GLUTEN-FREE WHOLEFOOD*
TOTAL CALORIES: ABOUT 1925

For low **salt**, replace the cheese with mushrooms – dried mushrooms go very well in a risotto. Use about $\frac{1}{2}$ ounce and soak them first for about half an hour. Their soaking water, strained, can be used for cooking the rice.
To reduce the **fat** and **cholesterol** levels to low, soften the onion in the oil alone, covering the pan to prevent it drying out, and add a teaspoon of butter with the rice. When the rice is cooked add only 2 teaspoons more butter, and $\frac{1}{4}$–$\frac{1}{2}$ cup cheese. (Calories lost: up to 654.)
For a **vegetarian** dish, cook the rice in vegetable stock. Brown rice will need more liquid.

Freezing: ✓ up to 3 months.

RISOTTO ALLA MILANESE

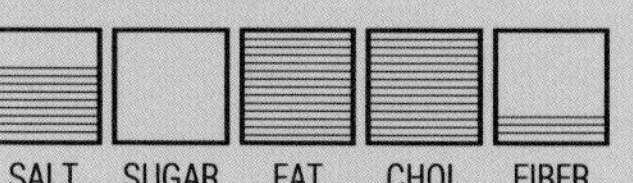

SALT SUGAR FAT CHOL FIBER

GLUTEN-FREE WHOLEFOOD*
TOTAL CALORIES: ABOUT 2880

For low **salt** use only $\frac{1}{2}$ cup Parmesan and unsalted stock.
To reduce the **fat** and **cholesterol** levels, cook the marrow and onion in a heavy pan brushed lightly with oil. Omit the remaining butter at the end, or add only 2–3 teaspoons so that each person gets about 2 teaspoonfuls fat. Together with reducing the Parmesan, as above, this will

give a very moderate fat and cholesterol level. (Calories lost: up to 472.)
If you are using brown rice for a high-**fiber** and **wholefood** dish, it will need more liquid and will take a lot longer to cook.
For a **vegetarian** dish omit the marrow; use vegetable stock.

Freezing: ✓ up to 3 months.

ORANGE RICE

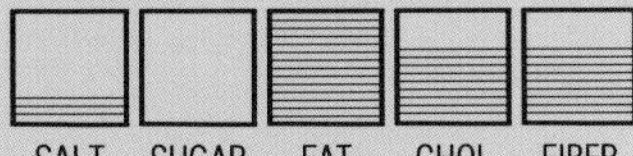

SALT SUGAR FAT CHOL FIBER

GLUTEN-FREE WHOLEFOOD* VEGETARIAN
TOTAL CALORIES: ABOUT 2290

To reduce the **fat** and **cholesterol** levels to low, cook the onion and celery in only 1 tablespoon butter, vegetable margarine or oil. Using either the margarine or oil will eliminate cholesterol from the dish. (Calories lost: up to 481.)

Freezing: ✓ up to 3 months.

RICE WITH GARLIC AND WALNUTS

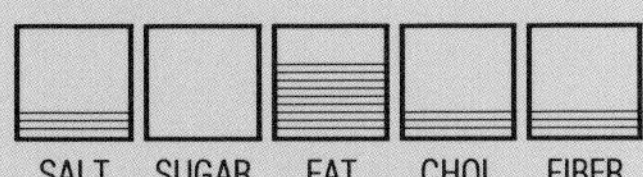

SALT SUGAR FAT CHOL FIBER

GLUTEN-FREE WHOLEFOOD*
TOTAL CALORIES: ABOUT 1600

For low **fat** use 1 tablespoon oil and half the Parmesan. (Calories lost: up to 322.)
For a **vegetarian** dish, cook the rice in a little more than its own volume of water. Brown rice will need about $2\frac{1}{4}$ times its own volume, and will give a high-**fiber** and **wholefood** dish.

Freezing: ✓ up to 2 months.

RICE WITH GARLIC AND WALNUTS

Plain boiled rice is a good substitute for potatoes and vegetables. Here the rice is given additional flavor, which makes it a good choice with goulash or curry.

PREPARATION TIME: *15 min*
COOKING TIME: *14 min*
INGREDIENTS *(for 4–6):*
1 cup Patna rice
2 heaping tablespoons finely chopped parsley
2 cloves garlic
$\frac{1}{3}$ cup shelled walnuts
$\frac{1}{2}$ cup grated Parmesan cheese
3 tablespoons olive oil
Salt and black pepper*
5 cups chicken stock
*1 tablespoon salt**
Juice of half lemon

Pound the parsley in a mortar with the peeled garlic and nuts until a smooth paste is achieved. Beat in the cheese until the mixture is thick, then gradually beat in the oil. Season to taste with salt and freshly ground pepper.

Pour the stock into a large saucepan and bring to the boil. Add the salt, lemon juice and rice, stirring until it returns to the boil. Cover and boil for 14 minutes or until the rice is just tender, adding more water only if necessary. Drain in a colander and rinse the rice by running hot water through it.

Drain the rice thoroughly and stir with a fork to separate the grains. Spoon it into a hot serving dish; season with a good grating of pepper. Blend the nut mixture into the rice and serve.

GREEK RICE RING

Particularly attractive when molded in a ring, this spicy rice dish, served hot or cold, makes a light meal on its own. Kebabs, shellfish or chicken make it even more substantial.

PREPARATION TIME: *20 min*
COOKING TIME: *20–40 min*
SETTING TIME: *1 hour*
INGREDIENTS *(for 6):*
1 cup long grain rice
Salt and black pepper*
Lemon juice
2 large ripe tomatoes
1 tablespoon finely chopped chives
1 tablespoon finely chopped parsley
8 green olives
½ teaspoon each, dried basil and marjoram
1 sweet red pepper
4 tablespoons olive oil
2 tablespoons tarragon vinegar
GARNISH:
Black olives

Cook the rice in a large pan of boiling salted water, with a teaspoon of lemon juice, for about 15 minutes or until the rice is just tender. Drain the rice in a colander and cover with a dry cloth to absorb the steam and keep the rice dry and fluffy.

While the rice is cooking, skin the tomatoes (page 160). Chop them finely and put in a large bowl together with the chives, parsley and finely chopped green olives. Blend in the dried herbs. Scald the pepper in boiling water for 5 minutes, cut off the stalk end and remove the seeds. Cut the pepper into narrow strips; set eight strips aside and chop the remainder finely. Add them to the tomato mixture.

Mix the still-warm rice into the tomato mixture. Blend the oil and vinegar together in a small bowl and season to taste with salt and freshly ground pepper. Add enough of this dressing to moisten the rice thoroughly; adjust seasoning and sharpen to taste with lemon juice. Press the rice firmly into a ring mold and leave to set in a cool place for at least 1 hour.

To serve hot, cover the rice mold with buttered foil or wax paper and place it in a roasting pan containing about ½ in of boiling water. Heat on top of the stove for 15–20 minutes, then remove the covering and place the serving dish over the mold. Turn it upside-down, and give a sharp shake to ease out the rice. Garnish with black olives and strips of red pepper.

Invert half a grapefruit in the center and skewer broiled lamb kebabs in a fan arrangement in the grapefruit.

For a cold lunch, unmold the rice ring, as already described, without re-heating it. For a more substantial meal, fill the center with cooked chicken, shrimp or lobster in mousseline sauce.

FRIED RICE WITH LEEKS

This unusual rice dish is especially good with meat courses that contain a lot of sauce, such as casseroles and braised oxtail stews.

PREPARATION TIME: *15 min*
COOKING TIME: *20 min*
INGREDIENTS *(for 6):*
2 pounds leeks
¾ cup Patna rice
*2 tablespoons salt**
¼ cup unsalted butter
½ teaspoon curry powder
Black pepper

Set a pan holding about 3½ quarts of water to boil for the rice, and a smaller one holding about 2½ cups for the leeks. Remove the coarse outer leaves, roots and tops from the leeks, wash well under cold running water, flushing away any dirt trapped in the ends; cut into ¼ in thick slices. Add a tablespoon of salt to each saucepan of boiling water, put the leeks in one and the rice in the other. Stir the rice until it comes back to the boil, cover and boil for 14 minutes. Meanwhile, simmer the leeks for about 5 minutes, then drain them in a colander. Melt the butter in a frying pan, and fry the leeks for about 8 minutes or until just tender.

When it is cooked, turn the rice into a sieve and wash thoroughly under hot running water. Add the drained rice to the leeks in the frying pan, blend with the curry powder; fry for a few minutes, stirring all the time. Season with freshly ground pepper and serve.

GREEK RICE RING

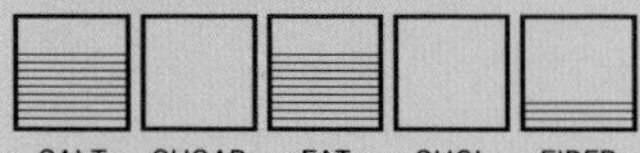

SALT SUGAR FAT CHOL FIBER

GLUTEN-FREE WHOLEFOOD* VEGETARIAN
TOTAL CALORIES: ABOUT 1430

The exact **salt** level depends on the number of black olives used for the garnish. For low salt, use not more than 6 or omit them entirely.
To reduce the **fat** level to low add only 2 or 3 tablespoons oil to the mixture, reducing the vinegar in proportion. (Calories lost: up to 270.)
Brown rice will take longer to cook but contributes more **fiber** and makes the dish **wholefood**.

Freezing: √ up to 3 months.

FRIED RICE WITH LEEKS

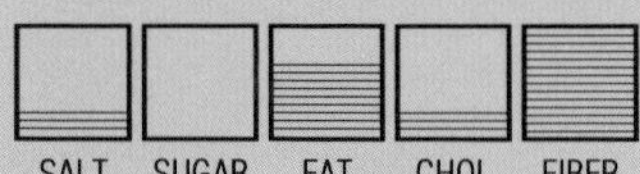

SALT SUGAR FAT CHOL FIBER

GLUTEN-FREE* WHOLEFOOD* VEGETARIAN
TOTAL CALORIES: ABOUT 1280

The low **salt** level assumes the rice and leeks are cooked in unsalted water.
To reduce the **fat** level to low, change the method of cooking the leeks. Put them in a large saucepan with 1 tablespoon butter and 3 tablespoons stock, and poach gently for about 8 minutes. (Calories lost: up to 265.)
Brown rice not only has more **fiber**, but more flavor even when cooked without salt. Check the curry powder is **gluten-free**.

Freezing: √ up to 2 months.

RAVIOLI WITH CHEESE

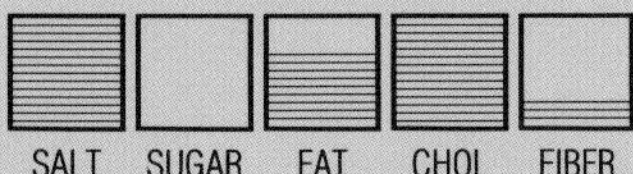

WHOLEFOOD* VEGETARIAN
TOTAL CALORIES: ABOUT 2485

To reduce the **salt** content to medium, use ¾ pound mushrooms, sliced and cooked in a heavy pan brushed with oil, then chopped, in place of half the ricotta cheese, and only 2 tablespoons of Parmesan, increasing the onion if wished. To reduce the **fat** and **cholesterol** content, use only 2 yolks to make the pasta and omit the yolks added to the filling, which should stick together enough without them. This will give low fat and cholesterol. Serve with low-fat sour cream or quark instead of butter. (Calories lost: up to 600.)

Freezing: ☑ up to 3 months.

RAVIOLI WITH CHEESE

This very rich pasta dough has a light filling, and is served simply with butter and grated cheese. Spinach is sometimes added to the ricotta.

PREPARATION TIME: *1 hour*
COOKING TIME: *10 min*
INGREDIENTS *(for 6–8):*
2 cups flour
6 egg yolks
*¾ teaspoon salt**
½–¾ cup warm water
1 pound ricotta cheese
1 cup grated Parmesan cheese
2 tablespoons grated onion

Sift the flour onto a board; make a well in the center and put 3 of the egg yolks in the well. Add ¼ teaspoon of the salt and 5 tablespoons of the water. Work it into the flour and knead until a stiff dough is formed, adding a little more warm water if necessary. Knead until smooth and elastic. Cover the dough and let it stand for 15 minutes.

Divide the dough in half, and roll out one half very thinly. In a bowl, mix the remaining egg yolks, the ricotta cheese, Parmesan cheese, onion, and remaining salt until well blended. Place 1 teaspoonful of the mixture on the center of the dough; repeat, spacing teaspoonfuls 2 in apart in each direction.

Roll out the remaining half of the dough and carefully position it as a top layer, brushing the outside edges lightly with water to seal the layers. Press the layers of dough together around each mound of the cheese mixture.

Cut into squares with a pastry wheel or a sharp knife. Drop into boiling salted water, and simmer for 10 minutes. Drain well. Serve with melted butter and additional grated Parmesan cheese.

LOBSTER RAVIOLI

Ravioli – little egg pasta cushions – are usually bought ready made and then filled with a savory stuffing. They bear little resemblance to fresh pasta, but here, for a special occasion, is a recipe for home-made ravioli, with a luxury filling. Crabmeat can be substituted for the lobster.

PREPARATION TIME: *1½ hours*
STANDING TIME: *2 hours*
COOKING TIME: *10 min*
INGREDIENTS *(for 4):*
RAVIOLI:
2 cups flour
*¼ teaspoon salt**
2 large eggs
3 tablespoons butter
1 small egg
FILLING:
½–¾ pound lobster or crabmeat
1 tablespoon heavy cream
Squeeze of lemon
Cayenne pepper
SAUCE:
1¼ cups white sauce
3 tablespoons heavy cream
1 heaping teaspoon tomato paste
Juice of half lemon
Cayenne pepper
GARNISH:
Parmesan cheese

Sift the flour and the salt into a mixing bowl and make a well in the center. Lightly beat the 2 eggs and pour into the flour; mix thoroughly. Melt the butter in a small saucepan and add to the flour. Knead the mixture to a stiff paste with a little cold water.

Turn the paste on to a floured surface and knead for 10 minutes until shiny. Set the paste aside to rest for at least 1 hour.

Meanwhile, make the filling for the ravioli; chop the lobster or crabmeat finely into a mixing bowl, add the cream and season to taste with lemon juice and cayenne pepper.

Roll out the paste, on a floured surface, to a paper-thin 24 in square. With a teaspoon, drop the filling over one half of the paste, at intervals of 1½ in. Brush between the fillings with lightly beaten egg. Turn over the other half of the paste and press down firmly with the fingers between the fillings. Cut through the filled squares with a pastry wheel. Dust the ravioli squares with flour and set them aside for about 1 hour before cooking.

When ready for cooking, bring a large pan of lightly salted water to the boil. Drop the ravioli into the water and cook for about 7 minutes. Drain on paper towels and keep them hot on a serving dish.

Serve the ravioli with a white sauce (page 166), enriched with cream and tomato paste. Season to taste with lemon and cayenne pepper. Heat the sauce through without boiling and serve in a sauce boat. Finally, grate Parmesan cheese into a separate bowl, and pass it around with the hot ravioli and sauce.

LOBSTER RAVIOLI

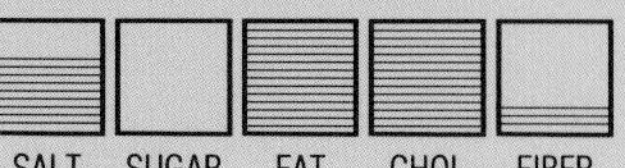

WHOLEFOOD*
TOTAL CALORIES: ABOUT 2685

The **salt** is natural to both lobster and crab. The only way to reduce it to low is to replace up to half with a less salty fish, such as monkfish.
The crab or lobster also account for much of the high **cholesterol** level, but this can be restricted to medium if some monkfish is used instead, as above, only 1 egg is used in making the pasta and the butter is replaced with 2 tablespoons oil. Omit the egg for brushing the pasta.
These moves will also reduce the **fat**. If, as well, the cream is replaced with quark or low-fat sour cream or yogurt, and skim milk is used in the sauce, the total fat level will be low. (Calories lost: up to 685.)

TAGLIATELLE ALLA CARBONARA

WHOLEFOOD*
TOTAL CALORIES: ABOUT 2045

The high **salt** content comes mainly from the bacon, with the ham, both cheeses, and eggs also contributing to the high total level. The only way to reduce it to moderate is to use half quantities of bacon, ham and cheese. You could omit the bacon which will almost halve the salt, giving a medium level, but bacon is very characteristic of this dish. In addition, ensure that

the pasta and butter are not salted.
Any reduction in the bacon, cheese or eggs will also reduce the **fat** and **cholesterol** (ham is not high in either). Cooking the bacon and ham in a pan lightly brushed with oil will save over half the fat entailed in using butter and oil for this job. The recipe will remain fairly high in cholesterol even if only 3 eggs are used. These changes can be made to the degree that suits your taste, giving a medium fat, medium salt and high cholesterol dish. For a low-fat dish, it is necessary to cut the eggs and cheese quite drastically. (Calories lost: up to 531.)

SPAGHETTI WITH EGGPLANT

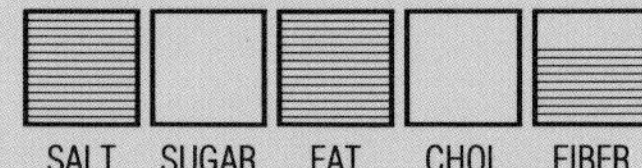

SALT SUGAR FAT CHOL FIBER

WHOLEFOOD* VEGETARIAN
TOTAL CALORIES: ABOUT 2265

To reduce the **salt** level to low, omit the salting stage for the eggplant. This is supposed to reduce the bitter taste of eggplant, but modern varieties seem not to need the treatment. What salting does do is reduce the need for so much oil when eggplants are fried, but broiling them as suggested below avoids this problem too.
For a low **fat** level, broil the eggplant strips on a generously greased oven sheet for a few minutes, tossing occasionally to coat with fat, under high heat. (Calories lost: up to 539.)

TAGLIATELLE ALLA CARBONARA

Alla carbonara means "in the style of the charcoal-burner's wife." She would probably have used all Parmesan or a mixture of Romano and Parmesan.

PREPARATION TIME: *10 min*
COOKING TIME: *15 min*
INGREDIENTS *(for 6):*
½ pound tagliatelle
2 ounces bacon
2 ounces cooked ham
2 tablespoons butter
1 tablespoon olive oil
4 eggs
½ cup grated Cheddar cheese
¼ cup grated Parmesan cheese
Salt and black pepper*

Chop the bacon roughly; dice the ham. Cook the tagliatelle in plenty of well-salted boiling water for 10–15 minutes or until just tender. Drain thoroughly in a colander.

While the tagliatelle is cooking, heat the butter and oil in a pan over moderate heat and fry the bacon and ham until they are crisp. Beat the eggs and cheeses together in a bowl.

Add the drained pasta to the bacon and ham and stir carefully until evenly coated with fat. Pour in the beaten eggs and cheese and continue stirring over gentle heat until the eggs thicken. Be sure to remove the pan from the heat before the eggs scramble.

Spoon the mixture into a warm dish and serve at once, with a bowl of grated Parmesan cheese.

SPAGHETTI WITH EGGPLANT

In Italy, pasta – and in particular spaghetti – frequently forms the main meal of the day. Often oil and garlic are the only additions, but eggplant gives the pasta an unusual flavor.

PREPARATION TIME: *10 min*
COOKING TIME: *15 min*
INGREDIENTS *(for 4–6):*
¾ pound spaghetti
1 large eggplant
2 tablespoons salt
6 tablespoons olive oil
Seasoned flour (page 184)
Black pepper

Remove the stalk end and wipe the eggplant. Cut it into thin round slices and place these in layers in a colander. Sprinkle salt over each layer and leave for 1 hour to draw out the excess water. Wipe the slices dry on absorbent paper towels, cut them into ¼ in wide strips and coat them lightly with seasoned flour.

Heat 4½ quarts of water in a large saucepan and, when boiling, add 1 tablespoon salt and the spaghetti. Stir continuously until the water returns to the boil. Continue boiling and stirring occasionally for 9 minutes, when the spaghetti should be tender but still slightly undercooked (*al dente*). While the spaghetti is cooking, heat 3–4 tablespoons of olive oil in a frying pan and sauté the eggplant strips until crisp.

Drain the spaghetti, toss in a colander to remove the last of the water, and pepper well. Warm the remaining olive oil in a saucepan, transfer the spaghetti to a warm serving dish and pour over the oil. Toss well and blend the eggplant strips into the spaghetti.

SPAGHETTINI WITH MUSSEL SAUCE

Fine thin strands of spaghetti, known as spaghettini, make a lighter-than-usual pasta dish. It is here served in an unusual sauce for a flavorful first course.

PREPARATION TIME: *1 hour*
COOKING TIME: *15 min*
INGREDIENTS *(for 4–6)*:
1 pound spaghettini
2½ quarts mussels
2 heaping tablespoons salt
8 tablespoons olive oil
3 cloves garlic
½ cup fish stock
Black pepper
1 tablespoon finely chopped parsley

Wash the mussels under cold running water, scrubbing the shells and scraping off the beards. Leave the mussels in a pail of cold water to which has been added 2 tablespoons salt.

Set a large pan of lightly salted water to boil. Meanwhile, heat 3 tablespoons oil in large sauté pan. Add 2 peeled and crushed cloves of garlic and fry in the oil until brown. Remove the garlic. Put the mussels in the pan, place over high heat, cover with a lid, and shake the pan for 5 minutes, or until the shells have opened. Remove the pan from the heat and discard any mussels that remain closed. Turn the contents of the pan into a bowl and ease the mussels from the shells, retaining the liquid.

Put the spaghettini into the pan of boiling salted water, stirring until the water boils again. Cook the spaghettini for 7–10 minutes, stirring occasionally until just tender. Drain the spaghettini

SPAGHETTINI WITH MUSSEL SAUCE

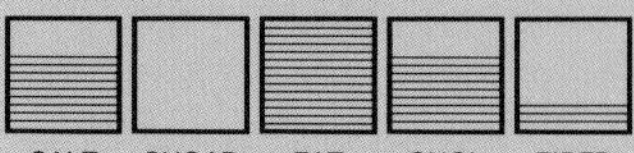

WHOLEFOOD*
TOTAL CALORIES: ABOUT 3375

The **salt** level comes mainly from the mussels, which are naturally high in sodium: 3½ ounces shelled mussels yield over 200 mg, so even if no salt is added elsewhere to the pasta or stock, the level cannot be reduced below medium.
The high **fat** level can be reduced to moderate by using only 2 or 3 tablespoons oil. If top quality oil is used, the flavor will still be good. (Calories lost: up to 809.) The **cholesterol** level cannot be changed either as this is due to the mussels (but see also the notes on the next recipe).

LUMACHINE CON COZZE

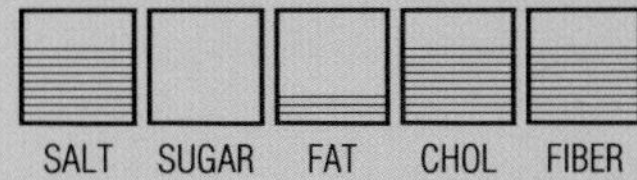

WHOLEFOOD*
TOTAL CALORIES: ABOUT 1785

The **salt** and **cholesterol** level are naturally present in the mussels, so cannot be reduced unless smaller portions are served. However, they are much lower than, for instance, in a bacon and egg breakfast. If a lower level of either is needed, replace half the mussels with mushrooms. This is, of course, a different dish, but still very good. (Calories lost: up to 238.)

Freezing: ✓ up to 3 months for the tomato sauce.

Microwave: ✓ for the tomato sauce.

SPAGHETTI WITH TUNA SAUCE

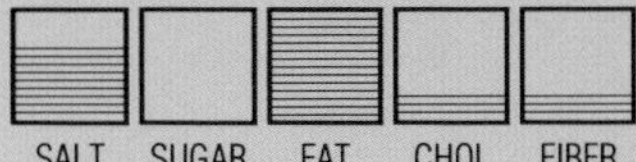

WHOLEFOOD*
TOTAL CALORIES: ABOUT 2720

The **salt** level comes from the salt added to canned tuna, whether in oil or brine. To give a low level, replace this with fresh tuna or monkfish.
The **fat** level can be reduced to low by cooking the garlic in a pan brushed with oil, omitting the remaining oil and butter. If wished, 2 tablespoons of butter can be tossed through the cooked pasta. Use tuna canned in brine, not in oil. Again, using fresh fish means an even lower fat level. (Calories lost: up to 653.)

thoroughly in a colander.

Heat the remaining oil in the sauté pan over low heat. Peel and crush the remaining garlic and fry until golden. Pour half the contents of the pan over the spaghettini and toss until it gleams. Return the mussels and their liquid to the sauté pan and heat through gently. Add the fish stock and continue cooking for 1–2 minutes until thoroughly heated. Pepper well, and stir in the parsley.

Spoon the mussels and liquid over the spaghettini, toss and serve at once, with slices of warm crusty bread.

LUMACHINE CON COZZE

This is an Italian dish of egg pasta shells (lumachine) and mussels. When fresh mussels are not available, bottled mussels, without their brine, may be used. Spaghetti or spaghettini can be used instead of the pasta shells, and baby clams (also available bottled) can replace the mussels, making this into a version of the popular spaghetti alle vongole.

PREPARATION TIME: *30 min*
COOKING TIME: *25 min*
INGREDIENTS *(for 4):*
2½ pints fresh mussels
1 pound ripe tomatoes
1 clove garlic
1 tablespoon olive oil
1 tablespoon chopped parsley
½ teaspoon each, dried marjoram and basil
5 tablespoons white wine
½ pound lumachine
Salt and black pepper*
Lemon juice

Scrub and clean the mussels thoroughly. Remove the beards, and discard any mussels with broken or open shells.

Skin the tomatoes (page 160) and chop them roughly. Peel and finely chop the garlic. Heat the oil in a frying pan and lightly fry the garlic. Add the tomatoes, parsley and herbs and bring this mixture to simmering point.

Put the cleaned mussels and the wine in a pan and cover with a lid. Cook over moderate heat, shaking occasionally, until the mussels open. Remove the mussels from the shells and set them aside. Strain the cooking liquid through cheesecloth to remove any sandy sediment, and stir it into the tomato mixture. Simmer over low heat for 20 minutes.

While the tomatoes are cooking, bring a large pan of water to the boil, add 2–3 teaspoons of salt and cook the pasta shells for 12 minutes or until tender, but not soft. Drain in a colander and cover with a clean cloth to keep the pasta warm.

Add the mussels to the tomato sauce and heat through. Season to taste with freshly ground pepper, adding salt only if necessary, and sharpen with lemon juice. Put the pasta shells in a warmed deep serving dish and pour the mussels and sauce over them. Serve at once, with crusty bread.

SPAGHETTI WITH TUNA SAUCE

Lighter and more summery than spaghetti with a tomato or meat sauce, this dish makes a good family meal. Serve it with crusty bread and a green salad, tossed in French dressing (page 167).

PREPARATION TIME: *10 min*
COOKING TIME: *15 min*
INGREDIENTS *(for 4–6):*
1 pound spaghetti
1 clove garlic (optional)
2 tablespoons olive oil
¼ cup butter
1 cup chicken stock
3 tablespoons dry white wine or vermouth
7-ounce can tuna fish
Salt and black pepper*
GARNISH:
2 tablespoons finely chopped parsley

Bring a large pan of salted water to the boil, add the spaghetti and bring back to the boil. Cook for 7–12 minutes or until the spaghetti is just resistant to the bite (*al dente*). Stir occasionally with a wooden spoon.

Peel and finely chop the garlic. Heat the oil and half the butter, and fry the garlic for 1–2 minutes, then stir in the stock and wine. Boil briskly over high heat until the liquid has reduced to about ½ cup. Drain the oil from the tuna fish, flake the meat and add it to the stock. Season with salt and freshly ground pepper.

When the spaghetti is cooked, drain it thoroughly in a colander and toss it in the remaining butter. Put the spaghetti in a serving dish, pour over the tuna sauce and sprinkle with the chopped parsley. Serve at once.

FETTUCCINE AL BURRO

This pasta dish is a specialty of many Roman restaurants and is ideally made from home-made noodles.

PREPARATION TIME: *8 min*
COOKING TIME: *10–15 min*
INGREDIENTS *(for 4–6):*
1 pound ribbon noodles
*1 tablespoon salt**
$\frac{1}{2}$ cup unsalted butter
6 tablespoons heavy cream
$1\frac{1}{2}$ cups grated Parmesan cheese
Black pepper

Boil $4\frac{1}{2}$ quarts of water in a large saucepan, and add the salt and the noodles, stirring until the water returns to the boil, to prevent the noodles from sticking together. Cover and continue to boil for 8 minutes until the noodles are tender. Meanwhile beat the softened butter in a bowl until it fluffs; gradually beat in the cream and half the cheese. Drain the noodles and toss them in a colander to remove the last drops of water.

Put the noodles in a hot serving dish, pour over the cheese and cream sauce and toss to coat the noodles thoroughly. Pepper well and serve the remaining cheese in a bowl.

FETTUCCINE AL BURRO

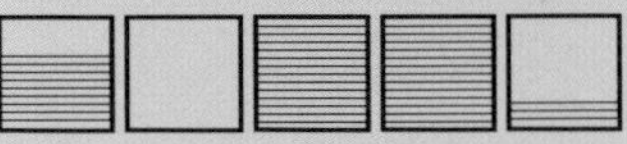

SALT SUGAR FAT CHOL FIBER

WHOLEFOOD* VEGETARIAN
TOTAL CALORIES: ABOUT 3430

The medium **salt** level comes almost all from the cheese, assuming that the pasta is cooked and made without salt. This is a huge amount of Parmesan, and many people will find that 1 tablespoon per person is enough, giving a low to medium salt level.
If this is done, and if the butter is replaced with quark and the cream with low-fat yogurt or sour cream, this will also give low overall **fat** and **cholesterol** levels. (Calories lost: up to 1159.)

RIGATONI WITH HARE SAUCE

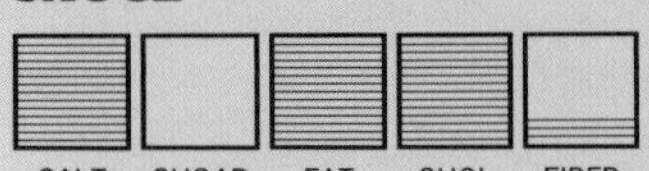

SALT SUGAR FAT CHOL FIBER

WHOLEFOOD*
TOTAL CALORIES: ABOUT 3500

The high **salt** level comes mainly from the bacon, with a substantial addition from the Parmesan. To reduce, use only 1 ounce bacon and $\frac{1}{4}$–$\frac{1}{2}$ cup cheese, giving a much lower though still medium/high level (325 mg per person from these items alone).
Hare is one of the leanest of all meats, and if the amount of bacon and cheese is reduced, as above, the dish will have a low **fat** level, especially if the lard is replaced with a brushing of oil in a heavy based pan. The **cholesterol** will also be low. (Calories lost: up to 582.)

Pressure cooker: ✓ for the sauce.

Freezing: ✓ up to 2 months for the sauce.

SCHINKENFLECKERL

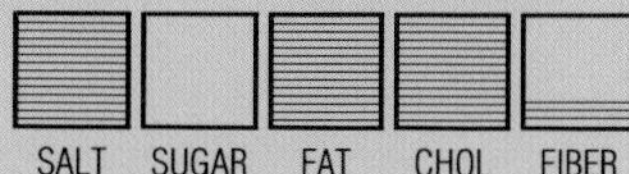

WHOLEFOOD*
TOTAL CALORIES: ABOUT 2600

The high **salt** level comes mainly from the ham, with some from the cheese. The only way to reduce this is to use less, but even if the amount of both is halved, the salt will still be high (just over 400 mg from these two ingredients alone).
The **fat** level can be reduced by cooking the shallots in a heavy based pan brushed lightly with oil, omitting the butter, and using quark or low-fat sour cream or yogurt (or any mixture of these) in place of the sour cream. To help stabilize these during baking, stir in a good teaspoonful of cornstarch, mixed to a smooth paste with cold water, before adding the mixture. (Calories lost: up to 917.)
The **cholesterol** will stay high because of the eggs, but the fat level will be low to medium.

RIGATONI WITH HARE SAUCE

This rich pasta dish from Tuscany with a thick sauce of wine and hare is an ideal way of using up the remains of a hare.

PREPARATION TIME: *25 min*
COOKING TIME: *$1\frac{1}{4}$ hours*
INGREDIENTS *(for 4)*:
$\frac{3}{4}$ pound rigatoni or broad noodles
4 hare or rabbit legs
$\frac{1}{4}$ pound bacon
1 clove garlic
1 onion
1 stalk celery
$\frac{1}{4}$ pound mushrooms
1 tablespoon lard or bacon fat
1 tablespoon flour
$\frac{1}{2}$ cup red wine or $\frac{1}{4}$ cup Marsala
Salt and black pepper*
Powdered thyme and marjoram
Rind and juice of half lemon
$\frac{3}{4}$–1 cup grated Parmesan cheese

Slice the meat off the legs of the hare and remove the tough tendons. Chop the meat into $\frac{1}{2}$ in pieces and set aside. Chop the bacon roughly. Peel and finely chop the garlic and onion. Scrub and chop the celery, and trim and slice the mushrooms.

Heat the lard or fat in a deep, heavy-based pan over moderate heat and fry the bacon, garlic, onion and celery for about 5 minutes, or until just taking color. Add the hare meat and mushrooms and cook for a few minutes until lightly browned.

Remove the pan from the heat and stir in enough flour to absorb all the fat. Return the pan to the heat and fry the mixture until brown, stirring continuously. Add the wine and gradually blend in 2 cups of water to make a thick sauce. Season to taste with salt, freshly ground pepper and a pinch of thyme and marjoram. Cover the pan with a lid and simmer over low heat for 1 hour. Add the grated lemon rind and sharpen with lemon juice.

Meanwhile, cook the rigatoni or noodles in a large pan of salted water for 12–15 minutes. Drain thoroughly in a colander. Arrange the rigatoni around the edge of a serving dish and spoon the hare sauce into the center. Sprinkle a little cheese over the sauce and serve the remainder in a separate bowl. Serve a tossed green salad with the pasta.

SCHINKENFLECKERL

This recipe for noodles with ham is traditional both in Austria and in Switzerland.

PREPARATION TIME: *15 min*
COOKING TIME: *40–45 min*
INGREDIENTS *(for 4)*:
$\frac{1}{2}$ pound pasta squares or short cut noodles
2 teaspoons olive oil
2 tablespoons toasted breadcrumbs
Salt and black pepper*
$\frac{1}{2}$ pound lean ham
2 shallots or 1 small onion
$\frac{1}{4}$ cup butter
1 cup sour cream
2 eggs
$\frac{1}{2}$ cup grated Gruyère or Cheddar cheese
GARNISH:
1 small green pepper

Grease a timbale mold or a round deep 6 in cake pan with the oil and coat it evenly with the breadcrumbs.

Bring a large pan of salted water to the boil and add the pasta

or noodles. Bring back to the boil and cook over high heat for 10 minutes. Drain well.

While the pasta is cooking, dice the ham, and peel and finely chop the shallots or the onion. Melt the butter in a small frying pan and cook the shallots over moderate heat for 5 minutes or until soft and transparent. Blend them into the pasta.

Blend the sour cream and eggs in a small bowl, stir in the ham and grated cheese, and add this mixture to the pasta. Blend well, and season to taste with salt and freshly ground pepper.

Spoon the pasta mixture into the prepared mold and put it in a roasting pan with enough cold water to reach 1 in up the sides of the mold. Bake in the center of an oven pre-heated to 400°F (200°C, mark 6) for 30 minutes, or until the mixture has set and is light brown on top.

Remove the mold from the oven and allow the mixture to cool and shrink slightly before unmolding it on to a warmed serving dish.

Garnish with wedges or squares of broiled green pepper.

LASAGNE VERDI AL FORNO

The district around Bologna in Italy is famous for its lasagne – pasta squares often colored with spinach (*pasta verde*). The pasta is usually baked in the oven with a Bolognese *ragù* or meat and vegetable sauce with alternating layers of thick béchamel sauce. This dish is an ideal main course for a small party as all the preparations can be done well in advance of baking.

PREPARATION TIME: *1 hour*
COOKING TIME: *20 min*
INGREDIENTS *(for 6):*

½ pound green lasagne
2 ounces fat ham or bacon
1 small onion
1 carrot
2 ounces button mushrooms
2 tablespoons butter
6 ounces ground beef
2–3 ounces chicken livers (optional)
1 rounded tablespoon tomato paste
½ cup dry white wine
1¼ cups beef stock or bouillon
1 teaspoon sugar
*Salt**
2 cups béchamel sauce
½ cup grated Parmesan cheese

Chop the ham or bacon. Peel and finely chop the onion and carrot and trim the mushrooms before slicing them thinly.

Melt half the butter in a large, heavy-based pan over low heat and fry the ham (or bacon) until the fat runs, then add the vegetables and fry them lightly. Crumble in the ground beef and add the cleaned and chopped chicken livers if used. Blend in the tomato paste. Continue frying, and stir continuously until the meat has browned. Add the wine and let the mixture bubble for a few minutes before adding the stock. Season to taste with sugar, and add salt if stock is used. Cover the pan with a lid and simmer over low heat for 30–40 minutes. Meanwhile make a thick béchamel sauce (page 166).

Cook the lasagne in a large pan of boiling salted water for 10–15 minutes or until just tender, stirring occasionally. Drain the pasta in a colander and drop it into a large basin of cold water to prevent it sticking together.

Thoroughly butter a shallow ovenproof dish, about 10 in by 8 in. Cover the bottom with a thin layer of the meat mixture, then béchamel sauce and lastly the drained lasagne. Repeat these layers until all the ingredients are used up, finishing with béchamel sauce. Sprinkle the top with the Parmesan cheese.

Bake in the center of the oven, pre-heated to 400°F (200°C, mark 6), for about 15–20 minutes or until the top is crisp and bubbly. Serve straight from the dish accompanied by a tossed green salad.

LUXURY PIZZA

The classic Italian pizza comes from Naples, and consists of a light yeast dough with a savory topping. The cheese should by tradition be Mozzarella (buffalo cheese), but any quick-melting cheese, such as Bel Paese, Fontina or Gruyère, is suitable.

PREPARATION TIME: *1¾ hours*
COOKING TIME: *20–25 min*
INGREDIENTS *(for 6):*
2 cups flour
*1 teaspoon salt**
8–10 tablespoons milk
½ cake fresh or 1 package active dry yeast
1 teaspoon sugar
3 tablespoons unsalted butter
1 large egg
TOPPING:
2 large onions
2 small cloves garlic
1 pound tomatoes
2 tablespoons olive oil
1 tablespoon chopped fresh marjoram or ½ teaspoon dried oregano
Salt and black pepper*
GARNISH:
6 ounces quick-melting cheese
1 can anchovy fillets
½–¾ cup black olives

Sift the flour and salt into a warm bowl and make a well in the center. Heat the milk until tepid and use a few drops to cream together the yeast and sugar. (If using dry yeast, follow the manufacturer's instructions.) Pour the yeast mixture and the rest of the milk into the flour, together with the melted butter and beaten egg. Work the dough with the hand until it is smooth and leaves the sides of the bowl clean. Shape the dough into a ball

LASAGNE VERDI AL FORNO

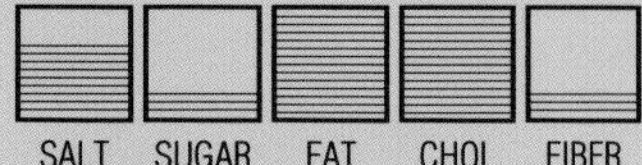

SALT SUGAR FAT CHOL FIBER

WHOLEFOOD*
TOTAL CALORIES: ABOUT 2700

The **salt** level comes mainly from the ham or bacon and cheese. Ham has 33% less than most types of bacon. Using 1 ounce each of ham and cheese, the level will be low, assuming that the remaining ingredients, such as tomato paste, stock and béchamel, as well as the pasta itself, are unsalted.
To reduce the **fat** and **cholesterol** levels to low, choose lean ham, make the béchamel sauce with only 1 tablespoon butter and skim milk, and select lean beef. The beef itself will produce enough fat to brown itself in if heated gently, and 1 tablespoon olive oil will be enough to replace the butter at this stage. (Calories lost: up to 363.)
While not high in fat, chicken liver, like other liver, is high in cholesterol. The amount here is not large enough to give a high cholesterol count once other sources, such as bacon, butter and some of the cheese, are avoided, but strict low-cholesterol dieters will want to omit it. The amount of mushrooms can be increased to compensate.

Freezing: ☑ up to 2 months.

LUXURY PIZZA

SALT SUGAR FAT CHOL FIBER

WHOLEFOOD*
TOTAL CALORIES: ABOUT 2320

To reduce the **salt** level to low, omit salt from the dough, use only 2 ounces of strong-flavored cheese, and replace the garnish with slices of green or sweet red pepper, sliced mushrooms and more fresh herbs, especially basil.
These changes will also reduce the **fat** level, which can be low if you add only 1 tablespoon butter to the pizza dough, omit the egg, and use only 1 tablespoon olive oil for the topping. (Calories lost: up to 905.)

Freezing: ✓ up to 3 months if uncooked, 2 months if cooked. The tomato sauce (topping) may be frozen separately for up to 3 months (up to 6 months if you omit the garlic).

CANNELLONI STUFFED WITH SPINACH

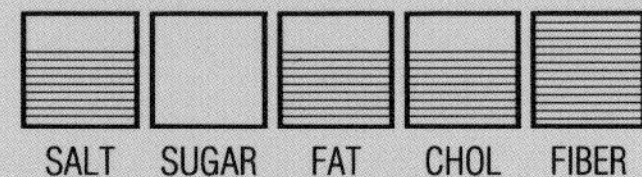

WHOLEFOOD*
TOTAL CALORIES: ABOUT 2190

The **salt** comes almost all from the cheese, assuming that the pasta, tomato sauce and chicken are unsalted. To reduce the level to low, use only 2–3 tablespoons cheese.
This will also reduce the **fat** level, which can be low if the chicken is skinned, skim milk is used, and the tomato sauce is made using only 1 tablespoon oil. Make the white sauce by the low-fat blending method (see page 166), omitting the butter. (Calories lost: up to 845.)

Food Processor: ✓ for the filling.

Freezing: ✓ up to 1 month.

and put it into an oiled plastic bag. Leave it in a warm place until it has doubled in size.

Meanwhile, prepare the topping: peel and roughly chop the onions and garlic. Skin the tomatoes (page 160) and chop them roughly. Heat the olive oil in a heavy-based pan and cook the onion and garlic over moderate heat until soft and transparent. Add the tomatoes to the pan. Cook for about 10 minutes, then stir in the marjoram or oregano. Season to taste. Set this sauce aside. Cut the cheese into thin wedge-shaped slices, and drain the anchovy fillets.

When the dough has risen, knead it lightly with the fingertips for 1–2 minutes. Shape it into a circle 12 in across. Put it on a greased and floured baking sheet. Cover the dough with the onion and tomato mixture to within 1 in of the outer edge. Arrange the cheese on top in a fan-like pattern, slightly overlapping the slices. Decorate the cheese with the anchovies and dot with olives.

Bake the pizza near the top of an oven pre-heated to 425°F (220°C, mark 7) for 20–25 minutes or until the cheese has melted and browned slightly, and the dough is well risen.

Pizza is best served straight from the oven, but it can also be served cold, or re-heated in the oven, at low heat. A crisp salad tossed in a well-seasoned dressing would be ideal with the pizza for a main course.

CANNELLONI STUFFED WITH SPINACH

Literally 'big pipes,' cannelloni are pasta tubes, about 3 in long and 1 in across.

PREPARATION TIME: *45–60 min*
COOKING TIME: *20–30 min*
INGREDIENTS *(for 4):*
8 cannelloni tubes
1 pound fresh bulk spinach
½ pound cooked chicken meat
2 tablespoons unsalted butter
2 tablespoons flour
1 cup milk
Salt and black pepper*
2–2½ cups tomato sauce (use the pizza topping in the previous recipe)
¾–1 cup grated Parmesan cheese

Wash the spinach and put it in a large saucepan – no water is needed. Cover and cook over low heat for about 10 minutes. Drain through a colander, squeezing with a spoon to remove all the moisture. Chop coarsely and set aside. Dice the chicken meat finely or put it through a grinder.

Melt the butter in a saucepan and stir in the flour; cook gently for 1 minute, then gradually blend in the milk, stirring continuously to get a smooth sauce. Bring to the boil and season to taste with salt and freshly ground pepper; simmer gently for 2–3 minutes or until the sauce has thickened. Take the pan off the heat and stir the spinach and chicken into the sauce; check seasoning.

Put the cannelloni tubes in a pan of boiling salted water and boil for 15 minutes or until the pasta is just tender. Drain and cool for a few minutes before stuffing the tubes with the spinach and chicken. Using a pastry bag, with a plain tube, pipe the stuffing into the tubes.

Arrange the cannelloni in a buttered ovenproof dish, pour the tomato sauce over them and sprinkle with half the grated cheese. Place the casserole above center in a pre-heated oven and cook at 350°F (180°C, mark 4) for 20–30 minutes or until bubbling hot and brown. Serve the cannelloni at once, with the remaining cheese in a bowl.

GNOCCHI ALLA ROMANA

Gnocchi are small dumplings made from a flour, semolina or potato paste. The Roman gnocchi are made from semolina and the paste should be left for several hours to rest. They are served with melted butter and plenty of Parmesan cheese.

PREPARATION TIME: *30 min*
COOKING TIME: *50 min*
INGREDIENTS *(for 6):*
3½ cups milk
1⅓ cups semolina
½ cup unsalted butter
1½ cups grated Parmesan cheese
Salt and black pepper*
Grated nutmeg
3 large eggs

Heat the milk to just below boiling point, then take the pan off the heat and sprinkle the semolina over the milk, stirring continuously. Return the pan to the heat and bring the mixture slowly to the boil, still stirring. Cook for 2 minutes; remove from the heat and stir in 5 tablespoons of butter and 1 cup of the grated cheese; season to taste with salt, pepper and nutmeg.

Lightly beat the eggs and gradually whisk them into the semolina mixture. Pour this paste into a buttered jelly roll pan and spread it evenly until ½ in thick. Set aside for several hours until it is firm and cold.

Cut the paste into 1½ in wide pieces with a cold, wet knife. Roll the pieces to the size and shape of walnuts (if necessary, roll them in a little semolina to ease shaping). Place them in a buttered ovenproof dish. Sprinkle with salt and pepper. Melt the remaining butter in a saucepan and pour it over the gnocchi; sprinkle with the remaining cheese and cook for 40 minutes or until pale golden, in the center of the oven pre-heated to 350°F (180°C, mark 4). Serve the gnocchi at once.

POTATO GNOCCHI

Served with a tomato sauce, these Italian gnocchi or potato dumplings would make a light supper dish on their own.

PREPARATION TIME: *30 min*
COOKING TIME: *12–15 min*
INGREDIENTS *(for 4):*
1 pound potatoes
Salt and black pepper*
¼ teaspoon ground nutmeg
1 cup flour
1 egg
¼ cup butter
½ cup grated Parmesan cheese

Peel the potatoes and cut them into 1 in pieces. Put in a saucepan, cover with cold salted water and bring to the boil. Cook for 15–20 minutes or until tender; drain and return the pan to the heat for a few minutes to dry the potatoes thoroughly.

Rub the potatoes through a coarse sieve into a large bowl. Season to taste with salt and freshly ground pepper, before mixing in the nutmeg and the flour. Beat the egg and stir it into the potatoes, using a wooden spoon; blend thoroughly until smooth. Turn the mixture out on to a floured working surface and knead lightly. Shape the mixture into a roll, cut it into 24 even pieces and shape them into balls.

Bring a large pan of water to the boil. Drop in the gnocchi, a few at a time, and simmer for 5 minutes. When cooked, the gnocchi will rise to the surface; lift them out carefully with a slotted spoon and put in a warm, buttered serving dish.

Sprinkle with the melted butter and grated cheese before serving.

GNOCCHI ALLA ROMANA

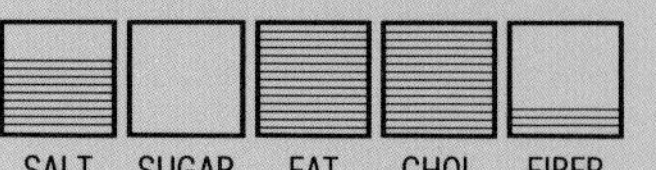

WHOLEFOOD VEGETARIAN
TOTAL CALORIES: ABOUT 3100

The **salt** level comes mainly from the cheese, and using only ¾ cup will reduce the level to low.
For low **fat** and **cholesterol** levels, use only 2 tablespoons of butter with the semolina and 1 or 2 eggs. The mixture will in fact work without any eggs, although it will obviously taste less interesting.
Instead of serving with more butter and cheese, provide a well-flavored sauce of mushrooms and low-fat sour cream or yogurt, with cumin or fresh herbs such as tarragon chopped in. (Calories lost: up to 1002.)
Gluten-free millet can be used in place of semolina.

POTATO GNOCCHI

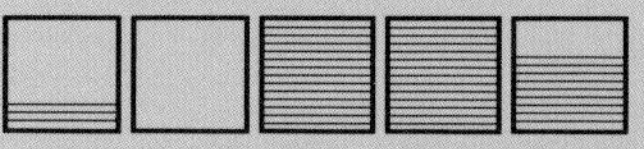

GLUTEN-FREE* WHOLEFOOD* VEGETARIAN
TOTAL CALORIES: ABOUT 1400

The **fat** and **cholesterol** levels can be reduced to low by serving the dish with only 2 tablespoons butter and ¼ cup cheese. If wished, these can be mixed with a few spoonfuls of quark, as the flavors combine well. (Calories lost: up to 287.)

Freezing: ✓ up to 3 months.

SPINACH GNOCCHI

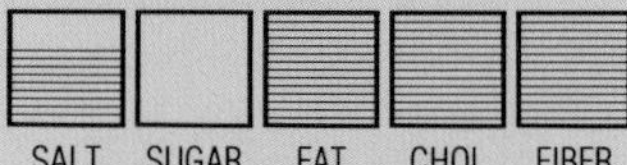

GLUTEN-FREE* WHOLEFOOD* VEGETARIAN
TOTAL CALORIES: ABOUT 2400

The **salt** level comes mainly from the cheese, and can be reduced to low by using unsalted quark instead of the cottage cheese or cream cheese, and only half the Parmesan. The **fat** and **cholesterol** levels can be low if the spinach is dried off in only 1 teaspoon of butter and oil, cottage cheese used rather than cream cheese, and the remaining butter reduced to 2 teaspoonfuls. The cream can be replaced with low-fat sour cream or more quark. (Calories lost: up to 1445.)

Microwave: ☑ for the spinach.

SPINACH GNOCCHI

The Italians take infinite trouble over their pasta dishes, and these small spinach dumplings require both patience and practice. They are, however, so light and tasty that they are worth mastering. The quantities are sufficient for a light main course for four or for a first course for six.

PREPARATION TIME: *20 min*
CHILLING TIME: *2 hours*
COOKING TIME: *15–20 min*
INGREDIENTS *(for 4–6):*
1 pound fresh bulk spinach
½ cup butter
¾ cup cottage or cream cheese
2 eggs
2 tablespoons heavy cream
3 tablespoons flour
¾ cup grated Parmesan cheese
Salt and black pepper*
Nutmeg

Wash the spinach thoroughly in several changes of cold water. Put the spinach in a large pan with a closely fitting lid. Cook, without extra water, over moderate heat for about 5 minutes or until the spinach is just soft. Drain in a sieve, pressing out all moisture. Chop the spinach finely.

Melt half the butter in a pan, add the spinach and cook, stirring constantly, for about 2 minutes or until all moisture has evaporated; if necessary squeeze the spinach in a sieve again. Rub the cottage cheese through a sieve, add to the spinach and cook for a further 3–4 minutes, stirring all the time. Remove the pan from the heat. Fold the lightly beaten eggs into the spinach. Stir in the cream, flour and ¼ cup of Parmesan cheese. Season to taste with salt, freshly ground pepper and grated nutmeg. Turn the gnocchi into a flat dish and chill for 2 hours or until firm.

Bring a large pan of lightly salted water to simmering point. Shape the gnocchi into small balls no more than ¾ in wide, between floured hands. Drop the balls into the simmering water, a few at a time. As soon as they puff up and rise to the surface, remove them with a slotted spoon.

Arrange the gnocchi in a buttered flameproof dish, melt the remaining butter and pour over them. Sprinkle with the remaining cheese and put the dish under a hot broiler until the cheese has melted and browned. Serve at once.

Vegetables

Ideally, vegetables should come straight from the field or the garden to the kitchen. Though this is seldom possible, there are many clues to the freshness or age of vegetables in the shops. Choose crisp and firm vegetables rather than hard ones, and avoid small vegetables which are probably immature and therefore lacking in flavor. Overlarge vegetables, on the other hand, are usually coarse.

Vegetables in the shops are displayed to appear as attractive as possible. To achieve this they will have been sprayed, fed with fertilizer and sometimes washed with detergent before being packaged. You may prefer to buy organically grown vegetables which have not had the benefit of such chemical treatment. If so, be prepared for them to look misshapen, often a little dirty and in general quite unlike the glossy, brightly colored, uniformly sized and neatly packaged produce in the average supermarket. They will also be more expensive, since growing crops organically is labour-intensive and relatively inefficient.

Usually vegetables are at their best in quality and lowest in price at the peak of their seasons. They are packed with vitamins and minerals and will be more nutritious, tastier, and retain their crisp texture if they are cooked only long enough to make them tender.

ROOTS AND TUBERS

Artichokes, Jerusalem

The potato-like tubers of Jerusalem artichokes have a sweet, delicate flavor, slightly reminiscent of the globe artichoke.

The vegetable is thought to have been taken to Europe from Massachusetts early in the 17th century, and certainly has nothing to do with the city of Jerusalem. It is a member of the sunflower family, and the name probably derives from the Italian name for that plant–girasole.

These tubers grow in a mass of twisted knobs and are covered with a thin white or purple skin. The crisp sweet flesh is white. Prime tubers are fairly regular in shape, and measure up to 4 in in length and 2 in across. Avoid artichokes which are misshapen, small or dirty.

Beets

These vegetables are sold by weight without leaves or in bunches with leaves. Choose deep red beets that are firm, round and smooth. Cooked beets should have fresh skin that looks slightly moist. Avoid any beets that are rough, shriveled, soft or flabby as these may be tough and woody. Soft, wet areas on beets are a sign of decay. Uncooked beets bleed easily, and care must be taken not to tear the skin when preparing beets for cooking. Beets are available all year.

Carrots

These orange-red root vegetables are among the most nourishing and inexpensive vegetables and a rich source of vitamin A. Young and slender carrots are usually sold in bunches with the leaves intact; they are tender and need only washing before cooking. Mature carrots are larger and coarser; they are sold without the leaves and by weight. Mature carrots require peeling before use. Early carrots showing green in the crown should be avoided, as they are not fully mature; and mature carrots should have no woody cores, nor should they be flabby or wilted. Avoid pitted and broken carrots.

Celeriac

This is the edible root of a variety of celery. Celeriac, which varies in size from an apple to a coconut, has a brown fibrous skin and creamy-white flesh with a celery flavor. Look for firm roots showing no signs of mushy flesh.

Celery

Celery grows wild in damp places in Europe, Asia, North and South Africa and South America. The Greeks cultivated it for the medicinal value of the seeds. Today, however, special forms are grown for their thick, crisp, juicy stalks, which may be eaten raw, mixed in salads, cooked as a vegetable or used to flavor soups and stews.

The most common variety is the *Pascal* celery. Choose thick crisp celery, plump at the base and with smooth branches that snap easily. The leaves indicate freshness: on prime celery the leaves are pale fresh green and straight.

Horseradish

Originally a native of south-east Europe, this hardy herb is now established along roadsides in many parts of the world.

Whether or not it occurs naturally in your area, it is a good idea to grow a few plants in a corner of the garden. As an accompaniment to roast beef and to some fish dishes, a sauce made from freshly grated horseradish root has no equal.

The fact that horseradish is easy to grow has its drawbacks, since if it begins to spread it is difficult to get rid of. The roots are deep and tough; if even a small piece is left in the ground a new plant will grow. Horseradish at its best has straight roots, 1–2 in thick at the top.

Kohlrabi

This has a swollen stem, with a mild turnip-like flavor.

The white or purple-skinned vegetables should be bought young, when they are the size of an orange. Avoid large kohlrabi, which may be tough, and any with decayed leaves.

Parsnips

The flavor of these winter vegetables is improved by a touch of frost, which makes them sweeter. They are at their best from October through January, before the central cores become woody. Buy parsnips with a crisp clean look; avoid any with a split or dried-up root, or with soft brown patches on the crown.

Potatoes

Despite the legends, it seems unlikely that Sir Walter Raleigh had much to do with the introduction of the potato to England, though he may well have planted some on his Irish estates in 1588, the year of the Armada. There is some evidence that it arrived some two years earlier in the holds of Sir Francis Drake's ships, fresh from their profitable raids on South America, where the vegetable originated.

Surprisingly, more than 150 years were to pass before the British regarded the potato as anything more than a novelty or cattle food. Only since the Irish and Scottish farmers of the 18th century, when its true value was realized, has it become a vitally important food crop in Britain and throughout the world.

There are generally three groups of potatoes. *New potatoes*, which are usually harvested during the late winter and early spring, are best for creaming or boiling. The name "new" is also applied to freshly dug but not fully matured potatoes.

General-purpose potatoes include the *Katahdin*, *Kennebec*, *Norgold Russet*, *Norland*, *Red Pontiac* and *White Rose*. These can be used for boiling, mashing, frying and baking.

The best known baking potato is the *Russet Burbank*, commonly called the Idaho. The area in which baking potatoes are grown, as well as the variety, are important factors that affect the baking quality. General-purpose and baking potatoes are available all year.

When buying any kind of potatoes, they should be firm, fairly smooth, well shaped and free from cuts, blemishes and decay. Avoid any that have green areas from light burn or that have sprouted or shriveled.

Radishes

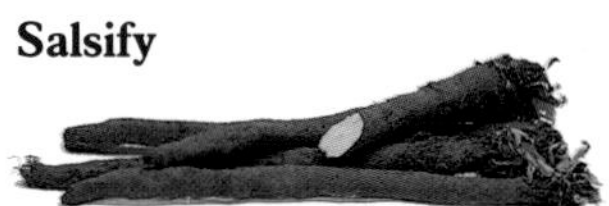

Small, pungent vegetables, used fresh in salads and for garnishing. Radishes may be round and bright red, tapering and pure white, bright red with white tips or black skinned with white flesh. Choose young, not too large radishes with a crisp look.

Salsify

This little-known root vegetable has soft white flesh. Look for young salsify roots with fresh gray-green leaves, which can be used in salads, and regular tapered roots.

Salsify is also known as the vegetable oyster, or the oyster plant, because of the flavor of its fleshy roots. This makes it a distinctive vegetable for use in June through February.

Scorzonera, black salsify

This long slender root vegetable, similar to salsify, has black skin and white flesh. Avoid small roots and any that have shriveled dry skins.

Rutabaga

These winter vegetables are similar to turnips, but the yellow flesh is milder in flavor. Avoid roots which are forked.

Sweet potatoes

These are not related to ordinary potatoes, the only resemblance being that they are both tubers. Sweet potatoes are globular or elongated and may be white, pink, red or purple. The white to yellow flesh is firm and sweet. They are sometimes incorrectly called yams – the true yam is the fruit of a tropical vine. Look for smooth-skinned firm potatoes; avoid any with shriveled, sunken or discolored areas.

Turnips

Although the turnip has been a favorite since Roman times, its popularity has little to do with its nutritional value. The root consists of about 90 per cent water, with some sugar and pectin – a jelly-like substance which helps jams to set. Nevertheless, it adds a fresh flavor to a dish of vegetables, particularly when accompanied by the season's first peas and carrots.

There are two types of turnip: early and mature. Early turnips have tender mustard-flavored flesh, which may be eaten both raw and cooked. Mature turnips have a somewhat coarser flesh, but are excellent boiled and in soups and stews. Avoid turnips with brown spots and holes, and any with spongy patches. Look for firm, small to medium, round turnips.

GREEN VEGETABLES

Beans

Most beans are eaten in the pod, but some are shelled.

Broad beans These comparative newcomers from Europe, also called *fava beans*, are similar to lima beans but their pods are longer, rounder and thicker. They are in season from mid-

April through June.

All pods should have a uniform bright green color, free from black markings. Avoid shriveled, dry-looking pods in favour of soft and tender pods. These beans are excellent for home-freezing; they must be shelled before cooking, although young broad beans are a delicacy cooked complete with pods.

Green beans Most green beans, or *snap beans*, are the green-podded varieties and are

on the market the year round. The large green *pole beans* and *yellow wax beans* are available only periodically.

Buy slender beans with a bright color. The best, freshest ones will snap easily when bent. Avoid flabby or wilted beans with serious blemishes.

Lima beans Sometimes available shelled, lima beans are usually sold in the shell. The shells should be dark green and well-filled with beans. Avoid any that are spotted, flabby or yellow. Lima beans are in season all year, and at their peak from June through September.

Beet Tops

These greens from the tops of beets are a very good source of vitamin A. They are cooked in the same way as spinach. Beet tops are available all year, and at their peak from June through October.

Broccoli

While cauliflower, a close relative, has one fused head of curds, broccoli develops thick, fleshy stalks that terminate in small florets. There are white or green sprouted, as well as purple broccoli. Choose broccoli with small, fresh-looking heads and brittle stalks which snap easily in the fingers. None of the buds should have opened enough to show the yellow flowers (a sign of age).

Broccoli is available all year, and is at its peak in March and April, October and November.

Brussels sprouts

Aristocrats of the cabbage family, these vegetables should be firm, compact and bright green. Avoid any that are puffy. Loose, yellow or wilting leaves are usually aged or stale. Ragged leaves or small holes in the sprouts may indicate worm damage. This is one of the vegetables often ruined by overcooking. Sprouts are in season all year, and at their best from September through February.

Cabbages

There are smooth-leaved green cabbages, crinkly-leaved green Savoys and red cabbages. All varieties are good for any use, although the red and Savoy cabbages are very popular raw.

Chinese cabbage Sometimes also known as **celery cabbage** or **pak choi**, this has some of the characteristics of both cabbage and romaine. It is usually eaten in salads but can be cooked like cabbage. The compact stalks range from 10–16 inches in length, but are normally 4 inches wide.

Red cabbages These cabbages are used for braising, marinating or for pickling as well as in salads and slaws. Fresh red cabbages have a good bloom. When red cabbage is cooked, an acid, such as vinegar, red wine, or apples, should always be added to retain the cabbage's color.

Savoy cabbages Look for firm green heads with crisp and curling outer leaves. Pale green savoys are almost certainly not fresh.

Spring cabbages Choose those with bright green and crisp leaves.

Summer and winter cabbages These follow spring cabbages, but have larger, more solid heads. Choose only firm, crisp-looking cabbages and check that the base of the stalk is clean. Avoid cabbages with slimy stalk ends and leaves pitted with holes.

White cabbages These cabbages have been in storage; they are trimmed of their outer leaves and are a lighter green. Excellent both for cooking and in salads. Choose firm, compact heads, and avoid any with loose curling leaves or those with brown smudges.

Collards Closely related to cabbage and to kale, this smooth broad-leaved vegetable is usually cooked with a piece of bacon or salt pork. Choose fresh, crisp leaves. In season all year.

Cauliflowers

Choose cauliflowers with the creamy-white heads not fully

developed and with clean white stalks. The leaves should be bright green. Small leaves extending up through the curds do not affect quality. Avoid any with limp leaves and loose, brown, gray or damaged curds. Spreading curds are a sign of age.

Endive, Belgian

A salad vegetable with a conical white or pale yellow head of crisp leaves packed firmly together. Choose heads that are firmly packed and avoid any which show yellow, curling leaves. The taste is slightly bitter. Although mainly used for salads it is also delicious cooked.

Chicory

The curly, narrow, ragged-edged leaves of chicory resemble dandelion leaves. The center of the head has yellowish leaves that have a milder flavor than the dark green outer leaves. *Escarole* has long wavy leaves that are broader and less crinkly than chicory leaves.

Look for crisp, fresh leaves with vivid green outer leaves. Avoid wilted leaves and any yellow or brown discolorations. Season: all year.

Kale

The broad leaves vary in color from dark green to purple. They are heavily crimped and have prominent pale green or white mid-ribs. Avoid kale with yellow, drooping or damaged leaves.

Lettuce

Although lettuces were popular with the Romans and Greeks – the philosopher Theophrastus identified three sorts in the 4th century BC – they are believed to have a much longer history, and may have been grown thousands of years earlier in the Far East.

Four types are generally available: *crisphead* (usually but incorrectly called iceberg), large, solid and round; *romaine* or *cos*, long and tapering with crisp dark green leaves; *butterhead* (which includes Boston and Bibb varieties), round with soft green leaves that have a buttery texture and delicate flavor; and *leaf*, a lettuce that does not form heads but has curled or smooth, broad, tender leaves arranged loosely around a stem. Choose lettuce with fresh and bright leaves and avoid any with brown or slimy patches on the hearts.

Okra

These vegetables are curved, generally ribbed seed pods. Select only the small, bright green, tender pods between 2 and 4 in long. The tips should bend with a slight pressure. Large pods will be tough. Avoid any shriveled pods.

Peas

Young peas have a delicious sweet flavor; overripe peas will be tough and starchy. Peas are in season all year, and at their best from February through July. Buy peas with bright crisp pods and avoid any which are so large that they show through the pods. Test for freshness by eating the peas raw, when they should be sweet and tender.

Snow peas or *sugar peas* are flat with edible pods. They are often used in Oriental dishes, and are expensive. They are available all year, and the peak time is May through September.

Spinach

There are two types of true spinach, the round-leaved summer variety and the wrinkly leaved winter spinach. Both have tender dark green leaves which must be handled carefully as they easily bruise. Spinach wilts quickly, and should be crisp to the touch. Look for dark green, unblemished leaves, avoiding any that are yellow, wilted, crushed or decayed.

Spinach is in season all year, but is at its peak from March through June.

Swiss chard, also called sea kale beet, has spinach-like dark green crisp and crinkled leaves with prominent white mid-ribs like celery stalks. The stalks as well as the leaves are used: the leaves should be cooked like spinach and the stalks like celery.

Swiss chard is in season from April through November, and is at its peak from June through October.

Watercress

This small-leaved peppery plant is mainly used in salads, soups and for garnishing. Avoid any in flower or with a high proportion of yellow or wilting leaves. Use within 24 hours of purchase.

OTHER VEGETABLES

Artichokes, globe

The artichoke is the leafy flower head of the plant. The gray-green, stiff leaves overlap each other, and the edible parts of the leaves are the fleshy bases of each leaf. Below the leaves is the fond (bottom), which has the finest flavor. Buy artichokes with stiff leaves which have a slight bloom.

Asparagus

Asparagus is a choice, but expensive, vegetable. It is sold loose or in bundles, and graded according to thickness of stem and plumpness of buds. Look for asparagus with tight, well-formed heads and avoid any with thin, woody, dry and dirty stems.

Eggplant

Oblong and near-round types of these distinctive, dark purple vegetables are available. Prime eggplants should be firm and heavy, with a satiny bloom to the shiny tough skin; the mealy flesh is yellow-green.

Avocados

These pear-shaped fruits are used as a vegetable rather than a dessert fruit. They have dark green skins. The oily, pale green, soft flesh surrounds a large seed. Avocados are not always ripe when bought: test for ripeness by pressing the flesh gently at the rounded end – it should yield slightly. Avoid avocados with blotched dry skins.

Corn

Corn kernels should be creamy and shiny within the bright green stiff husks; they should exude a milky liquid when punctured. Nutritional value and flavor are rapidly lost once the husks have been removed. The silk ends should be free from decay.

Cucumbers

Choose cucumbers that are firm over their entire length and have fresh green rinds. The surface may have many small bumps. Avoid cucumbers that are large or turning yellow. Most are grown in fields; others are produced in greenhouses.

Fennel, Florence fennel

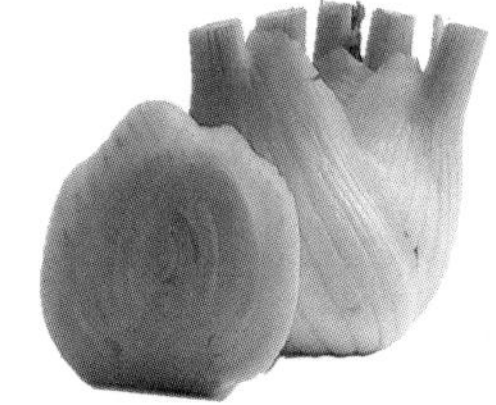

This vegetable, which looks like a root, is the swollen stem base. The leaves are bright green and feathery. It has a distinct licorice flavor. Choose well-rounded roots, of pale green to white color, avoiding any which are deep green.

Leeks

These thick-stem vegetables are composed of tightly packed skin layers which branch at the top into dark green leaves. The stems are white with a faint onion taste. Look for well-shaped, straight leeks, trimmed at the top and avoid those with yellow, discolored and slimy leaves.

Mushrooms

These are sold either as buttons, cups or flats according to age. White and brown types are available with no difference in taste. Large flat mushrooms have more flavor than the young buttons. Choose mushrooms carefully as they turn limp quickly and lose their flavor; use on the day of purchase. Avoid limp, broken mushrooms with a sweaty look.

Sprouted beans and peas

Delicious and nutritious, sprouts used to be seen only in meals in Chinese restaurants; now they are available in the produce section of the supermarket. Sprouts are crisp and crunchy, and full of flavor. Also, they are packed with vitamins—most sprouted peas and beans are five times more nutritious than in their dried form.

Sprouts can be used in all kinds of salads, in sandwiches, as a garnish for soup or any other dish and in stir-fry concoctions.

You can easily sprout seeds and beans at home, which is both fun and cost-saving. Try alfalfa seeds or mung beans, which are readily available at the supermarket or health food store, or choose dried chick peas, flaxseed, lentils or soybeans. Soak the seeds in warm water to cover for 8 hours or overnight, then drain. To sprout in a jar, cover the jar (a quart size jar) with cheesecloth or nylon net secured with a rubber band and lay it on its side in a warm, dark place. Two or three times a day, for 3–4 days, cover the seeds with fresh water, slosh it around and drain it off. Lay the jar on its side again after each rinsing. At the end of this period, give the sprouts a day of light on a windowsill. They will now be ready for use, and can be kept for 2–3 days in the refrigerator.

Another method of sprouting is to use a shallow glass or ceramic pan. Soak and drain the seeds as above. Line the bottom of the pan with cheesecloth or paper towels and scatter over the seeds in a single thick layer. Add enough water to wet the cloth or paper—but not to soak it—and cover the pan with plastic wrap. Store in a warm, dark place for 3–4 days, then move into the light for greening up. Keep moistenng during the sprouting period.

Onions

Onions vary in shape and color from flattish bulbs to round bulbs, with yellow, red or white skins. There are three general categories. *Maincrop* or *globe onions*, the most common type, are pungent and used primarily for cooking. *Bermuda-Granex-Granos* onions are milder, and thus are good for eating raw as well as cooking. The *Creole* types, such as Spanish onions, resemble globes but are much larger. They are also mild, and so are excellent for use in salads and sandwiches. Choose onions which are firm and

regular in shape, with feathery skins. Onions with shriveled skins and softness around the neck are almost certainly bad.

Small pickling onions, also called pearl onions, may be any of the above varieties.

Scallions or green onions Scallions are used to flavor other vegetables, but are essentially salad vegetables. The mild-flavored bulbs have a thin skin, which peels off easily. Choose scallions with small bulbs and fresh green foliage, and avoid any with wilting leaves. Scallions are available all year, but are best from May through July.

Parsley

This is the most versatile and useful of all garnishes, in sprigs or chopped. Wash freshly picked parsley as soon as possible, shake well and remove long stems. Place the parsley in a jar of water reaching to the base of the leaves, or put the parsley stems in a plastic bag, tied at the neck. Parsley will then stay crisp and green for several days. Change the water in the container daily.

Chopped parsley can be used as a garnish arranged in neat lines or at random; scissors can be used for chopping, but the result is coarser than when chopped with a knife. Gather the parsley into a tight bunch and with kitchen scissors snip off as much as is required straight on to the dish to be garnished.

To chop large quantities of parsley, place the stripped leaves on a chopping board. Using a sharp straight-bladed knife, hold the handle firmly with one hand and the tip of the knife blade with the other; lift the handle in a see-saw action, gradually chopping the parsley finely or coarsely as required. Alternatively, bunch the parsley leaves in one hand on the chopping board and, using the knife, gradually shred the parsley, moving the fingers back to reveal more parsley. Small wooden chopping bowls equipped with curved-bladed knives are available for chopping parsley, herbs, shallots and garlic. To preserve the vivid green, put chopped parsley in a piece of cheesecloth, tie loosely and hold the bag under cold water for a few minutes to rinse thoroughly. Squeeze dry, then shake the parsley out into a bowl. Chopped parsley will keep for a day or two in a lidded container in the refrigerator.

Peppers

These sweet peppers can have black, green, yellow or red skins. They are sold with the stalk ends attached, and before use these must be cut off and the inner white mid-ribs and seeds removed. Excellent for stuffing. Choose firm shiny peppers and avoid any which are misshapen and dull-looking, soft and flabby.

Shallots

These small onions are chiefly used to flavor sauces. The smooth and firm bulbs have a slight garlic flavor. Choose hard, rounded bulbs, avoiding any with shriveled skins or thick necks.

Squashes

Summer squash are harvested when they are young and tender. *Zucchini* are straight and cylindrical. Those no more than 6 in long are considered the best. *Yellow crooknecks* are moderately warted, have curved gooselike necks and are narrower at the top than at the base. *Straightnecks* are yellow squash, straighter than crooknecks. *Pattypans* are disk-shaped, with scalloped edges. They are pale green when young and white when mature.

Winter squash are harvested when fully mature, with hard shells. *Acorns* are small, widely ribbed and round in shape. Dark green, they turn mottled dull orange during storage. *Buttercups*, green pockmarked with gray, and faintly striped with dull gray, are turban-shaped at the blossom end. *Butternuts* are cylindrical with light brown or yellow skin. *Hubbards* are huge and globe-shaped with tapered necks. Their warted skin ranges from greenish-bronze to reddish-orange. *Pumpkins*, another member of the gourd family, vary from very small, about the size of a cantaloupe, to 100 pounds.

Tomatoes

Tomatoes are available throughout the year, but the best tomatoes are allowed to ripen completely on the vine before being picked. Tomatoes that are shipped for long distances must be harvested when they are green and therefore are not as juicy and flavorful as those that are home grown.

To ripen tomatoes properly, keep them in a paper bag in a dark place (not the refrigerator). Tomatoes stored in a sunny spot may wither and become pulpy.

The most familiar variety of tomato is the red one, which ranges in size from the big beefsteaks to the small, round cherry tomatoes, but there are also off-white, yellow, green and striped varieties, and they may be round, pear-shaped or flattened, with smooth or ridged skin.

Tomatoes should be firm and regular in shape and bright in color. The skin should have a matt texture; avoid any with blotched or cracked skins.

Pasta and rice

Dried foods such as pasta and rice are valuable kitchen standbys because they keep well and can be used for quick, filling, economical meals. Pasta, made mostly from wheat but sometimes from buckwheat, comes from Italy, with similar products being found in China and Japan. Rice is grown mainly in America, the Far East and the Mediterranean countries. Both can be rather bland in themselves but for this reason they combine well with many other types of food and with herbs, spices and other strong flavorings.

PASTA

In its simplest form pasta is a dough made from flour and water. The flour comes from durum wheat, or hard wheat, which is very high in gluten and grows particularly well in Italy. Ordinary or soft wheat can be used, but if you have ever tried making your own pasta you will see the difference at once between pasta made with strong (hard) flour and pasta made with ordinary flour. Eggs are often added to enrich it, and puréed spinach to color it green (*pasta verde*). A combination of yellow egg pasta and green spinach pasta is sold as *paglia e fieno* (straw and hay).

Dried pasta keeps indefinitely in a cool cupboard, but fresh pasta should be used within two or three days and preferably on the day it is made.

RICE

Most rice consists of polished white grains with the husks and brown cuticles removed. The two main types are long grain and short grain (or round grain) rice.

Long grain rice is used for curries and pilafs. The best is generally considered to be Basmati rice. Patna rice is cheaper and also good.

Short grain rice is much grown around the Mediterranean and is the kind used for risottos and paella, as well as for sweet puddings.

Brown or unpolished rice retains many valuable nutrients. It is now widely available, although less so in the rice-producing countries themselves. Both white and brown rice can be ground into flour: it has a pleasant nutty taste and is useful to those on gluten-free diets.

Wild rice is not related to rice at all: it is the seeds of a grass which grows wild in the northern United States.

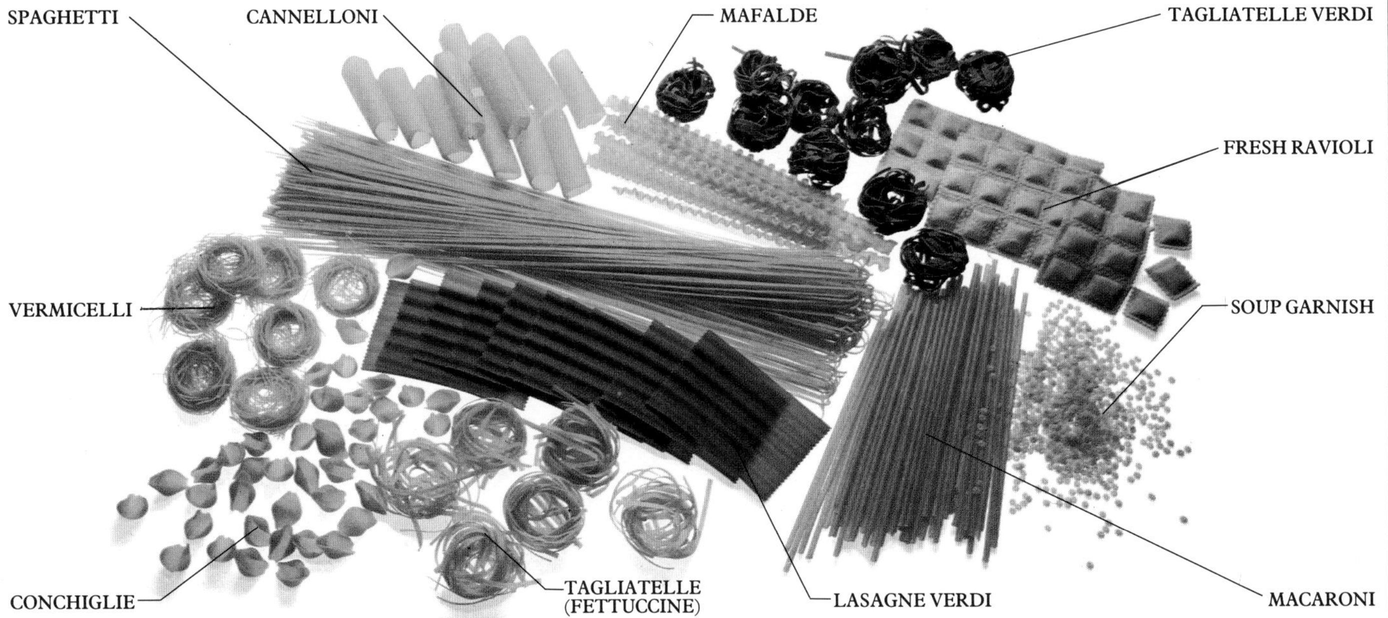

PASTA, IN ALL SHAPES AND SIZES Pasta can be divided into four main types: solid strings, which include vermicelli, noodles, spaghetti; hollow pasta tubes, such as macaroni and cannelloni; ribbon pasta, from tagliatelle to lasagne; and stuffed pasta, of which the best known is ravioli. Pasta is also made into a wide variety of small shapes, for garnishing soups.

Other dried foods, including cereals and the various dried beans, peas and lentils known collectively as legumes, are also valuable nutritionally as well as being useful standbys.

OTHER CEREALS

Barley Pearl barley, which is the polished grain, is used to thicken soups and in pilafs. Whole-grain barley is the unpolished grain, analogous to brown rice.

Rye Rye flour is used to make bread, usually mixed with wheat flour to help it rise, as gluten in rye is different from that in wheat.

Buckwheat This is gluten-free and is used for crêpes (in northern France) and noodles (in Japan and formerly in the countryside around Venice).

Millet Another gluten-free cereal which is an important crop in Asia and parts of Africa.

Oats The oat groat, or hulled berry, is commercially marketed in three basic forms. *Regular oatmeal* is rolled oats made by crushing the groat between steel rollers. It is available in various thicknesses. *Quick-cooking oatmeal* is partly cooked so it is quicker to prepare than regular oatmeal, but is inferior in both texture and flavor. *Scotch* or *Irish oatmeal* consists of coarsely cut groats that take longer to cook than regular oatmeal.

Semolina, sago and tapioca Semolina, coarsely milled hard wheat, is also made into gnocchi– savory dumplings, baked or poached and served as an appetizer. Sago is made from the pith in the trunk of the sago palm. Tapioca comes from the root of the West Indian cassava plant.

LEGUMES

Dried peas and beans of various types are known as legumes. The best known are black, navy and kidney beans.

Dried peas are a specially grown variety of garden pea, sometimes called blue peas. Lentils, one of the most nutritious legumes, are a type of pea widely grown in the south of Europe. Dried soybeans are sold in health food shops. They are also processed to make textured vegetable protein, which can be used on its own or mixed with fresh meat for hamburgers, ground meat dishes and stews.

A SELECTION OF CEREALS AND LEGUMES These foods tend to be bland on their own, but can easily be varied in flavor with the addition of spices and other ingredients. Wild rice, which is expensive, is the seed of an American grass and is served as an accompaniment to game. Chick peas are grown in the tropics and are used in soups and stews or cold in salads.

Herbs

Many herbs are best used fresh, but only a limited number are easily available unless they are grown at home. Bay leaves, chervil, fennel, parsley, rosemary, sage and thyme are sometimes sold fresh in markets, and are in season all the year round.

These herbs, as well as many less well-known ones, are also sold dried.

DRYING HERBS

Most herbs can be dried during the summer for use in winter. Pick the herbs just before flowering time when the flavor is best. Wash them thoroughly; then shake off the excess moisture. Tie the herbs into small bunches and hang them in a cool, airy place or spread them out on a clean cloth and put them to dry in a warm place such as an airing cupboard. Dry different types of herbs separately or the flavors will mingle. When they are dry and brittle, strip off the leaves and store them in airtight, labeled jars. Use within six months, before their flavor fades.

BASIL
Spicy herb that can be grown in pots or boxes. Does not lose pungency when it is dried.

FENNEL
The leaves and seeds of the herb are used to counteract the richness of oily fish and in sauces.

BAY
The leaves can be used fresh or dried to flavor savory dishes, particularly sauces and stews.

GARLIC
The very pungent cloves should be used sparingly. Garlic keeps for several months in a dry place.

PARSLEY
Mild-flavored parsley leaves are rich in iron and vitamins. Use them in sauces and as a garnish.

THYME
Widely used herb, fresh or dried. The strongly flavored leaves go well with most meat dishes.

SAGE
One of the best-known herbs, sage grows well in mild areas and can be used fresh or dried.

CAPERS
Flower buds, usually sold pickled, capers are most often used to make sauce for lamb or fish.

TARRAGON
Usually used dry, but the fresh leaves are particularly good for flavoring egg and tomato salads.

OREGANO
Wild marjoram, used in Greek and Italian dishes. Often sold as a dried powder.

MARJORAM
Spicy, bitter herb which can be used instead of basil, sprinkled on meat. More pungent dried.

CHIVES
Not widely available in the markets, chives are simple to grow and are best when they are freshly cut.

DILL
The leaves have a delicate, aniseed flavor, which enhances the flavor of broiled fish.

ROSEMARY
The shrub grows well in mild climates and the sweet, aromatic leaves are more pungent fresh.

BOUQUET GARNI
Ready-made bouquets garnis are available, in cheesecloth, and include bay leaf, thyme and parsley.

MINT
Widely grown, popular herb used in fruit tarts and cocktails as well as with meat and vegetables.

HERBS AND THEIR USES These fresh herbs are widely used in cooking. Many of them, not just the more usual ones, such as mint, parsley and thyme, can be grown in the garden or in pots on a sunny kitchen window-sill. This allows you to use them fresh, or to freeze or dry them at home. Remember that constant picking encourages the plants to grow.

DESSERTS CAKES AND BREADS

FRENCH APPLE TART

The open flans or tarts with a sweet filling of fruit or jam originate in the Alsace region of France. Remove the metal flan ring which holds the pastry in shape before serving the tart.

PREPARATION TIME: *1 hour*
COOKING TIME: *45 min*
INGREDIENTS *(for 4–6):*
2 pounds cooking apples
2 red-skinned eating apples
1½ cups flour
*Salt**
½ cup unsalted butter
¾ cup sugar
1 large egg yolk
Juice of a lemon
1 tablespoon apricot jam

Sift the flour and a pinch of salt into a mixing bowl. Cut 6 tablespoons of the butter into small pieces and rub it into the flour until the mixture resembles breadcrumbs. Mix in 2 tablespoons sugar. Make a well in the center of the flour, drop in the egg yolk and mix to a stiff dough with a little cold water.

Wrap the pastry in wax paper and leave to rest for 30 minutes. Meanwhile, peel and core the cooking apples and cut them up roughly. Melt the remaining butter in a saucepan and add the apple pieces and 7 tablespoons of sugar. Cover with a lid and cook gently for 10 minutes. Drain the apples, saving the juice. Rub the cooking apples through a coarse sieve, then allow this purée to cool. Wash the eating apples; core them before cutting them into ¼ in rings. Sprinkle with a little lemon juice to prevent them going brown.

Roll out the pastry, ¼ in thick, on a floured surface and use to line a 7 in flan ring set on a greased baking sheet. Trim the pastry edges and prick the bottom with a fork. Spoon the apple purée over the pastry and smooth the top. Arrange the apple rings in an overlapping pattern on top.

Put the apple juice, 2 tablespoons lemon juice, and jam and remaining sugar in a saucepan. Cook over low heat until the sugar has dissolved, then bring to the boil and boil briskly for 4 minutes. Brush a little of this glaze over the apple slices.

Bake the flan for 45 minutes in the center of an oven pre-heated to 400°F (200°C, mark 6). If the apple slices brown too quickly, cover the flan with foil. Remove the flan from the oven, brush with the remaining glaze and serve it hot or cold, with cream.

DEEP-DISH APPLE PIE

An alternative filling for this traditional pie could be 1 pound apples and ½ pound blackberries. Other fruits, such as halved and pitted apricots, plums, peaches, pears, black currants or blueberries, also make good pies.

PREPARATION TIME: *20 min*
COOKING TIME: *35 min*
INGREDIENTS *(for 4–6):*
1 quantity standard pastry (page 171)
1½ pounds cooking apples
¼–⅓ cup granulated or ⅓–½ cup brown sugar
Milk

Peel and core the apples and cut them into chunky slices. Place a pie funnel in the center of a 2 pint pie dish, arrange half the apple slices in the dish, sprinkle over the sugar and add the remaining fruit with 3 tablespoons of water.

Cover the pie with the rolled-out pastry, decorate it and brush the top with milk. Dust with granulated sugar. Make a slit in the center of the pastry lid for the steam to escape. Set the pie on a baking sheet and bake in the center of the oven pre-heated to 400°F (200°C, mark 6) for 35–40 minutes. If the pastry browns too quickly, cover it with a double layer of moistened wax paper.

For variation, the water may be replaced with orange juice and the grated rind of half an orange mixed with the sugar.

Gluten-free pastry

This is slightly adapted from an original recipe which also includes raw cane sugar.

INGREDIENTS
¼ cup polyunsaturated soft margarine
⅔ cup ground brown rice
1 small eating apple
¼ cup ground almonds

Blend the margarine and ground rice, using a fork. Grate the apple and work it in together with the ground almonds. This makes an excellent crust for sweet pies and pastries. It needs to be pressed into a pan as it is very difficult to roll, so it is suitable for flans and tarts, not double-crust or covered pies. It is simple to make and does not go hard or tough. The pectin in the apple binds it and moistens it, and the texture is slightly crunchy, like shortbread.

FRENCH APPLE TART

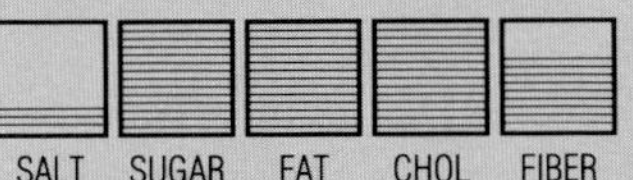

GLUTEN-FREE* WHOLEFOOD*
TOTAL CALORIES: ABOUT 2565

To reduce the **sugar** content to low, use eating apples throughout. Cook and purée them, then sweeten to taste with about 2 tablespoons honey or fruit sugar (fructose), both of which tend to give more sweetness for the same weight than ordinary sugar. (Calories lost: up to 293.)
The pastry is high in both **fat** and **cholesterol**. The cholesterol can be avoided completely by using vegetable fat, preferably soft margarine, in place of butter. To reduce the fat by more than a quarter is difficult without losing the properties of pie pastry, but you could use the recipe for low-fat pastry on page 95. (Calories lost: up to 1082.)
The **fiber** level is moderate, as given, if 6 are served, but high if 4 are served.
Gluten-free flour can be used, or you can use the gluten-free recipe suggested on this page.

Freezing: ✓ up to 3 months.

DEEP-DISH APPLE PIE

GLUTEN-FREE* WHOLEFOOD*
TOTAL CALORIES: ABOUT 2175

Reduce the **sugar** content to moderate by using eating apples rather than cookers. The variation using orange juice will help to reduce the need for sugar, and a tablespoon of

honey could replace up to 2 tablespoons sugar. (Calories lost: up to 253.)
See notes on the previous recipe for **fat** and **cholesterol** levels and for **gluten-free** pastry. (Calories lost: up to 1229.)
Whole wheat flour makes delicious pastry for a **wholefood** diet. The dough may need slightly more water than when refined flour is used.

Freezing: ✓ up to 3 months if unbaked, 6 months if baked.

APPLE AND ALMOND PARADISE PUDDING

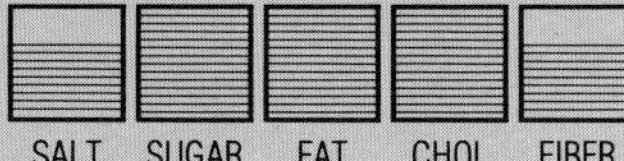

SALT SUGAR FAT CHOL FIBER

GLUTEN-FREE WHOLEFOOD*
TOTAL CALORIES: ABOUT 2080

For low **sugar**, use 1 tablespoon honey to sweeten the rice. Choose eating apples rather than cookers and poach them in half the amount of water, not in syrup; sweeten with 1 tablespoon of honey. Use apricot jam made without added sugar for the base of the pudding. One tablespoon of sugar will be enough for the topping. (Calories lost: up to 486.)
Reduce **fat** and **cholesterol** to low by substituting skim milk or soy milk; use quark or low-fat sour cream instead of heavy cream. (Calories lost: up to 391.)
Using brown rice will make this **wholefood:** cook it in twice its volume of water for 30 minutes; or use millet, cooked as white rice.

APPLE AND ALMOND PARADISE PUDDING

The combination of creamed rice, fruit and crisp topping makes this pudding a great favorite with children. Pears or other autumn fruit can be used instead of apples.

PREPARATION TIME: *30 min*
COOKING TIME: *35 min*
INGREDIENTS *(for 4):*
⅓ cup long grain rice
2 cups milk
¼ teaspoon vanilla
½–⅔ cup sugar
1½ pounds cooking apples
6 tablespoons heavy cream
3–4 rounded tablespoons apricot jam
TOPPING:
1 large egg white
2 tablespoons ground almonds
2 tablespoons sugar
2 tablespoons flaked almonds

Put the rice and milk in a heavy-based saucepan and bring slowly to simmering point. Cover with a lid, and cook over low heat for about 25 minutes or until the rice is cooked, but still slightly nutty in texture. Stir frequently during cooking to prevent sticking. Sweeten the rice to taste with vanilla and a little sugar. Leave to cool.

Peel, core and slice the apples. Put ½ cup of sugar with 1¼ cups of water in a saucepan over low heat and stir until all the sugar has dissolved. Bring this syrup to simmering point, then add the apple slices. Cook gently for 5 minutes or until just tender and retaining their shape. Lift the slices carefully into a colander to drain and cool.

Whip the cream lightly and fold it into the cooled rice. Spread the apricot jam over the bottom of a shallow, 7 in wide ovenproof dish or pie plate. Cover the jam with apple slices and spoon over creamed rice.

Beat the egg white for the topping until stiff. Mix together the ground almonds and sugar and fold in the egg white. Spoon this mixture over the rice and scatter the flaked almonds on top. Put the dish under a hot broiler for a few minutes until the almonds are crisp and golden. Serve at once.

APPLE-RUM MERINGUE

Meringue is a favorite topping for many desserts. In this recipe, it covers tart cooking apples over rum-soaked amaretti. Macaroons or ladyfingers may be used instead of amaretti.

PREPARATION TIME: *30 min*
COOKING TIME: *15 min*
INGREDIENTS *(for 6):*
¼ pound amaretti
4 tablespoons white rum
1½ pounds cooking apples
2 tablespoons unsalted butter
½ teaspoon cinnamon
⅔ cup dark brown sugar
3 egg whites
*¼ teaspoon salt**
¾ cup granulated sugar

Cover the bottom of a china flan dish with the amaretti, and pour the rum over them. Peel, core and thinly slice the apples into a saucepan; add the butter, cinnamon, brown sugar and 2–3 tablespoons water. Simmer for 10–15 minutes or until the apples are just cooked. Leave to cool, then spoon the apples over the amaretti.

Beat the egg whites with the salt until stiff, but not dry. Stir in half of the granulated sugar and beat for about 2 minutes or until the meringue mixture is smooth and glossy. Fold in the remaining sugar, and immediately spoon the meringue over the apples in the flan dish. Swirl the meringue into soft peaks with a spatula.

Bake the flan for 10–15 minutes, in the center of an oven pre-heated to 350°F (180°C, mark 4) until the meringue is pale beige. Serve hot or cold with a bowl of cream.

Macaroons

PREPARATION TIME: *10 min*
COOKING TIME: *15 min*
INGREDIENTS *(for 24 cookies):*
Rice paper
1 cup ground almonds
¾ cup sugar
2 egg whites
1 tablespoon cornstarch
¼ teaspoon vanilla
12 blanched almonds

Line two or three baking sheets with rice paper. Mix the ground almonds with the sugar and add the unbeaten egg whites, setting 1 tablespoon aside. Using a wooden spoon, work the mixture until the ingredients are evenly blended. Stir in the cornstarch, vanilla and 2 teaspoons of water. Spoon the mixture into a pastry bag fitted with a ½ in plain nozzle. Pipe the cookies on to the rice paper in large round buttons; top each with half an almond. Brush lightly with the remaining egg white.

Bake the macaroons just above or in the center of a pre-heated oven, at 375°F (190°C, mark 5), for about 15 minutes or until lightly browned, risen and slightly cracked. Cut the rice paper to fit around each macaroon and leave to cool on a wire rack. This recipe makes double the quantity required for the apple-rum meringue, but the macaroons will keep for a day or two in a tightly closed tin, although they are best if eaten on the day of baking.

APPLE TURNOVERS

These apple turnovers, sold ready-made in most French 'boulangeries', or pastry shops, provide an easily made dessert.

PREPARATION TIME: *25 min*
COOKING TIME: *30 min*
INGREDIENTS *(for 4–6):*
2 large cooking apples
1 tablespoon unsalted butter
¼ teaspoon grated lemon rind
¼ cup sugar
1 tablespoon golden raisins
¾ pound prepared puff pastry
1 egg
Confectioners' sugar

Peel, core and thinly slice the apples. Melt the butter in a saucepan, add the apples and lemon rind. Cover with a lid and cook over low heat until the apples are soft. Beat the apples to a purée, add sugar and raisins. Set aside until cold.

Roll out the puff pastry ¼ in thick. Using a 3 in round, fluted pastry cutter, stamp out circles from the pastry; gently roll each circle with a rolling pin to form an oval about ⅙ in thick. Spoon the apple mixture equally over half of each pastry shape. Brush the edges with beaten egg and fold the pastry over. Press the edges firmly to seal. Slash the top of each pastry with a knife, brush with beaten egg and leave for 15 minutes.

Bake the pastries on wet baking sheets, above the center of an oven pre-heated to 425°F (220°C, mark 7), for 10 minutes. Lower to 375°F (190°C, mark 5) and continue baking until golden brown. Dust with sifted confectioners' sugar and serve warm or cold with cream.

APPLE-RUM MERINGUE

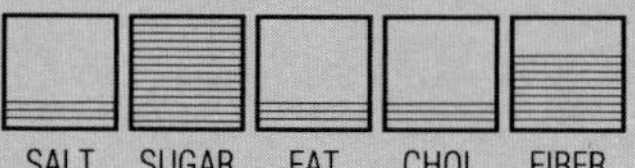

GLUTEN-FREE WHOLEFOOD*
TOTAL CALORIES: ABOUT 1850

For a medium **sugar** level choose eating apples and use honey to sweeten as in the notes on the previous recipes. Make the meringue using only ¼–⅓ cup sugar. (Calories lost: up to 664.)

MACAROONS

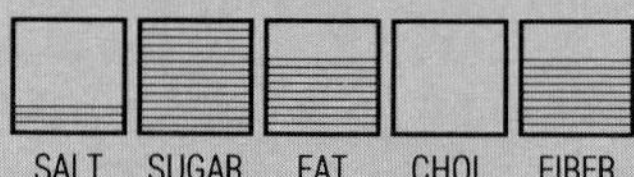

GLUTEN-FREE WHOLEFOOD*
TOTAL CALORIES: ABOUT 1140

Reduce the **sugar** to moderate by using only ½ cup. The results, though unconventional, will still be very good. (Calories lost: up to 296.)

Freezing: √ up to 3 months.

APPLE TURNOVERS

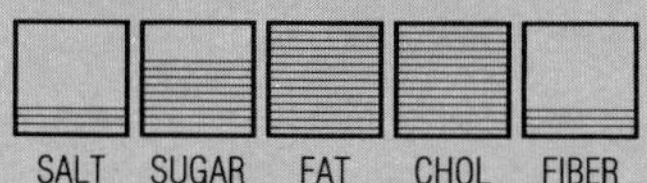

TOTAL CALORIES: ABOUT 4330

The **sugar** can be reduced to very low by substituting a tablespoon of honey for the sugar and using eating apples; instead of dusting the finished pastries with confectioners' sugar, brush with a little apple juice concentrate or apricot jam made without added sugar. For extra sweetness use up to one extra tablespoon raisins. (Calories lost: up to 225.)

The problem with both **fat** and **cholesterol** is mainly in the puff pastry – the butter content in the apple mixture could be omitted but is hardly enough to worry about, and the whole egg can be replaced with just white of egg. But puff pastry needs a large quantity of fat, for which there is no substitute. An alternative is the strudel dough in the next recipe. (Calories lost: up to 2530.)

Freezing: ✓ up to 3 months if unbaked, 6 months if baked.

APPLE AND NUT STRUDEL

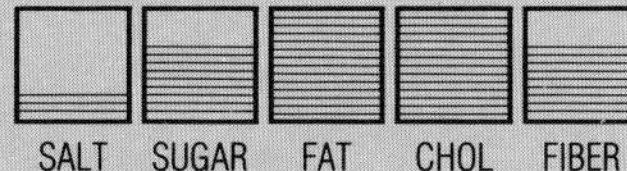

WHOLEFOOD*
TOTAL CALORIES: ABOUT 2520

The **sugar** content can be reduced to fairly low by using a tablespoon of honey instead of the sugar and eating apples instead of cookers. (Calories lost: up to 166.)
Fat levels can be reduced to low by using only 1 tablespoon of oil for making the dough and a further tablespoon butter for brushing it. Toast the breadcrumbs in the oven and mix with ¼ cup ricotta or cottage cheese. (Calories lost: up to 549.)
Cholesterol can be reduced by reducing fat as above, or eliminated by using oil and vegetable margarine.
Strudel dough can never be **gluten-free** as gluten is needed to give it its characteristic stretch; but a **wholefood** version using strong whole wheat flour is excellent.

Freezing: ✓ up to 3 months if unbaked, 6 months if baked.

APPLE AND NUT STRUDEL

Austria, and particularly Vienna, is renowned for its rich pastries and cakes. Among them all, the strudel recipe is probably the most popular. This famous pastry should be almost transparent, or as the Austrians say, 'thin enough to read your love letters through.'

PREPARATION TIME: *1 hour*
COOKING TIME: *40 min*
INGREDIENTS *(for 6):*
1 cup flour
3½ tablespoons vegetable oil
Flour for rolling out
Oil for brushing
¼ cup unsalted butter
FILLING:
¼ cup unsalted butter
1½ cups soft breadcrumbs
½ cup hazelnuts or walnuts
1 pound cooking apples
1 teaspoon ground cinnamon
¼ cup sugar
⅓ cup golden raisins
Grated rind of half lemon

Sift the flour into a warmed bowl; make a well in the center and stir in the vegetable oil mixed with 3 tablespoons warm water. Work the mixture into a soft dough, adding more warm water as required. Knead the dough thoroughly on a lightly floured surface, then roll it into a long sausage shape. Pick up the strudel dough by one end and hit it against the pastry board. Repeat this lifting and hitting process, picking it up by alternate ends, for about 10 minutes or until bubbles appear under the surface of the dough.

Knead the elastic strudel dough into a ball and leave it to rest on a plate for 30 minutes under an inverted, warm bowl.

Meanwhile, heat the butter for the filling, and gently fry the breadcrumbs until golden. Chop the nuts roughly. Peel, core and roughly chop the apples.

Spread a large, clean dish towel over the table top and sprinkle it evenly with flour. Roll out the strudel dough on the cloth, as thinly as possible, and brush it with a little warm oil to keep it pliable. Place the hands under dough and stretch it over the backs of the hands by pulling them away from each other until the dough is paper-thin. Work on one area at a time, until all the dough is nearly transparent.

When the dough is thin enough, trim off the uneven edges with a sharp knife or scissors. Melt the remaining butter; brush it over all the dough; spread the fried breadcrumbs on top. Cover these with the chopped apples to within 2 in of the edges. Mix the cinnamon and sugar, and sprinkle over the apples, together with the chopped nuts, raisins and grated lemon rind. Fold the lower edge of the dough over the filling, then lift the edge of the cloth and roll the strudel up like a jelly roll. Seal the join with water, and tuck under the ends.

Lift the strudel and roll it off the cloth on to a greased baking sheet, with the join underneath. Curve the strudel into a horseshoe shape and brush the top with the remaining melted butter. Bake in the center of a pre-heated oven, at 425°F (220°C, mark 7), for 10 minutes, then lower the heat to 400°F (200°C, mark 6) for about 30 minutes or until golden brown.

Serve hot or cold, dredged with confectioners' sugar.

APPLE CRUMBLE

A simple but well-loved and always popular dessert. The crisp and crunchy topping contrasts with the soft apple filling.

PREPARATION TIME: *25 min*
COOKING TIME: *45 min*
INGREDIENTS *(for 4–6):*
$1\frac{1}{2}$ pounds cooking apples
2 tablespoons sugar
Grated rind of half lemon
TOPPING:
$1\frac{1}{2}$ cups flour
6 tablespoons margarine
$\frac{1}{4}$ cup granulated sugar
$1\frac{1}{2}$ tablespoons light brown sugar

Peel, core and slice the apples thinly. Put them, sprinkled with sugar, into a $1\frac{1}{2}$ quart baking dish; top with lemon rind.

For the topping, sift the flour into a mixing bowl, cut up the margarine and rub it lightly into the flour with the tips of the fingers. Mix in the granulated sugar. Spoon the crumble mixture over the apples and press it down lightly. Sprinkle the brown sugar on top. Place the dish on a baking sheet and bake in the center of the oven at 400°F (200°C, mark 6) for 45 minutes.

Wholefood topping
Use whole wheat flour, and $\frac{1}{4}$ cup light brown sugar. This makes a wonderfully satisfying, nutty-flavored topping which will be preferred by many people who are not necessarily wholefood addicts themselves. Another excellent addition is 2 tablespoons of sesame seeds. This is the topping shown in the picture.

Ground almonds can be used instead of some or all of the sugar, with a little butter.

APPLE CRUMBLE

SALT SUGAR FAT CHOL FIBER

GLUTEN-FREE* WHOLEFOOD*
TOTAL CALORIES: ABOUT 1755

For low **sugar** level use eating apples, half the sugar used to sweeten, and ground almonds in place of sugar in the topping. (Calories lost: up to 129.)
The **wholefood** topping is also very low in **fat**. (Calories lost: up to 203.)
Millet flakes make a good **gluten-free** alternative to flour in the topping.

Freezing: ☑ up to 3 months.

Microwave: ☑ except for browning the top.

CHEESY APPLE PIE

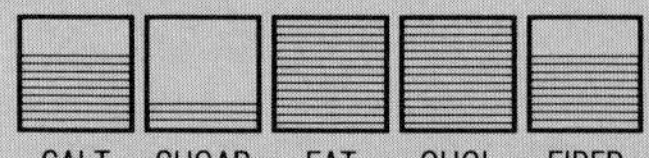

SALT SUGAR FAT CHOL FIBER

GLUTEN-FREE* WHOLEFOOD*
TOTAL CALORIES: ABOUT 2435

The **salt** content comes from the cheese, which is essential.
The **sugar** can be reduced still further by using eating apples and no added sugar, or perhaps a little honey or apple juice concentrate. (Calories lost: up to 77.)
To reduce the **fat** to low, use a biscuit dough (page 142) or the very low-fat pastry on page 95. Use reduced-fat Cheddar, or substitute Edam. This will also reduce **cholesterol** to low, especially if you glaze with skim milk. (Calories lost: up to 890.)
See page 10 for a **gluten-free** pastry.

Freezing: ☑ up to 3 months if unbaked, 6 months if baked.

APRICOT SHERBET

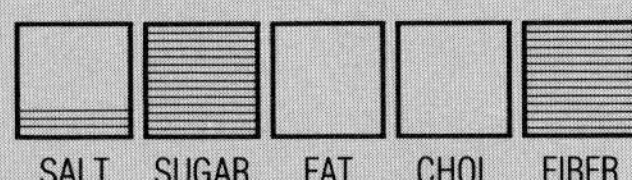

GLUTEN-FREE WHOLEFOOD*
TOTAL CALORIES: ABOUT 2650

The very high **sugar** content of this recipe can easily be reduced to low: as dried apricots have quite a lot of sweetness, there is no need to poach them in a sugar syrup. Instead, use 1½ cups water and 2 tablespoons of apple juice concentrate. (Calories lost: up to 1761.)
Wholefood: if you are using sugar, it is important to crush it as finely as possible.

Food processor: √ to purée the apricots.
Freezing: √ up to 6 months.

BRANDY APRICOT TRIFLE

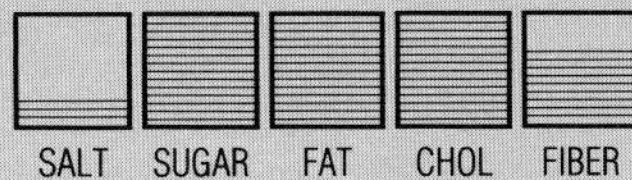

GLUTEN-FREE WHOLEFOOD
TOTAL CALORIES: ABOUT 2435

To reduce the **sugar** to moderate, use a tablespoon of apple juice concentrate to sweeten the liquid in which the apricots cook, and use the honey ratafias on page 127. (Calories lost: up to 191.)
For low levels of both **fat** and **cholesterol**, use the low-fat custard recipe suggested on pages 104–5. Omit the whipped cream or substitute a low-fat small curd cottage cheese, beaten with 2–4 tablespoons apricot jam, preferably made without added sugar.(Calories lost: up to 494.)

CHEESY APPLE PIE

A popular combination is apple pie and slices of cheese. This pie is a variation on that theme; the cheesy taste is more prominent if the apples are slightly sour.

PREPARATION TIME: *30 min*
COOKING TIME: *35–40 min*
INGREDIENTS *(for 4–6):*
2 cups flour
*½ teaspoon salt**
½ cup unsalted butter
1 cup grated Cheddar cheese
2 pounds cooking apples
1 tablespoon sugar
1 egg
1–2 tablespoons milk

Sift the flour and salt into a mixing bowl. Cut the butter into small pieces and rub them into the flour until the pastry mixture is crumbly. Blend in the cheese and knead the pastry to a stiff dough with a little cold water. Divide the pastry in half, roll out one half on a floured surface and use to line a pie plate. Peel, core and slice the apples. Pile them over the pastry and sprinkle with the sugar.

Roll out the remaining pastry; moisten the edge of the lining and cover the pie with pastry. Press the edges well down to seal, and use the trimmings to decorate the 7 in pie. Make an air vent in the center. Beat the egg lightly with 1–2 tablespoons of milk and brush over the pie to give it a glaze. Bake for 35–40 minutes in the center of the oven pre-heated to 425°F (220°C, mark 7).

Serve the pie cold.

APRICOT SHERBET

A tart, beautifully flavored sherbet is a perfect dessert after a heavy meal.

PREPARATION TIME: *2½ hours*
FREEZING TIME: *2 hours*
INGREDIENTS *(for 6):*
1 pound dried apricots
2 cups sugar
2 tablespoons cognac, apricot liqueur, or kirsch

Cover the apricots in warm water and soak for 2 hours. Drain. Cook the sugar in 1 cup water until the mixture boils; boil for 10 minutes. Add the apricots and cook an additional 10 minutes. Put the apricots and the liquid through a food mill or purée them in a blender. Add the cognac, apricot liqueur, or the kirsch.

Pour the mixture into freezer trays and place in the freezer compartment of the refrigerator. When the mixture has become partially frozen, remove it from the refrigerator and turn into a chilled bowl. Beat thoroughly with a whisk or heavy fork. The mixture should be almost thin enough to pour; it if is too thick, whisk in a little ice water. Return the mixture to the trays. Put in the freezer until firm but not hard, or freeze packed with ice and coarse salt in a crank freezer until the mixture is frozen but still soft.

BRANDY APRICOT TRIFLE

Fresh apricots form the basis of this rich dessert, suitable for a dinner party.

PREPARATION TIME: *20 min*
COOKING TIME: *30 min*
CHILLING TIME: *2 hours*
INGREDIENTS *(for 4–6):*
1 pound fresh apricots
2½ cups custard sauce (page 169)
½ cup white wine
¼ cup sugar
6 tablespoons brandy
½ pound ladyfingers
½ cup heavy cream

Prepare the custard and set aside to cool. Wash and dry the apricots, cut them in halves and remove the pits. Put the wine and sugar in a pan and bring slowly to the boil. When the sugar has dissolved, add the apricot halves and cook them in this syrup, over low heat, until softened; set aside to cool.

Put the apricots in a glass bowl or serving dish and pour over the syrup and brandy. Set aside 2–3 ladyfingers for decoration and crush the remainder with a rolling pin. Sprinkle them over the apricots and brandy, stirring carefully to let the cookies absorb the liquid. Spoon the custard, which should now be almost at setting point, over the apricots and chill the trifle in the refrigerator for about 2 hours.

Just before serving, whip the cream until stiff and pipe it in swirls over the trifle. Decorate the top with the remaining cookies.

CROÛTES AUX ABRICOTS

A croûte is a classic French garnish of bread. For a dessert, the croûtes should be sweet bread, and brioches (page 140) are the most suitable. Slices of currant bread or milk loaf can also be used.

PREPARATION TIME: *10 min*
COOKING TIME: *20 min*
INGREDIENTS *(for 6):*
12 ripe apricots
¾ cup sugar
3 brioches
¾–1 cup clarified butter
½ cup heavy cream
1 liqueur glass kirsch (optional)
GARNISH:
Angelica

Cut the apricots in half and remove the pits. Bring the sugar and 2 tablespoons of cold water to the boil in a saucepan, then add the apricots and poach them gently for 6–8 minutes; they should be tender and retain their shape. Carefully lift out the apricots and keep them warm. Turn up the heat and boil the syrup rapidly until it has reduced to a thick syrup. Do not allow it to caramelize. Let the syrup cool.

Trim the crusts from the brioches or bread and cut into six slices, ½ in thick; fry them in clarified butter (page 182) on both sides until golden brown. Keep warm. Whip the cream lightly and flavor it to taste with the apricot syrup and kirsch.

To serve, arrange the fried bread on a dish and put four apricot halves on each slice. Top with a swirl of cream and garnish with finely chopped angelica.

POACHED APRICOTS

Apricots, like other fruit with a strongly characteristic taste, do not need elaborate cooking to show them at their best. This very simple recipe is an excellent way of presenting early apricots which are perhaps not quite ripe and sweet enough to eat raw. The cinnamon goes particularly well with apricots.

PREPARATION TIME: *10 min*
COOKING TIME: *15 min*
INGREDIENTS *(for 4):*
1 pound fresh apricots
6–8 tablespoons sugar
Lemon rind or cinnamon stick

Wash and dry the apricots. Put the sugar with 1¼ cups of water and thinly pared lemon rind or cinnamon in a saucepan and place over low heat until the sugar has dissolved. Bring to the boil and cook for 2 minutes. Strain this syrup through a sieve.

Cut the apricots in half with a small sharp knife. Twist the two halves to separate. Discard the pits. Return the syrup to the pan, place the apricot halves, rounded side down, in the syrup and bring slowly to the boil. Reduce the heat, cover and simmer gently until the fruit is tender, about 15 minutes. Leave to cool.

Cook plums in a similar way; they cook more quickly and should be poached for 10 minutes only.

CROÛTES AUX ABRICOTS

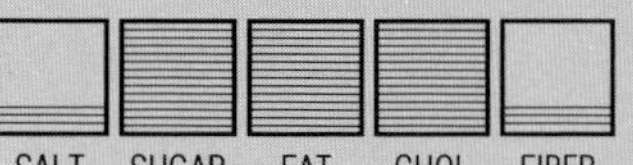

SALT SUGAR FAT CHOL FIBER

TOTAL CALORIES: ABOUT 3710

Reduce **sugar** to moderate by using only 2–4 tablespoons with 1–2 tablespoons of honey for the syrup; omit the angelica. (Calories lost: up to 423.)
Both **fat** and **cholesterol** can be reduced to low if the bread is baked or toasted rather than fried, and low-fat thick yogurt or sour cream is used instead of the whipped cream. Or, use apple purée sweetened with the apricot syrup for a sauce. (Calories lost: up to 2480.)
Gluten-free brioche dough is not successful; use an ordinary gluten-free bread.
Wholefood: as well as using whole wheat bread, omit the angelica.

POACHED APRICOTS

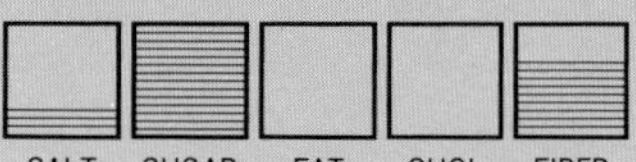

SALT SUGAR FAT CHOL FIBER

GLUTEN-FREE WHOLEFOOD*
TOTAL CALORIES: ABOUT 500

To reduce the **sugar** to moderate, use only 2 tablespoons and substitute apple or grape juice for the water. Dried apricots will be sweeter than fresh ones and can be successfully used instead. Soak them for an hour or two beforehand. Using dried apricots will increase the salt content slightly. (Calories lost: up to 187.)

Microwave: ☑ for poaching the apricots.

AVOCADO FOOL

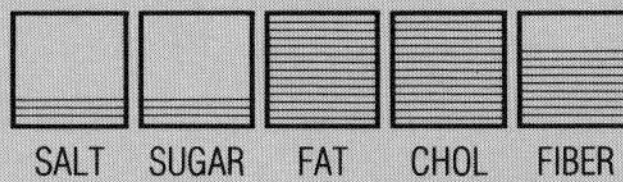

SALT SUGAR FAT CHOL FIBER

GLUTEN-FREE WHOLEFOOD*
TOTAL CALORIES: ABOUT 1345

Although avocados are very high in **fat**, both this and the **cholesterol** can be reduced to low if the cream is replaced with low-fat small curd cheese such as quark or fromage blanc, or with low-fat thick yogurt. (Calories lost: up to 395.) The oatcakes on page 127 make a very good alternative to ladyfingers and are both low-fat and low-sugar.

Food processor: ✓ for blending to a smooth purée.

BANANA AND RHUBARB COMPÔTE

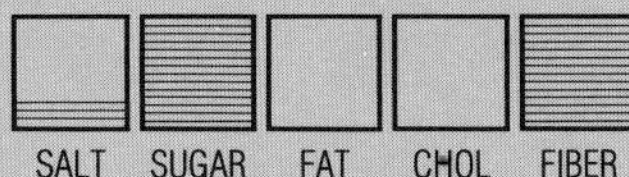

SALT SUGAR FAT CHOL FIBER

GLUTEN-FREE WHOLEFOOD*
TOTAL CALORIES: ABOUT 950

This only needs a reduction in the **sugar** level to be a very healthy dessert. The amount of sugar given here makes it very sweet indeed, as bananas are naturally sweet. Try using only ¼ cup sugar or 2 tablespoons of honey, with a teaspoon or two of apple juice concentrate if you like the taste. You could replace up to half the rhubarb with chopped dried dates for extra sweetness: they go well with the rhubarb and bananas. (Calories lost: up to 369.)

AVOCADO FOOL

The origin of the word 'fool' to describe a purée of pressed fruit mixed with cream or custard goes back to the 16th century. It was a synonym for a trifling thing – of small consequence. This avocado fool is an unusual, refreshing sweet, best flavored with lime.

PREPARATION TIME: *20 min*
CHILLING TIME: *2 hours*
INGREDIENTS *(for 6):*
3 large avocados
2 limes or 1 large lemon
1 rounded tablespoon confectioners' sugar
½ cup heavy cream

Peel the avocados and remove the seeds. Dice the avocado flesh finely. Cut a thin slice from the middle of one lime or the lemon and divide the slice into six small wedges; set aside. Squeeze the juice from the fruit and put it into a liquidizer, together with the confectioners' sugar.

After 30 seconds add the diced avocado and liquidize until the mixture has become a smooth purée. Whip the cream and fold it into the purée, adding more sugar and fruit juice to taste.

Spoon the avocado fool into six individual glasses and chill in the refrigerator for at least 2 hours. Garnish with the reserved lime or lemon wedges, and serve with ladyfingers.

BANANA AND RHUBARB COMPÔTE

Pink tender rhubarb is readily available early in the year. It should be cooked slowly to keep its shape for a compôte.

PREPARATION TIME: *15 min*
COOKING TIME: *35 min*
CHILLING TIME: 2 hours
INGREDIENTS *(for 4):*
1 pound rhubarb
¾ cup sugar
Juice of an orange
1 pound bananas

Trim tops and bottoms off the rhubarb, wash the stalks and cut them into 1 in lengths. Place in a casserole or ovenproof dish and add the sugar and strained orange juice. Stir to blend the ingredients thoroughly, and cover with a lid. Bake for 35 minutes in the center of the oven pre-heated to 325°F (170°C, mark 3). Remove from the oven and leave the casserole to stand, covered, for 5–10 minutes.

Peel and thinly slice the bananas into a serving dish. Pour over the hot rhubarb and the juices. Cool and then chill in the refrigerator. A bowl of cream or vanilla ice cream could be served with the compôte.

BERRY LEMON PUDDING

The large cultivated blackberries now available go well with the lemon flavor of this pudding, which can be eaten hot or cold.

PREPARATION TIME: *25 min*
COOKING TIME: *45 min*
INGREDIENTS *(for 4):*
½ pound blackberries
2 tablespoons unsalted butter
½ cup sugar
1 lemon
2 eggs
¾ cup milk
¼ cup flour
¾ cup heavy cream

Cream together the butter and 2 tablespoons of the sugar in a mixing bowl. Wash the lemon and finely grate the rind into this mixture; squeeze the juice from the lemon and strain it in as well. Beat thoroughly.

Separate the eggs and beat the milk into the yolks. Add this little by little to the creamed mixture, alternately with the sifted flour and remaining sugar, beating until the mixture is thoroughly blended. Whisk the egg whites until stiff, but still moist, and fold them into the lemon mixture.

Hull the blackberries, setting a few large ones aside for decoration. Put the remaining berries in the bottom of a 2½ cup soufflé dish. Pour the creamed mixture over the berries and set the dish in a roasting pan containing 1 in of hot water. Bake the pudding in an oven pre-heated to 375°F (190°C, mark 5) for 40–45 minutes or until the top is golden brown and set. Test by pressing the top with a finger – the pudding is cooked if it leaves no imprint.

The top of the pudding will have set to a sponge-like mixture over a creamy lemon sauce covering the berries. If the pudding is served hot, sprinkle it generously with sugar and decorate with the remaining berries. Offer a bowl of whipped cream separately. For a cold dessert, pipe whipped cream over the top and garnish with the blackberries.

BLACKBERRY SWISS CHARLOTTE

The classic charlotte, which probably originated in France, is a cold dessert of cooked fruit, set in a mold of ladyfingers. In this version, cultivated blackberries are used, but autumn raspberries or loganberries are equally suitable. The Swiss meringue topping is crisp on top with a soft marshmallow texture underneath.

PREPARATION TIME: *40 min*
COOKING TIME: *25 min*
INGREDIENTS *(for 4–6):*
1 pound cultivated blackberries
½ cup sugar
1 tablespoon cornstarch
2 small egg yolks
5 tablespoons heavy cream
Lemon juice
¼ pound ladyfingers
MERINGUE TOPPING:
2 small egg whites
1 cup confectioners' sugar
5 tablespoons blackberry syrup

Hull the blackberries and set aside a dozen large berries for decoration. Put the sugar and 1¼ cups of water in a pan over low heat until the sugar has dissolved to a syrup. Add the blackberries to the syrup and cook over very low heat for 10 minutes, or until tender but still whole. Drain the syrup into a measuring cup, and set the blackberries aside.

Put the cornstarch into a small pan and gradually blend in 1¼ cups of the blackberry syrup; cook over low heat for 3–4 minutes, stirring constantly, until the mixture is clear and beginning to thicken. Remove from the heat.

Separate the eggs, setting the whites aside for the meringue. Beat together the yolks and cream and gradually stir this into the thick syrup mixture. Sharpen and sweeten to taste with lemon juice and sugar.

Cut one rounded end off each of the ladyfingers. Put a ½ in layer of the blackberry cream in the bottom of a 2½ cup soufflé dish. Stand the ladyfingers, cut edge downwards, closely around the inside of the dish to make a casing. Put a single layer of blackberries over the cream, followed by another layer of cream and so on, finishing with a layer of blackberry cream.

For the meringue topping, put the egg whites in a mixing bowl with the confectioners' sugar and blackberry syrup. Place the bowl over a pan of boiling water and whisk the mixture steadily until it stands in soft peaks. Remove the bowl from the pan and continue whisking until the meringue is cool. Swirl or pipe it over the blackberry cream.

Bake the charlotte in the center of a pre-heated oven at 300°F (160°C, mark 2) for 20 minutes or until the meringue is delicately colored. Serve the dessert cold, decorated with the reserved fresh blackberries.

BERRY LEMON PUDDING

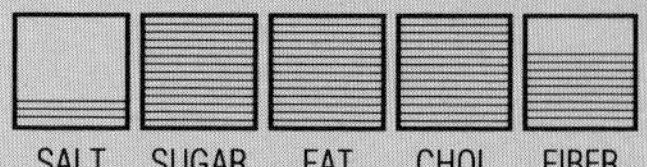

GLUTEN-FREE* WHOLEFOOD*
TOTAL CALORIES: ABOUT 1510

Reduce **sugar** to moderate by using only the 2 tablespoons that are creamed with the butter. Replace the rest of the sugar with 2 tablespoons honey. Using soy milk will give it a little extra sweetness. (Calories lost: up to 196.)
For moderate **fat** and **cholesterol**, use half the butter and only 1 egg yolk. Use skim milk or soy milk. (Calories lost: up to 255.) The cholesterol can be still further reduced by using vegetable margarine or oil instead of butter.
Cornstarch is a suitable **gluten-free** flour to use here.

BLACKBERRY SWISS CHARLOTTE

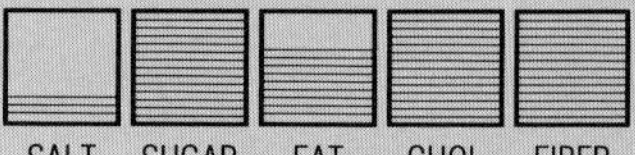

TOTAL CALORIES: ABOUT 2080

For moderate **sugar**, use 1 tablespoon honey for the syrup and replace the water with apple juice. The meringue topping can be made quite successfully with half the quantity of sugar and syrup and could even be omitted altogether. (Calories lost: up to 443.)
For low **fat** and **cholesterol**, make the blackberry cream using only 1 egg yolk and skim milk (or soy milk, which will give a slightly creamy texture) instead of cream. If you are omitting the meringue topping and don't want a leftover egg

white, use one whole egg in order to thicken the cream. (Calories lost: up to 375.)
The honey ratafias on page 127 make a good **gluten-free** and **wholefood** alternative to ladyfingers.

BLACK CURRANT AND MINT PIE

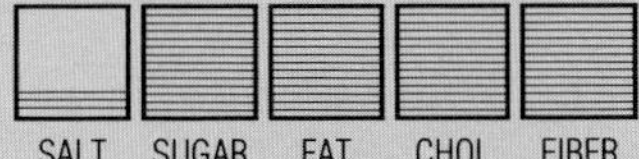

GLUTEN-FREE* WHOLEFOOD*
TOTAL CALORIES: ABOUT 2125

Half the amount of **sugar** will give a moderate sugar level and should be quite enough to sweeten the fruit, but you could also add 2–3 tablespoons of finely chopped dates. (Calories lost: up to 73.)
For a very low-**fat** pastry, see page 95; for low **cholesterol** and **gluten-free** alternatives to standard pastry, see notes on page 82.

Freezing: ✓ up to 6 months.

BLACK CURRANT AND MINT PIE

Fresh black currants are best when in season, but at any time of year whole frozen black currants can be used for this sharp, refreshing dessert.

Blueberries can be used in exactly the same way, but in this case you should omit the chopped mint.

PREPARATION TIME: *30 min*
COOKING TIME: *35–40 min*
INGREDIENTS *(for 6)*:*
1 pound black currants
1 tablespoon chopped mint
½ cup sugar
1 quantity standard pastry (page 171)

Top and tail the black currants and wash them in a colander, dipping it into several lots of cold water. Drain the black currants thoroughly and put them in a shallow, 7 in wide pie pan. Mix the finely chopped mint with the sugar and sprinkle it evenly over the black currants.

Roll out the prepared pastry on a floured surface, to a thickness of about ¼ in. Cover the pie pan with the pastry and decorate with pastry leaves or flowers from the trimmings (pages 173 and 174).

Make a slit in the center of the pastry for the steam to escape. Brush the surface lightly with water and sprinkle over a little extra sugar.

Bake the pie on the middle shelf of an oven pre-heated to 400°F (200°C, mark 6) for 35–40 minutes or until golden.

Serve the pie cold, with fresh cream or with vanilla or maple ice cream.

BLACK CURRANT BRÛLÉE

This can be made with other fruits: blueberries and cherries (pitted) are particularly successful. A tablespoon or two of liqueur can be added to the fruit if you like: crème de cassis is the obvious choice for black currants, kirsch for cherries.

PREPARATION TIME: *12 min*
COOKING TIME: *8–10 min*
INGREDIENTS *(for 4):*
½ pound stripped black currants
½ cup light brown sugar
1½ teaspoons arrowroot
½ cup sour cream
Extra light brown sugar
Ground cinnamon

Simmer the stripped black currants in 4 tablespoons of water until tender; add the brown sugar, bring to the boil and simmer for a few more minutes. Blend the arrowroot with 1 tablespoon of water, stir it into the currants and boil gently, stirring all the time, for 1–2 minutes.

Cool the black currant mixture before spooning it into four small flameproof dishes. When it is quite cold, top the fruit with sour cream and cover with a thin layer of brown sugar mixed with a pinch of ground cinnamon. Put in the refrigerator for an hour or two to chill. Set the dishes under a hot broiler for a minute or two until the sugar bubbles and caramelizes. There should be a delicious contrast between the crunchy hot topping and the cool, refreshingly fruity base.

BLACK CURRANT SHERBET

The taste of black currants is exceptionally refreshing in a sherbet or water ice. Blueberries can be used instead; both black currants and blueberries give a wonderful color to the ice.

PREPARATION TIME: *30 min*
FREEZING TIME: *3–4 hours*
INGREDIENTS *(for 6):*
1¼ cups water
½ cup sugar
½ pound fresh or frozen black currants
1 teaspoon lemon juice
2 egg whites

Put the water in a saucepan together with the sugar. Heat over low heat until the sugar has dissolved, then bring to the boil and boil gently for 10 minutes. Set aside to cool.

Meanwhile, strip and wash the fresh black currants if you are using them. Put the fresh or frozen currants, with 2–3 tablespoons of water, in a pan and cook over low heat for 10 minutes. Rub the currants through a sieve and make up the purée with the sugar syrup and extra water to make a total of 2½ cups. Leave until quite cool. Stir in the lemon juice and pour the mixture into ice cube trays or a shallow freezing container. Place in the freezer until nearly firm.

Whisk the egg whites until stiff, but not dry. Turn the frozen mixture into a chilled bowl, break it down thoroughly with a fork, and carefully fold in the egg whites. Return the sherbet mixture to its container and freeze until firm. Take it out of the freezer and put into the refrigerator to soften slightly about half an hour before serving.

CLAFOUTI LIMOUSIN

A clafouti is a sweet crêpe batter baked with fresh fruit. In the Limousin province of France, where the pudding originates, it is traditionally made with black cherries.

PREPARATION TIME: *15 min*
COOKING TIME: *30 min*
INGREDIENTS *(for 6):*
1½ pounds black cherries
3 eggs
3 tablespoons flour
*Salt**
5 tablespoons sugar
2 cups milk
1 tablespoon dark rum (optional)
2–3 tablespoons unsalted butter

Remove the stalks from the cherries, pit, wash and drain the fruit thoroughly. Beat the eggs in a bowl; blend in the sifted flour and a pinch of salt before adding 3 tablespoons of sugar. Heat the milk until lukewarm and gradually pour it into the egg mixture, stirring continuously. Add the rum if used.

Butter a wide, shallow, fireproof dish thoroughly. Put in the cherries, pour the batter over them and dot with the remaining butter. Bake in the center of an oven, pre-heated to 425°F (220°C, mark 7) for 25–30 minutes. When the dish is cooked, the cherries will have risen to the top and the batter will have set like a baked custard.

Sprinkle the pudding with the remaining sugar and serve lukewarm.

BLACK CURRANT BRÛLÉE

GLUTEN-FREE WHOLEFOOD
TOTAL CALORIES: ABOUT 815

Black currants do need some added sweetening; however, for low **sugar**, if apple juice is used instead of water (apples and black currants make a good combination) 2 tablespoons sugar or 1 tablespoon honey should be enough to sweeten the fruit. (Calories lost: up to 234.)
For low **fat** and **cholesterol** substitute low-fat plain yogurt for the sour cream. (Calories lost: up to 160.)

BLACK CURRANT SHERBET

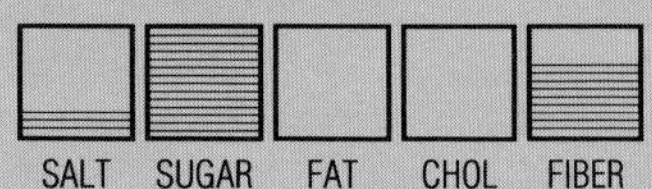

GLUTEN-FREE WHOLEFOOD
TOTAL CALORIES: ABOUT 485

As with the previous recipe, using apple juice instead of water and only half the quantity of **sugar** should make it quite sweet enough and will reduce the sugar level to moderate. You could also mix the fruit with ⅓–½ cup dried apricots, cooked and beaten to a thick purée. (Calories lost: up to 89.)

Freezing: √ up to 6 months.

CLAFOUTI LIMOUSIN

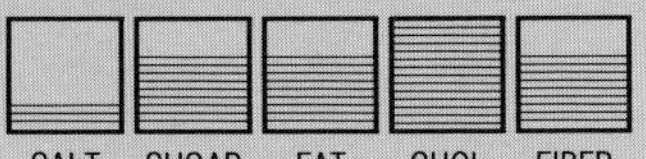

SALT SUGAR FAT CHOL FIBER

GLUTEN-FREE* WHOLEFOOD*
TOTAL CALORIES: ABOUT 1545

The **sugar** level can be reduced to low quite easily: if soy milk, which is slightly sweet, is used for the batter, it will need no more than 1 tablespoon of sugar to sweeten it and another tablespoon for sprinkling over the top. (Calories lost: up to 177.)
The **fat** and **cholesterol** can be reduced to moderate by omitting one egg yolk, using skim milk (or soy milk) and using no more than 1 tablespoon butter for greasing the dish; omit the dotting with butter. For still lower cholesterol, replace the butter with vegetable margarine. (Calories lost: up to 442.)
Soy flour, fine cornmeal or a mixture of the two make good **gluten-free** alternatives to flour for the batter, but the cooking time may be longer. Test after about 25–30 minutes.

FRESH FIGS AND YOGURT

Purple, black and green figs are available for a short season—August through October. This refreshing dessert may evoke memories of the Mediterranean, especially if fig or vine leaves are arranged beneath the dessert glasses.

PREPARATION TIME: *15 min*
CHILLING TIME: *2 hours*
INGREDIENTS *(for 4):*
8 fresh figs
$\frac{1}{2}$ cup heavy cream
$\frac{1}{2}$ cup plain yogurt
3–4 tablespoons brown sugar

Put the figs in a large bowl of hot water for 1 minute. Drain them thoroughly, peel off the skins and quarter each fig. Whisk the cream lightly and blend it into the yogurt.

Spoon a little of the cream mixture into four small serving glasses. Top with a layer of figs, followed by more cream and figs and finish with a layer of cream mixture. Sprinkle each layer with brown sugar.

Chill in the refrigerator for at least 2 hours to allow the sugar to melt into the cream.

FIG PIE

An unusual way of using this familiar dried fruit—or fresh figs if available—is as a pie filling.

PREPARATION TIME: *45 min*
COOKING TIME: *35 min*
INGREDIENTS *(for 6):*
$\frac{3}{4}$ quantity standard pastry (page 171)
$\frac{1}{2}$ pound figs (fresh or dried)
2 teaspoons cornstarch
$\frac{1}{2}$ teaspoon ground allspice
2 tablespoons currants
2 teaspoons molasses or corn syrup

Roll out the pastry, on a floured surface, to a thickness of $\frac{1}{8}$ in. Line a deep 8 in pie plate with the pastry. Cut the stalks off the figs and place the fruit in a shallow saucepan with just enough water to cover them; cook over low heat until tender. Fresh figs need 5–15 minutes' cooking time depending on their ripeness; dried figs should first be soaked for 12 hours with a squeeze of lemon juice before being stewed for 20 minutes in their soaking liquid.

Drain the figs and retain $1\frac{1}{4}$ cups of the liquid; top up with hot water if necessary. Pour a little of the juice into a basin, add the cornstarch and mix until it resembles a thin smooth cream. Gradually add the rest of the liquid, stirring well. When well mixed, return it to the saucepan and place over moderate heat. Stir until thickened, then cook for another 2 minutes. Mix in the spice, currants and syrup and remove from the heat.

Arrange the figs over the pastry; pour over the thickened fig liquid, making sure that the currants are evenly distributed. Bake the pie on the middle shelf

FRESH FIGS AND YOGURT

SALT SUGAR FAT CHOL FIBER

GLUTEN-FREE WHOLEFOOD
TOTAL CALORIES: ABOUT 1150

For low **sugar**, make sure your figs are really ripe: one teaspoon of sugar or a dribble of honey for each serving will then be enough. (Calories lost: up to 156.)
For low **fat** and **cholesterol** levels, use low-fat yogurt and replace the cream with quark, fromage blanc or low-fat sour cream. (Further calories lost: up to 555.)

FIG PIE

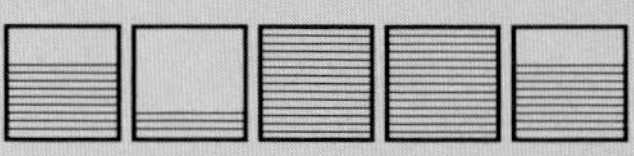

SALT SUGAR FAT CHOL FIBER

GLUTEN-FREE*
TOTAL CALORIES: ABOUT 1805

The moderate **salt** content can be reduced to low if the molasses or syrup is replaced by honey and fresh figs used. This will also reduce the **sugar** content further. (Calories lost: up to 387.)
For a very **low-fat** pastry see page 95; for low **cholesterol** and **gluten-free** alternatives to standard pastry, see notes on page 82. Serve with yogurt or low-fat sour cream instead of cream or ice-cream. Honey and molasses make **wholefood** alternatives to corn syrup.
This recipe is medium **fiber** if fresh figs are used, or high fiber if the figs are dried.

Freezing: ✓ up to 6 months.

GOOSEBERRY TART

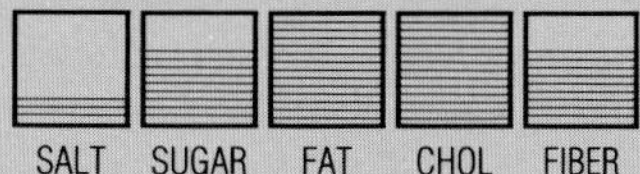

GLUTEN-FREE* WHOLEFOOD*
TOTAL CALORIES: ABOUT 2400

For a low **sugar** level, choose very ripe, sweet gooseberries. Cook them in apple or grape juice instead of water, and sweeten them with 1–2 tablespoons of honey. (Calories lost: up to 287.)
You can eliminate the eggs and most of the butter, and thus reduce the **fat** and **cholesterol** in the filling to very low, by using tofu. Blend the gooseberry purée with about 11 ounces silken tofu to a smooth consistency. (Calories lost: up to 663.)
Try replacing ¼ pound of the gooseberries with the same weight of dried apricots, soaked for 30 minutes. The taste of apricots blends very well with tofu, and you may need a little less added sweetening.
For a very low-**fat** pastry, see this page; for low **cholesterol** and **gluten-free** alternatives to standard pastry, see notes on page 10.

Freezing: √ up to 3 months.

GRAPE GELATIN

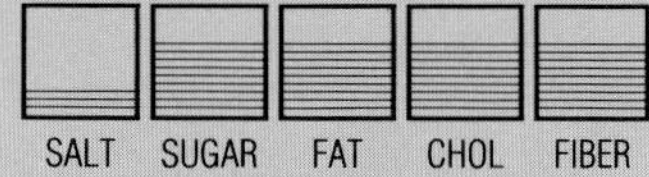

GLUTEN-FREE WHOLEFOOD*
TOTAL CALORIES: ABOUT 820

To reduce the **sugar** to very low, use 1 tablespoon of honey. (Calories lost: up to 78.)
For low **fat** and **cholesterol**, use low-fat sour cream or yogurt instead of cream. (Calories lost: up to 240.)

GOOSEBERRY TART

This dessert is based on an English recipe from the 18th century when puréed, wine-flavored fruits were popular.

PREPARATION TIME: *1 hour*
COOKING TIME: *15 min*
INGREDIENTS *(for 6):*
1½ pounds gooseberries
1 cup flour
1 rounded tablespoon confectioners' sugar
11 tablespoons unsalted butter
1 large egg yolk
3 large eggs
Sugar
1 tablespoon orange-flower water or 2 tablespoons muscat-flavored white wine

Sift together the flour and confectioners' sugar into a large bowl. Cut up 5 tablespoons of the butter and rub into the flour until the mixture resembles fine breadcrumbs. Add one egg yolk and sufficient water to bind the pastry.

Roll the pastry out, on a lightly floured surface, to ¼ in thickness and use to line a buttered 7 in wide, loose-bottomed flan pan. Prick the pastry with a fork and bake it blind in the center of a preheated oven, at 350°F (180°C, mark 4) for 15 minutes.

Wash and drain the gooseberries, but do not top and tail the fruit. Put them in a large saucepan with 5 tablespoons of water. Cover the pan with a lid and cook over low heat for 10 minutes, then increase the heat and cook until the gooseberries have burst and are soft.

Rub the gooseberries through a sieve and sweeten this purée with sugar to taste. Put the purée in a clean pan. Stir over low heat, adding the remaining butter in small pieces. Beat the eggs.

Remove the pan from the heat and stir in the eggs. Return the pan to the heat and cook, stirring continuously, until the purée thickens. It should not be allowed to boil. Cool slightly, then add orange-flower water or wine to taste.

If necessary, re-heat the pastry case. Spoon the gooseberry purée into the pastry case and serve it warm, with cream.

Low-fat pastry

This recipe is similar to the wartime recipes evolved when butter was scarce. Although it does not have the same flavor as pastry made with fat, it is quite good if eaten hot. Using skim milk powder gives a slightly better result than using skim milk.

INGREDIENTS
1 cup flour
4–5 tablespoons skim milk or 2 heaping tablespoons skim milk powder
1½ teaspoons baking powder
*Salt**

Mix all the ingredients together to a smooth dough. If you are using skim milk powder, add just enough water to bind the mixture. Do not try to roll out but press into a flan or tart pan.

of the oven heated to 400°F (200°C, mark 6) for 30–35 minutes.

Serve hot or cold, with cream or vanilla ice cream.

GRAPE GELATIN

A lovely, cool-looking dessert, this is even easier to make if you can find sweet seedless grapes.

PREPARATION TIME: *40 min*
SETTING TIME: *about 3 hours*
INGREDIENTS *(for 4):*
1¼ pounds large green grapes
Juice of 2 oranges
Juice of a lemon
2 tablespoons sugar
4 tablespoons water
1½ teaspoons unflavored gelatin
½ cup light cream

Dissolve the sugar with 2 tablespoons of water in a small pan over low heat, and dissolve the gelatin in a cup with the remaining water. Stir the hot sugar liquid into the gelatin, blend thoroughly and stir it all into the strained fruit juices. The liquid should now measure 1¼ cups; make up with cold water if necessary. Leave to cool until it has jelled to the consistency of unbeaten egg white.

Peel and seed the grapes (page 152); this is easiest done by dipping the whole bunch in boiling water for 30 seconds, then stripping off the skin and extracting the seeds from the stalk ends.

Divide the grapes equally between four sundae glasses, and spoon the gelatin over them. Leave in the refrigerator until set, and just before serving float a thin layer of cream on top of each or serve the cream separately.

GRAPEFRUIT IN BRANDY

The slightly acid flavor of grapefruit is equally refreshing both before and after a rich main course. Slices of grapefruit, poached in syrup and doused with brandy, give a clean taste to the palate.

PREPARATION TIME: *12 min*
COOKING TIME: *8 min*
INGREDIENTS *(for 6):*
4 large grapefruit
½ cup sugar
1 teaspoon cinnamon
4 tablespoons brandy

Cut off all the peel and pith from the grapefruit and carefully poke out the pithy core with the little finger. Slice the fruit into ½ in thick rounds. Put the sugar in a large saucepan with ½ cup cold water and the cinnamon. Cook over low heat, stirring frequently, until the sugar has dissolved, then boil this syrup briskly for 2 minutes. Lower the heat, add the grapefruit slices and poach them gently in the syrup for 6 minutes, turning once.

Arrange the grapefruit slices in a serving dish, pour over the brandy and serve hot or chilled.

GRAPEFRUIT IN BRANDY

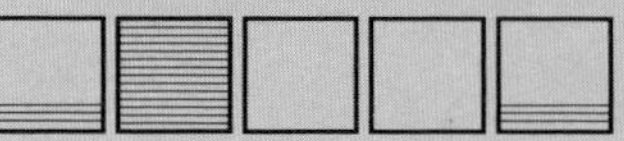

SALT SUGAR FAT CHOL FIBER

GLUTEN-FREE WHOLEFOOD*
TOTAL CALORIES: ABOUT 665

To reduce the **sugar** content to low, poach the grapefruit in water or grape juice to which 2 tablespoons of honey or fruit sugar (fructose) have been added. Pink grapefruits hardly need sweetening. (Calories lost: up to 314.)

Freezing: ☑ up to 6 months.
Microwave: ☑

GREENGAGES WITH APRICOT PURÉE

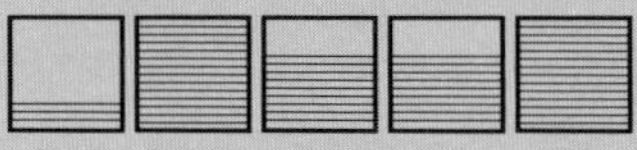

SALT SUGAR FAT CHOL FIBER

GLUTEN-FREE* WHOLEFOOD*
TOTAL CALORIES: ABOUT 1370

For low added **sugar**, use dried apricots: they are very sweet and will make it unnecessary to add sugar to the fruit purée. Use only 2 tablespoons vanilla sugar, or 2 tablespoons honey, on top of the greengages. (Calories lost: up to 197.)
To reduce the **fat** and **cholesterol** content, replace the bread-and-butter base under the fruit with a biscuit dough (see page 142). This should be baked at around 400°F (200°C, mark 6) for the first ten minutes, then continue at 350°F (180°C, mark 4). (Calories lost: up to 325.)
A **gluten-free** alternative to bread could be rice pudding, if the baking dish is well sealed with foil during baking to prevent a crust forming.

Food processor: ☑ for the purée.
Freezing: ☑ up to 4 months for the purée.

QUICHE REINE-CLAUDE

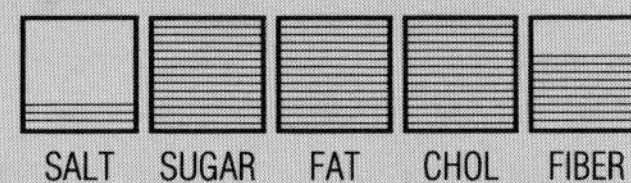

SALT SUGAR FAT CHOL FIBER

GLUTEN-FREE* WHOLEFOOD*
TOTAL CALORIES: ABOUT 2635

It is easy to eliminate some of the **sugar** and reduce the level to low. Use the gluten-free pastry on page 82 which tastes sweet but does not include sugar; use greengage (or plum) jam made without added sugar; and try the alternative pastry cream suggested below. (Calories lost: up to 262.)
For low **fat** and **cholesterol**, omit the accompanying cream and use the alternative pastry cream given. Use the very low-fat pastry on page 95 or a low-cholesterol one as suggested in the notes on page 82. (Calories lost: up to 726.)

ALTERNATIVE PASTRY CREAM
1¼ cups milk
2 tablespoons brown sugar
2 tablespoons soy flour
2 tablespoons cornmeal
1 large egg
Heat the milk in a pan over low heat. Blend together the sugar, soy flour, cornmeal and egg; gradually stir in the warm milk. Return the mixture to the pan over low heat and stir continuously until it thickens. Remove from the heat, pour into a bowl and cover with wet wax paper. Allow to become quite cold.

Freezing: ☑ up to 2 months.

GREENGAGES WITH APRICOT PURÉE

The small, round, golden-yellow greengage plums make their brief appearance in late summer. They are excellent as dessert fruits, and for puddings.

PREPARATION TIME: *25 min*
COOKING TIME: *30 min*
INGREDIENTS *(for 4):*
1 pound greengages
½ pound fresh or ¼ pound dried apricots
2 tablespoons sugar
½ teaspoon grated lemon rind
4 slices bread
3–4 tablespoons unsalted butter
2–4 tablespoons vanilla sugar (page 184)

Wash and dry the apricots, cut them in half and remove the pits. Leave dried apricots to soak overnight in cold water.

Put the apricots in a pan, cover with fresh cold water and cook until tender. Drain thoroughly and rub the apricots through a coarse sieve; flavor this purée with sugar and lemon rind.

Wash and dry the greengages, and cut them in half. Remove the pits. Cut the crusts from the bread and spread the slices with half the butter. Lay the slices, buttered side up, in a greased ovenproof dish. Arrange the greengages on top with a tiny piece of butter in each half; sprinkle with the vanilla sugar.

Bake in the center of the oven, pre-heated to 350°F (180°C, mark 4), for about 30 minutes, or until the greengages are tender.

Serve the greengage pudding warm, and offer the warmed apricot purée separately.

QUICHE REINE-CLAUDE

Lorraine is the land of quiches and Alsace of guiches. Both are names for an open tart with a cream filling combined with sweet or savory ingredients. This tart is filled with greengage plums (Reine-Claudes) on a base of crème pâtissière (confectioner's custard).

PREPARATION TIME: *40 min*
COOKING TIME: *30 min*
INGREDIENTS *(for 6):*

1 pastry case
½ pound greengages
4 tablespoons greengage jam
1 tablespoon lemon juice
½ cup heavy cream

CRÈME PÂTISSIÈRE:
2 eggs
¼ cup sugar
2 tablespoons flour
1¼ cups milk
½ teaspoon vanilla or 4 teaspoons lemon juice

Bake or buy a 7 in pastry case, made from sweet standard or pâte sucrée pastry. Leave the baked case to cool completely before assembling the tart.

Make the crème pâtissière next as this too should not be used until quite cool: put 1 whole egg and 1 egg yolk in a mixing bowl (set aside the remaining egg white). Whisk the sugar with the eggs until creamy and near white, then whisk the sifted flour into the eggs, and gradually add the milk. Pour the mixture into a small saucepan and bring to the boil, whisking continuously.

Simmer this custard-cream over very low heat for 2–3 minutes to cook the flour. Flavor to taste with vanilla or lemon juice and pour the cream into a shallow dish to cool. Stir from time to time to prevent a skin forming.

Spread the cold crème pâtissière over the bottom of the pastry case. Cut the greengages in half, remove the pits and arrange the fruit over the cream.

Put the greengage jam in a small, heavy-based pan, with 3 tablespoons of water and the lemon juice. Cook over low heat, stirring until the jam has dissolved and the mixture is clear. Increase the heat and boil rapidly to form a glaze. Do not over-boil–the glaze is ready when it will coat the back of the spoon and falls off in heavy drops. Rub the glaze through a coarse sieve.

Spoon the glaze over the greengages, covering them completely; brush the top edge of the tart with the remaining glaze to give a smooth finish. Set the tart in a cool place until the glaze has set.

Just before serving, whisk the remaining egg white until stiff, but still moist. Whip the cream into soft peaks and fold in the white; sweeten to taste with a little sugar and serve in a separate bowl to accompany the quiche.

LEMON MOUSSE

When shiny, firm lemons are plentiful and good value, they can be used for a light and refreshing mousse.

PREPARATION TIME: *30 min*
CHILLING TIME: *2 hours*
INGREDIENTS *(for 4):*
Juice and rind of 2 large lemons
1 tablespoon unflavored gelatin
3 eggs
½ cup sugar
½ cup heavy cream
GARNISH:
½ cup whipping cream

Sprinkle the gelatin over 2 tablespoons of water in a small pan and set aside. Separate the eggs, putting the yolks into a large bowl and the whites into another. Finely grate the rind from the lemons, and mix it into the egg yolks, together with the sugar. Squeeze the lemons and strain the juice into the gelatin. Place the saucepan over low heat, stirring continuously. Do not allow to boil, and immediately the gelatin has dissolved remove the pan from the heat.

Whisk the egg yolks and sugar until pale and creamy. Slowly pour in the dissolved gelatin, whisking all the time. Continue to whisk the mixture until it is cool and beginning to thicken. Lightly beat the heavy cream and fold into the mixture. Beat the egg whites until stiff, then blend them in evenly and lightly.

Spoon the mousse into a serving dish or individual dishes and chill until set. Serve a bowl of whipped cream separately or pipe whipped cream over the mousse.

LEMON SYLLABUB

In Elizabethan times, one of the favorite wines in Britain was a still dry wine produced around Sillery in the Champagne district of France. Bub was a slang term for a bubbly drink, and by association syllabub came to describe a drink or dessert made by mixing frothy cream with still wine.

PREPARATION TIME: *20 min*
STANDING TIME: *6 hours*
CHILLING TIME: *3 hours*
INGREDIENTS *(for 6):*
1 lemon
3–4 tablespoons brandy
6 tablespoons sugar
1¼ cups heavy cream
½ cup sweet white wine
GARNISH:
Rind of a lemon

Peel the lemon thinly with a potato peeler. Squeeze out the juice and add enough brandy to make the liquid up to 5 tablespoons. Pour the liquid into a small bowl, add the lemon peel and leave to stand for at least 6 hours.

Strain the liquid through a fine sieve and stir in the sugar until it has dissolved completely. Whip the cream until it holds its shape. Mix the wine into the lemon and brandy, then add this liquid to the cream a little at a time, whisking continuously. The cream should absorb all the liquid and still stand in soft peaks. Pile the mixture into individual glasses and chill for several hours.

For the garnish, thinly peel the lemon rind and cut into narrow strips; blanch for 2–3 minutes.

Serve the syllabub with a cluster of drained lemon strips.

GLAZED LEMON TART

The fresh sharp flavor of this tart is welcome after a rich main course. Preparations for the tart, which can also be served as a pastry with morning coffee, should begin a day in advance.

PREPARATION TIME: *1¾ hours*
COOKING TIME: *25–30 min*
INGREDIENTS *(for 6):*
½ quantity standard pastry (page 171)
1 tablespoon flour
½ cup ground almonds
¼ cup unsalted butter
¼ cup sugar
1 egg
Rind of a lemon
TOPPING:
2 small lemons
1 vanilla bean
1 cup sugar

Prepare the topping first: scrub the two lemons thoroughly in cold water, then cut them into slices about ⅛ in thick. Remove the seeds carefully and put the slices in a bowl. Cover with boiling water and leave to soak for 8 hours.

Drain the lemon slices, put them in a saucepan and cover with fresh cold water; bring briskly to the boil. Lower the heat, cover the pan with a lid and simmer gently for 1 hour or until the lemon slices are soft. Remove from the heat and let the slices cool in the liquid.

Roll the pastry out on a lightly floured surface, to a circle about 9 in across. Line a 7–8 in flan pan with the pastry and prick lightly with a fork. Bake the tart blind for 5 minutes, then set it aside while preparing the filling.

Mix the flour and ground

LEMON MOUSSE

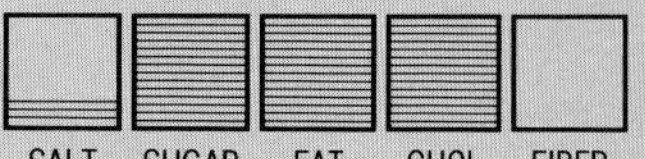

GLUTEN-FREE WHOLEFOOD*
TOTAL CALORIES: ABOUT 1870

To reduce the **sugar** content by half, to medium, beat the egg yolks with 3 tablespoons of fruit sugar or clear honey for a considerable time until creamy. (Calories lost: up to 264.)
For low **fat**, replace the heavy cream with ½ cup quark beaten with ⅔ cup thick low-fat yogurt or sour cream. To decorate the mousse, use piped sweetened quark and curls of lemon rind instead of more cream.
Use only 2 yolks with 3 or even 4 whites to reduce the **cholesterol:** this will however remain fairly high unless you use only 1 yolk. (Calories lost: up to 1032.)

Freezing: ✓ up to 2 months.

LEMON SYLLABUB

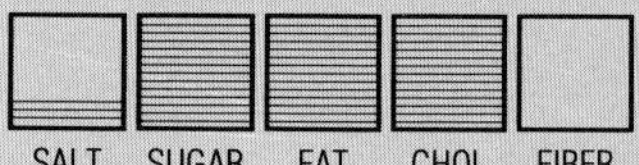

GLUTEN-FREE WHOLEFOOD*
TOTAL CALORIES: ABOUT 1890

The amount of **sugar** can be cut to medium if it is replaced with 2 tablespoons honey or fruit sugar. Extra sweetness will be given by the wine. (Calories lost: up to 216.)
Reducing the amount of **fat** and **cholesterol** to medium is difficult as this dish is traditionally flavored cream, but one way of doing so is to make the dish just before serving, and replace half the cream with 2 large stiffly beaten egg whites, beating these

separately and then folding them into the mixture. (Calories lost: up to 641.)

GLAZED LEMON TART

GLUTEN-FREE* WHOLEFOOD*
TOTAL CALORIES: ABOUT 2545

To reduce the amount of **sugar** in this dish involves changing the topping method completely. The easiest way to achieve this clear topping is to make a fruit juice gelatin, using $1\frac{1}{4}$ cups of unsweetened, cloudy apple juice. Warm a little of this with 2 scant teaspoons unflavored gelatin until completely clear, then mix with the remaining cold juice. Cool, taste, and add a teaspoonful or two of honey or fruit sugar if wished; then, when the gelatin is thick in texture, spoon it over the tart. The lemon slices can be replaced with orange ones, poached as suggested, but not cooked in syrup as these are already sweet enough. In the filling use half the sugar. This gives a low sugar level. (Calories lost: up to 785.)
The high **fat** level can only be reduced to medium by changing the pastry to a biscuit dough base or using the very low-fat pastry on page 95; the filling cannot be altered substantially, although the **cholesterol** level can be reduced by exchanging some or all of the butter for soft vegetable margarine, and using only the egg white. (Calories lost: up to 502.)
The **gluten-free** pastry on page 82 is excellent for this.

Freezing: ☑ up to 3 months.

almonds; beat the butter and sugar until soft and light. Beat the egg lightly and blend in the finely grated lemon rind. Gradually stir the egg into the butter mixture, then add the flour and ground almonds. Spread this mixture evenly in the pastry case. Place the tart just above center of a preheated oven at 375°F (190°C, mark 5) and bake for 25–30 minutes or until the tart has risen and is golden brown and firm to the touch. Remove from the oven and leave to cool.

Drain the liquid from the lemon slices, setting aside $1\frac{1}{4}$ cups. Add the vanilla bean and the sugar to the lemon liquid and cook in a saucepan over low heat until the sugar has dissolved. Add the lemon slices and simmer gently for about 5 minutes, then carefully lift the soft lemon slices on to a plate. Continue to boil the syrup rapidly until the mixture sets–test by spooning a little on to a saucer. Arrange the lemon slices in a circular pattern over the tart. When the syrup is setting, draw the pan off the heat, remove the vanilla bean, and as soon as the bubbles have subsided, spoon all the syrup over the lemon slices.

Leave the tart to chill in the refrigerator before serving it cold, cut into wedges.

LEMON MERINGUE PIE

A classic combination of pastry, tangy smooth lemon cream, and crisp airy meringue.

PREPARATION TIME: *30 min*
COOKING TIME: *40 min*
INGREDIENTS *(for 4–6):*
½ quantity standard pastry (page 171)
1 large thin-skinned lemon
2–3 tablespoons granulated sugar
2 tablespoons cornstarch
2 eggs
1 tablespoon unsalted butter
½ cup superfine sugar

Roll out the pastry and line an 8½ in pie plate or a 7 in flan ring. Bake the pastry case blind in the center of a pre-heated oven, at 400°F (200°C, mark 6) for about 15 minutes or until the pastry is crisp and golden. When cold, remove the pastry from the pie plate or ease away the flan ring.

Meanwhile, peel the rind from the lemon in thin slivers, carefully omitting all white pith. Squeeze the juice from the lemon and set it aside. Put the lemon peel, granulated sugar and 1¼ cups of water in a pan; cook over low heat until the sugar has dissolved, then bring this syrup to the boil. Remove the pan from the heat. Blend the cornstarch in a bowl with 3 tablespoons lemon juice, then pour in the syrup through a strainer, stirring thoroughly. Separate the eggs, and beat in the egg yolks, one at a time, together with the butter. The mixture should be thick enough to coat the back of a wooden spoon; otherwise return it to the pan and cook for a few minutes without boiling. Spoon the lemon mixture into the cooked pastry case, set on a baking sheet.

Whisk the egg whites until stiff, then add half the superfine sugar and continue whisking until the meringue holds its shape and stands in soft peaks. Fold in all but 1 teaspoon of the remaining sugar, using a metal spoon.

Pile the meringue over the lemon filling; spread it from the edge towards the center, making sure that the meringue joins the pastry edge to prevent the meringue 'weeping.' Sprinkle the meringue with the remaining sugar. Reduce the heat to 300°F (150°C, mark 2) and bake the pie in the center of the oven for 20–30 minutes, or until the meringue is crisp. Serve the pie warm.

COLD LEMON SOUFFLÉ

The clean taste of lemon is particularly good in soufflés. It can be enhanced and given an unusual overtone by adding a few drops of fresh lime juice, if you have it.

PREPARATION TIME: *25 min*
CHILLING TIME: *1–2 hours*
INGREDIENTS *(for 4):*
2 lemons
3 eggs
6 tablespoons sugar
2 teaspoons unflavored gelatin
½ cup heavy cream

Grate the rind from the lemons and squeeze out the juice. Separate the eggs, and beat the egg yolks, sugar, lemon rind and juice in a bowl until thick.

In a small bowl, mix the gelatin with 2 tablespoons of cold water and set the bowl in a pan of hot water until the gelatin has dissolved and is clear. Allow the gelatin to cool slightly, then pour it into the lemon mixture. Beat the cream until it just holds its shape, then fold it into the lemon mixture. Whisk the egg whites until stiff and fold them carefully into the mixture when nearly set. Spoon the lemon soufflé into a prepared 6 in or 1 quart soufflé dish and chill until set.

LEMON MERINGUE PIE

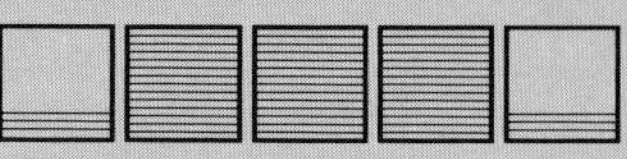

SALT SUGAR FAT CHOL FIBER

GLUTEN-FREE* WHOLEFOOD*
TOTAL CALORIES: ABOUT 1700

The high level of **sugar** added to the meringue topping can be reduced to 2 tablespoons, reducing the sugar content of this recipe to low. (Calories lost: up to 295.)
The high **fat** content of the pastry cannot be reduced, except by substituting a biscuit dough or yeast pastry base, or the very low-fat pastry on page 95. However, if wished, 1 egg yolk only can be used in the filling, reducing the **cholesterol**; if you are using the standard pastry base, cholesterol can be reduced to low by substituting vegetable fat, preferably soft margarine. (Calories lost: up to 502.)

Freezing: ☑ up to 2 months if you want to make the pie and filling in advance; the meringue itself does not freeze.

COLD LEMON SOUFFLÉ

SALT SUGAR FAT CHOL FIBER

GLUTEN-FREE WHOLEFOOD*
TOTAL CALORIES: ABOUT 1265

The high **sugar** content can be reduced by half, to moderate; in this case use only 2 egg yolks. This will also reduce the **cholesterol** level to some extent, but it will still be high. (Calories lost: up to 308.)
To reduce the **fat** and cholesterol levels to low requires a change to the nature of the recipe, mixing ¼ cup

heavy cream, whipped with 3 tablespoons of low-fat quark or fromage blanc, before folding in first the lemon mixture and then the beaten egg whites. (Calories lost: up to 412.)

Freezing: ✓ up to 2 months.

MELON ICE CREAM

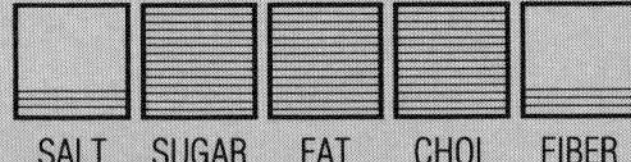

GLUTEN-FREE WHOLEFOOD*
TOTAL CALORIES: ABOUT 3000

The high **sugar** level can be reduced to low by finding a very sweet melon, and adding only 2 tablespoons sugar or honey to it. (Calories lost: up to 295.)
The high **fat** and **cholesterol** level involved in the egg yolks and heavy cream can only be reduced by changing the nature of the recipe, although the lighter result can be tasty and refreshing. Use only 1 egg yolk added to the pulp, and only ½ cup heavy cream, folding in as the recipe suggests. When mixture is mushy, beat smooth and fold in 3 stiffly beaten egg whites. These changes reduce the fat and cholesterol levels to medium. (Calories lost: up to 1379.)

Freezing: ✓ up to 3 months.

MELON ICE CREAM

The Italians introduced water ices or sherbets to Britain during the reign of Charles I, at least two centuries before cream ices became known. Today, virtually any sweetened fruit juice can be made into ice cream with egg custard and cream.

PREPARATION TIME: *30–40 min*
CHILLING TIME: *3 hours*
INGREDIENTS *(for 4):*
1 large cantaloupe melon
½ cup sugar
4 egg yolks
5 tablespoons ginger wine
2 tablespoons lemon juice
2 cups heavy cream

Slice about 1½ in off the top of the melon; remove the seeds and fibers with a small spoon. Scoop all the melon pulp into a small saucepan, taking care not to pierce the shell. Add the sugar and place the pan over low heat until the sugar has melted into the melon, and the mixture is a soft pulp. Mash with a fork.

Beat the egg yolks until light and creamy, and add them to the melon pulp, stirring well. Continue cooking and whisking over low heat, so that the eggs will not curdle, until the mixture has the consistency of thin cream.

Pour the melon mixture into a bowl and leave it to cool completely. Stir in the ginger wine and lemon juice, mix thoroughly, then fold in the lightly whipped cream. Cover the bowl with foil and chill in the refrigerator for 30 minutes.

Spoon the melon cream into a freezing tray or container, cover with foil or the lid, and freeze for 2–3 hours. Stir the ice cream several times during freezing to prevent crystals forming.

Pile the ice cream into glasses or the chilled melon shell and serve at once. Any surplus ice cream can be stored for several months in the home freezer.

ORANGE SOUFFLÉS

A light fluffy soufflé is a good choice for rounding off a meal. These individual soufflés are baked in orange shells and should be served straight from the oven before they collapse.

PREPARATION TIME: *30 min*
COOKING TIME: *20 min*
INGREDIENTS *(for 4):*
4 large oranges
1 lemon
2 tablespoons unsalted butter
2 tablespoons flour
3 tablespoons sugar
3 eggs
GARNISH:
Confectioners' sugar

Wash the oranges and cut them in half crosswise. Take out all the orange flesh and remove the white pith; set the shells aside.

Squeeze the orange flesh to extract all the juice and strain it into a bowl together with the strained juice from the lemon. Melt the butter in a saucepan over low heat, stir in the flour and cook for a few minutes until this roux is lightly colored. Gradually add the fruit juice, stirring continuously, until the mixture has thickened to a smooth sauce. Bring to the boil, simmer for 1–2 minutes, then take the pan off the heat. Stir in the sugar, and let the sauce cool slightly.

Separate the eggs, and beat one yolk at a time into the sauce, stirring well before adding the next (all these preparations can be made in advance). Whisk the egg whites until stiff, then fold them into the sauce carefully but thoroughly, using a metal spoon.

Fill the orange shells with the soufflé mixture and set them on a baking sheet (or in a muffin pan to keep them steady). Bake the oranges in a pre-heated oven for 20 minutes at a temperature of 400°F (200°C, mark 6).

Serve the oranges immediately, dusted generously with sifted confectioners' sugar.

FRUITS RAFRAÎCHIS

A fresh-fruit salad is easily prepared from a selection of fruit whose flavors and colors harmonize. Chill the salad for a few hours so that the flavors can develop.

PREPARATION TIME: *30 min*
CHILLING TIME: *2–3 hours*
INGREDIENTS *(for 6):*
2 oranges
½ pound purple grapes
½ ripe honeydew melon
2–3 ripe pears
2 bananas
½ cup sugar
½ cup dry white wine
2 tablespoons kirsch

Choose a deep glass bowl as the serving dish, and arrange the prepared fruit in layers in the bowl.

With a sharp knife, cut a slice from the top and base of each orange, then cut down each orange in strips to remove the peel and all white pith. Ease out each orange segment and peel off the thin skin. Peel and halve the grapes and remove the seeds (page 152). Place in the bowl on top of the oranges and sprinkle with a little of the sugar. Remove the seeds from the melon, cut it in quarters lengthwise, cut away the peel and dice the flesh. Add the melon to the bowl with another sprinkling of sugar. Quarter, peel and core the pears, then slice them thinly. Peel the bananas and cut them in half lengthwise before dicing them. Put them in the bowl with the remaining sugar.

Mix the fruit carefully; pour over the white wine and the kirsch. As the fruit soaks in the liquid, press it down so that it is covered with juice and less likely to discolor.

Chill in the refrigerator for 2–3 hours. A jug of cream may be served separately.

CANDIED ORANGES GRAND MARNIER

A tangy dinner-party dessert becomes even more attractive to the hostess when it can be prepared the day before. It should be left to chill in the refrigerator.

PREPARATION TIME: *15 min*
COOKING TIME: *45 min*
CHILLING TIME: *2–3 hours*
INGREDIENTS *(for 6):*
6 oranges
¾ cup sugar
Juice of half lemon
2 tablespoons Grand Marnier

Cut a slice from the top and bottom of each orange, so that it will stand upright. Slice downwards through the orange skin, cutting away the peel and all the white pith, leaving only the orange flesh. Cut the oranges crosswise into slices and place them in a serving dish.

Select six of the larger pieces of peel and carefully cut away the pith. Shred the peel finely and put it in a saucepan. Cover with cold water, bring to the boil, then drain – this removes the bitter flavor of the peel. Cover the peel

ORANGE SOUFFLÉS

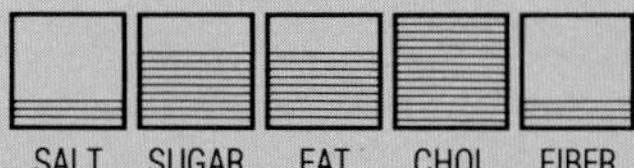

SALT SUGAR FAT CHOL FIBER

GLUTEN-FREE* WHOLEFOOD*
TOTAL CALORIES: ABOUT 925

The **sugar** can be reduced to 1 tablespoon, a very low level, provided the orange juice is only briefly heated: it tends to go sour if cooked. (Calories lost: up to 99.)
The high **cholesterol** level can be reduced to low by using only 1 egg yolk in the soufflé, with all the whites. The **fat** in the soufflé roux cannot be reduced, but can be rendered cholesterol-free by using vegetable fat, preferably soft margarine. (Calories lost: up to 160.)

FRUITS RAFRAÎCHIS

SALT SUGAR FAT CHOL FIBER

GLUTEN-FREE WHOLEFOOD*
TOTAL CALORIES: ABOUT 1030

The high added **sugar** level of this recipe can be reduced to nil, provided the fruit chosen is ripe. A small amount of sugar will be added by the kirsch, but too little to worry about. (Calories lost: up to 394.)

Freezing: ☑ if the bananas are omitted (they can be added just before serving).

CANDIED ORANGES GRAND MARNIER

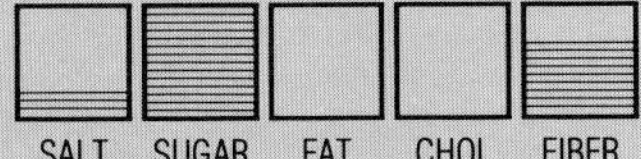

GLUTEN-FREE WHOLEFOOD*
TOTAL CALORIES: ABOUT 1030

The high **sugar** content of this recipe can be reduced simply by serving less caramel with each portion. ¼ cup sugar will produce enough to give the dish a characteristic flavor. If wished, add a little more lemon or orange juice, or Grand Marnier, and use a deep dish which will allow more of the fruit to be immersed in the liquid. This will give a medium sugar level. (Calories lost: up to 493.)

with fresh cold water; bring to the boil and simmer for about 30 minutes or until the orange peel is tender. Drain and set aside.

Put the sugar into a heavy-based saucepan, then stir with a wooden spoon over moderate heat until the sugar has melted and turned to caramel. Remove from the heat and add ½ cup of water: it will boil furiously. When the bubbling stops, return the pan to the heat and stir until the caramel has dissolved and a syrup has formed. Add the shredded peel and bring to the boil. Simmer for 2–3 minutes until the peel is glazed. Draw off the heat, cool for a few moments, then add the lemon juice and the Grand Marnier.

Spoon the syrup and candied peel over the oranges. Set aside until cold, basting the oranges occasionally with the syrup. Chill for several hours before serving with vanilla ice cream (page 125).

CRÈME CARAMEL À L'ORANGE

Caramel custard is a favorite international dessert, especially after a rich or spicy main course. In this Spanish recipe, the caramel custard is given additional flavor by fresh or frozen orange juice.

PREPARATION TIME: *30–35 min*
COOKING TIME: *25 min*
CHILLING TIME: *2 hours*
INGREDIENTS *(for 4):*
Rind of an orange
1¼ cups orange juice
3 eggs plus 3 egg yolks
2 tablespoons sugar
CARAMEL:
½ cup sugar

Finely grate the rind from the orange and leave it to steep in the orange juice.

Meanwhile, warm but do not grease four dariole molds (page 183) and make the caramel. Put the sugar and 1½ tablespoons of cold water in a small, heavy-based pan over low heat; stir gently until the syrup is clear. Turn up the heat and boil briskly, without stirring, until the syrup turns a golden caramel color. Pour a little caramel into each dariole mold. Twist the molds quickly until they are evenly coated with the caramel (use thick oven gloves to handle the molds as they will be very hot).

Heat the orange juice and rind in a pan over low heat. Whisk the whole eggs, egg yolks and sugar until creamy and when the orange juice is on the point of boiling, strain it into the eggs, stirring briskly. Pour the orange cream into the prepared dariole molds and set them in a roasting pan with 1 in of hot water.

Cover the molds with buttered wax paper and bake in the center of a pre-heated oven at 350°F (180°C, mark 4) for about 30 minutes or until completely set.

Remove the molds from the oven, leave them to cool and then chill in the refrigerator for at least 2 hours. Just before serving, unmold the caramel custards on to individual plates and serve with a jug of cream.

BAKED ORANGES

Orange sections are delicious baked in a rich, orange-flavored custard.

MARINATING TIME: *overnight*
PREPARATION TIME: *15 min*
COOKING TIME: *50 min*
INGREDIENTS *(for 4):*
4 navel oranges, sectioned
½ cup sugar
4 tablespoons orange liqueur
3 eggs
6 tablespoons heavy cream
*⅛ teaspoon salt**

Sprinkle the orange sections with half the sugar and layer them in a rectangular 1½ quart baking dish. Add the liqueur, cover, and refrigerate overnight.

Preheat the oven to 350°F (180°C, mark 4). Bake the oranges, covered, for 20 minutes. Drain and save ½ cup of the juice. Beat the eggs with the cream, the remaining sugar, the salt, and the reserved juice. Pour this mixture over the oranges and bake, uncovered, for 25 minutes or until the custard is slightly thickened.

Serve this dessert warm, rather than hot or cold.

CRÊPES SUZETTE

Crêpes with lemon are traditionally served on Shrove Tuesday in Britain. For a small dinner party, Crêpes Suzette are more interesting, especially cooked in a chafing dish.

PREPARATION TIME: *30 min*
COOKING TIME: *2–3 min*
INGREDIENTS *(for 6):*
1 cup all-purpose or self-rising flour
*Pinch of salt**
1 egg
1½ cups milk
3–4 tablespoons unsalted butter
¼ cup sugar
Juice of 2 oranges
Juice of half lemon
2–4 tablespoons orange liqueur

Sift the flour and salt into a large bowl. Using a wooden spoon make a hollow in the center of the flour and drop in the lightly beaten egg. Slowly pour half the milk into the flour, gradually working the flour into the milk. When all the flour is incorporated, beat the mixture with a wooden spoon, whisk, or rotary beater, until it becomes smooth and free of lumps. Allow it to stand for a few minutes. Then add the remainder of the milk, beating continuously until the batter is bubbly and has the consistency of light cream.

It is not necessary to leave the batter to stand for a while before being cooked, although this may be done if you wish. The batter may be left, covered, at room temperature for any time up to 4 hours, or up to 24 hours in a refrigerator. It may be necessary to add a little more liquid to restore the batter to its original

CRÈME CARAMEL À L'ORANGE

GLUTEN-FREE WHOLEFOOD*
TOTAL CALORIES: ABOUT 1090

The custard itself does not contain a large amount of **sugar**, although even this may be reduced by half if you prefer a less sweet flavor. The main sugar content, in the caramel, can only be reduced by putting less caramel in each small dish. A reasonable coating can be achieved with only ¼ cup sugar, but the total level for the dish is still fairly high. (Calories lost: up to 256.)
The **fat** and very high **cholesterol** levels come from the eggs and extra yolks, and these can be reduced if wished to 3 whole large eggs – still fairly high levels. (Calories lost: up to 195.)
Serve the dish with poached apricots in place of cream.

BAKED ORANGES

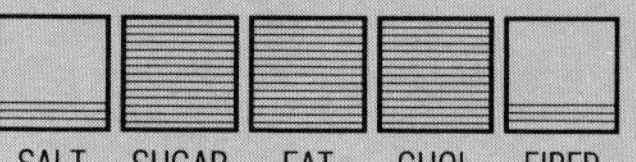

GLUTEN-FREE WHOLEFOOD*
TOTAL CALORIES: ABOUT 1350

The **sugar** level can easily be reduced to low by simply using only ½ tablespoon of brown sugar or honey or fruit sugar, sprinkled over the oranges before baking, and omitting sugar from the marinade. (Calories lost: up to 167.)
To reduce the **fat** and **cholesterol**, the egg-cream custard can be made less rich, using 2 eggs, ½ tablespoon sugar

or honey, and ½ cup thick low-fat yogurt or sour cream with the juice. If a more solid mixture is wanted, work 1 teaspoon cornstarch or arrowroot into the mixture. Omit the salt.
This gives the mixture a low fat and sugar content, but it still has a medium cholesterol level from the eggs. (Calories lost: up to 514.)

CRÊPES SUZETTE

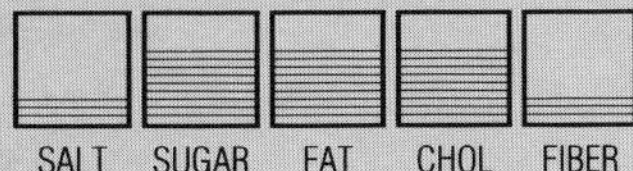

SALT SUGAR FAT CHOL FIBER

GLUTEN-FREE* WHOLEFOOD*
TOTAL CALORIES: ABOUT 1245

The amount of **sugar** can be reduced to low simply by adding only 4 teaspoonfuls to the sauce. (Calories lost: up to 117.)
To reduce the **fat** level to low, use skim milk in the batter, cook in a heavy pan brushed very lightly with oil and use only 1 teaspoon butter or vegetable margarine for the sauce. Make up the necessary volume of liquid with extra orange and lemon juice, if needed. (Calories lost: up to 246.)
For a strict low **cholesterol** regime, use the white of egg but not the yolk in making the crêpes. (Calories lost: up to 65.)
Gluten-free crêpes can be made by blending 6 tablespoons gluten-free flour with 2 tablespoons oil, 3 small eggs and about 1½ cups skim milk, or enough to make a thin batter.

Freezing: ✓ up to 2 months.

pouring consistency.

To make the crêpes, use a 6 in heavy-based shallow frying pan with sloping sides. Add just enough butter to gloss the pan to prevent the batter sticking. Fierce heat is necessary, and the pan should be really hot before the batter is poured in.

Pour in just enough batter to flow in a thin film over the bottom – tilting the pan to spread it. Use a jug or ladle for pouring in the batter. The heat is right if the underside of the crêpe becomes golden in 1 minute; adjust the heat to achieve this. Flip the crêpe over with a palette knife or spatula, or toss by flicking the wrist and lifting the pan away from the body. The other side of the crêpe should also be done in about 1 minute. (See the illustrations on page 170.)

Keep the crêpes hot between two plates over a saucepan of gently boiling water. Melt the butter in a large frying pan, stir in the sugar and cook gently until it is a golden-brown caramel. Add the strained orange and lemon juice and stir until the caramel has dissolved and become a thick sauce. Drop a flat crêpe into the pan, fold it in half and then in half again. Push to the side of the pan and add the next crêpe. When all the crêpes are in the hot sauce, add the orange liqueur and set it alight when hot. Shake the pan gently to incorporate the flamed liqueur evenly in the sauce.

Transfer the crêpes to a hot serving dish, pour over the sauce from the pan and serve at once.

PEACH MELBA

During the 1892-3 opera season Escoffier, then chef at the Savoy Hotel, London, created this now classic sweet for Dame Nellie Melba, the famous Australian opera singer. It originally consisted of peaches and vanilla ice cream, the raspberry purée being a later addition.

PREPARATION TIME: *12 min*
INGREDIENTS *(for 4)*:
2 large peaches
2 cups fresh raspberries
¼ cup sugar
1 pint vanilla ice cream

Put the peaches in a bowl and cover with boiling water. Leave for no more than 1 minute, then drain and peel them. Cut the peaches in half, carefully remove the pits and set the fruit aside. Rub the raspberries through a fine sieve into a mixing bowl; sweeten the resulting purée with the sugar.

Assemble the dessert by placing two scoops of vanilla ice cream (page 125) in each individual serving glass; place one peach half on top, rounded side up, and spoon over part of the raspberry purée. Serve at once.

PEACHES IN WINE

A very simple way to prepare peaches or nectarines, but one of the best if the fruit is really ripe. Nectarines, of course, need no peeling.

PREPARATION TIME: *20 min*
CHILLING TIME: *20 min*
INGREDIENTS *(for 4)*:
4 ripe yellow peaches
4 teaspoons sugar
6–8 tablespoons sweet white wine

Peel the peaches, cut them in half and remove the pits. Slice the peaches into individual serving glasses, sprinkle with sugar and spoon the wine over them. Chill for about 20 minutes.

PEACHES WITH GINGER

A good dessert for a dinner party as it is unusual and can be prepared well in advance.

PREPARATION TIME: *15 min*
CHILLING TIME: *3 hours*
INGREDIENTS *(for 4)*:
½ cup freshly squeezed orange juice
2 tablespoons honey
*Pinch of salt**
4 large, ripe peaches
2 tablespoons finely chopped candied ginger
Flaked coconut
Mint sprigs

Peel the peaches, cut them in half and remove the pits. Slice the peaches. Mix the orange juice, honey, and salt. Add the peach slices and ginger. Toss gently to mix. Cover and chill for about 3 hours. Spoon into sherbet glasses. Sprinkle with coconut and garnish with mint sprigs.

PEACH MELBA

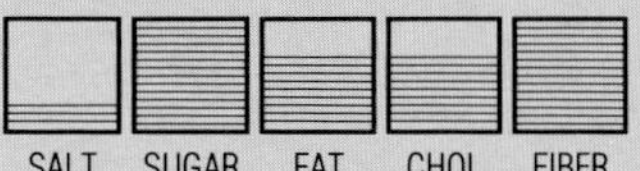

GLUTEN-FREE WHOLEFOOD*
TOTAL CALORIES: ABOUT 1875

Added **sugar** can be omitted as raspberries are sweet enough alone for most tastes. (Calories lost: up to 197.)
For low-**sugar**, low-**fat** and low-**cholesterol** versions of home-made ice cream, see the notes on page 125, or serve with fromage blanc instead. (Calories lost: up to 548.)

Freezing: ✓ up to 6 months for the raspberry purée and ice cream.

PEACHES IN WINE

GLUTEN-FREE WHOLEFOOD*
TOTAL CALORIES: ABOUT 355

You may prefer to omit the sugar, gaining any sweetness required from the wine, or replace it with clear honey drizzled over the peaches.

PEACHES WITH GINGER

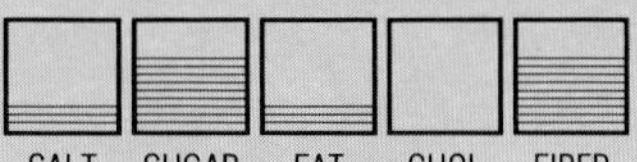

GLUTEN-FREE WHOLEFOOD
TOTAL CALORIES: ABOUT 385

To reduce the **sugar** level to low, halve the amount of honey added, or use only 2 teaspoonfuls. (Calories lost: up to 40.)

PEACHES WITH SOUR CREAM

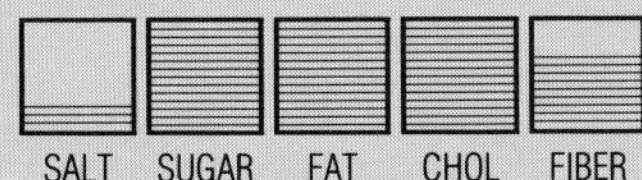

GLUTEN-FREE WHOLEFOOD*
TOTAL CALORIES: ABOUT 1970

The amount of **sugar** is difficult to calculate as the peaches will only absorb some of the sugar in the syrup in which they are poached. For a lower amount, poach peaches in a very little water (an ideal job for a microwave or pressure cooker), then, if they are not sweet enough, drizzle with a very little honey or fruit sugar before covering. (Calories lost: up to 807.)
In place of sour cream, which can be around 18% fat, use low-fat sour cream (5–10% fat), or thick low-fat yogurt blended if wished half and half with quark. This will give low to medium **fat** and **cholesterol**. (Calories lost: up to 449.)

Freezing: ✓ up to 3 months.

BAKED STUFFED PEACHES

GLUTEN-FREE* WHOLEFOOD*
TOTAL CALORIES: ABOUT 980

The cookies can be fairly high in **sugar** unless you make them yourself, using the recipe on page 127, which will give a moderate overall sugar level. (Calories lost: up to 328.)

PEACHES WITH SOUR CREAM

Golden firm peaches are at their best and least expensive in the summer. They make refreshing summer desserts – on their own, poached in white wine or cooked in a pastry case. Here, poached peaches are served lightly chilled with a sour cream topping.

PREPARATION TIME: *35 min*
CHILLING TIME: *30 min*
INGREDIENTS *(for 6):*
6 large peaches
1 cup vanilla sugar (page 184)
Granulated sugar
1¼ cups sour cream
GARNISH:
3 tablespoons light brown sugar or ¼ cup toasted sliced almonds

Dissolve the vanilla sugar in 1¼ cups of water in a small pan and cook over moderate heat. Simmer this syrup for 5 minutes.

Wash and dry the peaches thoroughly, then poach them lightly in the syrup for 5–10 minutes, depending on the ripeness of the fruit.

Lift the peaches from the syrup, leave to cool slightly, then peel off the skin and cut the peaches in half. Remove the pits, and slice the peaches into a serving bowl, one layer at a time, sprinkling each layer with a little granulated sugar. Strain the syrup and set aside for another use.

Cover the top of the peaches with a thick layer of sour cream and chill for 30 minutes. Just before serving, sprinkle the top with brown sugar or toasted flaked almonds.

BAKED STUFFED PEACHES

Traditionally this Italian dessert is made with amaretti – tiny macaroons made from apricot kernels or bitter almonds. If these are unobtainable, ratafia cookies make a good substitute (see recipes on pages 84 and 127).

PREPARATION TIME: *20 min*
COOKING TIME: *20–30 min*
INGREDIENTS *(for 4–6):*
4 large peaches
4 teaspoons sugar
1 tablespoon unsalted butter
1 egg yolk
2 ounces amaretti or ratafia cookies

Cream together the sugar, butter and egg yolk in a small bowl. Crush the cookies with a rolling pin and add these to the creamed mixture.

Pour boiling water over the peaches and leave for 2–3 minutes. Peel off the skin, halve the peaches and remove the pits. Enlarge the cavities slightly by scooping out some of the flesh with a pointed teaspoon. Add this pulp to the egg mixture and blend well.

Pile the stuffing into the peach halves and arrange them in a buttered fireproof dish. Bake on the center shelf of a pre-heated oven, at 350°F (180°C, mark 4), for 20–30 minutes or until the peaches are soft, but still shapely.

Serve the peaches warm, with a bowl of cream.

PEARS IN CHOCOLATE JACKETS

Large ripe winter pears, such as 'Comice,' are ideal for this attractive dessert of chocolate-covered pears. It makes a good choice for a dinner party as it can be prepared a day in advance and left in the refrigerator.

PREPARATION TIME: *20min*
COOKING TIME: *20 min*
CHILLING TIME: *2–3 hours*
INGREDIENTS *(for 4)*:
4 ripe dessert pears
1½ tablespoons shelled walnuts
2 tablespoons glacé cherries
4 ounces semisweet chocolate
3 tablespoons cold black coffee
2 tablespoons unsalted butter
2–4 teaspoons rum
2 eggs
GARNISH:
Angelica, or whipped cream and chopped pistachio nuts

Peel the pears thinly and cut out the cores from the base of the fruit, leaving the stem and top intact. Cut a small sliver from the base of each pear so that it will stand upright. Roughly chop and mix together the walnuts and cherries and press a little of this mixture into the core cavities of the pears. Stand the pears upright in one large or four small shallow serving dishes.

Break up the chocolate and put it in a bowl with the coffee. Stand the bowl over a saucepan of boiling water and stir occasionally until the chocolate has melted. Remove the bowl from the heat and stir in first the butter and then the rum. Separate the eggs and beat the yolks, one at a time, into the chocolate mixture. Whisk the egg whites until stiff, but still moist, and fold them carefully into the chocolate. The consistency should be similar to that of a mousse.

Spoon the chocolate mixture over the pears until they are evenly coated. Soften the angelica strips in hot water, cut into ½ in lengths and slice them crosswise into eight diamond shapes. Make a small slit on either side of each pear stalk and insert an angelica diamond, twisting them to resemble small leaves.

Chill the chocolate pears in the refrigerator for 2–3 hours or overnight.

Piped whipped cream and chopped pistachio nuts are also attractive garnishes.

PEARS IN CHOCOLATE JACKETS

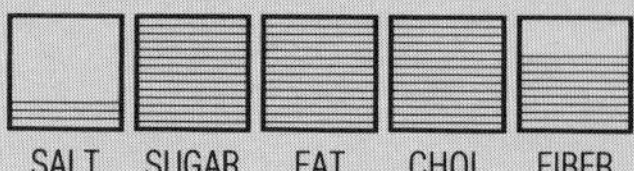

GLUTEN-FREE
TOTAL CALORIES: ABOUT 1145

For a low added **sugar** content, omit the glacé cherries, which are preserved by heavy sugaring, and replace the chocolate (typically 56% sugar) with no-added-sugar carob. (Calories lost: up to 34.)
These two changes will also render this dessert **wholefood**, as cherries are artificially colored red. (Angelica is also colored, but often remains uneaten.)
The **fat** and **cholesterol** level can be limited to medium only by giving the pears a thinner coating. (Calories lost: up to 234.)

POIRES FLAMBÉES

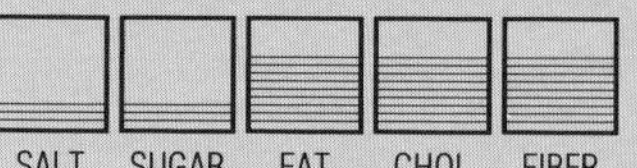

GLUTEN-FFREE WHOLEFOOD
TOTAL CALORIES: ABOUT 735

The **fat** level can be reduced to low by replacing the heavy cream with 2 tablespoons quark or low-fat sour cream. (Calories lost: up to 111.)
For low **cholesterol**, replace the cream as suggested above, and use 1 teaspoon of butter and 2 of vegetable margarine for cooking the pears.

CHINESE PEARS

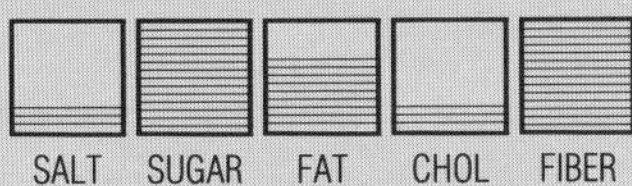

GLUTEN-FREE WHOLEFOOD
TOTAL CALORIES: ABOUT 1750

Most of the added **sugar** comes from the red currant jelly. To avoid this, make the sauce from puréed currants or raspberries, lightly sweetened with a very small amount of sugar or honey if necessary. The high-sugar ginger syrup can also be reduced, adding a little ground ginger or grated fresh ginger if liked to step up the ginger flavor. This will give a low sugar level. (Calories lost: up to 315.)
The **fat** level comes mainly from the pine nuts, and these can be reduced by half if wished, giving a low fat level. (Calories lost: up to 241.)
Cholesterol can be eliminated or reduced by replacing butter with vegetable fat completely or in part.

POIRES FLAMBÉES

This French recipe for pears in brandy is an ideal dessert to cook in a chafing dish at the table. Fresh firm peaches and apricots are also excellent cooked in this way.

PREPARATION TIME: *15 min*
COOKING TIME: *10 min*
INGREDIENTS *(for 4):*
4 ripe firm dessert pears
4 pieces stem ginger
2 tablespoons unsalted butter
2 tablespoons brandy
1–2 tablespoons ginger syrup
2 tablespoons heavy cream

Peel the pears thinly, cut them in half and carefully scoop out the cores with a pointed teaspoon. Quarter each piece of stem ginger and set aside.

Heat the butter in a chafing dish, a shallow flameproof dish, or a frying pan over moderate heat. Fry the pears, cut side down, until golden brown. Turn the pears over and fry the other side. Fill a warmed tablespoon with brandy, set it alight and pour it over the pears. Repeat with the remaining brandy.

Arrange the pears on individual plates, placing two ginger pieces in each cavity. Add the ginger syrup and cream to the pan juices and stir over gentle heat until well blended and heated through. Spoon a little sauce over each portion and serve the pears immediately.

CHINESE PEARS

Despite its name this unusual and aromatic dessert is French in origin. It is sweet and rich, suitable for a dinner party. Bartlett or other squat dessert pears are excellent for this recipe.

PREPARATION TIME: *35 min*
COOKING TIME: *35 min*
INGREDIENTS *(for 6):*
6 large ripe pears
½ cup golden raisins
¾ cup pine nuts
2 tablespoons honey
2 tablespoons unsalted butter
½–1 cup dry white wine
2 tablespoons ginger syrup
½ cup red currant jelly

Peel the pears thinly and cut a small slice from the base of each, so that it will stand upright. Remove a ¾–1 in lid from the top of each pear and scoop out the core and seeds. Roughly chop the raisins and pine nuts, mix with the honey and spoon the mixture into the pear cavities. Replace the lids.

Grease an ovenproof dish with the butter and stand the pears in the dish together with any remaining raisin mixture. Pour over the white wine and cover the dish with foil. Bake the pears in the center of an oven pre-heated to 350–375°F (180–190°C, mark 4–5) for about 30 minutes or until tender – the time varies according to the type and ripeness of the pears.

When cooked, place the pears in individual serving bowls and keep them warm in the oven. Pour the cooking juices into a small saucepan and add the ginger syrup and red currant jelly. Boil over moderate heat until the jelly has dissolved. Pour this sauce carefully over the pears and serve at once.

FRUIT SALAD IN A PINEAPPLE

This uses the pineapple shell itself as a container which is very effective. Although the more homely apples and pears have not been used here, there is no reason why they should not be.

PREPARATION TIME: *30 min*
STANDING TIME: *1–2 hours*
INGREDIENTS *(for 6):*
½ cup sugar
2 tablespoons lemon juice
1 tablespoon orange liqueur or kirsch
½ pound green or purple grapes (optional)
1 pineapple
2 oranges
2 bananas

Put the sugar, with ½ cup of water, in a small pan, heat gently to dissolve the sugar, then bring to the boil for 2–3 minutes. Set aside until cold, then add the lemon juice and liqueur and pour into a large serving bowl.

Peel the grapes if used and remove the seeds (page 152). Add the grapes to the sugar syrup in the bowl. Peel and cut oranges into segments, and squeeze the orange membranes into the bowl. Peel and slice the bananas and add, with the oranges, to the bowl. Turn the fruit in the syrup. Cover and leave in a cool place, preferably not the refrigerator, for 1–2 hours to develop the flavors.

When fresh strawberries are available, include 1½–2 cups hulled and halved small strawberries. Pitted cherries, plums, halved apricots, sliced peaches and red currants are also good for fresh fruit salads, as are kiwi fruit, grapefruit and melon.

CRÊPES GEORGETTE

These crêpes with a rum-flavored pineapple filling are said to have been created for Georgette Leblanc, close friend of the Belgian poet Maeterlinck.

PREPARATION TIME: *30 min*
COOKING TIME: *30 min*
INGREDIENTS *(for 6):*
1½ cups crêpe batter (page 170)
6 pineapple rings
1¼ cups vanilla-flavored confectioner's custard (page 97)
3–4 tablespoons rum
¼ cup melted butter
Confectioners' sugar

Prepare the crêpe batter and use it to make 12 very thin crêpes. Drain and finely chop the pineapple rings. Make the confectioner's custard (crème pâtissière) and flavor it with 2–4 teaspoons rum. Mix the chopped pineapple into the cream. Put a tablespoon or so of the warm cream mixture in the center of each crêpe and fold the two sides over it.

Place the stuffed crêpes side by side in a well-buttered, warmed, flameproof dish. Brush them with melted butter, and dredge generously with sifted confectioners' sugar. Heat a metal skewer and press it in a criss-cross pattern on to the sugar.

Set the dish under a hot broiler for about 5 minutes to glaze the sugar topping. Just before serving, warm the remaining rum in a small pan, set it alight and pour it over the crêpes.

FRUIT SALAD IN A PINEAPPLE

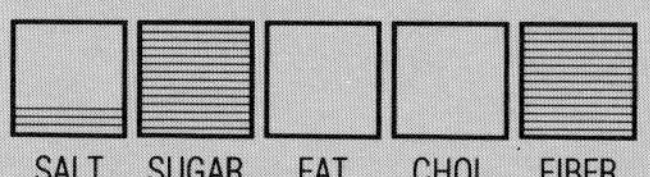

SALT SUGAR FAT CHOL FIBER

GLUTEN-FREE WHOLEFOOD*
TOTAL CALORIES: ABOUT 935

Reduce the added **sugar** level to very low (only that contained in the liqueur) by omitting the sugar syrup, using apple juice to provide extra liquid if wished. (Calories lost: up to 394.)

Freezing: ✓ up to 2 months if bananas are not included.

CRÊPES GEORGETTE

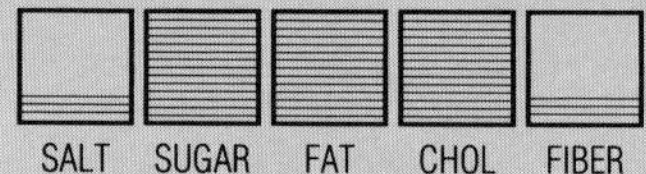

SALT SUGAR FAT CHOL FIBER

GLUTEN-FREE* WHOLEFOOD*
TOTAL CALORIES: ABOUT 2330

For low **sugar**, make the alternative confectioner's custard or pastry cream suggested in the notes on page 97, and instead of dredging with confectioners' sugar, trickle a little jam made without added sugar over the crêpes. Put under the broiler for 5 minutes for the jam to melt and form a glaze. (Calories lost: up to 338.)
For low **fat** and **cholesterol**, see the notes on crêpes on page 105, and on pastry cream on page 97. Instead of brushing with the melted butter, use a tablespoon or two of low-fat sour cream. (Calories lost: up to 739.)

Freezing: ✓ up to 1 month.

BAKED PINEAPPLE FLAMBÉ

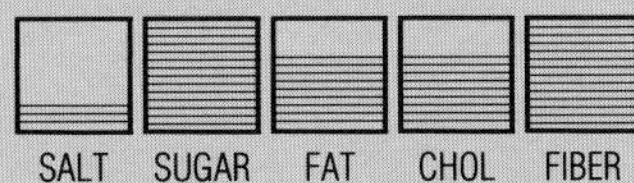

GLUTEN-FREE WHOLEFOOD
TOTAL CALORIES: ABOUT 1530

For low **sugar**, add only 2 tablespoons sugar to the mixture, and use marmalade made with no added sugar. (Calories lost: up to 290.)
The butter can be reduced to 1 tablespoon, giving an overall low **fat** and **cholesterol** content. (Calories lost: up to 259.)

Freezing: ✓ up to 2 months.

PLUMS IN WINE

GLUTEN-FREE WHOLEFOOD*
TOTAL CALORIES: ABOUT 1160

For low **sugar**, poach the fruit in wine only, in two batches or more to enable the liquid to cover the fruit.
If wished, add a spoonful of honey to the wine and 2 tablespoons of water. Using this method, the syrup will not have the volume to require boiling down. As it will not thicken without sugar, stir in 1 heaping teaspoonful of arrowroot that has been moistened to a smooth paste with cold water, and simmer for a few minutes until mixture clears. (Calories lost: up to 246.)
Serve with low-fat yogurt or sour cream in place of light cream.

Freezing: ✓ up to 2 months.

BAKED PINEAPPLE FLAMBÉ

A very successful combination of fruit. Any marmalade can be used, but grapefruit marmalade gives an interesting flavor. Greengages or apricots could be used instead of red plums.

PREPARATION TIME: *30 min*
COOKING TIME: *20 min*
INGREDIENTS *(for 6):*
1 medium pineapple
1 pound plums
4 tablespoons marmalade
Grated rind and juice of a lemon
½ teaspoon ground cinnamon
⅔ cup dark brown sugar
¼ cup unsalted butter
4 tablespoons white rum

Slice, peel and core the pineapple. Cut the slices in half. Cut the plums in half, and remove the pits. Place the pineapple and plums in a wide shallow casserole with a lid.

In a small pan, heat together the marmalade, lemon rind and juice, cinnamon, sugar and butter. Stir well and pour the mixture over the fruit. Cover and cook in a pre-heated oven at 400°F (200°C, mark 6) for about 20 minutes. Just before serving, place the rum in a warm ladle, ignite with a match and pour it flaming over the fruit.

PLUMS IN WINE

The flavor of plums is brought out to the full by poaching them in a syrupy wine and serving them while still warm.

PREPARATION TIME: *5 min*
COOKING TIME: *30 min*
INGREDIENTS *(for 6):*
1½–2 pounds firm red-fleshed plums
6 tablespoons sugar
1¼ cups tawny port, medium dry sherry or Madeira
2 tablespoons sliced almonds

Dissolve the sugar in 1¼ cups of water and simmer for 10 minutes. Stir in the wine and bring the syrup gently up to simmering point again.

Remove the stalks from the plums, wash and dry them. Add the plums, one at a time, to the simmering syrup. Cover the pan with a lid and remove from the heat. Leave the plums in the syrup for 10 minutes.

Lift out the plums with a slotted spoon and put them in a serving dish. Cover the dish with a plate or foil, and leave in a warm place. Boil the syrup over high heat until it has reduced by about one-third and thickened slightly. Pour it over the plums.

Meanwhile, toast the sliced almonds for about 5 minutes in the oven until golden. Scatter these over the plums and serve at once, with a jug of light cream.

PLUM AND CINNAMON PIE

You could also use fresh plums for this, poached in the same way as the apricots on page 88.

PREPARATION TIME: *5 min*
COOKING TIME: *40 min*
STANDING TIME: *1 hour*
INGREDIENTS *(for 6):*
1 quantity stirred pastry (page 172)
2 16-ounce cans yellow plums
1 tablespoon fine tapioca
¼ teaspoon powdered cinnamon
2 tablespoons butter
1 egg white
Granulated sugar

Drain the plums, reserving the syrup, and remove the pits. Blend the tapioca and cinnamon in a bowl with 6 tablespoons of the plum syrup and leave it to stand for 30 minutes.

Roll out half the prepared pastry and use it to line a 10 in pie plate. Mix the plums with the tapioca mixture and spoon it over the pastry base; dot with butter. Roll out the remaining pastry for the lid and cover the pie. Seal the edges and make a slit in the lid. Brush the top with beaten egg white and dust generously with sugar. Chill for 30 minutes.

Set the pie on a heated baking sheet and bake in the center of a pre-heated oven at 400°F (200°C, mark 6) for about 40 minutes. Serve the pie warm, with whipped cream.

RASPBERRY YOGURT SHERBET

A sherbet is welcome on a hot summer's evening. One of the most delicious is made from raspberries. Adding yogurt to this sherbet enhances its flavor.

PREPARATION TIME: *15 min*
CHILLING TIME: *2–3 hours*
INGREDIENTS *(for 6):*
2 cups raspberries
4–6 tablespoons sugar
1¼ cups plain yogurt
Juice of half lemon
1 envelope unflavored gelatin
2 egg whites

Make a thick purée from the raspberries by rubbing them through a sieve and into a bowl. Sweeten to taste with the sugar. Stir the yogurt and the lemon juice into the sweetened purée.

Put 4 tablespoons of cold water in a small bowl and sprinkle the gelatin over it. Leave the gelatin to stand for 5 minutes and then set the bowl over a pan of hot water. Stir until the gelatin has dissolved and the liquid is clear.

Add the liquid gelatin to the raspberry purée. In a separate bowl, beat the egg whites until stiff but not dry, and then fold them into the purée.

Spoon the mixture into a container, cover with a lid and set in the freezer. When almost frozen, beat the purée with a rotary whisk. Then allow the mixture to freeze firmly.

PLUM AND CINNAMON PIE

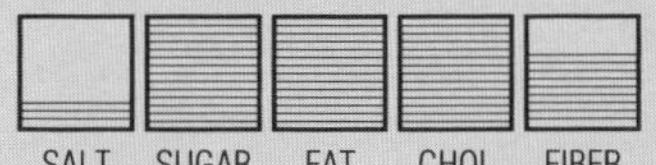

SALT SUGAR FAT CHOL FIBER

GLUTEN-FREE* WHOLEFOOD*
TOTAL CALORIES: ABOUT 3330

The high level of **sugar** typical of canned fruit can be avoided by using fresh fruit, briefly poaching in a little water, then sweetening to taste with as little honey or sugar as possible. This should give a low to medium sugar level depending on how sweet the fruit is. Alternatively, poach with 1 cup dates, pitted, which have been stewed and liquidized to a thick purée. These will give sweetness to the plums without adding sugar as such. Be sparing with sugar sprinkled on pie. (Calories lost: up to 446.)
Stirred pastry has even more **fat** than standard. To reduce, switch to standard pastry using 1 part fat to 2 of flour or use a biscuit dough instead. (Calories lost: up to 1105.)
If the fat used is vegetable, the dish will be low in **cholesterol**. Dotting with butter can be omitted. Using millet flakes would provide a more nutritious filling than tapioca.

Freezing: ✓ up to 6 months.

RASPBERRY YOGURT SHERBET

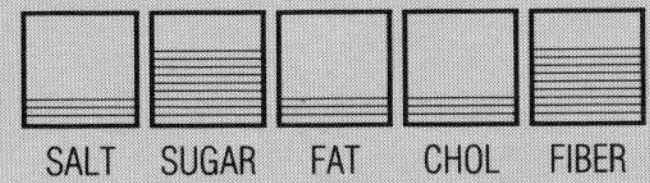
SALT SUGAR FAT CHOL FIBER

GLUTEN-FREE WHOLEFOOD*
TOTAL CALORIES: ABOUT 575

If wished, little or no **sugar** can be added to the raspberries, reducing the sugar level to low or nil. (Calories lost: up to 296.)

Freezing: ☑ up to 1 month.

HAZELNUT GANTOIS

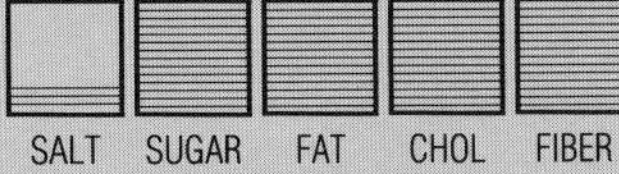
SALT SUGAR FAT CHOL FIBER

GLUTEN-FREE* WHOLEFOOD*
TOTAL CALORIES: ABOUT 2995

For a moderate **sugar** content, use only 3 tablespoons sugar in the dough, and halve the amount used for the caramel topping. (Calories lost: up to 187.)
For low **fat** and **cholesterol**, use only ¼ cup butter (or replace some or all of it with vegetable margarine); use quark or fromage blanc instead of cream. (Calories lost: up to 950.)

Freezing: ☑ up to 3 months (cookie layers only).

HAZELNUT GANTOIS

A gantois, or Flemish pastry, consists of crunchy cookies layered with fresh fruit and whipped cream. The pudding is topped with crisp golden caramel.

PREPARATION TIME: *1 hour*
CHILLING TIME: *30 min*
COOKING TIME: *25–30 min*
INGREDIENTS *(for 4–6):*
1 cup shelled hazelnuts
1 cup plus 2 tablespoons flour
¼ cup plus 1 teaspoon sugar
6 tablespoons unsalted butter
2 pints raspberries or 6–8 peaches
1¼ cups whipping cream
CARAMEL TOPPING:
6 tablespoons sugar

Put the hazelnuts in the broiler pan and broil under medium heat, shaking the pan frequently, until the nuts are toasted. Rub them in a colander with a dry cloth to remove the skins. Measure ¼ cup of the nuts, chop them coarsely and set aside. Grind the remainder in a coffee mill or chop them very finely.

Sift the flour into a mixing bowl and add the ground nuts and the sugar. Rub in the butter until the mixture resembles fine breadcrumbs, then knead lightly for a few minutes. Chill the dough in a refrigerator for at least 30 minutes, or until quite firm.

Meanwhile, pick over the raspberries and hull them, or peel the peaches and cut them into thin slices.

Shape the firm dough into a thick sausage, on a lightly floured board. Divide the dough into four equal pieces and roll each piece out to a 7 in circle, about ⅛ in thick. Lift the circles carefully onto greased baking sheets. Bake in the center of a pre-heated oven, at 350°F (180°C, mark 4) for 15 minutes or until the cookies are golden brown and firm. Remove to a wire rack and leave to cool.

For the caramel topping, put the sugar and 2 tablespoons water in a small pan over low heat. Stir until the sugar has completely dissolved. Turn up the heat and boil the syrup briskly, without stirring, until it is caramel-colored.

Pour enough of the caramel over one cookie circle to cover it, spreading it evenly with an oiled knife. Sprinkle the coarsely chopped nuts around the edge of the caramel-covered cookie, and arrange a quarter of the raspberries or peach slices in the center. Trickle over the remaining caramel or pull this into thin threads to make a spun sugar veil on top of the cookies.

Whip the cream and sweeten to taste with a little sugar. Assemble the cake by spreading the cream in equal layers over the remaining three cookies; arrange the fruit evenly on each layer. Put the cookies on top of each other, finishing with the caramel-topped cookie. Serve at once.

RASPBERRIES WITH COEUR À LA CRÈME

A classic French summer dessert is this combination of soft fruit and home-made cream cheese. Traditionally, the cheese is set in little heart-shaped molds (which are now widely available) and served with cream poured over. Strawberries can be served in the same way.

PREPARATION TIME: *20 min*
CHILLING TIME: *12 hours*
INGREDIENTS *(for 4–6):*
1 quart raspberries
1 cup unsalted cream cheese or cottage cheese
1¼ cups heavy cream
4 teaspoons sugar
2 egg whites
½ cup light cream

Rub or press the cheese through a fine sieve and mix with the heavy cream before stirring in the sugar. (Cream cheese makes a richer, denser mixture than cottage cheese.) Beat the egg whites until stiff, but not dry, and fold them into the cheese and cream.

Line the heart-shaped molds with the fine cheesecloth (to make unmolding easier). Alternatively, use a 6 in wide, shallow cake pan as a mold. Pierce a few holes in the base for draining, and line the pan with cheesecloth.

Spoon the cheese and cream mixture into the prepared molds and place them on a wide plate or in a sieve. Leave in the refrigerator overnight to drain and chill.

Just before serving, unmold the cream cheese on to a serving plate. Pour over the light cream, and serve with the fresh raspberries or other soft fruit, or with a sweetened fruit sauce.

RASPBERRY MOUSSE

The texture of this mousse is light and creamy; for a firmer set increase the gelatin to 4 teaspoons.

PREPARATION TIME: *45 min*
SETTING TIME: *2 hours*
INGREDIENTS *(for 6):*
2 pints raspberries
3 whole eggs
2 egg yolks
½ cup sugar
1 envelope (1 tablespoon) unflavored gelatin
3 tablespoons water
1¼ cups heavy cream
Grated chocolate

Set eight raspberries aside for garnish and put the remainder (hulled and washed) in a pan and simmer for about 5 minutes until soft. Rub the raspberries through a sieve – the purée should measure about 1 cup.

Put the whole eggs and the egg yolks in a bowl, together with the sugar. Place the bowl over a pan of hot water and whisk the eggs until thick and fluffy. Take the bowl from the pan and set in a basin of chilled water or ice cubes. Whisk the egg mixture until cool.

Dissolve the gelatin in the water, stir it quickly into the raspberry purée, and then whisk this into the egg mixture. Whip the cream lightly and fold it into the raspberries when beginning to set. Spoon into a serving dish and chill until set.

Just before serving, sprinkle coarsely grated chocolate over the mousse and decorate with the whole raspberries.

SUMMER PUDDING

The origin of this classic English pudding is unknown, but as early as the 18th century it was served to patients who were not allowed rich pastry desserts. This does not in the least make it invalid food–it is a delicious composition of fresh summer fruits.

PREPARATION TIME: *30–40 min*
CHILLING TIME: *8 hours*
INGREDIENTS *(for 6):*
6–8 slices stale, crustless bread, ½ in thick
1½ pounds mixed soft fruits
½ cup sugar

Strawberries, raspberries, red and black currants, as well as black cherries, are all suitable for this dish, and can be mixed according to taste and availability. The more varied the fruits, the tastier the result, but avoid using too many black currants as their flavor and color will tend to dominate the pudding.

Line the bottom of a 1 quart soufflé dish or pudding basin with one or two slices of bread to cover the bottom completely. Line the sides of the dish with more bread, if necessary cut to shape, so that the bread fits closely together.

Hull and carefully wash the fruit, and remove the pits from the cherries. Put the fruit in a wide heavy-based pan and sprinkle the sugar over it. Bring to the boil over very low heat, and cook for 2–3 minutes only, until the sugar melts and the juices begin to run. Remove the pan from the heat and set aside 1–2 tablespoons of the fruit juices. Spoon the fruit and remaining juice into the prepared dish and cover the surface closely

RASPBERRIES WITH COEUR À LA CRÈME

GLUTEN-FREE WHOLEFOOD*
TOTAL CALORIES: ABOUT 2980

For very low **sugar**, sweeten with 2 teaspoons honey instead of sugar. (Calories lost: up to 52.)
For low **fat** and **cholesterol**, use cottage cheese rather than cream cheese and quark or fromage blanc instead of heavy cream; replace the light cream with puréed soft fruit. (Calories lost: up to 2161.)

RASPBERRY MOUSSE

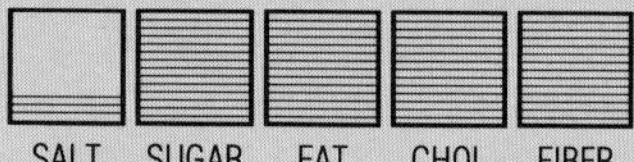

GLUTEN-FREE WHOLEFOOD*
TOTAL CALORIES: ABOUT 2800

To reduce the amount of added **sugar** to medium, simply halve the amount added to the egg mixture. You cannot eliminate the sugar, as the sweetness of the raspberries will not cover the large volume of other ingredients. (Calories lost: up to 197.)
This recipe is high **cholesterol** because each person eats almost a whole egg yolk plus a substantial amount of heavy cream. To reduce cholesterol to low, use only 2 egg yolks beaten with about 2–3 ounces silken tofu plus 1 egg white. Beat 2 more whites stiff and fold into the mixture after the cream. This will also reduce the amount of **fat** in the recipe, partly through using fewer yolks and partly because the amount of cream can be halved,

with the stiff egg whites making up the volume. For a lower fat dish, replace the remaining cream with quark mixed half and half with thick yogurt. (Calories lost: up to 1489.) Increase the amount of gelatin to 4 teaspoons to give a firmer set, as egg whites are less stable when beaten than cream.

Freezing: ✓ up to 2 months.

SUMMER PUDDING

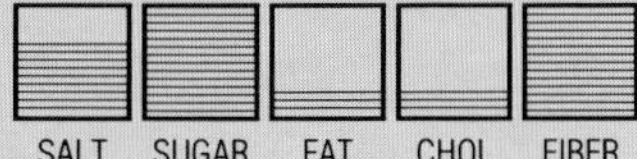

GLUTEN-FREE* WHOLEFOOD*
TOTAL CALORIES: ABOUT 1290

To reduce the amount of added **sugar** to low or zero, replace ½ pound of the fruit with ¼ pound dried apricots, stewed and puréed. This will sweeten the fruit without overpowering its flavor. Then taste and only add sugar cautiously if needed. (Calories lost: up to 172.)

Freezing: ✓ up to 2 months.

with the rest of the bread.

Put a plate that fits the inside of the dish on top of the pudding and weight it down with a heavy can or jar. Leave the pudding in the refrigerator to chill for 8 hours.

Before serving, remove the weight and plate. Cover the dish with the serving plate and turn upside-down to unmold the pudding. Use the reserved fruit juice to pour over any parts of the bread which have not been soaked through and colored by the fruit juices.

SOFT FRUIT GÂTEAU

This dessert cake consists of a sponge case filled with fresh fruit and cream. It can be assembled to look like a jewelry box by setting the sponge lid at an angle and letting strawberries, raspberries or stalks of red currants appear over the edge.

PREPARATION TIME: *50–60 min*
COOKING TIME: *15 min*
INGREDIENTS *(for 6–8):*
4 eggs
$\frac{1}{2}$ cup granulated sugar
1 cup self-rising flour
*$\frac{1}{4}$ teaspoon salt**
$\frac{1}{2}$–$\frac{3}{4}$ pound mixed soft fruit (strawberries, raspberries, red currants)
$1\frac{1}{4}$ cups heavy cream
$\frac{3}{4}$ cup confectioners' sugar

Lightly grease and flour a rectangular cake pan, approximately 14 in by 8 in. Put the eggs and sugar into a deep mixing bowl, and whisk until the eggs are pale and thick enough for the whisk to leave a trail. Sift the flour and salt together, and fold gently into the creamed egg mixture.

Spoon this sponge mixture into the prepared pan, spreading it evenly and making sure the

SOFT FRUIT GÂTEAU

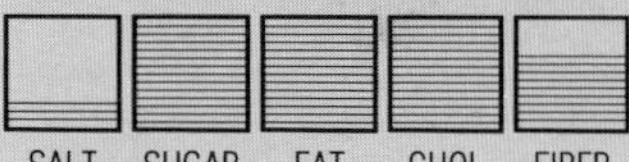

GLUTEN-FREE* WHOLEFOOD*
TOTAL CALORIES: ABOUT 2820

To reduce the amount of **sugar** in this dish is impossible, as it is necessary to the structure of the sponge. Alternatives are to make a smaller sponge base, using 2 eggs, $\frac{1}{4}$ cup sugar and $\frac{1}{2}$ cup flour, and/or increase the amount of fruit topping.
This will give a low sugar content, and halves the **cholesterol** from the eggs.
Most of the **fat** comes from the cream, and this can be replaced with quark, blended smoothly with honey to taste (about 1 pound quark with 2 tablespoons honey), and a few drops of vanilla if wished. This gives a more cheesecake-like base. Some of the quark can be piped, just like cream, to decorate. These changes give a low-fat, low-cholesterol dish. (Calories lost: up to 1751.)
Gluten-free sponge cake can be made, using the same amount of sugar and eggs with $\frac{1}{2}$ cup plus 2 tablespoons gluten-free flour.

Freezing: √ up to 6 months (sponge only).

RHUBARB CRUMBLE

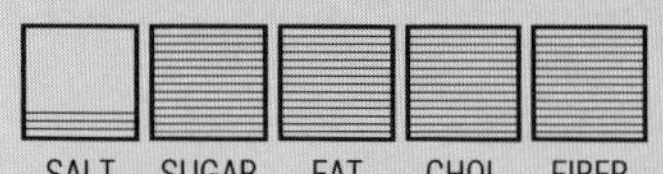

GLUTEN-FREE* WHOLEFOOD*
TOTAL CALORIES: ABOUT 2635

The high level of added **sugar** can be reduced to low by these changes: mix $1\frac{1}{2}$ pounds

rhubarb with ½ pound stewed dried apricots, dates or golden raisins (¼ pound dried weight) that have been puréed. This will reduce the need for sugar to 1–2 tablespoons, with either honey or fruit sugar giving excellent results. Dates are the sweetest of the three. In the topping, the amount of sugar need only be 2 tablespoons. (Calories lost: up to 315.)
For a medium **fat** level rub only 3 tablespoons fat into the flour. The remaining fat from the cream can be avoided by replacing this with quark, flavored with honey and ginger, or for a softer consistency, mixed with low-fat yogurt. (Calories lost: up to 833.)
If this is done, and vegetable fat (such as soft vegetable margarine) is used, the **cholesterol** will be very low.

Freezing: ✓ up to 3 months.
Microwave: ✓

STRAWBERRY SYLLABUB TRIFLE

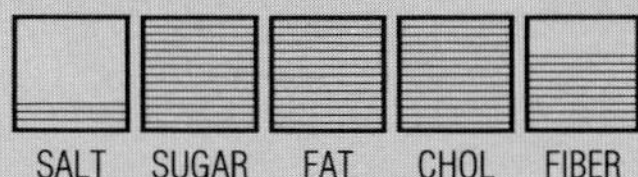

GLUTEN-FREE* WHOLEFOOD*
TOTAL CALORIES: ABOUT 3185

The **sugar** can be reduced to medium by adding only ¼ cup to the egg whites. (Calories lost: up to 493.)
The **fat** and **cholesterol** can be reduced to low by replacing the cream with ½ cup quark whipped with ½ cup thick low-fat sour cream or yogurt, flavoring with honey if wished. (Calories lost: up to 1192.)
Macaroons are often **gluten-free**, made with rice and almonds, but check the ingredients list on the package.

corners are filled. Bake just above the center of a pre-heated oven at 375°F (190°C, mark 5) for 15 minutes, or until the sponge is golden and firm to the touch.

Turn the sponge on to a wire rack and leave to cool completely, preferably overnight. Meanwhile, clean the fruit and wash and drain it thoroughly on absorbent kitchen paper towels. Whip the heavy cream until it is thick and fluffy.

Carefully cut the sponge across into two halves, with a sharp knife. Spread just over half of the whipped cream over one half. Cut an oblong out of the other half, leaving an outer, unbroken edge, 1 in wide, all around.

Carefully lift this frame on to the cream-covered base and fill the box, or cavity, with the fruit, reserving a few pieces for decoration. Sprinkle the confectioners' sugar over the fruit, and cover the box with the lid set at a slight angle. Pipe the remaining cream on to the lid and decorate with the reserved fruit.

The cake will keep for 2–3 hours in a refrigerator, but it should not be assembled too far in advance, or the fruit will become mushy and stain the cream.

RHUBARB CRUMBLE

In late spring, rhubarb is larger and slightly tougher than the tender early forced rhubarb. The tart flavor is more pronounced and blends well with a topping of sweet crumble.

PREPARATION TIME: *20 min*
COOKING TIME: *40 min*
INGREDIENTS *(for 4–6):*
2 pounds rhubarb
¾ cup sugar
1½ cups flour
6 tablespoons unsalted butter
½ cup heavy cream
1 piece preserved ginger
1 teaspoon ginger syrup

Wash the rhubarb stalks, top and tail them, discard any damaged pieces and remove tough strings. Chop the stalks into ½ in sections. Put the rhubarb in a deep baking dish, sprinkle over half the sugar and add 2 tablespoons of cold water. Sift the flour and rub the butter in until it forms a crumbly mixture; blend in the remaining sugar. Cover the rhubarb with this crumble, patting it down well. Bake in the center of an oven pre-heated to 375°F (190°C, mark 5) for about 40 minutes or until crisp and golden on top.

Whip the cream until it stands in soft peaks; flavor with chopped ginger and the syrup.

Serve the crumble warm or cold and offer the cream in a bowl separately.

STRAWBERRY SYLLABUB TRIFLE

There is a recipe for macaroons on page 84, or you could use the ratafia recipe on page 127.

PREPARATION TIME: *30 min*
RESTING TIME: *4 hours*
INGREDIENTS *(for 6–8):*
3 cups strawberries
½ pound green grapes
6 ounces small macaroons
3 egg whites
¾ cup sugar
½ cup dry white wine
Juice of half lemon
2 tablespoons brandy
1¼ cups heavy cream

Hull, wash and drain the strawberries, and remove the seeds from the grapes (page 152). Set 6–8 strawberries aside, and arrange half the remainder together with half the grapes over the bottom of a glass dish. Set 8 macaroons aside, and lay half of the remainder over the fruit. Cover with the rest of the strawberries and grapes and lay the remaining macaroons over them.

Whisk the egg whites with half the sugar until stiff, but not dry, then fold in the remaining sugar with a metal spoon. Mix the wine, lemon juice and brandy, and blend it carefully into the egg whites. Whisk the cream until it just holds its shape, set a little aside for decoration, and fold the egg-white mixture into the remaining cream.

Spoon the cream over the macaroons, smoothing it neatly, and leave in a cool place, not the refrigerator, for several hours.

Decorate the trifle with the reserved strawberries and macaroons sandwiched with cream.

STRAWBERRY SHORTCAKE

This makes a wonderful ending for a summer luncheon party.

PREPARATION TIME: *25 min*
COOKING TIME: *20 min*
INGREDIENTS:
2 cups flour
1 teaspoon cream of tartar
½ teaspoon baking soda
*Pinch of salt**
¼ cup butter or margarine
3 tablespoons sugar
1 egg
3–4 tablespoons milk
FILLING:
1½–2 cups hulled strawberries
1¼ cups heavy cream
1 tablespoon milk
Sugar
Butter

Sift together the flour, cream of tartar, baking soda and salt into a bowl. Cut the butter into small pieces and rub into the flour until the mixture resembles fine breadcrumbs. Blend in the sugar. Make a well in the center, stir in the beaten egg and enough milk to give a soft but manageable dough. Knead lightly and roll out into a 7 in circle.

Place on a greased baking sheet, dust lightly with flour and bake towards the top of an oven pre-heated to 425°F (220°C, mark 7) for about 20 minutes. Cool slightly on a wire rack.

For the filling, slice the strawberries thickly. Whisk together the cream and the milk, sweetened with sugar to taste, until it holds its shape. Cut the warm shortcake into three layers, horizontally, with a serrated knife, and lightly butter each. Spread the cream over all three circles, then top with the sliced strawberries and sandwich the cake together. Decorate the top with piped cream.

STRAWBERRY ICE

Fruit ices are both easy and economical to make. They are refreshing at any time of day and make a perfect summer dessert after a rich main course.

PREPARATION TIME: *10 min*
FREEZING TIME: *minimum 3 hours*
INGREDIENTS *(for 4–6):*
1½–2 cups strawberries
¼ cup confectioners' sugar
2 cups lemonade
2 egg whites

Wash and hull the strawberries, drain them thoroughly in a colander, then cut them into small pieces. Rub the strawberries through a sieve and stir the sugar into the purée. (Alternatively, put the fruit and sugar in a liquidizer to purée.) Add enough lemonade to the purée to make 2 cups liquid. Spoon the mixture into an ice cube tray or a plastic freezing container, cover with foil or a lid and put in the freezer.

When the mixture is beginning to freeze around the sides of the container, remove from the freezer. Scrape the frozen bits into the center of the container with a fork to break up any ice crystals. Whip the egg whites until stiff, but not dry, and fold them into the strawberry mixture. Return to the freezer, either in the original container or spooned into small molds. Cover and freeze the ice until set.

Serve the ice spooned into glasses or in the molds.

STRAWBERRY SHORTCAKE

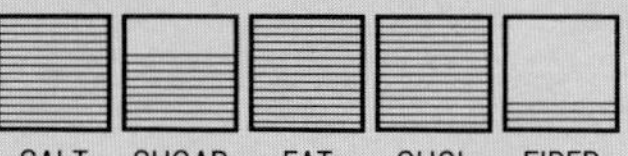

SALT SUGAR FAT CHOL FIBER

GLUTEN-FREE* WHOLEFOOD*
TOTAL CALORIES: ABOUT 3150

The high **salt** level is due to the astonishingly high level in baking soda. To avoid this, low-salt baking powder can be bought at health food stores: it is used just like conventional baking powder, replacing both soda and cream of tartar.

If no **sugar** is beaten into the cream, or only 1 tablespoon (taken from the amount in shortcake base mixture) this recipe will be low sugar, especially if it serves more than 4 people. (Calories lost: up to 99.)

The shortcake base is much lower in **fat** than a usual shortcrust pastry, and is worth using for other dishes, including savories if sugar is omitted. The amount of fat can be reduced to 3 tablespoons, and vegetable margarine chosen to avoid the **cholesterol** of the butter (or a mixture used). (Calories lost: up to 78.)

The remaining high fat level comes from the cream, which can be replaced by a half-and-half mixture of 1 cup thick low-fat yogurt with 1 cup low-fat quark, and from the butter spread over the layers, which can be painlessly omitted. (Calories lost: up to 1196.)

These changes give a low-fat, low-cholesterol dish.

A **gluten-free** base can be made, using a mixture of wheat starch, gluten-free flour and buckwheat flour for flavor.

Freezing: ☑ up to 2 months.

STRAWBERRY ICE

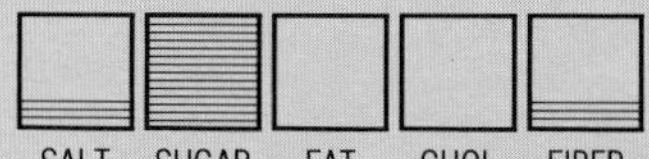

SALT SUGAR FAT CHOL FIBER

GLUTEN-FREE WHOLEFOOD
TOTAL CALORIES: ABOUT 275

For low **sugar** use home-made lemonade, with no more than 2 tablespoons sugar to each 2½ cups. (Calories lost: up to 65.)

Food processor: √ for the purée.
Freezing: √ up to 3 months.

STRAWBERRY ICE CREAM

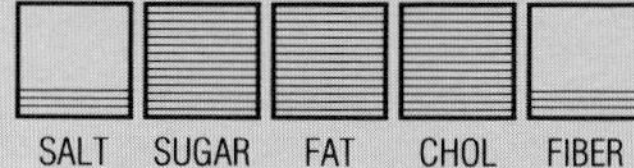

SALT SUGAR FAT CHOL FIBER

GLUTEN-FREE WHOLEFOOD
TOTAL CALORIES: ABOUT 1370

Less **sugar** can be used, say 2 tablespoons, giving a low sugar level. (Calories lost: up to 197.) The high **fat** level from the cream cannot be changed without changing the character of the ice cream. However, a mixture of 1 cup low-fat quark blended with 1 cup thick low-fat yogurt, or ½ cup yogurt and ½ cup low-fat sour cream will give a delicious if different ice, with low to moderate fat and **cholesterol**. (Calories lost: up to 699.)
The result will be harder, so thaw slightly before serving.
Wholefood: use a pale type of sugar as otherwise the flavor may overwhelm that of the strawberries.

Food Processor: √ for the purée.
Freezing: √ up to 3 months.

STRAWBERRY ICE CREAM

This dessert is best if prepared the day before.

PREPARATION TIME: *15–20 min*
FREEZING TIME: *12 hours*
INGREDIENTS *(for 6):*
1½–2 cups strawberries
¾ cup confectioners' sugar
Squeeze lemon juice
½ cup heavy cream
½ cup light cream
GARNISH:
6–8 large strawberries

Hull and wash the strawberries in a colander, drain them thoroughly and cut them into small pieces. Put them in the liquidizer, with the sifted sugar and lemon juice (alternatively, rub the strawberries through a fine sieve and add the sugar and lemon juice to the purée). Whisk the two creams until thick, but not stiff; blend this well into the strawberry purée.

Spoon the strawberry mixture into a plastic freezing container, cover with a lid and leave to freeze for 12 hours. One or two hours before serving, remove the ice cream from the freezer and thaw slightly in the refrigerator.

Scoop the ice cream into individual glasses and decorate with slices of fresh strawberries.

ICED TANGERINES

For a special dinner party, this refreshingly tangy and impressive looking ice cream is a fitting ending. Prepare the ice cream a day ahead.

PREPARATION TIME: *30 min*
COOKING TIME: *25 min*
INGREDIENTS *(for 6):*
8 medium-sized tangerines
¾ cup sugar
1¼ cups water
Juice of half lemon
1 egg yolk
1¼ cups heavy cream
GARNISH:
Crystallized violets
Tangerine slices
Camellia leaves
Langues de chat

Wipe the tangerines, cut off the tops and carefully scoop out the flesh from both tops and bottoms. Place six of the empty tangerine skins in a plastic bag in the refrigerator and set the remaining two aside. Squeeze 1¼ cups of juice from the tangerine pulp. Boil the sugar and water in a saucepan over a high heat for 10 minutes to make a syrup. Remove and allow to cool. Stir into the syrup the tangerine and lemon juices. Beat the egg yolk and stir into the syrup. Return to the heat and cook gently for 5 minutes, stirring continuously. Cool, pour into a freezing container, cover tightly with a lid and place in the freezer until lightly set, for approximately 1½–2 hours.

Grate the rind of the remaining two tangerines and beat the cream until stiff. Break the frozen syrup into a bowl and beat vigorously with a fork until it has an even texture. Beat in the cream and tangerine rind until the color is uniform and the rind evenly distributed. Spoon this ice cream back into the freezing container, cover with a lid and freeze for a further 2½ hours.

Turn out the mixture, break it down as before and beat until the texture is even; return to the freezer. One hour before serving, scoop the ice cream into the empty tangerine skins and fix on the lids at an angle.

Brush the outsides of the tangerines with water and place in the freezer. Ten minutes before serving, remove the tangerines from the freezer in order to let the frost on the skins settle.

Serve on a tray decorated with well-washed camellia (or other glossy evergreen) leaves, crystallized violets and tangerine slices. A dish of langues de chat could be served separately.

ICED TANGERINES

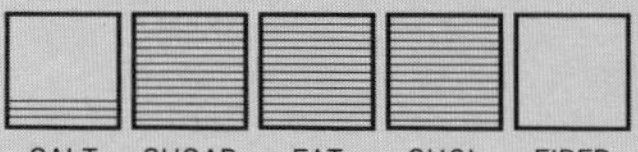

GLUTEN-FREE WHOLEFOOD
TOTAL CALORIES: ABOUT 2380

This method is based on a tangerine-flavored sugar syrup. Instead, you can sweeten 2½ cups of juice, mixing tangerine and apple juice if wished, with about ¼ cup sugar, or honey. This reduces the **sugar** level to medium. (Calories lost: up to 408.)
To reduce the **fat** and **cholesterol** levels to low, replace the cream with 1 cup low-fat quark mixed with ½ cup low-fat sour cream and ½ cup low-fat yogurt, lightly sweetened with a spoonful of honey and a few drops of pure vanilla extract if liked. (Calories lost: up to 969.)
This dish is not **wholefood** because of the garnishes, which are likely to carry colorings, preservatives and sugar. Instead, garnish the dish with fresh fruit slices, or flowers (ideally orange blossom or scented jasmine).
An alternative treatment of this recipe would be to replace some of the juice with jasmine tea.

Freezing: ☑ up to 3 months.

TUTTI FRUTTI PUDDING WITH ORANGE FOAM SAUCE

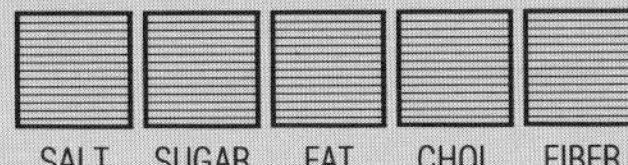

SALT SUGAR FAT CHOL FIBER

GLUTEN-FREE* WHOLEFOOD*
TOTAL CALORIES: ABOUT 2795

Low-salt baking powder would reduce the **salt** level to low.
For low **sugar**, omit both butter and sugar from the sponge. Instead, beat 3 eggs with 3 tablespoons honey and the orange rind in a bowl over a pan of hot water until thick and fluffy. The sauce can be made with half the quantity of sugar. Coat the bottom of the steaming mold with honey instead of light corn syrup. (Calories lost: up to 882.)
This will also give a medium **fat** level, but the **cholesterol** will remain medium to high because of the eggs. For low to moderate cholesterol, replace the foam sauce with 6 tablespoons of marmalade, made without added sugar, heated gently with the grated rind and juice of an orange and, if liked, a little lemon juice and/or apple juice concentrate. (Calories lost: up to 404.)
For a **wholefood** pudding, replace the glacé cherries and angelica with fresh cherries. If you have fresh angelica, this can be used.
Commercial **gluten-free** flour makes quite a satisfactory sponge.

Pressure cooker: ✓ for the pudding.
Freezing: ✓ up to 3 months (the pudding only).
Microwave: ✓ for the pudding.

TUTTI FRUTTI PUDDING WITH ORANGE FOAM SAUCE

A steamed pudding is an ideal winter dessert especially when it is composed of a light-textured sponge and colorful fruit. It is served with a feather-light orange-flavored sauce.

PREPARATION TIME: *40 min*
COOKING TIME: *2 hours*
INGREDIENTS *(for 6):*
½ cup prunes
½ cup dried apricots
⅓ cup glacé cherries
2 tablespoons candied angelica
½ cup unsalted butter
½ cup sugar
Grated rind and juice of an orange
2 eggs
¾ cup self-rising flour
1 cup fresh breadcrumbs
2 tablespoons light corn syrup
6 canned apricot halves or 6 pitted prunes
ORANGE FOAM SAUCE:
2 tablespoons unsalted butter
Grated rind and juice of an orange
2 teaspoons flour
¼ cup sugar
1 egg
Lemon juice

Finely chop the dried prunes, apricots, glacé cherries and angelica. Thoroughly grease a 1-quart steaming mold. Cream together the butter and sugar until light and fluffy, then add the grated orange rind. Whisk the eggs lightly and gradually beat them into the butter. Mix the sifted flour and the breadcrumbs together and lightly fold them into the pudding mixture. Add the orange juice and fold in the chopped fruit.

Coat the bottom of the steaming mold with light corn syrup and arrange the six apricot halves or soaked pitted prunes in a circle over the syrup. Spoon over the pudding mixture and cover the bowl with buttered foil or a double layer of wax paper. Tie securely with string. Place the mold in a steamer or in a pan with boiling water reaching two-thirds up the sides of the mold. Steam for 1¾–2 hours or until the pudding has risen and is set.

While the pudding is steaming, prepare the sauce: cream the butter with the grated orange rind and gradually beat in the flour mixed with the sugar. Separate the egg and beat the yolk into the butter and flour mixture, add the orange juice–made up with water to ¾ cup. Do not worry if the mixture curdles at this stage; it will become smooth again as it cooks.

Cook the sauce in a small heavy saucepan over low heat, stirring constantly, until the sauce thickens and the flour is cooked through. Add a little extra water if necessary to keep the sauce to a pouring consistency. Remove the pan from the heat and cover with a lid to keep warm.

Just before serving, fold the stiffly beaten egg white into the sauce and sharpen with a little lemon juice.

Unmold the cooked pudding on to a hot serving dish, and serve the orange foam sauce separately.

BREAD PUDDING

The genuine Welsh bread pudding is packed with fruit, spices and peel. It is served warm as a pudding; any left-overs can be served cold as a snack.

PREPARATION TIME: *35 min*
COOKING TIME: *2 hours*
INGREDIENTS *(for 4–6):*
½ pound stale bread
1¼ cups milk
⅓ cup chopped candied peel
Peel of a small orange
Peel of a lemon
¾ cup currants
⅓ cup golden raisins
6 tablespoons shredded beef suet
⅓ cup light brown sugar
2 teaspoons allspice
1 large egg
Milk
Butter
Grated nutmeg
Granulated sugar

Cut away all the crust from the bread; break the bread into small pieces. Place in a large mixing bowl and pour over the milk; leave to soak for 20 minutes. Finely chop the candied peel, grate the orange and lemon peel, add to the bread and mix in. Add the dried fruit, suet, sugar and mixed spice; blend well. Beat the egg and stir it into the mixture which should have a dropping consistency. If necessary, add a teaspoon or two of milk.

Spoon the bread mixture into a well-greased 1-quart deep pie dish and grate a little nutmeg over it. Bake on the middle shelf of an oven heated to 350°F (180°C, mark 4) for 1¾–2 hours or until browned.

Serve hot or cold, liberally sprinkled with granulated sugar. You can also serve custard sauce or cream separately in a bowl to accompany the pudding.

BREAD AND BUTTER PUDDING

Slightly stale buttered bread is the basis for this traditional English nursery pudding.

PREPARATION TIME: *15 min*
COOKING TIME: *30 min*
INGREDIENTS *(for 4):*
8 slices buttered bread
⅓ cup golden raisins
Grated rind of a lemon
2 eggs
3 tablespoons sugar
2½ cups vanilla-flavored milk

Remove the crusts and cut the bread into 1 in squares. Place them in a lightly buttered fireproof dish, with alternate layers of raisins mixed with grated lemon rind.

Beat the eggs lightly with 2 tablespoons of the sugar and all the milk. Pour this custard over the bread. Sprinkle the remaining sugar over the top, and bake the pudding in a pre-heated oven, at 350°F (180°C, mark 4) for about 30 minutes.

STEAMED JAM PUDDING

The simple steamed puddings never lose their appeal for children and adults. Fresh breadcrumbs give this suet pudding a particularly light texture.

PREPARATION TIME: *15 min*
COOKING TIME: *2–2½ hours*
INGREDIENTS *(for 4–6):*
1½ cups self-rising flour
1 teaspoon baking powder
*Salt**
1½ cups fresh breadcrumbs
½ cup shredded beef suet
½ cup sugar
1 egg
Milk to mix
1 tablespoon red jam
SAUCE:
2 rounded tablespoons red jam
¼ cup sugar

Sift the flour, baking powder and a little salt into a mixing bowl, add the breadcrumbs, suet and sugar, and mix well. Lightly beat the egg and stir into the flour, with sufficient milk to make the dough a soft dropping consistency. Blend thoroughly. Butter a 1-quart steaming mold and put 1 tablespoon red jam in the bottom. Spoon in the pudding mixture until the mold is two-thirds full. Cover with a double thickness buttered wax paper and fold a pleat in this to allow the pudding to expand as it cooks. Secure the paper with string.

Set the pudding in a steamer over a saucepan half-filled with simmering water, or put the mold on an upturned saucer in a saucepan and fill the pan with boiling water to come two-thirds up the side of the mold. Cover the pan with a tightly fitting lid and

BREAD PUDDING

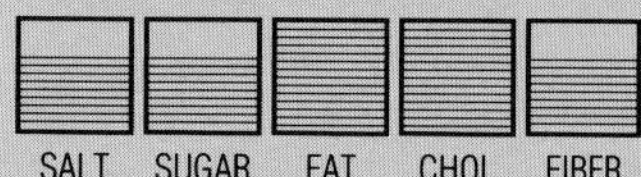

GLUTEN-FREE* WHOLEFOOD*
TOTAL CALORIES: ABOUT 2410

The **salt** level will be low if unsalted bread is used.
The **sugar** content is medium if the pudding serves 6 people, high if it serves 4. It can be avoided by puréeing about ⅓ of the dried fruit in the milk (you can use soy milk which is a little sweeter) and omitting the added sugar. If wished, a little brown sugar can be sprinkled on top when serving. (Calories lost: up to 197.)
For low **fat** and **cholesterol**, use skim milk (or soy milk) and only 2 tablespoons soft vegetable margarine instead of the suet; for very low cholesterol, use only the egg white. (Calories lost: up to 608.)
The **fiber** level is medium if the pudding serves 6, high if it serves 4. Using whole wheat bread makes it very high fiber.
Wholefood: some may like to replace the candied peel with fresh rind grated finely from a very well scrubbed orange.

Freezing: √ up to 2 months.

BREAD AND BUTTER PUDDING

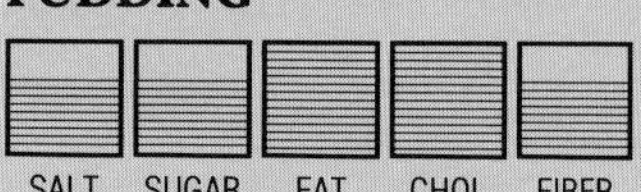

GLUTEN-FREE* WHOLEFOOD*
TOTAL CALORIES: ABOUT 1900

The **salt** level will be low if unsalted bread is used.
To reduce the **sugar** content to low, use only 1 tablespoon

beaten with the eggs. Sprinkle the top with extra raisins, or add some chopped dates, instead of sugar. Soy milk is slightly sweet and could be used instead of ordinary milk. (Calories lost: up to 55.)
For low **fat** and **cholesterol**, omit the butter on the bread, use skim milk (or soy milk), and omit one egg yolk. (Calories lost: up to 662.)

STEAMED JAM PUDDING

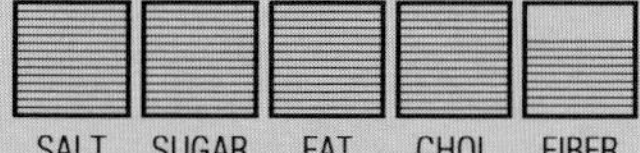

SALT SUGAR FAT CHOL FIBER

GLUTEN-FREE* WHOLEFOOD*
TOTAL CALORIES: ABOUT 2425

The high **salt** level can be reduced to low by using low-salt baking powder and breadcrumbs made from unsalted bread.
The **sugar** and **fat** level in the pudding can be reduced to 6 tablespoons each and the sauce made much lower in sugar by using jam made without added sugar, heated very gently. This still gives a moderately high fat and sugar level and high **cholesterol**, especially as the egg is needed for the texture. The jam in the sponge can also be the no-added-sugar variety, which has roughly half as much sugar as conventional jam but tastes perfectly sweet enough. (Calories lost: up to 367.)

Pressure cooker: √

Freezing: √ up to 3 months.

Microwave: √

steam for 2 to $2\frac{1}{2}$ hours. Top the pan up with more boiling water if it has evaporated before steaming is finished.

About 10 minutes before the pudding is cooked, prepare the sauce: put the jam, sugar and 2 tablespoons of water into a pan, stir over low heat to dissolve the sugar, then bring to the boil. Simmer the sauce for 2–3 minutes or until thick and syrupy.

Loosen the sides of the pudding with a knife and turn out on to a hot serving dish. Pour the sauce into a bowl and serve separately.

CRÈME BRÛLÉE

This rich but delicious pudding, ideal for an important dinner party, is a traditional specialty of Trinity College, Cambridge. Be very careful when cooking the cream not to let it boil. If you keep a jar of sugar with a vanilla bean in it, use this sugar and omit the vanilla extract.

PREPARATION TIME: *20 min*
CHILLING TIME: *4 hours plus 2–3 hours*
INGREDIENTS *(for 12):*
1½ quarts light cream
12 egg yolks
2 tablespoons granulated sugar
½ teaspoon vanilla
4 tablespoons light brown sugar

Put the cream in the top half of a large double boiler or in a bowl over a pan of gently simmering water. Carefully stir the egg yolks, beaten with the granulated sugar and vanilla, into the warm cream. Continue cooking gently until the cream has thickened enough to coat the back of the wooden spoon. Strain the cream through a fine sieve into a large soufflé dish or mold and leave to chill for at least 4 hours.

Sprinkle the sifted brown sugar on top of the chilled cream. Set the dish or mold on a bed of ice cubes on the broiler pan and place under a hot broiler until the sugar has caramelized. Remove the dish and chill in the refrigerator for 2–3 hours. Serve with fruit – any fresh fruit in season – as a foil for the richness of the dish.

ZABAGLIONE

This Italian dish is probably a more popular dessert in countries outside its homeland where it is chiefly served as a tonic. It is quickly made, but care must be taken to prevent it from curdling while cooking.

PREPARATION AND COOKING TIME: *10 min*
INGREDIENTS *(for 4):*
4 egg yolks
¼ cup sugar
4–6 tablespoons Marsala wine
GARNISH:
Ladyfingers

Put the egg yolks in a mixing bowl, together with the sugar and Marsala wine. Place the bowl over a saucepan half filled with water kept simmering. Whisk the egg mixture continuously over the heat until thick and fluffy (about 5–7 minutes). On no account must the egg mixture reach boiling point.

Remove the bowl from the heat and pour the thickened mixture into warmed serving glasses. Serve at once, garnished with ladyfingers.

CRÈME BRÛLÉE

GLUTEN-FREE WHOLEFOOD*
TOTAL CALORIES: ABOUT 4315

Crème brûlée is by its nature extremely high in **fat** and **cholesterol** so that apart from eating very tiny portions there is no way to reduce the levels to anything approaching moderate. There are however alternatives, which are just as good. You can make the black currant brûlée on page 20, using other soft fruits if you prefer; or you can fill half the dish with fresh peaches, nectarines or apricots before adding the custard cream – using half the quantity given will give a medium to high fat and cholesterol level. Replacing some or all of the custard cream with thick Greek yogurt gives a delicious, if rather different, result. (Calories lost: up to 3784.)

ZABAGLIONE

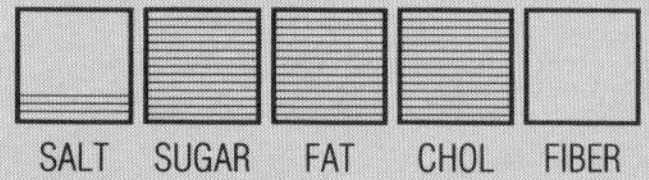

GLUTEN-FREE* WHOLEFOOD
TOTAL CALORIES: ABOUT 655

This recipe cannot be materially altered or it won't work. However, as it is quite rich, you could use only 3 egg yolks with 3 tablespoons sugar among 4 people, and garnish with fingers of fresh fruit, ideally pears, rather than sponge fingers. This would give a medium to high **sugar** level and medium **fat**, but the **cholesterol** would be still quite high. (Calories lost: up to 144.)

VANILLA ICE CREAM

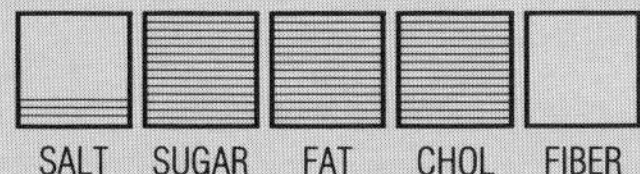

GLUTEN-FREE WHOLEFOOD*
TOTAL CALORIES: ABOUT 2050

For medium **sugar** simply make the custard less sweet: for many people, adding 2 tablespoons sugar or honey would provide plenty of sweetness. (Calories lost: up to 197.)
The **fat** and **cholesterol** in this recipe can be reduced to medium by making the custard with skim milk, and thickening with 2 whole eggs rather than one egg with 2 extra yolks. Half the cream can be replaced with ½ cup quark, folding it in with the cream. For extra volume, fold in a stiffly beaten large egg white when the mixture is just setting. (Calories lost: up to 715.)

Freezing: ☑ up to 3 months.

BROWN BREAD ICE CREAM

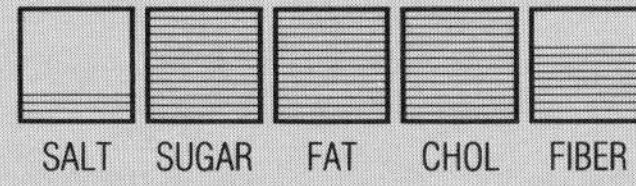

GLUTEN-FREE* WHOLEFOOD*
TOTAL CALORIES: ABOUT 1900

For medium **sugar** add only 2 tablespoons to the crumbs. (Calories lost: up to 197.)
To reduce the **fat** level, replace the heavy cream with ½ cup quark, ½ cup low-fat sour cream and two egg whites, stiffly beaten and folded in when the ice cream is nearly set and crumbs are added. This will also give a low **cholesterol** level. (Calories lost: up to 1127.)

Freezing: ☑ up to 2 months.

VANILLA ICE CREAM

Delicious on its own or as an accompaniment to raspberries, strawberries or other soft fruit.

PREPARATION TIME: *25 min*
FREEZING TIME: *about 3 hours*
INGREDIENTS *(for 6):*
1¼ cups milk
Vanilla bean
1 whole egg
2 egg yolks
6 tablespoons sugar
1¼ cups heavy cream

Bring the milk almost to the boil with the vanilla bean, then leave to infuse off the heat for about 15 minutes. Remove the vanilla bean. Cream the whole egg, yolks and sugar until pale. Stir in the vanilla-flavored milk and strain this mixture through a sieve into a clean pan. Heat the custard mixture slowly over gentle heat, stirring all the time, until the mixture thickens just enough to coat the back of a wooden spoon. Pour into a bowl and leave to cool.

Whip the cream lightly and fold it carefully and thoroughly into the cooled custard. Spoon into ice cube trays or a suitable freezing container, cover and set in the freezer until half-frozen. Whisk the ice cream thoroughly, then freeze until firm.

Remove from the freezer and put in the refrigerator for 20 minutes before serving to soften slightly.

BROWN BREAD ICE CREAM

For a picnic treat, spoon this crunchy ice cream straight into a wide-necked thermos, and pack any spaces with sliced peaches or pears.

PREPARATION TIME: *20 min*
FREEZING TIME: *2–3 hours*
INGREDIENTS *(for 6):*
1¼ cups heavy cream
2 tablespoons vanilla sugar (page 184)
3 thick slices stale, crustless brown bread
½ cup dark brown sugar

Blend the cream and vanilla sugar in a bowl and whisk until fluffy. Spoon the mixture into shallow ice trays or a plastic container, cover with foil or the lid, and put into the freezer. When the mixture has begun to set around the edges, take it out of the freezer and stir the sides into the middle to prevent ice crystals forming. Repeat this twice during freezing.

Reduce the bread to fine crumbs and mix with the brown sugar. Spread the crumbs on a lightly oiled baking sheet and put this into the center of an oven, pre-heated to 400°F (200°C, mark 6). Leave until the sugar caramelizes and the crumbs are golden brown; stir them occasionally. When cool, break up into crumbs again with a fork.

When the ice cream is nearly set, turn it into a chilled bowl, beat with a wire whisk and stir in the crumbs. Spoon the mixture into the ice trays and return them, covered, to the freezer. Freeze until firm.

BISCUIT TORTONI

During the 19th century, Tortoni's restaurant in Paris was famous for its buffet table, patronized by many great writers.

PREPARATION TIME: *15 min*
FREEZING TIME: *3 hours*
INGREDIENTS *(for 6–8):*
2 cups heavy cream
½ cup light cream
½ cup confectioners' sugar
*Salt**
12 macaroons
6 tablespoons cream sherry
GARNISH:
Wafers or ratafia cookies

Whip the creams together with the sugar and a pinch of salt, until the mixture is firm but not stiff. Spoon into a 9 in loaf pan or plastic box, cover with a lid or a double layer of foil and freeze the cream until nearly solid.

Put the macaroons into a plastic bag and crush them to fine crumbs with a rolling pin. Set aside a third for decoration.

Break up the frozen cream mixture into a basin and blend in the sherry and remaining macaroon crumbs with a hand whisk. The mixture should stay light and bulky; add a little more sugar and sherry if necessary. Spoon the cream mixture into the washed and dried container, cover and return to the freezer.

When the cream has frozen quite firm again, remove it from the freezer and invert the container on to a serving plate. Rub the container with a cloth wrung out in very hot water until the ice cream drops out. Press the macaroon crumbs lightly into the top and sides of the ice with a broad-bladed knife.

GRANITA AL CAFFÈ

Strong, bitter black coffee, preferably a continental roast, should be used for this Italian ice. It is sometimes served with whipped cream.

PREPARATION TIME: *10 min*
CHILLING TIME: *3–4 hours*
INGREDIENTS *(for 4):*
2 cups strong black coffee
4½ tablespoons sugar
½ cup whipping cream

Melt 4 tablespoons of sugar in ½ cup of water over moderate heat, stirring until the sugar has completely dissolved. Bring this syrup to the boil and boil steadily for 5 minutes. Remove from the heat and leave the syrup to cool.

Stir the strained coffee into the cold syrup, and pour the mixture into ice cube trays. For the best texture, the dividers should be left in the trays so that the ice will set in cubes. Put the trays into the freezer for at least 3 hours. Stir the ice occasionally with a fork to scrape the frozen crystals around the edges into the center.

Turn the frozen cubes into a bowl and crush them lightly with a pestle or break them up with a fork. Spoon the ice into individual glasses and serve at once with a separate bowl of whipped cream, sweetened with the remaining sugar.

BISCUIT TORTONI

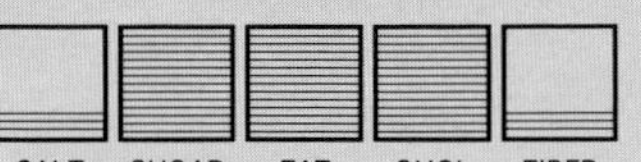

SALT SUGAR FAT CHOL FIBER

GLUTEN-FREE WHOLEFOOD
TOTAL CALORIES: ABOUT 3215

This alternative recipe is very low in **sugar**, **fat** and **cholesterol**.

1 cup small curd cottage cheese (12% fat variety)
1¼ cups thick low-fat yogurt
2 egg whites
2 tablespoons honey
2–3 tablespoons sherry
12 macaroons

Mix the cottage cheese, yogurt and honey, and freeze for about 1 hour until mushy. Beat egg whites until stiff. Beat frozen mixture smooth, stir in the sherry, and 8 crushed macaroons, and then fold in the egg whites. Freeze and continue with recipe.
Transfer to refrigerator about 1 hour before serving to soften. A drop of almond extract could be mixed with the sherry.

Freezing: ✓ up to 2 months.

GRANITA AL CAFFÈ

SALT SUGAR FAT CHOL FIBER

GLUTEN-FREE WHOLEFOOD
TOTAL CALORIES: ABOUT 785

The **sugar** level can be reduced slightly but will still be fairly high, as for most people's tastes at least 3 tablespoons will be needed to sweeten the coffee. The **fat** and **cholesterol** are all in the cream, and this can be omitted completely as the granita is very good on its own. (Calories lost: up to 597.)

Freezing: √ up to 2 months (the coffee ice only, not the cream).

CHAMPAGNE CHARLIE AND OAT COOKIES

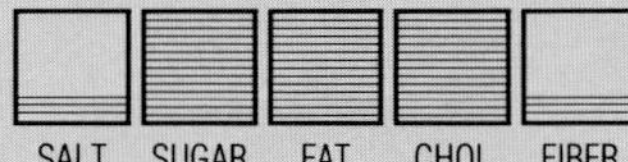

SALT SUGAR FAT CHOL FIBER

GLUTEN-FREE* WHOLEFOOD*
TOTAL CALORIES: ABOUT 4665

The **sugar** in the ice cream can be reduced to ½ cup, still high, with 7 tablespoons water, but the sugar and light corn syrup in the oat cookies can be omitted. (Calories lost: up to 650.)
About half the heavy cream can be replaced with quark, and 2 stiffly beaten egg whites will help make up the lost bulk, folded in when the mixture is just setting. This will give medium **fat** and **cholesterol**. (Calories lost: up to 1080.)
Ratafias are usually **gluten-free**, but check ingredients list.

Freezing: √ up to 3 months (both ice cream and cookies).

MIRIAM'S HONEY RATAFIAS

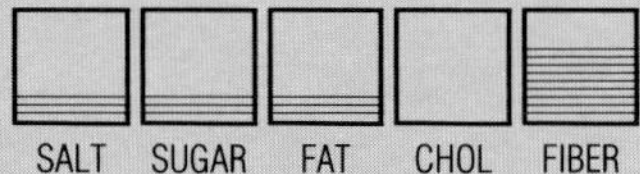

SALT SUGAR FAT CHOL FIBER

GLUTEN-FREE WHOLEFOOD
TOTAL CALORIES: ABOUT 240

This recipe is specifically designed to conform to healthy guidelines.

CHAMPAGNE CHARLIE

George Leybourne, star of the English music hall of the 1890s, often ordered champagne for his audiences, a gesture which earned him the nickname of 'Champagne Charlie.' This ice cream, named after him, is a superb dessert for a special occasion.

PREPARATION TIME: *30 min*
COOKING TIME: *10 min*
FREEZING TIME: *5 hours*
INGREDIENTS *(for 6):*
¾ cup sugar
2 oranges and 2 lemons
2½ cups chilled champagne
2½ cups heavy cream
8 tablespoons brandy
36 ratafia cookies
GARNISH:
Langues de chat or oat cookies
Lemon peel

Put the sugar in a pan with ½ cup of water. Bring to the boil and boil rapidly for 6 minutes to make a syrup. Meanwhile, grate the rind from one orange and squeeze the juice from the oranges and lemons. Add the rind and the strained juice to the syrup and leave to cool. Stir in the chilled champagne.

Pour the mixture into a plastic container, and cover with the lid or a double layer of foil. Freeze for 1½–2 hours or until frozen around the edges. Scoop the mixture into a chilled bowl and whip until smooth. In a separate bowl, beat the cream until stiff, and blend it slowly into the champagne syrup until it is smooth and uniform in color. Blend in 2 tablespoons of the brandy.

Spoon the mixture into the container, cover and freeze for about 3 hours.

About 30 minutes before serving, place six ratafia cookies in the bottom of each champagne glass. Pour 2 teaspoons of brandy over the cookies and leave them to soak. Scoop the ice cream into the glasses. Hang a thin spiral of lemon peel from the rim of each glass and pour a teaspoon of brandy over each portion.

Serve immediately, with a separate plate of langues de chat or oat cookies made as in the following recipe.

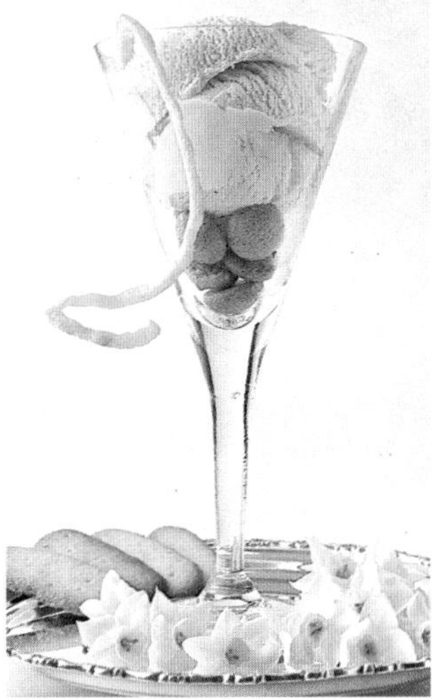

Oat Cookies

PREPARATION TIME: *15 min*
COOKING TIME: *20–25 min*
INGREDIENTS *(for 24 cookies):*
¾ cup flour
½ teaspoon baking soda
½ cup light brown sugar
1 cup rolled oats
6 tablespoons unsalted butter
1 tablespoon rum
1 tablespoon light corn syrup

Sift the flour and baking soda into a bowl; add the sugar and the oats, blending thoroughly. Heat the butter with the syrup and the rum in a small pan until the butter has just melted. Pour into the flour mixture and blend thoroughly with a wooden spoon.

Shape the dough into balls, 1 in wide, between floured hands. Set the balls well apart on greased baking sheets. Bake in the center of the oven, pre-heated to 325°F (170°C, mark 3), for 20–25 minutes or until golden brown. Allow to cool before serving.

MIRIAM'S HONEY RATAFIAS

PREPARATION TIME: *10 min*
COOKING TIME: *12–15 min*
INGREDIENTS *(for about 15 ratafias):*
1 egg white
2 tablespoons clear honey
6 tablespoons ground almonds
Few drops pure almond extract (optional)
Sheets of rice paper

Beat the egg white until it forms stiff, but not hard, peaks. Continue beating while drizzling in the honey, then the ground almonds and flavoring (if used). Spoon in very small heaps on rice paper, allowing only a little room for spreading. Bake in a pre-heated oven at 350°F (180°C, mark 4) for 12–15 minutes. Cool on a wire rack. They will crisp up as they cool.

TREACLE TART

British country cooking is justly famous for its variety of sweet and savory tarts and pastries. The popularity of this traditional lattice tart has never diminished. It is, in spite of its name, always made with golden syrup.

PREPARATION TIME: *20 min*
COOKING TIME: *25–30 min*
INGREDIENTS *(for 6):*
1¾ cups flour
*½ teaspoon salt**
1 egg yolk
10 tablespoons unsalted butter
5 rounded tablespoons imported golden syrup
3 heaping tablespoons fresh breadcrumbs
1 teaspoon finely grated lemon rind
1 tablespoon lemon juice

Sift the flour and salt into a mixing bowl. Cut the butter into small pieces and rub into the flour until the mixture resembles breadcrumbs. Mix in the egg yolk with a fork, and add just enough cold water to make a dough. Knead this pastry on a lightly floured surface before rolling it out, ⅛ in thick. Line an 8 in shallow pie plate with the pastry and prick the base lightly with a fork. Mix the other ingredients together and spread over the pastry. Roll out the pastry trimmings, cut them into ½ in wide strips and lay them in a lattice pattern over the tart; trim the edges neatly. Bake the tart on the middle shelf of an oven preheated to 400°F (200°C, mark 6) for 25–30 minutes.

LINZERTORTE

This classic Austrian torte, or tart, named after the town of Linz, is popular both as a dessert and as an accompaniment to morning or afternoon coffee. It is traditionally served with *Schlagsahne*. This consists of sweetened whipped cream into which stiffly beaten egg white is sometimes folded just before serving.

PREPARATION TIME: *30 min*
CHILLING TIME: *1½ hours*
COOKING TIME: *1 hour*
INGREDIENTS *(for 6):*
¾ cup flour
½ teaspoon ground cinnamon
6 tablespoons sugar
¾ cup unblanched ground almonds or hazelnuts
Grated rind of half lemon
½ cup unsalted butter
2 egg yolks
¼ teaspoon vanilla
1 cup thick raspberry jam
GLAZE:
1 egg yolk
1 tablespoon heavy cream

Sift the flour, cinnamon and sugar into a mixing bowl. Add the ground almonds and finely grated lemon peel; blend thoroughly before rubbing in the butter until the mixture resembles breadcrumbs.

Beat the egg yolks with the vanilla and stir into the flour and almond mixture. Using a wooden spoon, work it into a soft dough. Wrap in wax paper or foil, and chill for 1 hour in the refrigerator.

Grease a loose-bottomed flan pan 8 in wide by 1½ in deep. Knead the dough to soften it slightly, then press it with the fingers over the bottom of the pan

TREACLE TART

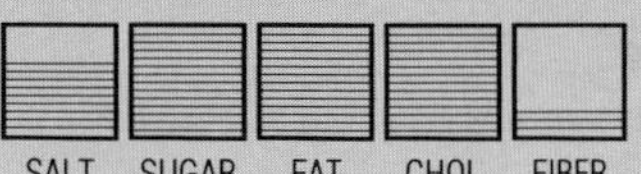

GLUTEN-FREE*
TOTAL CALORIES: ABOUT 1950

Golden syrup has a significant sodium level. The alternative is to use honey, in the same amount, giving a low **salt** dish. To reduce the **sugar** level is virtually impossible, given the character of the recipe. If wished, the amount of treacle topping could be halved, and spread over a layer of cooked fruit purée. If sweet fruit, such as eating apples or dried apricots were used, almost no sugar would be needed for this, resulting in a medium sugar dish. (Calories lost: up to 94.) To reduce the **fat** also requires a basic change to the recipe, using some other type of pastry, such as a yeast or a biscuit dough, as standard pie pastry does not adapt to using lower fat: it just becomes hard. However, a very low fat pastry (as on page 95) is acceptable if the dish is eaten straight from the oven. (Calories lost: up to 1043.)
For very low **cholesterol** use pastry made with oil or vegetable margarine.

Freezing: ✓ up to 6 months.

LINZERTORTE

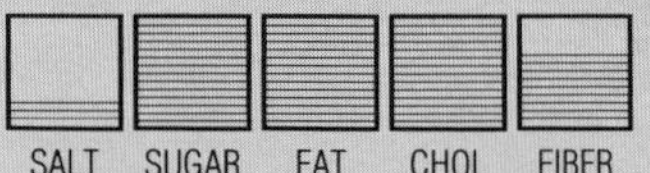

GLUTEN-FREE* WHOLEFOOD*
TOTAL CALORIES: ABOUT 2900

For low **sugar** omit the sugar from the dough, and use jam made with no added sugar.

(Calories lost: up to 772.)
Reducing the **fat** is more difficult, since it involves changing the type of pastry used, ideally to a yeast type. There is still a substantial amount of fat from almonds, which are roughly half oil. If hazelnuts are used instead, the amount of fat from the nuts will be reduced by about ⅓ or to a medium level for the dish, if combined with low fat pastry. However, almonds have twice as much **fiber** as hazels.
(Calories lost: up to 493.)
To reduce the **cholesterol** level almost to zero, vegetable fat can be used in the pastry and the egg yolks wholly or partly replaced by egg whites. Serve with slightly sweetened yogurt or quark in place of cream.
If the above changes to the jam are made, this recipe can be considered **wholefood**.

Freezing: √ up to 6 months.

SHOO FLY PIE

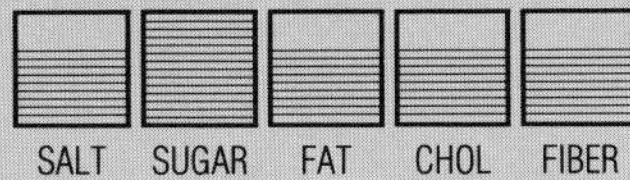

SALT SUGAR FAT CHOL FIBER

GLUTEN-FREE* WHOLEFOOD*
TOTAL CALORIES: ABOUT 2160

This can be low **salt** if you use a low-salt baking powder.
For low to medium **sugar** use chopped dates to mix with the raisins, and substitute ground almonds for some or all of the sugar in the topping. (Calories lost: up to 137.)
For low **fat**, use a low-fat pastry as suggested on page 82 and use only half the amount of butter in the topping; for low **cholesterol**, replace the butter with vegetable margarine.
(Calories lost: up to 612.)

Freezing: √ up to 6 months.

and up the sides. The lining should be not more than ¼ in thick, and the surplus dough should be pushed up over the top edge and trimmed off neatly with a knife. Spread the jam evenly over the bottom of the tart case.

Knead the pastry trimmings together and roll them out on a well-floured board to a rectangle 8 in by 3 in. Cut this into six strips, each ½ in wide. Lift the strips, one at a time, with a palette knife, and lay them across the raspberry filling in a lattice pattern. Press the ends of the strips into the pastry lining. Run a sharp knife around the top of the pan to loosen the pastry that extends above the lattice pattern, then fold it inwards and down on to the strips to make a ½ in wide border.

For the glaze, beat the egg yolk and cream together and brush it over the lattice and border. Chill the tart for 30 minutes in the refrigerator, then bake it in the center of a pre-heated oven at 350°F (180°C, mark 4) for about 1 hour or until crisp and lightly browned.

Leave the tart to cool and shrink slightly, then loosen the edge with a knife. Place the pan on a jar and gently push down the rim of the pan. Slide the tart on to a serving plate, and serve it warm or cold with a bowl of *Schlagsahne*.

SHOO FLY PIE

This pie, a favorite in the deep south, takes its name from its extreme sweetness. Flies and bees are so attracted to the pie that it is necessary to shoo them away while the pie is cooling.

PREPARATION TIME: *30 min*
COOKING TIME: *35 min*
INGREDIENTS *(for 6):*
½ quantity standard pastry (page 171)
⅔ cup raisins
⅓ cup brown sugar
¼ teaspoon baking soda
TOPPING:
1 cup flour
½ teaspoon cinnamon
¼ teaspoon ground nutmeg
¼ teaspoon ground ginger
¼ cup unsalted butter
⅓ cup brown sugar

Prepare the standard pastry and roll it out thinly on a lightly floured board. Line a 7 in flan pan or shallow pie plate with the pastry. Crimp the edges between finger and thumb for a decorative finish. Prick the bottom of the pastry all over with a fork and cover with the raisins. Mix the brown sugar with 3 tablespoons of hot water and the baking soda; pour over the raisins.

For the topping, sift together the flour and spices. Cut the butter into small pieces and rub them into the flour until the mixture resembles fine breadcrumbs. Stir in the brown sugar and sprinkle over the filling.

Bake the pie on the shelf above the center of a pre-heated oven, at 425°F (220°C, mark 7), until the pie begins to brown. Reduce the heat to 325°F (170°C, mark 3) and bake for a further 20 minutes, or until the topping has set.

Cut the pie into wedges and serve it warm or cold. A jug of cream may be offered although it is not traditional.

PROFITEROLES

Do not disturb these little buns while they are cooking, or the steam will escape thus causing them to collapse.

PREPARATION TIME: *1 hour*
COOKING TIME: *15 min*
INGREDIENTS *(for 20–25):*
1 quantity choux pastry (page 174)
1¼ cups heavy or whipping cream
Confectioners' sugar
4 ounces semisweet chocolate
1 small can evaporated milk

Make up the choux pastry and spoon it into a pastry bag fitted with a plain ½ in vegetable nozzle. Pipe 20–25 small bun shapes, well apart, on to greased baking sheets, and bake in a pre-heated oven, in the center or just above, at 425°F (220°C, mark 7) for about 15 minutes until well risen, puffed and crisp. If the profiteroles are not thoroughly dry after 15 minutes, reduce the heat to 350°F (180°C, mark 4) and continue baking for a further 10 minutes. Cool on a wire rack.

Split the buns not quite in half, lengthwise. Fill the hollow centers with whipped cream and dust the tops with confectioners' sugar. To serve, carefully pile the profiteroles into a pyramid on a serving dish and pour a little chocolate sauce over them; serve the remainder separately.

To make the sauce, melt the chocolate, broken into pieces, in a bowl over a pan of hot water. Stir in the evaporated milk and beat thoroughly.

SOUR CREAM TART

This tart, whose texture is reminiscent of cheesecake, makes a good weekday dessert and may be served hot or cold. For a more elaborate dessert, a chilled apricot purée could be served with it.

PREPARATION TIME: *30 min*
COOKING TIME: *40 min*
INGREDIENTS *(for 6):*
¾ quantity standard pastry (page 171)
3 eggs
⅔ cup sugar
1⅓ cups golden raisins
½ teaspoon ground cinnamon
¼ teaspoon ground cloves
*¼ teaspoon salt**
¾ cup sour cream
Grated rind of a lemon

Roll out the prepared pie pastry, ⅙ in thick, on a floured surface. Line a 9 in flan ring with the pastry. Prick the bottom with a fork and leave it to rest in the refrigerator.

Separate the eggs and beat the yolks thoroughly with the sugar until pale yellow and thick enough to leave a trail. Finely chop the raisins and beat them into the eggs, together with the cinnamon, cloves, salt, sour cream and lemon rind. Beat the egg whites in a separate bowl until stiff, but not dry. Fold the egg whites carefully and evenly into the yolk mixture, and spoon it into the tart case. Bake for 15 minutes on a shelf low in the oven, pre-heated to 425°F (220°C, mark 7), then reduce the heat to 350°F (180°C, mark 4) for a further 25 minutes.

Leave the tart for about 10 minutes before removing the ring and serving the tart.

PROFITEROLES

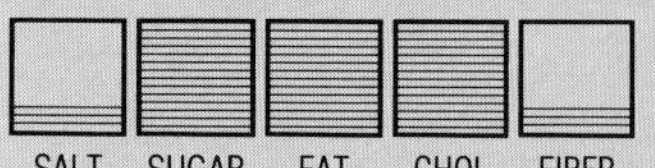

WHOLEFOOD*
TOTAL CALORIES: ABOUT 3000

For low **sugar** use carob bars without added sugar and unsweetened evaporated milk. (Calories lost: up to 13.)
The **fat** and **cholesterol** will be moderate to fairly high, if some or all of the heavy cream filling is replaced with quark lightly sweetened with honey. Less chocolate can also be used, and water instead of the milk-and-water mixture in the pastry. (Calories lost: up to 1250.)
Choux pastry made with either commercial **gluten-free** or **whole wheat** flour is excellent.

Freezing: ☑ up to 3 months (profiteroles and sauce should be frozen separately).

SOUR CREAM TART

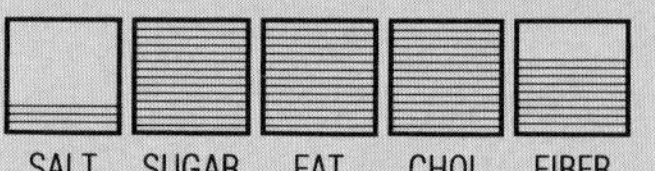

GLUTEN-FREE* WHOLEFOOD*
TOTAL CALORIES: ABOUT 2950

For medium **sugar** use only half. (Calories lost: up to 296.) For a low **fat** level, replace the sour cream with low-fat sour cream (or, for a very low-fat filling, quark) and use only 1 egg yolk with 2 ounces tofu. Use a low-fat pastry. (Calories lost: up to 415.) This, plus the use of vegetable fat in whatever pastry is used, will give low **cholesterol**.

Freezing: ☑ up to 1 month.

CHOCOLATE CREAM PIE

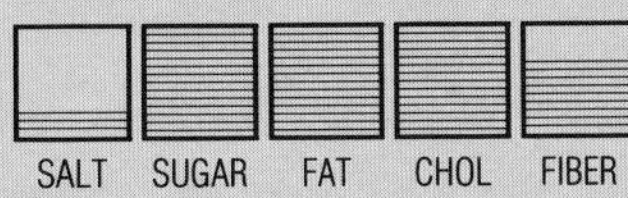

GLUTEN-FREE* WHOLEFOOD*
TOTAL CALORIES: ABOUT 4445

For medium **sugar** use oatcakes instead of graham crackers, omit sugar from the filling and only a little for the dusting. (Calories lost: up to 355.)
The **fat** and **cholesterol** will be medium if you use crumbled cookies, such as gingersnaps, which have less fat, and no binding fat. Use skim milk, together with only 1 tablespoon butter for the sauce, and make the topping with quark or only half the cream, into which a stiffly beaten egg white is folded just before serving. (Calories lost: up to 1721.)

Food processor: ✓ for the crumb crust.

Freezing: ✓ up to 2 months.

PARIS-BREST

WHOLEFOOD*
TOTAL CALORIES: ABOUT 2535

For low **sugar** omit sugar in the pastry and use 1 tablespoon honey in the filling. (Calories lost: up to 119.)
To reduce the **fat** level to low, use skim milk and replace the heavy cream with quark. The **cholesterol** level will remain high because of the eggs. Use thinly sliced hazelnuts instead of almonds. (Calories lost: up to 1205.)

Freezing: ✓ up to 3 months.

CHOCOLATE CREAM PIE

The crumb crust for this light fluffy pie should be chilled for 2 hours before filling.

PREPARATION TIME: *20 min*
CHILLING TIME: *1 hour*
INGREDIENTS *(for 6):*
1 quantity crumb crust (page 172)
FILLING:
1¼ cups milk
2 tablespoons granulated sugar
¼ cup flour
1½ teaspoons cornstarch
2 eggs
2 tablespoons unsalted butter
3–3½ ounces semisweet chocolate, grated
2 teaspoons brandy or rum
Confectioners' sugar
TOPPING:
½ cup heavy cream
1 tablespoon milk
Grated chocolate (optional)

Make up the crumb crust according to the basic recipe and line an 8½ in fluted flan dish.

Heat the milk. Blend the sugar, flour, cornstarch and beaten egg together in a bowl, then stir in the milk. Return this mixture to the pan and cook over low heat, stirring continuously, until the mixture thickens and just comes to the boil. Remove the pan from the heat and stir in the butter, cut into small pieces, the chocolate and brandy. Stir until smooth, then leave to cool slightly. Spoon the filling into the crumb crust, and dust it with confectioners' sugar to prevent a skin forming. Chill.

Just before serving, whip the cream with the milk until thick enough to hold its shape. Spoon this over the filling and dust with a little coarsely grated chocolate if you are using it.

PARIS-BREST

In the late 19th century, this dessert was created in honor of a famous bicycle race which was run on a circular route from Paris to Brest and back again. It is a concoction of choux pastry filled with Chantilly cream.

PREPARATION TIME: *30 min*
COOKING TIME: *30 min*
INGREDIENTS *(for 4):*
2 tablespoons unsalted butter
1 teaspoon sugar
¾ cup milk
1 cup flour
3 eggs
⅓ cup sliced almonds
CHANTILLY CREAM:
1¼ cups heavy cream
3 tablespoons confectioners' sugar
1 egg white

For the choux pastry, put the butter, sugar and milk into a saucepan over moderate heat, and bring to the boil. Stir in the sifted flour, remove the pan from the heat, and beat vigorously with a wooden spoon until the dough leaves the sides of the pan clean. Beat 2 eggs, one by one, into the dough. Then add the yolk of the third egg, beating vigorously until the dough is smooth and shiny. If necessary, beat in the remaining egg white.

Spoon the dough into a pastry bag fitted with a large plain nozzle. Pipe a ring, about 1½ in wide and 8 in across, on to a greased baking sheet. Sprinkle the almonds over the dough and bake for 30 minutes on the middle shelf of an oven pre-heated to 425°F (220°C, mark 7) for 30 minutes, or until dark brown. Cool on a wire rack, then split in half, horizontally.

For the Chantilly cream, whip together the heavy cream, 2 tablespoons confectioners' sugar and an egg white until light and fluffy. Spoon the cream into the hollow bottom half of the ring. Cover with the lid, and dust with the remaining confectioners' sugar.

CHEESE CAKE

This cheese cake is not baked like the European version, but set with gelatin. It is chilled and decorated with fruit for an unusual dessert.

PREPARATION TIME: *35 min*
CHILLING TIME: *3 hours*
INGREDIENTS *(for 6):*
1 cup cottage cheese
½ cup cream cheese
4–6 tablespoons unsalted butter
1½ cups crushed graham crackers
½ cup sugar
2 envelopes unflavored gelatin
Rind and juice of a small lemon
2 eggs
*Salt**
½ cup heavy cream
GARNISH:
Black grapes and mandarin orange segments

Melt the butter in a small saucepan over low heat. Remove the pan from the heat and with a fork stir in the cracker crumbs and 2 tablespoons of sugar. Press this mixture over the bottom of an 8 in loose-bottomed flan or cake pan. Put the base in the refrigerator to chill while preparing the cheese mixture.

Put 3 tablespoons of cold water in a small pan and sprinkle the gelatin evenly on the surface. Set aside to soak for 5 minutes. Meanwhile, rub the cottage cheese through a coarse sieve into a large basin and add the cream cheese. Finely grate the lemon rind and mix in well.

Separate the eggs; add 3 tablespoons of sugar and a pinch of salt to the yolks and beat until creamy and light. Gently heat the pan of soaked gelatin, stirring continuously, but do not allow it to boil. Remove from the heat once the gelatin has dissolved, and add the strained lemon juice. Gradually whisk this liquid into the egg yolks, before blending it all into the cheese mixture. Whisk the egg whites until thick, then whisk in the remaining sugar and beat until stiff. Fold the beaten egg whites and the lightly whipped cream into the cheese mixture. Pour into the prepared chilled cake base and level the top. Chill in the refrigerator for 2–3 hours or until firm.

When ready to serve, loosen the sides of the cheese cake with a knife blade. Remove the cake from the pan and decorate the top with halved black grapes and mandarin orange segments.

Serve cut into wedges.

CHEESE CAKE

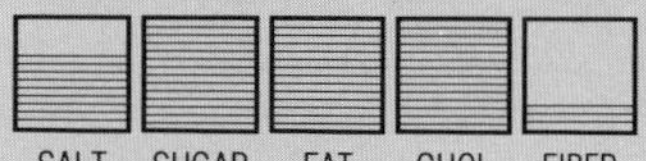

SALT SUGAR FAT CHOL FIBER

GLUTEN-FREE WHOLEFOOD*
TOTAL CALORIES: ABOUT 2840

For low **salt** use crushed Shredded Wheat instead of graham crackers, and unsalted soft cheese. If this is difficult to obtain, drain thick yogurt through coarse cloth.
Reduce **sugar** to moderate by substituting ground almonds in the base mixture and using only 2 tablespoons in the yolks and again to beat with the whites. (Calories lost: up to 129.)
For a low **fat** level, use skim milk cheese such as quark throughout. (If making at home, about 2 quarts of thick low-fat yogurt will be needed to yield ¾ pound (1½ cups) firm cheese.) Use only 2 tablespoons butter with the crushed cereal (Grapenuts make a good base, and contain no added sugar), and substitute low-fat sour cream or thick yogurt (1¼ cups of either) for the cream. (Calories lost: up to 782.)
For a low **cholesterol** level also omit 1 yolk.
Using Grapenuts or a similar cereal will give a **wholefood** dish.

Freezing: √ up to 1 month.

LAYER CAKE

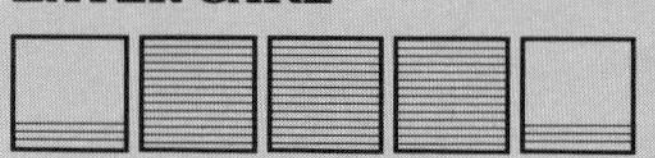

SALT SUGAR FAT CHOL FIBER

WHOLEFOOD*
TOTAL CALORIES: ABOUT 1655

For medium **sugar** replace the fillings with fruit purées, mixed with quark if wished. (Calories lost: up to 569.)

The amount of **fat** can be reduced by making what is known as a fatless sponge (see Strawberry Cream Sponge, on the next page) where the only fat comes from the eggs. This is very satisfactory if eaten the same day, or frozen. Using quark in place of cream in fillings gives a low fat content; or for medium fat, replace half the cream with quark, and fold in a beaten egg white. (Calories lost: up to 1115.)
The **cholesterol** remains high because of the eggs.

Freezing: ✓ up to 6 months.

GINGERBREAD

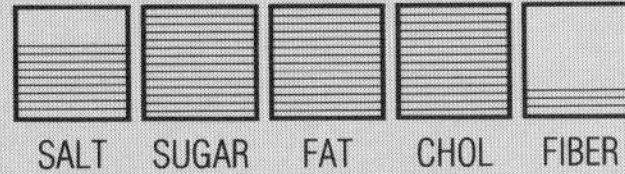

GLUTEN-FREE*
TOTAL CALORIES: ABOUT 5015

For low **salt** use honey instead of golden syrup, unsalted butter and low-sodium baking powder. For a less rich cake use skim milk and halve the sugar, butter, molasses and syrup. If wished, ⅔ cup raisins can be liquidized in the milk to give a moist sweetness and more bulk (also more fiber). The levels of **fat**, **cholesterol** and **sugar** will of course depend on the size of the slice you cut, but will then be between medium and low. (Calories lost: up to 1428.)
Gluten-free buckwheat flour can be used successfully.
This kind of cake is excellent made with **whole wheat** flour, with a spoonful of water added to the mix before putting in the pan.

Freezing: ✓ up to 6 months.
Microwave: ✓

LAYER CAKE

In this traditional layer cake, the fat is creamed before the flour is beaten in, giving a rich cake with a close, even grain and soft crumb.

PREPARATION TIME: *15 min*
COOKING TIME: *25 min*
INGREDIENTS:
½ cup butter or margarine
½ cup sugar
2 large eggs
Vanilla extract or grated lemon or orange rind
1 cup self-rising flour

Grease two 7 in straight-sided layer cake pans and line the bottoms with buttered wax paper. In a bowl, beat the butter until soft, then add the sugar and cream until light and fluffy. Beat in the eggs, one at a time, then add a few drops of vanilla or finely grated lemon or orange rind. Beat in the sifted flour.

Divide this mixture equally between the two pans, and level off the surface. Bake the cakes side by side, if possible, in the center of the oven pre-heated to 350°F (180°C, mark 4) for about 25 minutes. Cool on a wire rack.

Layer the two cakes with jam or a butter cream filling and dust the top lightly with granulated or sifted confectioners' sugar.

GINGERBREAD

This is best if made 4–7 days in advance, to give the flavor time to mellow. Cut into chunks just before serving.

PREPARATION TIME: *15 min*
COOKING TIME: *1½ hours*
INGREDIENTS:
2 cups flour
1 tablespoon ground ginger
1 tablespoon baking powder
1 teaspoon baking soda
*1 teaspoon salt**
1⅓ cups light brown sugar
¾ cup butter
½ cup molasses
½ cup imported golden syrup or dark corn syrup
1¾ cups milk
1 large egg

Grease a 9 in square cake pan, about 2 in deep, and line with buttered wax paper. Sift all the dry ingredients, except the sugar, into a large bowl. Warm the sugar, butter, molasses and syrup in a pan over low heat until the butter has just melted. Stir the melted ingredients into the center of the dry mix, together with the milk and beaten egg. Beat thoroughly with a wooden spoon. Pour the mixture into the prepared pan and bake in the center of an oven, pre-heated to 350°F (180°C, mark 4), for about 1½ hours, or until well-risen and just firm to the touch. Leave to cool in the pan for 15 minutes, then turn out to cool on a wire rack. When cold, wrap in foil, without removing the lining paper, and store in a tin.

HUNGARIAN HAZELNUT TORTE

Hungarian dessert cakes – or *torten* – are internationally famous, and several of them were perfected by Dobos, a 19th-century Hungarian confectioner. This classic hazelnut cake has a chocolate cream filling and a caramel topping. It improves in flavor if kept for a day or two in a completely airtight tin.

PREPARATION TIME: *30 min*
COOKING TIME: *30–40 min*
INGREDIENTS *(for 6)*:

1 cup unblanched hazelnuts
4 eggs
⅔ cup sugar
FILLING:
¼ cup unsalted butter
½ cup confectioners' sugar
2 rounded teaspoons chocolate powder
1 rounded teaspoon instant coffee
TOPPING:
6 tablespoons sugar
12 hazelnuts

Lightly grease two round 7 in layer cake pans. Grind the unblanched hazelnuts finely in a liquidizer or coffee grinder. Separate the eggs and whisk the whites until stiff, but still moist. Whisk the egg yolks with the sugar until pale lemon in color and the mixture trails off the whisk in ribbons.

Fold the ground nuts and whisked egg whites alternately into the egg yolks. Divide the mixture equally between the two cake pans and bake in the center of an oven pre-heated to 350°F (180°C, mark 4) for 30 minutes, or until set. Test by pressing the top of the cakes with a finger – it should leave no impression. Remove the cakes from the oven, and allow them to shrink slightly before turning them out to cool on a wire rack.

Meanwhile, prepare the filling: cream the butter until fluffy and sift the confectioners' sugar, chocolate and coffee together; beat it gradually into the butter. When the cakes are cool, sandwich them together with the filling. Set aside while you prepare the caramel topping.

Put 2 tablespoons of water and the sugar in a small, heavy-based saucepan. Stir the contents over low heat until dissolved into a clear syrup. Increase the heat and boil the syrup rapidly, without stirring, until it is a rich golden color.

Remove the pan from the heat immediately and pour most of the caramel over the top of the cake. Spread it evenly with an oiled knife and mark the topping into portions with the same knife. Decorate the top quickly with the whole nuts before the caramel hardens. As the remaining caramel cools it can be trickled over the nuts or pulled into a spun sugar veil and arranged on top of the cake.

STRAWBERRY CREAM SPONGE

A very light cake which uses no fat, its texture depending entirely on the incorporated eggs.

PREPARATION TIME: *20 min*
COOKING TIME: *15 min*
INGREDIENTS:
¾ cup flour
*Pinch of salt**
3 eggs
6 tablespoons sugar
Strawberry jam
½ cup heavy or whipping cream
Granulated or confectioners' sugar for dusting

Butter and dust with flour and sugar two 7 in straight-sided cake pans. Sift the flour with the salt twice into a bowl. Place a deep mixing bowl over a pan of hot water, break the eggs into the bowl and gradually whisk in the sugar. Continue whisking until the mixture is pale, and thick enough to leave a trail. Carefully fold in the sifted flour and salt. Divide the mixture equally between the two pans, putting any scrapings from the bowl at the side of the pans, not in the middle. Bake just above the center of an oven, pre-heated to 375°F (190°C, mark 5), for about 15 minutes or until pale brown and springy to the touch.

Carefully ease away the edges of the baked cakes with a palette knife, and cool on a wire rack.

When cold, spread the bases of both sponges with a thin layer of jam, cover one sponge with whipped cream and place the other cake, jam downwards, on top. Press lightly together and dust with granulated or confectioners' sugar. Chill until serving.

HUNGARIAN HAZELNUT TORTE

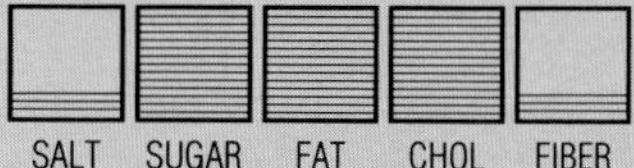

SALT SUGAR FAT CHOL FIBER

GLUTEN-FREE WHOLEFOOD*
TOTAL CALORIES: ABOUT 2295

For slightly lower **sugar** halve the amount of caramel topping, or replace with a brushing of warmed honey when the cakes are still warm. The filling can be made by combining quark with the chocolate and coffee powder and just 1 tablespoon honey; fill just before serving. (Calories lost: up to 704.)

The amount of **fat** cannot be reduced as the hazelnut 'flour' acts as the main base in this cake. However, the fat in the filling can be reduced to low by the change from butter to quark, suggested above. (Calories lost: up to 331.)

The **cholesterol** level will stay high because of the eggs.

STRAWBERRY CREAM SPONGE

SALT SUGAR FAT CHOL FIBER

GLUTEN-FREE* WHOLEFOOD*
TOTAL CALORIES: ABOUT 1600

Eliminate added **sugar** in the filling by using strawberry jam made without added sugar, or mashed strawberries or for a variation, mashed raspberries (which will give a high **fiber** content). (Calories lost: up to 21.)

This kind of sponge, with its only fat coming from the eggs, is preferable in health terms to the ordinary type.

The **fat** and **cholesterol** content from the eggs can be reduced by omitting 1 or 2 egg yolks, although this will change the color and flavor of the cake. One egg yolk plus 3 whites works well, but the cooking time is less, only 7–10 minutes. (Calories lost: up to 130.)

Freezing: ✓ up to 6 months.

DANISH LAYER CAKE

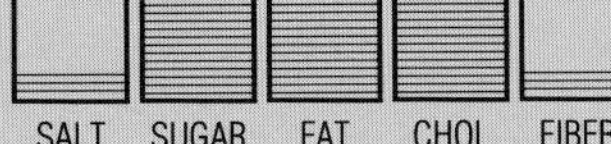

SALT SUGAR FAT CHOL FIBER

GLUTEN-FREE* WHOLEFOOD*
TOTAL CALORIES: ABOUT 4440

The **sugar** in the cake cannot be reduced, but the amount in the filling can be halved, as the chocolate and pineapple (if using canned, choose fruit canned in juice, not sugar syrup) will add sweetness. If wished, the sponge recipe on the facing page can be substituted. This gives medium sugar. (Calories lost: up to 514.)
The high **fat** level can be reduced to moderate by substituting quark for the heavy cream. If the cream flavor is still wanted, replace only half the cream with quark, and fold in 1 large stiffly beaten egg white when the mixture is just setting. Soft cheese fillings work very well for this type of cake. (Calories lost: up to 2109.) The **cholesterol** level remains high because of the eggs.
Wholefood: if using whole wheat flour, sift and retain the bran in the sieve. Use to 'flour' the greased cake pans, mix into the filling, or keep for another time.

Freezing: ✓ up to 3 months.

DANISH LAYER CAKE

There are numerous versions of the Danish layer cake, from a simple jam sandwich to a huge eight-layer concoction of wafer-thin sponge cakes in alternating layers of thick cream and fruit. It is served with morning coffee and afternoon tea, as an after-dinner sweet or with evening coffee.

PREPARATION TIME: *45 min*
COOKING TIME: *25 min*
CHILLING TIME: *1 hour*
INGREDIENTS *(for 6):*
4 eggs
Rind and juice of half lemon
$1\frac{1}{4}$ cups confectioners' sugar
$\frac{3}{4}$ cup flour
$\frac{1}{4}$ cup cornstarch
$\frac{1}{2}$ teaspoon baking powder
FILLING:
1 envelope unflavored gelatin
$2\frac{1}{2}$ cups heavy cream
4 teaspoons vanilla sugar (page 184)
4 slices fresh or canned pineapple
3 ounces unsweetened or bittersweet chocolate

Separate the eggs and put the yolks in a large bowl, together with the lemon rind and juice. Sift the confectioners' sugar into the yolks and beat until fluffy and pale cream in color. Whisk the egg whites in a separate bowl until they stand in soft peaks, then fold them carefully into the yolk mixture. Sift the two flours and baking powder together and blend into the sponge mixture.

Grease a loose-bottomed round deep cake pan, 8 in wide, and line with buttered wax paper. Spoon the sponge mixture into the pan, smoothing it level around the sides. Bake in the center of a pre-heated oven at 350°F (180°C, mark 4) for 25 minutes or until the sponge is golden and well risen.

Loosen the edges of the sponge with a sharp knife and turn the cake out on a wire rack to cool. When completely cold, cut the cake into three thin layers.

Dissolve the gelatin in a few spoonfuls of warm water and leave to cool slightly. Whip the cream, setting one-third aside for decoration. Fold the cooled gelatin into the remaining cream and sweeten with the vanilla sugar. Peel and trim the pineapple slices (or drain thoroughly if using canned pineapple); set one slice aside and chop the other three finely. Grate the chocolate and blend into the cream with the chopped pineapple. Leave the filling to set.

Assemble the layer cake about 2 hours before serving. Divide the filling equally over the sponge layers and spread it evenly; sandwich the layers together. Pipe the rest of the whipped cream through a narrow rosette nozzle, around the edge and down the sides of the cake. Garnish the top with the reserved pineapple, cut into small chunks.

Chill the layer cake in the refrigerator for about 1 hour and serve it cut into wedges.

CARROT CAKE

The natural sweetness of carrots is brought out in this moist cake with its rich orange color.

PREPARATION TIME: *25 min*
COOKING TIME: *35–40 min*
INGREDIENTS:
1 cup butter
2 cups sugar
1 teaspoon ground cinnamon
½ teaspoon ground mace or nutmeg
½–1 teaspoon grated orange rind
4 eggs
1½ cups grated carrots
¾ cup finely chopped toasted walnuts
2½ cups flour
1 tablespoon baking powder
*½ teaspoon salt**
⅓ cup warm water

Cream the butter and sugar together until light and fluffy. Beat in the cinnamon, mace (or nutmeg) and the grated orange rind. Add the eggs one at a time, beating well after each addition. Gradually stir in the grated carrots and chopped nuts.

Sift together the flour, baking powder and salt. Add them, with the warm water, to the creamed mixture. Do not beat it but fold in the flour to the point where it is just well moistened.

Pour the batter into a buttered 11 by 15 in cake pan and bake in a pre-heated oven at 350°F (180°C, mark 4) for 35–40 minutes, or until the cake springs back when it is pressed lightly in the center.

Leave the cake for just a few minutes after removing it from the oven, then loosen it from the sides of the pan and turn it out on a rack to cool.

FARMHOUSE FRUIT CAKE

This recipe uses soft margarine, which cuts the preparation time, as there is no need to beat it until creamy as is the case with butter. An electric mixer can be used instead of beating with a wooden spoon; switch it off from time to time and scrape the cake mixture down into the bowl before you continue.

PREPARATION TIME: *10 min*
COOKING TIME: *about 1½ hours*
INGREDIENTS:
¾ cup soft margarine
¾ cup sugar
½ cup golden raisins
½ cup raisins
½ cup chopped glacé cherries
3 cups self-rising flour
*Pinch of salt**
1 teaspoon apple pie spice
4–6 tablespoons milk
3 eggs

Grease an 8 in round deep cake pan and line it with buttered wax paper. Mix the margarine and all the dry ingredients in a bowl, then add the milk and eggs and beat with a wooden spoon until well mixed, for 2–3 minutes. Turn into the prepared pan and level the top.

Bake in the center of the oven pre-heated to 350°F (180°C, mark 4) for about 1½ hours. When a skewer comes away clean, the cake is cooked. Leave the cake in the pan for 15 minutes before turning out on a rack to cool.

TYROL CAKE

This is an example of a plain, rubbed-in cake, the easiest type of all to make. They are best eaten within 2 or 3 days of baking.

PREPARATION TIME: *25 min*
COOKING TIME: *1¾ hours*
INGREDIENTS:
2 cups flour
*Pinch of salt**
1 teaspoon ground cinnamon
7 tablespoons margarine
¼ cup sugar
⅓ cup currants
⅓ cup golden raisins
1 teaspoon baking soda
¾ cup milk
3 tablespoons clear honey

Grease a 6 in round deep cake pan. Sift the flour, salt and cinnamon into a bowl, cut up the margarine and rub into the flour until the mixture resembles fine breadcrumbs. To keep the mixture cool, raise the hands high when letting the crumbs drop back into the bowl. Stir in the sugar, currants and raisins and made a well in the center. Dissolve the baking soda in the milk, stir in the honey and pour this mixture into the well in the flour. Using a wooden spoon, gradually work in the dry ingredients, adding more milk if necessary to give a firm dropping consistency.

Spoon the cake mixture into the prepared pan and level the top. Bake in the center of the oven, pre-heated to 325°F (170°C, mark 3), for 1¾–2 hours or until well risen.

Test with a fine skewer – if it comes away clean, the cake is cooked. Cool on a wire rack.

CARROT CAKE

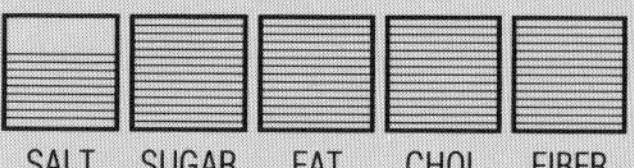

SALT SUGAR FAT CHOL FIBER

GLUTEN-FREE* WHOLEFOOD*
TOTAL CALORIES: ABOUT 5195

Reduce the **salt** to low by using a low-salt baking powder.
Using only ½ cup **sugar** with the same amount each of ground almonds and (optional) chopped dates will make the cake quite sweet enough and gives an overall low to medium level. (Calories lost: up to 566.)
For moderate **fat** and **cholesterol**, use half the amount of butter and only 2 egg yolks, with an extra egg white. (Calories lost: up to 937.)

Freezing: √ up to 6 months.

FARMHOUSE FRUIT CAKE

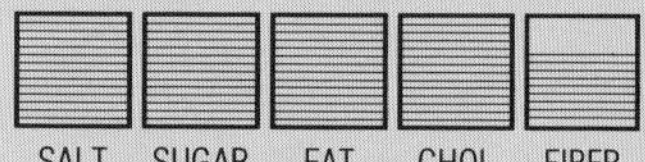

SALT SUGAR FAT CHOL FIBER

GLUTEN-FREE*
TOTAL CALORIES: ABOUT 3985

For medium **salt** use unsalted baking powder and margarine.
To reduce **fat** to low use only 2–4 tablespoons. (Calories lost: up to 639.)
For medium **sugar** reduce it by half and add an extra ⅔ cup dried fruit. (Calories lost: up to 99.)
For medium **cholesterol** omit 2 yolks and add a fourth egg white plus an extra spoonful of milk, if needed.
For a **wholefood** cake, use whole wheat flour, honey in place of sugar and chopped dried apricots in place of cherries.

Freezing: √ up to 6 months.

TYROL CAKE

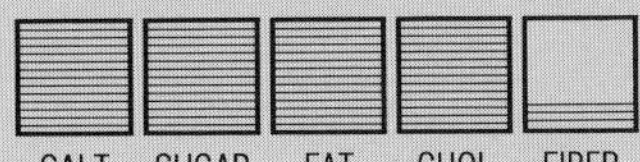

GLUTEN-FREE* WHOLEFOOD*
TOTAL CALORIES: ABOUT 2170

To reduce **salt** level to low, use low-sodium margarine and baking powders.
The amount of **sugar** can be halved, adding a spoonful of extra milk if needed. (Calories lost: up to 99.)
Both salt and **fat** levels can also be reduced by halving the amount of fat added. Skim milk can also be used, which with reduction of fat will produce a low-fat recipe with virtually no **cholesterol** provided the margarine is vegetable. (Calories lost: up to 376.)

Freezing: ✓ up to 6 months.

ANADAMA BREAD

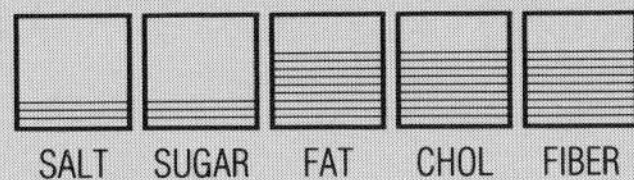

GLUTEN-FREE* WHOLEFOOD*
TOTAL CALORIES: ABOUT 2700

The low **salt** level assumes unsalted butter or oil is used. The **fat** level can be reduced to very low by omitting the butter from the dough, and covering loosely with plastic wrap when rising, rather than greasing: both measures are intended to stop surface drying from contact with air, which will stop bread rising fully. However, fat-free bread stales quickly, so 1–2 tablespoons butter or oil is worth adding, and will still give low fat and **cholesterol**. (Calories lost: up to 211.)

Freezing: ✓ up to 3 months.

ANADAMA BREAD

This is a variation, using molasses, on the cornbread that is popular in the southern states.

PREPARATION TIME: *20 min (plus rising)*
COOKING TIME: *55 min*
INGREDIENTS *(for 2 loaves):*
2½–3 cups flour
1 cup cornmeal
2 packages active dry yeast
1 tablespoon salt
2 cups water
5 tablespoons butter
½ cup molasses

Heat the water until it feels warm to the hand. Mix a little of it (about half a cup) with the yeast and stir until well blended. Leave for 10 or 15 minutes until frothy.

Combine 2½ cups flour, the cornmeal and salt in a large bowl. Mix the rest of the warm water with the butter and molasses. Add this to the flour mixture together with the yeast. Beat for 3 minutes with an electric mixer set at medium speed, or beat by hand – about 150 strokes with a wooden spoon. Add flour as necessary to make a stiff dough.

Turn the dough on to a floured surface and knead for about 10 minutes until it is no longer sticky. Place the dough in a buttered bowl, turning it over in the bowl 2 or 3 times until it is well greased. Set aside to rise in a warm place for 1–1½ hours, or until the dough has doubled in size.

Punch down the dough, divide it into 2 balls, and place each in a buttered 8 in round cake pan. Allow to rise again until doubled in size, then bake in the center of a pre-heated oven at 375°F (190°C, mark 5) for about 55 minutes or until deep brown. The bread is done if the bottom of the bread sounds hollow when rapped with the knuckles.

SALLY LUNN

This can be baked in an ordinary cake pan, as below, or in a tube pan or plain ring mold, which looks attractive and is easy to slice.

PREPARATION TIME: *25 min (plus rising)*
COOKING TIME: *15–20 min*
INGREDIENTS *(for 2 loaves):*
4 cups flour
¼ cup butter
1 cup milk
1 teaspoon sugar
1 package active dry yeast
2 eggs
*1 tablespoon salt**
SUGAR TOPPING:
1 tablespoon sugar
1 tablespoon water

Melt the butter in a small pan, then add the milk and sugar. Put the yeast in a bowl, beat the eggs and add them, with the warm milk mixture, to the yeast: blend thoroughly until the yeast has dissolved.

Sift the flour and salt into a large bowl, make a well in the center and pour in the milk mixture. Gradually incorporate the flour with the fingers of one hand and beat the dough against the bowl until it leaves the sides clean. Knead the dough on a lightly floured surface until smooth.

Divide the dough into two equal portions, knead each piece into a ball and place it in a greased 15 in round cake pan. Slide each pan into an oiled plastic bag and leave in a warm place for about 1 hour or until the dough has risen almost to the top of the pans.

Remove the plastic and set the pans on baking sheets. Bake just above the center of a pre-heated oven at 450°F (230°C, mark 8) for 15–20 minutes. Meanwhile, make the sugar topping by heating the sugar and water in a small pan over low heat until the sugar has dissolved: boil rapidly for 1–2 minutes.

Turn the Sally Lunns out on to a wire rack and, while still warm, brush the tops with the sugar.

BABAS

These are traditionally flavored with rum, but if you do not have any to hand you could use brandy instead. Although unorthodox, it is quite successful.

PREPARATION TIME: *40 min (plus rising)*
COOKING TIME: *15–20 min*
INGREDIENTS *(for 16 babas):*
2 cups flour
2 packages active dry yeast
6 tablespoons warm (110°F, 43°C) milk
*½ teaspoon salt**
2 tablespoons sugar
4 eggs
½ cup butter
⅔ cup currants
Lard
SYRUP:
4 tablespoons clear honey
4 tablespoons water
3 tablespoons rum (approx.)
GARNISH:
1¼ cups whipped cream

Blend the yeast, milk and ½ cup of the measured flour together in a large bowl and beat with a wooden spoon until smooth. Leave the yeast in a warm place for about 20 minutes or until frothy. Sift the remaining flour and the salt into the yeast and blend in the sugar, the lightly beaten eggs, softened butter and the currants. Beat the mixture, which should be fairly soft, with a wooden spoon for 4 minutes.

Grease 16 small ring molds with lard and, using a teaspoon, spoon in the dough until the molds are half full. Set the ring molds on baking sheets and cover them with sheets of lightly oiled plastic wrap.

Leave the babas to rise in a warm place until the dough has risen about two-thirds up the sides of the molds.

Bake the babas just above the center of an oven pre-heated to 400°F (200°C, mark 6) for 15–20 minutes or until golden brown.

Meanwhile, prepare the syrup: heat the honey and water in a small pan over low heat; stir in rum to taste. Leave the baked babas to cool for a few minutes in the molds before turning them out on to a plate. While the babas are still hot, spoon the warm syrup over them until it has soaked in. Leave to cool, then transfer the rum-soaked babas to a serving dish and fill the centers with spooned or piped whipped cream.

Serve at once.

SALLY LUNN

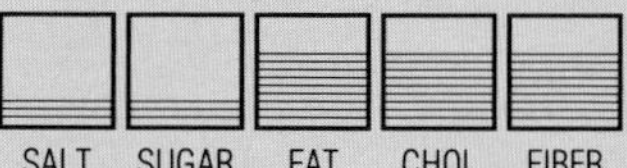

GLUTEN-FREE* WHOLEFOOD*
TOTAL CALORIES: ABOUT 2290

The low **salt** level assumes unsalted butter is used.
The **sugar** can be replaced by honey if wished, adding ½ tablespoon of water to make the topping. (Calories lost: up to 25.)
The **fat** and **cholesterol** levels can be reduced to low by adding only 2 tablespoons butter, using skim milk and 1 egg only. (Calories lost: up to 342.)
The **fiber** content depends on the flour used: it will be medium, as shown, if refined flour is used, but high if whole wheat flour is used.

Freezing: ✓ up to 3 months.

BABAS

GLUTEN-FREE* WHOLEFOOD*
TOTAL CALORIES: ABOUT 3865

The low **salt** level depends on unsalted fat being used.
The **sugar** content will only be low if strict level spoonfuls of honey are used. If wished, use only 3 carefully measured spoonfuls and ½ in dough, for an overall low sugar level. (Calories lost: up to 60.)
The **fat** and **cholesterol** levels can be reduced to low by using skim milk, only 2 tablespoons butter and only 1 egg yolk but all the whites. (Calories lost: up to 779.)

Freezing: ✓ up to 3 months.

CHELSEA BUNS

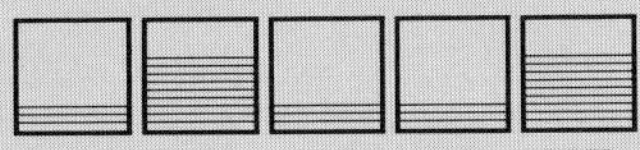

GLUTEN-FREE* WHOLEFOOD*
TOTAL CALORIES: ABOUT 1695

The amount of **sugar** will depend on how much honey is used. To minimize, make your own chopped peel from well-scrubbed citrus rind (which will not be soaked in sugar, and will also be free from preservative), and replace the sugar with 2½ tablespoons clear honey, which tends to give a sweeter flavor, weight for weight. Use honey for brushing sparingly, heating gently before applying to get a thinner coating. This will give a low sugar level. (Calories lost: up to 133.)

Freezing: √ up to 1 month.

CHELSEA BUNS

This is a not too rich version of these famous small buns. A little apple pie spice – about half a teaspoon – can be added.

PREPARATION TIME: *20 min (plus rising)*
COOKING TIME: *30–35 min*
INGREDIENTS *(for 9 buns):*
2 cups flour
½ teaspoon granulated sugar
1 package active dry yeast
¾ cup warm (110°F, 43°C) milk
*½ teaspoon salt**
1 tablespoon margarine or lard
1 egg
½ cup dried fruit (golden raisins, currants or raisins)
2 tablespoons chopped mixed peel
⅓ cup light brown sugar
1–2 tablespoons melted butter
Clear honey

Sift ½ cup of the measured flour into a bowl and add the granulated sugar and yeast. Beat in the milk with a wooden spoon. Leave this yeast mixture in a warm place for about 20 minutes or until frothy. Sift together the remaining flour and the salt and rub in the margarine. Make a well in the center, add the beaten egg and pour in the yeast mixture. Using one hand, gradually work in the flour.

Beat the dough in the bowl until it leaves the sides clean; it should be fairly soft and pliable. Turn the dough on to a lightly floured surface and knead it for 10 minutes, until smooth. Put it in a lightly oiled plastic bag and leave it to rise at room temperature for 1–1½ hours or until it has doubled in size.

Knead the risen dough on a lightly floured surface until smooth, then roll it out with a well-floured rolling pin, to a rectangle 12 by 9 in. Mix the dried fruit, peel and brown sugar together, brush the dough with melted butter and spread the fruit mixture on top to within ½ in of the longer edges. Roll up the dough, starting with one of the long sides, and press the join to seal it.

Cut the roll into nine equal slices and lay them flat, in rows of three, in a greased 7 in square cake pan. Leave to rise in a plastic bag, in a warm place, for about 30 minutes.

Remove the plastic bag and bake the buns in the center of a pre-heated oven at 375°F (190°C, mark 5) for 30–35 minutes. Turn the buns on to a wire rack and, while hot, brush with honey.

BARN BRACK

An Irish tea bread, similar to the Welsh bara brith and the Manx bonnag. The word "barn" comes from the Irish for loaf and its resemblance to the Saxon word "barm," meaning yeast, is coincidental. This has caused some confusion, especially since this bread would originally have been made using yeast. The word "brack" means speckled.

SOAKING TIME: *overnight*
PREPARATION TIME: *10 min*
COOKING TIME: *1¾ hours*
INGREDIENTS:
3 cups golden raisins
3 cups raisins
3 cups brown sugar
1 quart black tea or 2½ cups tea and 1 cup Irish whiskey
4 cups flour
3 eggs
1 tablespoon baking powder
1 tablespoon apple pie spice (optional)
Honey

Soak the raisins and sugar in the tea (or tea and whiskey) overnight. The next day add, gradually, the flour and the lightly beaten eggs to the fruit and sugar mixture. Blend in the baking powder and spice.

Spoon the mixture into three greased loaf pans, 8 in long by 4 in wide by 3 in deep. Bake in the center of a pre-heated oven at 300°F (150°C, mark 2) for 1¾ hours.

Leave the loaves to cool on a wire rack. Glaze the tops lightly by brushing with melted honey.

POTATO CAKES

These originated in Ireland, but are also known in Scotland and parts of the north of England.

PREPARATION TIME: *15 min*
COOKING TIME: *30 min*
INGREDIENTS *(for 10–12 cakes):*
2 cups self-rising flour
*1 teaspoon salt**
6 tablespoons butter or margarine
¾ cup mashed potatoes
½ cup milk
Caraway seeds (optional)

Sift the flour with the salt and rub in the butter or margarine. Mix in the mashed potatoes, which should be warm, and add the milk to make a soft dough (you may not need quite all the milk). Roll out about ½ in thick and cut into 10 or 12 rounds, 3 in across. If liked, sprinkle with caraway seeds. Bake on lightly floured baking sheets in a pre-heated oven at 450°F (230°C, mark 8) for 20–30 minutes. Serve the potato cakes split and spread with butter.

BRIOCHES

Special brioche pans, large or small, with sloping fluted sides are available for making this delicious sweet yeast bread.

PREPARATION TIME: *25 min (plus rising)*
COOKING TIME: *10 min*
INGREDIENTS *(for 12 brioches):*
2 cups flour
*½ teaspoon salt**
1 tablespoon sugar
1 package active dry yeast
1½ tablespoons warm water
2 eggs
¼ cup butter, melted

Sift the flour and salt into a bowl and add the sugar. Mix the yeast with the water in a small bowl, and stir it, together with the beaten eggs and the melted butter, into the flour with a wooden spoon. Beat the dough until it leaves the sides of the bowl clean, then turn it out on to a lightly floured surface and knead for 5 minutes.

Put the dough in an oiled plastic bag and leave it to rise at room temperature for 1–1½ hours or until it has doubled in

BARN BRACK

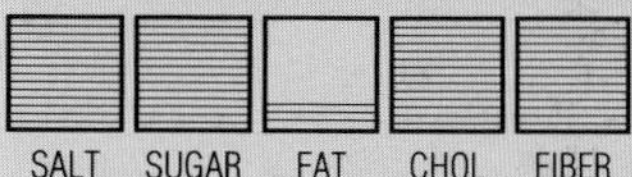

GLUTEN-FREE* WHOLEFOOD*
TOTAL CALORIES: ABOUT 6635

To reduce the **salt** level to low, use low-sodium baking powder.
The high added **sugar** level can be replaced with about 4 tablespoons honey, or by liquidizing one-quarter of the dried fruit in the tea. (Calories lost: up to 1210.)
The high **cholesterol** level can be reduced to low by using only 1 egg yolk with all the whites. The spice is advisable here, as the removal of the yolks also diminishes flavor.
(Calories lost: up to 130.)

Freezing: ✓ up to 6 months.

POTATO CAKES

GLUTEN-FREE* WHOLEFOOD*
TOTAL CALORIES: ABOUT 1575

For a low **fat** level, reduce the amount of butter or margarine to ¼ cup and use skim milk to mix. If vegetable margarine is used, the **cholesterol** will be almost nil. Serve spread with low-fat cottage cheese instead of butter. (Calories lost: up to 209.)

Freezing: ✓ up to 3 months.

BRIOCHES

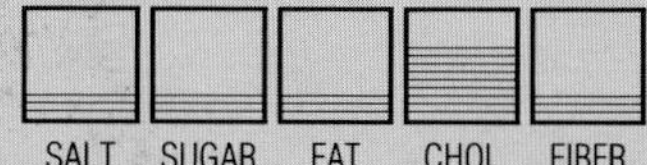

WHOLEFOOD*
TOTAL CALORIES: ABOUT 1370

The **fat** level can be further lowered, and the **cholesterol** level reduced to low, by using only 1 egg, and either reducing butter to 2 tablespoons or replacing with 2 tablespoons vegetable margarine. (Calories lost: up to 275.)

Freezing: √ up to 1 month.

DANISH PASTRIES

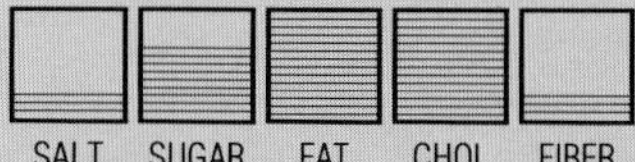

GLUTEN-FREE* WHOLEFOOD*
TOTAL CALORIES: ABOUT 3655

To keep **sugar** level to the low level given by the amount in the pastries themselves, brush with jam made with no added sugar, slightly warmed, in place of icing. Decorate with sliced almonds if wished. (Calories lost: up to 565.)
To reduce the **fat** level, use only ¼ cup unsalted butter, and omit lard from dough. In filling, replace almond paste with raisins or stewed whole dried apricots, or thick apple purée. The low fat level will give a less 'flaky' texture to the pastries, but they can still be delicious.
For low **cholesterol**, use less butter, as above, and egg whites only, both in the mixture and for the glaze. (Calories lost: up to 1093.)

Freezing: √ up to 1 month.

size. Turn the risen dough on to a lightly floured surface and knead it until smooth. Shape the dough into a sausage and divide it into 12 equal pieces.

Brush 3 in fluted patty pans with oil and shape three-quarters of each piece of dough into a ball; place it in a patty pan. Using a floured finger, press a hole in the center of the dough as far as the base of the pan. Shape the remaining piece of dough into a knob and insert it in the hole. Press lightly with the fingertip to unite the two pieces of dough. When all 12 brioches have been shaped, set the patty pans on a baking sheet and cover them with oiled plastic wrap. Leave to rise until the dough is puffy and just below the tops of the pans.

Remove the plastic wrap and bake the brioches in the center of a pre-heated oven at 450°F (230°C, mark 8) for 10 minutes or until golden brown.

DANISH PASTRIES

These can be made in a variety of shapes, including squares, crescents and pinwheels.

PREPARATION TIME: *45 min (plus rising)*
RESTING TIME: *50 min*
COOKING TIME: *10 min*
INGREDIENTS:
2 cups flour
*Pinch of salt**
2 tablespoons lard
1 tablespoon sugar
1 package active dry yeast
5 tablespoons cold water
2 eggs
10 tablespoons unsalted butter
FILLINGS:
Almond paste
2 tablespoons butter
2 tablespoons sugar
1 teaspoon cinnamon
Currants and chopped mixed peel
GARNISH:
Glacé icing

Sift the flour and salt into a large bowl. Cut up the lard and rub it into the flour with the fingertips; add the sugar and make a well in the center of the flour. Blend the yeast with the water in a small bowl until creamy and smooth, then add it to the flour together with 1 lightly beaten egg. Gradually work in the flour, then beat the soft dough until it leaves the sides of the bowl clean.

Turn the dough out on to a lightly floured surface and knead it until smooth. Put it inside a lightly oiled plastic bag and chill for 10 minutes.

Beat the butter with a wooden spoon until soft but not oily, then shape it into a rectangle about 5 in by 9½ in. On a floured board, roll out the dough to a 10–11 in square and place the butter in the center. Fold the two unbuttered sides over so that they just overlap the butter. Seal the open sides with the rolling pin, then roll the dough into an oblong strip, about three times as long as it is wide; fold in three.

Place the dough in a lightly oiled plastic bag and leave in the refrigerator for 10 minutes. Remove the plastic and roll out the dough, in the opposite direction, to an oblong strip and fold in three. Repeat the resting, rolling and folding twice more. Finally, rest the dough for 10 minutes in the refrigerator before rolling it out to any of the traditional shapes.

Almond Squares Roll out half the dough to a 10 in square, then cut it into four equal pieces. Fold two corners of each square to meet in the center, envelope style, and repeat with the other two corners. Press down firmly to seal. Place a small round of almond paste in the center.

Crescents Roll out the dough as for almond squares, and cut each square diagonally in half. Place a small piece of almond paste at the base of each triangle, then roll it up from the base and curve into a crescent shape.

Pinwheels Roll out half a portion of pastry dough to a rectangle 12 in by 8 in. Cream the butter with the sugar and cinnamon and spread over the dough to within ¼ in of the edges. Scatter a few currants and a little mixed peel over the butter. Cut the dough in half, lengthwise, and roll each piece, from the shorter end, into a thick roll. Cut this into 1 in thick slices.

Alternatively, make cuts, 1 in apart, through three-quarters of the depth of the rolls. Ease the near-cut pinwheels apart so that they overlap each other slightly; bake for about 30 minutes.

Set the pastry shapes well apart on greased baking sheets and cover with sheets of oiled plastic wrap. Leave the pastries to rise in a warm place for 20 minutes. Remove the plastic and brush the pastries with lightly beaten egg. Bake near the top of a pre-heated oven, at 425°F (220°C, mark 7), for about 10 minutes or until golden. Leave on a wire rack and, while still warm, brush almond squares, crescents and pinwheels with glacé icing. Leave to set before serving.

OVEN SCONES

If you like fruited scones, you can add about $\frac{1}{3}$ cup dried fruit – raisins, currants or golden raisins – to the mixture.

PREPARATION TIME: *15 min*
COOKING TIME: *10 min*
INGREDIENTS *(for 10–12 scones):*
2 cups flour
*Pinch of salt**
$\frac{1}{2}$ teaspoon baking soda
1 teaspoon cream of tartar
3 tablespoons firm margarine
About 4 tablespoons each milk and water mixed
Milk for glazing

Sift together the flour, salt, baking soda and cream of tartar into a wide bowl. Cut up the margarine and rub it into the flour. Gradually add the milk and water and mix with a round-bladed knife to give a soft but manageable dough.

Knead the dough quickly on a lightly floured surface, to remove all cracks. Roll the dough out $\frac{1}{2}$ in thick, and cut out 2 in rounds with a plain or fluted pastry cutter. Knead the trimmings together, roll them out and cut out as many scones as possible. Set the scones on a heated, ungreased baking sheet, brush them with milk and bake them near the top of a preheated oven at 450°F (230°C, mark 8) for about 10 minutes, until well risen and light golden brown.

SODA BREAD

Another Irish specialty, soda bread does not keep well and should be eaten on the day it is made.

PREPARATION TIME: *15 min*
COOKING TIME: *30 min*
INGREDIENTS:
4 cups flour
2 teaspoons baking soda
2 teaspoons cream of tartar
*1 teaspoon salt**
2 tablespoons lard
1–2 teaspoons sugar (optional)
$1\frac{1}{2}$ cups soured milk, or 1 cup buttermilk and $\frac{1}{2}$ cup ordinary milk

Sift the flour, baking soda, cream of tartar and salt into a bowl. Cut up the lard and rub it into the flour with the fingertips until the mixture resembles fine breadcrumbs. Mix in the sugar if used. Make a well in the center of the flour, add the milk (soured with 1 tablespoon of lemon juice) or the buttermilk, and mix to a soft but manageable dough, working the ingredients with a round-bladed knife. Add more milk if necessary.

Turn the dough on to a floured surface, knead it lightly and shape it into a 7 in round; flatten it

OVEN SCONES

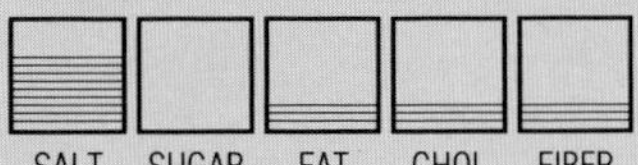

GLUTEN-FREE* WHOLEFOOD*
TOTAL CALORIES: ABOUT 1140

The **salt** level can be reduced to low by using low-sodium baking powder in place of soda plus tartar and unsalted fat.
If wished, the margarine can be reduced to 2 tablespoons for a very low **fat** content, and skim milk used. (Calories lost: up to 109.)

Freezing: ✓ up to 6 months.

SODA BREAD

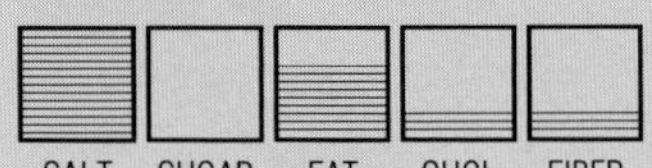

GLUTEN-FREE* WHOLEFOOD*
TOTAL CALORIES: ABOUT 1975

To reduce **salt** content to low, use low-sodium baking powder.
The medium **fat** content assumes full cream milk is used: if buttermilk (which is very low in fat) or skim milk is used, the fat level will be low. The lard can be replaced with unsalted butter, soft vegetable margarine or oil if preferred. The last two will give an even lower **cholesterol** level. (Calories lost: up to 41.)

PANCAKES

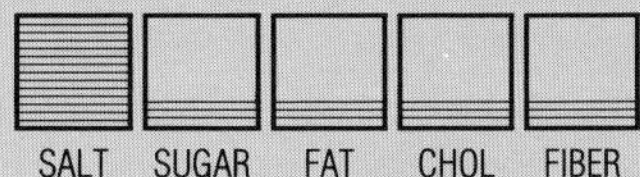

GLUTEN-FREE* WHOLEFOOD*
TOTAL CALORIES: ABOUT 810

The **salt** level can be reduced to low by using low-sodium baking powder with plain flour. Use skim milk and the minimum of oil for cooking to keep the **fat** and **cholesterol** levels very low. For an even lower cholesterol level, use the egg white only. (Calories lost: up to 225.)

Freezing: ✓ up to 6 months.

APRICOT AND WALNUT LOAF

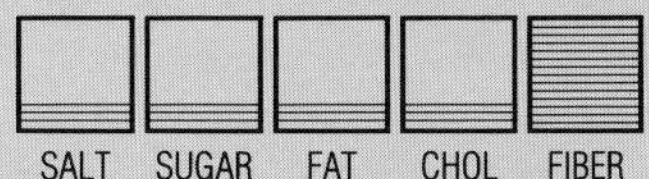

GLUTEN-FREE* WHOLEFOOD*
TOTAL CALORIES: ABOUT 1740

Sugar in the topping can be replaced with fruit sugar if wished.
To reduce the **fat** level even more, use fewer walnuts, or replace with hazelnuts which have less oil; use only 1 tablespoon fat in topping. (Calories lost: up to 184.). If you use vegetable margarine, here and in the dough in place of lard, the **cholesterol** content will be zero.
The high **fiber** content comes as much from the apricots and walnuts as from the use of brown flour.

Freezing: ✓ up to 1 month.

slightly. Mark the round into four with the back of a knife, set it on a floured baking sheet and bake in the center of a pre-heated oven at 400°F (200°C, mark 6) for about 30 minutes.

Cool on a wire rack and serve.

PANCAKES

Although traditionally these are made on an iron griddle, a heavy frying pan works very well.

PREPARATION TIME: *5 min*
COOKING TIME: *3–5 min per batch*
INGREDIENTS *(for 15–18 pancakes):*
1 cup self-rising flour
*Pinch of salt**
1 tablespoon sugar
1 egg
About ¾ cup milk
Lard for cooking

Set a griddle or heavy frying pan over heat. While it is warming, sift the flour and salt into a bowl and stir in the sugar. Make a well in the center and drop in the egg; gradually add the milk, working in the flour with a spoon until a smooth batter is formed.

Grease the heated surface lightly with a little lard. When a slight haze appears, pour on small rounds of batter, well apart, either from a jug or with a spoon to give perfect rounds. As soon as the pancakes are puffed, bubbling on the surface and golden on the undersides, turn them over with a palette knife to brown on the other side. Serve at once, or place the pancakes between folds in a clean dish towel until serving time.

APRICOT AND WALNUT LOAF

A simple way of turning a basic loaf into a fruity tea bread which keeps well.

PREPARATION TIME: *30 min (plus rising)*
COOKING TIME: *40–45 min*
INGREDIENTS *(for one 1 lb loaf):*
Half quantity quick wheatmeal dough (page 178)
⅔ cup dried apricots
2 tablespoons sugar
½ cup chopped walnuts
TOPPING:
2 tablespoons butter or firm margarine
2 tablespoons sugar
⅓ cup flour

Cut the dried apricots roughly with scissors and put them in a bowl or on a floured board, with the risen dough, the sugar and walnuts. Work the mixture together until no streaks can be seen. Line the bottom of a 5×3×2 in loaf pan with buttered wax paper and grease the sides of the pan. Put the dough in the pan and set in a lightly oiled plastic bag; leave in a warm place for about 1 hour or until the dough has risen to within ½ in of the rim of the pan.

Meanwhile, make the topping. Rub together the butter, sugar and flour in a small bowl until the mixture resembles coarse breadcrumbs. Cover the risen dough evenly with the crumb mixture, and set the pan on a baking sheet. Bake in the center of a pre-heated oven at 400°F (200°C, mark 6) for 40–45 minutes. Leave the baked loaf in the pan for 10 minutes, then turn it out to cool on a wire rack.

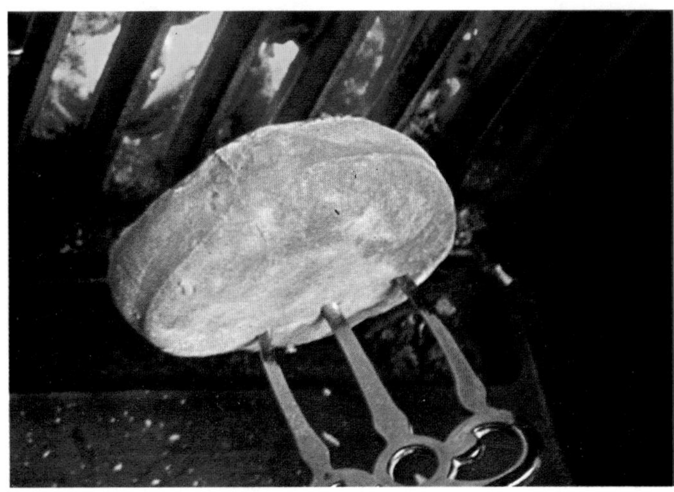

YORKSHIRE TEA CAKES

These are similar to the recipe for floury baps, but are sweeter and contain dried fruit.

PREPARATION TIME: *20 min (plus rising)*
COOKING TIME: *20 min*
INGREDIENTS *(for 5 cakes):*
4 cups flour
1 teaspoon salt
2 tablespoons sugar
2 tablespoons lard
⅓ cup currants
1 package active dry yeast
1½ cups warm (110°F, 43°C) milk

Sift the flour and salt together into a large bowl, add the sugar and rub in the lard until evenly blended. Stir in the currants, then make a well in the center. In a small bowl, blend the yeast with the milk until smooth and creamy. Pour this liquid into the well, mix the ingredients together, beating the dough against the bowl until it leaves the sides clean (add a little extra flour if you think it is necessary).

Turn the dough out on to a lightly floured surface and knead for about 10 minutes. Put the dough in a lightly oiled plastic bag and set aside to rise at room temperature for about 1½ hours or until it has doubled in size. Remove the plastic, place the risen dough on a lightly floured surface and knead well. Divide the dough into five equal portions and shape each portion into a round; roll each of these into a 6½ in wide, flat cake.

Set the cakes well apart on lightly greased baking sheets and brush the tops with milk. Cover the cakes with sheets of oiled plastic wrap. Leave the cakes to rise in a warm place for 45 minutes or until doubled in size.

Bake the cakes at or just above the center of the oven, pre-heated to 400°F (200°C, mark 6), for about 20 minutes. Cool on a wire rack and serve the cakes split in half, either cold or toasted, and with plenty of butter.

BRAN TEABREAD

A good bread to make if you have time to spare, as it keeps well and can be made in advance.

PREPARATION TIME: *10 min*
RESTING TIME: *8 hours*
COOKING TIME: *1¼–1½ hours*
INGREDIENTS:
3 cups All Bran
1⅓ cups golden raisins
1⅓ cups light brown sugar
1½–1¾ cups milk
1½ cups self-rising flour
1 teaspoon baking powder

Mix the All Bran, raisins, sugar and milk in a bowl and leave to stand overnight, covered with a cloth.

Grease and line a loaf pan measuring 9 by 5 in at the top. Sift the flour and baking powder into the soaked ingredients, blend thoroughly and spoon into the prepared pan. Level the top of the mixture and bake in the center of a pre-heated oven, at 375°F (190°C, mark 5) for about 1¼ hours until the bread is well risen and just firm to the touch. If the loaf browns too quickly, cover it with a double sheet of wax paper.

Turn out the loaf, remove the paper and cool on a wire rack. Serve the loaf sliced and buttered. It is best left for a day or two to mature before serving, and will keep for 1 week in a tin.

YORKSHIRE TEA CAKES

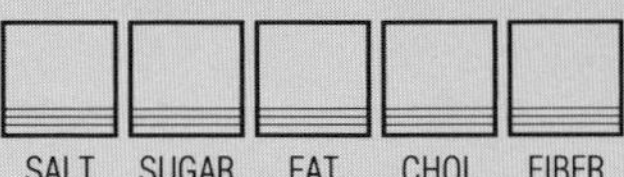

GLUTEN-FREE* WHOLEFOOD*
TOTAL CALORIES: ABOUT 2160

This recipe needs no adaptation.

Freezing: √ up to 6 months.

BRAN TEABREAD

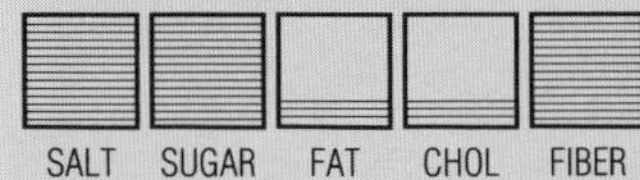

GLUTEN-FREE*
TOTAL CALORIES: ABOUT 2445

All Bran is the highest of all breakfast cereals in **salt**. To reduce the salt level, use low-sodium baking powder and replace the All Bran with an unsweetened bran granola containing pieces of compressed bran.
The high **sugar** level will also be reduced in this way (All Bran is 15% sugar). To reduce it further, omit the sugar entirely, increasing the amount of raisins (or other dried fruit) to 3 cups and liquidizing half of this in the milk before mixing. (Calories lost: up to 253.)
To give a very low **fat** content, use skim milk. (Calories lost: up to 96.)
Using another cereal will give a lower **fiber** content, but adding extra dried fruit and using whole wheat flour will still give a high-fiber teabread.

Freezing: √ up to 6 months.

FLOURY BAPS

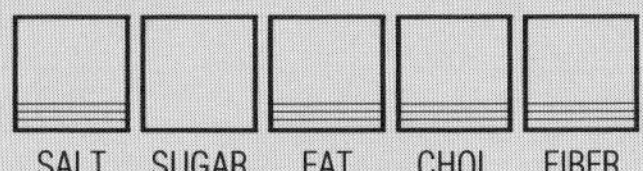

GLUTEN-FREE* WHOLEFOOD*
TOTAL CALORIES: ABOUT 2065

The **fat** and **cholesterol** levels are low because each of the baps will be large enough for 2 portions. The level can be reduced further by using skim milk and only 2 tablespoons fat, replacing lard with other fats if wished. (Calories lost: up to 271.)

Freezing: ✓ up to 1 month.

FLOURY BAPS

Split in half and toasted in front of a fire, these are most comforting on a dreary winter day.

PREPARATION TIME: *15 min (plus rising)*
COOKING TIME: *25 min*
INGREDIENTS *(for 4 baps):*
4 cups flour
1 package active dry yeast
$1\frac{1}{2}$ cups milk and water, mixed
*1 teaspoon salt**
$\frac{1}{4}$ cup lard

Blend the yeast with all the liquid until smooth; sift the flour and salt into a wide bowl and rub in the cut-up lard. Stir in the yeast liquid and work the dough until firm, adding a little extra flour if needed. Turn the dough out on to a lightly floured surface and knead for about 5 minutes. Place in an oiled plastic bag and leave to rise at room temperature for $1\frac{1}{2}$ hours or until the dough springs back when lightly pressed with a finger.

Divide the risen dough into four, shape into balls and roll out to flat rounds, $\frac{1}{2}$–$\frac{3}{4}$ in thick. Set the rounds on a well-floured baking sheet, dredge the tops with more flour and cover with plastic wrap. Leave to rise at room temperature until doubled in size, about 45 minutes.

Press each bap lightly in the center with the knuckles. Bake just above the center of a preheated oven, at 400°F (200°C, mark 6) for 25 minutes. Cool on a rack.

Fruit

Fresh fruit makes delicious eating on its own, in fruit salads and with cheese. Fruit is also used for jams and jellies, pickles and chutneys.

With crop-spraying so widespread in modern fruit farming, it is essential that all fruit should be washed in running water before serving, especially if it is to be eaten fresh. Apart from soft fruits such as blackberries, most fruit will keep in good condition for up to a week if stored in a refrigerator.

Top fruit, the term used by fruit growers for all tree fruits, includes apples and pears, and also stone fruits such as cherries, nectarines, plums, peaches and nuts. Buy only enough to last a few days, as fruit does not keep for long at room temperature. Apples and pears will store for a couple of weeks if they can be kept in a cool airy cellar or pantry, but all stone fruit, with the exception of plums and nuts, are best eaten on the day of purchase.

Strawberries, raspberries and currants are all soft fruits which are best used on the day of purchase. All soft fruit, with the exception of gooseberries, leave stains on the bottom of the containers in which they are sold; avoid any badly stained containers as the fruits are bound to be mushy and often moldy. As soon as possible after buying, tip berries carefully on to a plate, pick out any moldy berries and set the remainder well apart on a tray until serving.

Citrus fruits, which include grapefruit, lemons, limes and oranges, are grown mainly in the Mediterranean countries, South Africa, the West Indies, Florida and California. Although citrus fruits are much used in cooking, they are at their best when served fresh, with the exception of lemons and limes which are too acid.

As all citrus fruits have a fairly thick skin, it is sometimes difficult to tell the state of the fruit. In general, all fruits should have bright, taut and slightly moist skins with a definite aroma. Many supermarkets display fruits cut in half to enable customers to gauge the condition of flesh and juice content and the thickness of the skin. When buying citrus fruit, avoid any that is dry-looking or has soft indentations and blemishes to the skin.

Citrus fruits store fairly well. Lemons and grapefruit can be kept in the vegetable compartment of the refrigerator for 1–2 weeks, and other types can be stored in a cool place for about 1 week. They must, however, be used before the skins shrivel. Before cutting or serving the fruits, they should be rolled between the palms or on a flat surface to get an even distribution of juice within the fruit.

Other fruits range from the well-known bananas, grapes and melons to the more exotic mango, papaya and passion fruit, and include dates, figs, kiwi fruit, litchis or lychees and pineapples. Most of these are eaten fresh, but dates and figs are also used dried.

Apples

These are probably the most popular fruit. Apples are divided into dessert (or eating) and cooking apples. Look for apples with smooth skins and avoid any with brownish bruises.

Apples are available all year round, even in summer, but are at their most plentiful from September through March.

Favorite varieties include: (winter) *Cortland*, shiny red with delicate snow-white flesh; *Delicious*, brilliant red with fine-grained, juicy flesh; *Golden Delicious*, bright yellow to gold with sweet flesh; *McIntosh*, bright red with very juicy, sweet flesh when ripe; *Newton*, bright yellow to greenish-yellow with aromatic, crisp flesh; *Northern Spy*, glossy pinkish-red with tender flesh; *Rhode Island Greening*, bright green to greenish-yellow with rich, fairly acid flesh; *Rome Beauty*, bright red; *Winesap*, glossy bright red with firm, coarse flesh; *York Imperial*, light red with firm flesh; (summer) *Gravenstein*, greenish-yellow with crisp acid flesh; *Granny Smith*, bright green, hard and crunchy; (fall) *Jonathan*, bright red with juicy aromatic flesh.

While cooking apples can only be used for culinary purposes, many eating apples, especially if firm, are also excellent for cooking. They can be baked, stewed, made into purées or used as fillings for pastry, baked and steamed puddings, cream-based foods and mousses. Dip sliced apples for decoration in lemon juice to prevent discoloration.

For a purée, wash, peel and core 1 pound of apples. Cook them over gentle heat, with a piece of lemon peel and 2–3 tablespoons of water, until soft. Liquidize the apple pulp or rub it through a sieve; sweeten to taste with sugar. This makes about 1 cup.

Apricots

Small stone fruits with yellow, juicy and sweet flesh. Buy firm fruits, avoiding any with bruised or squashy, brown skins.

Perfect ripe fruit are excellent served as a dessert fruit. They can also be poached or used in pie fillings.

Bananas

These are normally picked and shipped green, then stored and sold in varying stages of ripeness. The mealy flesh becomes sweeter as it matures. Choose bananas from a bunch rather than buying them loose. Preferably they should be golden-yellow, flecked with brown.

Avoid any with black spots or patches, and damaged and squashy fruit. For cooking purposes, choose underripe green bananas, as they slice better and can be kept in a cool place for up to one week.

Slice bananas as close to serving time as possible, or leave them in fresh or canned grapefruit juice or lemon, lime or orange juice to prevent discoloration.

Blackberries

The large purple to black, juicy and sweet berries grow wild but are also cultivated. Being extremely soft, they deteriorate quickly and must be used as soon as possible after purchase. Avoid containers with too many red and unripe berries.

These berries go well with apples, and are used as pie fillings, in apple snow, fruit puddings, jams and jellies. Hull the berries before use.

Blueberries

Originally a wild fruit collected by the Indians during colonial times, blueberries are now grown commercially. They grow in clusters. Blueberries are sometimes incorrectly called "huckleberries;" these berries belong to a different genus.

Blueberries are delicious eaten raw as a breakfast fruit or added to crêpes, waffles, biscuits, and muffins. They also make good pies, cobblers, puddings, jams, sauces and jellies.

Look for berries that are dark blue and have a silvery bloom. This is the best sign of quality. The bloom is natural waxy protective coating. Choose berries that are uniform in size and free from stems and leaves. Avoid damp containers; the fruit at the bottom may be moldy.

Cherries

Most sweet cherries on the market come from the western US and Canada. Tart or sour cherries, used mainly in cooking, are usually sold frozen or canned. Good cherries are bright, glossy and plump with fresh-looking stems. Avoid those that are shriveled, with a dull appearance or brown discolorations. Sweet varieties include *Bing*, *Schmidt*, *Royal Ann* and *Lambert*. Sour varieties include *Morello*, *Early Richmond* and *Montmorency*.

Cranberries

The fruits vary in size. The skins are lustrous, varying in color from medium red to blackish red. The berries, which have a sharp, slightly bitter flavor and are used for preserves and sauces, should be firm and plump. They are in season September through December.

Currants

These may be black, red or white. Black currants are usually sold stripped from their stalks. Look for containers with large berries and no more than 15 per cent dark red and 5 per cent green berries turning red. Black currants are used as fillings for pies and sponge puddings, and make excellent jams, jellies, ice creams and sherbets. The berries are dark, almost black, with fairly tough skin and juicy, slightly acid flesh.

Red currants are always sold on their stalks, and must be stripped before being served fresh as a dessert. Avoid punnets with wet berries and with a high proportion of leaves. These bright red, glossy berries are also suitable for compôtes, fruit salads, pastries, jams and jellies. White currants, an albino strain of red currant, are usually eaten fresh.

Dates

Fresh dates are plump and shiny, yellow-red to golden brown and with smooth skins. The pulpy flesh has a sweet sugary flavor. Serve them as a dessert fruit or use in fresh fruit salads. Squeeze the stem end to remove the date from its slightly tough skin.

Dried dates should be plump, 1–2 in long and shiny; avoid any with a shriveled look or with sugary crystals.

Figs

Figs are highly perishable so should be eaten as soon as ready. The squat, pear-shaped fruits are soft to the touch when ripe, and the skin, which is either greenish-yellow, purple or black, has a bloom to it. The juicy pulp is sweet, and heavily seeded. These dessert fruits are served fresh; cut them open with a knife and fork and eat only the soft flesh inside. Cream may be served with them.

Dried figs should come easily out of the box and not be too sticky.

Gooseberries

Dessert varieties are served on their own, but acid gooseberries are usually cooked. They may be served as a sauce with meat and fish, and they are used for delicious desserts such as gooseberry fool and in pies, puddings and tarts, and for jam and jelly-making. Avoid squashy berries or any with splits and blemishes to the skin.

When available, these berries usually appear in farmers' markets or through local suppliers. They may be green, red, yellow or white, smooth or hairy, and may grow as large as 1 in across and $1\frac{1}{2}$ in long. Gooseberries are in season, in limited quantities, from May through August with their peak in June and July.

Grapes

These delicious fruits are served plain or as a good addition to fresh fruit salads. They are not cooked, except for the classic garnish known as à la Véronique. The juicy, thin-skinned grapes should have a distinct bloom to them. When possible, buy in bunches and avoid any with shriveled, split or squashed grapes, or those which show mold near the stems. They are available as purple, black, red and green grapes. Table grape varieties, grown mainly in California and Arizona, include *Thompson Seedless*, *Emperor*, *Tokay* and *Ribier*. Varieties such as *Catawba*, *Concord*, *Delaware* and *Niagara* are mostly used to make jelly, juice and wine.

Grapefruit
The largest of the citrus fruits, it is a squat, round fruit. The skin may be pale yellow, bronze or russet, and the juicy flesh ranges from pale yellow to pink to red. A spongy skin is often an indication of thick peel and lack of fruit juice and flesh. Grapefruit contain few or no seeds, and where they are present they are so large that they can be easily seen and removed. Grapefruit is usually served fresh as a breakfast dish or an appetizer; it is also used in marmalade making and in salads.

Popular varieties include *Duncan*, *Marsh* (seedless), *Foster*, *Thompson* (Pink Marsh) and *Ruby*. Grapefruit are grown in California, Florida and Arizona.

Kiwi fruit (Chinese gooseberries)

Egg-shaped or oblong, with brownish-red, hairy skins, these have soft, juicy, sweet, green flesh, pitted with seeds. Avoid any with shriveled skins. Peel before eating. They are especially attractive as part of a fruit salad, with the pattern of black seeds against the pale green; or cut them in half across and scoop out the juicy flesh with a teaspoon. They can also be used for jams and jellies.

Kumquats
A small, oval, orange-like fruit with bright yellow skin and juicy, slightly bitter flesh. It may be served fresh, when it is eaten whole, including the skin, or used for marmalades, bottled and preserved in sugar syrup. It is also used fresh as a garnish for duck. Originally the kumquat was a Chinese and Japanese fruit, but it is now grown in California and Florida.

Lemons
Lemons are large or small with smooth and thin or thick and knobbly skin.

Generally, plump lemons, heavy for their size and with smoothy oily skins, have less peel and more juice than large, knobbly skinned lemons. Grown in California and Florida, they are available all year round.

Lemon is one of the most useful fruits in the kitchen and both the rind and juice are used in a large number of dishes. It makes an attractive garnish for food and long drinks. Rub sugar cubes over the skin of a lemon until they are well colored and use the cubes whole or crushed in iced drinks.

Lemon juice can be substituted for vinegar in any recipe, except pickling, and can be used to sour fresh or evaporated milk or fresh cream: add 1 tablespoon juice to ½ cup.

Lemons can be stored in the refrigerator, but if they are cut wrap them in plastic film.

Limes
These are small fruit, similar to lemons but rounder, and with green thin skin and tart greenish-yellow flesh. The flavor is very distinctive. They are used in a similar way to lemons, and lime juice is particularly good squeezed over melon and papaya wedges. It also gives a fresh tangy flavor to salad dressings. Limes are much used in curry dishes. Avoid limes with dull, dry skins, with soft spots, skin punctures and mold.

Litchis, lychees

Of Chinese origin, these stone fruits are the size of large cherries, with hard, scaly skins, turning through pink to brown. The white pulpy flesh is firm, juicy and slippery. Buy when skin is red, but avoid any with shriveled dry skins.

Litchis are served as a dessert fruit on their own or added to fruit salad. Pinch the parchment-like outer skin to crack it and then peel it off.

Loganberries

These tangy juicy fruits have the shape of blackberries, but the color of raspberries. They are tapering and seedless. They are highly perishable. Use in making pies, tarts, jams and preserves, or sprinkle on cereal.

Loquats
These stone fruits, also known as Japanese medlars, are similar in shape and size to plums, with smooth, golden-yellow, orange or red-brown skins. The juicy cream-colored flesh is slightly tart. Choose firm fruit.

Mangoes

These large tropical stone fruits come in different shapes and sizes; some are round, others long and narrow, kidney or pear-shaped. The largest fruits may weigh up to 3 pounds, and the smallest are the size of an average peach. The tough hard skins range in color from green to yellow, orange and red, flushed with pink. The orange-yellow, juicy flesh has a delicate fragrance and spicy taste. Fresh mangoes are served as dessert fruits; avoid mushy-looking fruits with blemishes. Mangoes are also made into chutney and served as a side dish with curries.

Melons
These refreshing juicy fruits come in different sizes and shapes. When buying melons, always insist on touching them to check for ripeness; a ripe melon will yield to pressure applied

gently at the stalk end. Melons are generally available throughout the year, with the exception of watermelons which are at their best in the summer.

The *Cantaloupe* melon may be oval, oblong or round, and the rind has a coarse thick netting or veining. The skin beneath the netting should be yellow when fully ripe.

Casabas are normally pumpkin-shaped, slightly pointed at the stem end. They have shallow ridges running from the stem to blossom end, and range from light green to yellow.

Honeydews are large and oval, with a smooth skin that ranges from yellow to creamy white. The flesh is sweet and fine-grained.

Persians resemble cantaloupes but are rounder and have a finer netting. The green rind has a yellow tint when ripe.

Watermelon is the largest of all melons. Glossy dark skin surrounds the scarlet and juicy, almost watery, flesh and prominent black seeds.

Cool ripe melon is served as a first or last course, with sugar, finely chopped stem ginger or a squeeze of fresh lemon or lime juice. Refrigerate melon only long enough to chill it, or the delicate flavor will be lost.

Nuts

Almonds Small, oval, flat nuts in light brown pitted shells. They are available bitter and sweet, shelled and unshelled, and are best bought with the thin brown skin on.

Brazil nuts Hard, dark brown, three-edged shells enclose firm, slightly oily nuts of coconut and hazelnut flavor. They are sold unshelled and shelled. Avoid any which feel light or rattle in the shells.

Chestnuts The shiny brown fruits of the sweet chestnut are enclosed in a fleshy outer covering which breaks open when the nuts are ripe. Avoid any that look dry and shriveled. The large French chestnuts, 'marrons,' are sold canned or preserved.

Coconuts These large nuts have a hard, dark brown outer shell closely covered with tough fibers. At the top of each nut are three small indentations which must be punctured so that the colorless liquid can be shaken out. This is served chilled as a drink. Crack the tough shell by hitting it with a cleaver about one-third of the way down from the top. Pry the shells open, and cut out the tough flesh with a small sharp knife. To test a whole coconut for freshness, shake it to make sure it contains liquid.

Hazel or cob nuts The small, gray-brown nuts are partly covered with leafy husks. Ripe, fresh nuts should have firm, not shriveled, husks.

Filbert nuts These are a variety of hazelnut, but the fruits are more oblong and should be completely covered by firm husks.

Peanuts The two major types are the Virginia and the Spanish. The former has a longer shell, larger nut, and more pronounced flavor. Available shelled, plain or roasted; or unshelled.

Pecans These nuts, related to walnuts and native to North America, are grown in the southeastern United States as far north as Indiana, as far west as Texas, and in northern Mexico. Available in the shell. Shelled, they are sold roasted, dry-roasted, salted or plain.

Walnuts The brown shells should have a faint damp sheen. Avoid any which rattle, as they will be dry and shriveled. Green or under-ripe walnuts are sometimes seen in early autumn. They may be eaten fresh, but are more often used for pickling.

Oranges

The most widely available citrus fruits, oranges can be both bitter and sweet.

The most popular bitter orange is the *Seville orange*, or bigarade, a thin-skinned, orange-red fruit with an acid, deep yellow flesh and numerous seeds. The flesh is too acid for dessert use, but it is excellent and almost exclusively used for making marmalade. Seville oranges are imported from Mexico and the West Indies and are only available in February and March.

The *Navel* and *Valencia* are the leading varieties of sweet orange, from California and Arizona. The seedless Navel is easier to peel and separate into segments than the Valencia, and the former is especially well suited for eating as a whole fruit. Valencias are good for juicing and slicing for salads, but they have a few seeds.

The oranges from Florida and Texas, grown especially for juice, are the *Parson Browns*, *Hamlins* and *Pineapple*. The *Florida Temples* peel and section easily and have an excellent flavor.

Blood oranges are small, with slightly rough skin flushed with red, and have sweet juicy flesh, flecked with red, usually with a number of seeds. There is also the oval, thick-skinned *Jaffa*.

Oranges are served fresh on their own and in fruit salad. They are much used in cooking, especially in sauces and stuffings.

Ortaniques

This cross between an orange and tangerine has orange-yellow thin skin and sweet, juicy, orange-colored flesh. Use flesh as a dessert fruit. It is also good for marmalade.

Passion fruit

These tropical fruits are similar in shape and size to large plums. The tough skin is purple and deeply wrinkled when ripe. The aromatic orange pulp is sweet and juicy, and deeply pitted with small black seeds which are eaten with the flesh.

The sharp tangy juice is used to flavor cocktails, punches or fresh fruit cups, as well as fruit pies. It may also be served as a dessert fruit and the flesh eaten with a little sugar.

Papayas

Large tropical fruits, papayas have smooth skins which ripen through green to yellow or orange. The sweet flesh is orange-pink and melon-like in texture; the brown-black seeds lie in the center. Avoid fruits with dry or blemished skins.

Peaches and Nectarines

Free-stone peaches have juicy soft flesh which comes easily away from the stone. Cling stone peaches have firmer flesh adhering tightly to the stone. Free-stone peaches are considered to have a better flavor and are good for eating fresh or freezing. Avoid any which have split or those with bruised skins and brown or soft spots.

Peaches are usually served whole as a dessert, but are also excellent in fruit salads, tarts and pies. Peach purée can be used as a base for ice creams, soufflés and other sweet recipes.

Nectarines are a smooth-skinned variety of peach. Their skin is usually orange-yellow with red areas, and the flesh is sweet and juicy. Like peaches, nectarines are particularly suited for use in fruit salads, ice cream and pies. Nectarines are usually sold when fully ripe and perfect; use on the day of purchase.

Pears

Pears bruise easily and should be handled with care; they are best bought before fully ripe and left at room temperature for 2–3 days. Ripe pears will yield when gently pressed at the stalk end. Avoid misshapen, shriveled, bruised or blackened fruit with dull-looking skin.

Bartlett, the most popular variety and first of the season, is an excellent all-purpose pear. It is ideal for eating raw, for poaching, and for canning. Look for a pale yellow to rich yellow skin with red blush. Other popular varieties are *Clapp Favorite*, greenish-yellow (August through October); *Seckel*, yellowish-brown (late August through November); *Anjou*, greenish-yellow (October through April); the long necked *Bosc*, greenish-yellow to brownish-yellow (October through March); *Comice*, greenish-yellow to yellow with red (October through March); and *Winter Nelis*, green to yellow with brown mottling (October through April).

Really ripe pears can be eaten on their own or served in fruit salads. They may also be poached and served chilled with a raspberry or hot chocolate sauce. To prepare pears for poaching, cut them in half lengthwise with a sharp knife. Fresh pears discolor quickly and stainless steel or silver tools should be used in the preparation. Scoop out the core and seeds with a pointed spoon. Poach the pears at once before they turn brown.

Persimmons

These tropical fruits look like large tomatoes with their leathery skins which turn from yellow to bright red. The orange-yellow juicy and soft flesh has a sharp flavor and may often taste astringent even when ripe. Fruits with pitted or cracked skins should be avoided.

For serving fresh, wash and lightly chill the fruits and serve with a pointed spoon, to dig the juicy flesh out of the skin. A squeeze of lemon or lime may be added, and the skin can be marked in quarters and peeled back for an attractive presentation. The pulp may be used as a basis for ice creams, milk drinks, gelatins and sauces.

Pineapples

Large oval fruits with hard, knobbly top skin, varying from deep yellow to almost orange-brown. The firm, yellow to cream flesh is sweet and juicy. Look for fruits with stiff leaves.

Plums

Plums include both eating and cooking varieties. Gages are a type of plum, round and green to yellow in color. Damsons, too, are plums with dark blue to black skin; they are oval in shape and smaller than gages, and should only be used cooked and for jam-making. Eating plums should be firm or slightly soft to the touch, with a bloom on the skin; they are often sold slightly under-ripe and can be kept in a cool place for 1–3 days before serving. Avoid any plums with skin breaks, punctures or any that are very hard. Varieties include: *Santa Rosa*, *Laroda*, *El Dorado*, *Greengage* and *Stanley*.

There are also a few varieties of fresh prunes on the market. They are all similar in shape and color, ranging from bluish-black to purple. Varieties include: *Italian*, *French* and *Imperial*. They are in season from July through October.

Plums and fresh prunes are excellent for use in pies, fruit salads, tarts, baked and steamed puddings, jams, jellies, chutneys and pickles.

Ripe greengages are often served fresh as a dessert and are also delicious halved and pitted as pie fillings.

Pomegranates
These are the size of oranges with thin but tough rind. In prime fruits, the rind is deep red or purple, and the juicy flesh crimson. The seeds, flesh and juice are all edible. The fruit is excellent served fresh as a dessert: slice the top off and provide a spoon for eating. Choose fruits that are heavy for their size, with fresh unbroken skins.

Quinces
These fruits have tough bright yellow or golden yellow skin when ripe, and the firm acid flesh is highly aromatic. Indigestible if eaten raw, they make excellent jams and jellies. Choose firm but not hard fruit, and avoid any with bruises or soft spots.

Raspberries

Like other soft fruit, ripe raspberries should be used as soon as possible after purchase. If it is necessary to wash them, put them in a colander and let water flow gently through them. Drain and use at once. They are less juicy than most other soft fruit, and are always sold hulled. Avoid berries which show cracks or pits near the top and any that are squashy and moldy. Raspberries are usually served fresh as a dessert, with cream; they may also be used for jams and preserves.

Raspberries grow wild but are also cultivated. They may be red, black, purple, yellow or amber. Raspberries can be substituted in most recipes calling for strawberries. They are in season in June and July, and at their peak in July.

To make raspberry purée, rub the fruit through a nylon sieve, pressing it with a wooden spoon, or use an electric liquidizer and sieve the purée to remove the seeds – 2 pints fresh raspberries will give approximately 1 cup of raspberry purée.

Rhubarb

Although in fact a vegetable, rhubarb is used as a fruit. It is extremely acid and must be stewed or poached before eating. The leaves are highly poisonous. Hothouse or forced rhubarb has tender, pink and delicately flavored stalks which do not require peeling. Maincrop rhubarb has a stronger flavor and tough brittle stalks. Avoid limp and split stalks.

Particularly suited for pie fillings, in baked puddings, fools and jams, rhubarb blends well with many other flavors, such as grated orange rind, ginger and cinnamon. Forced tender rhubarb needs little preparation apart from cutting off the root ends and the leaves. Older rhubarb is somewhat coarser, and tough strings of skin must be peeled off. Wash and drain thoroughly before use.

Satsumas
Similar to tangerine, this round and squat orange has smooth, fairly thick skin and pale orange-yellow flesh without seeds. The *Clementine*, a cross between an orange and a tangerine, has a stiff orange-red pebbly skin.

Strawberries

The most popular and eagerly awaited fruit of the berry season. Fresh strawberries are served with cream and sugar, used fresh in cakes and tarts, eaten with ice cream and water ices and used for jams. The sweet and juicy red berries should be used on the day they are bought. Choose berries that are clean and bright, with bright green caps, and avoid over-ripe and under-ripe fruit and those with gray mold. Stained containers indicate spoilage. Berries with large, seedy areas have poor flavor and texture. Usually small to medium strawberries are of better quality than large ones.

About 70 varieties of strawberries are planted commercially in the United States. Popular types include: *Sequoia*, *Ozark Beauty*, *Tioga*, *Tufts*, *Fresno*, *Midway*, *Blakemore*, *Hood*, *Florida Ninety*, *Surecrop*, *Headliner*, *Guardian* and *Raritan*. Some varieties are available all year, but strawberries are at their best from April through June.

Like raspberries, these soft fruits must be eaten soon after picking. Serve whole or sliced (use a stainless-steel knife to prevent discoloration). Strawberry purée is made in the same way as raspberry purée and yields the same amount.

Tangerines
A small type of sweet orange distinguished by its loose, bright-orange to red skin and small, juicy segments. It contains numerous seeds, but is a delicious dessert fruit and can be successfully used for marmalades.

Ugli Fruit

This fruit is approximately the size of a large grapefruit. It has a thick knobbly and greenish yellow skin; the juicy yellow flesh is sweeter than that of grapefruit and has only a few seeds. It is mainly grown in Jamaica, although small quantities are also produced in Florida.

Ugli fruit may be prepared and served as grapefruit halves; as they are sweet, they do not need any sugar.

Preparation of fruit

This section gives some hints, with illustrations, of how to prepare fruit for eating raw or for cooking.

Apricots
Pit apricots by cutting them in half with a sharp knife, following the slight indentation line. Twist the two halves in opposite directions to separate them; remove the pit.

CUTTING APRICOTS IN HALF

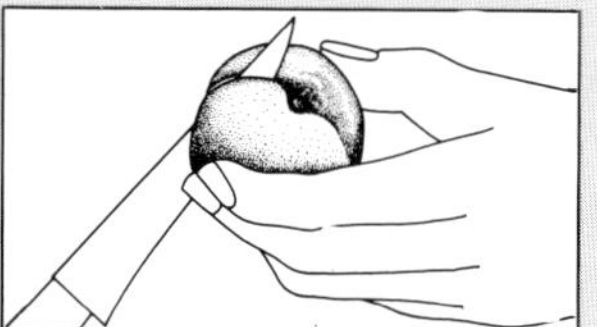

Split the fruit lengthwise

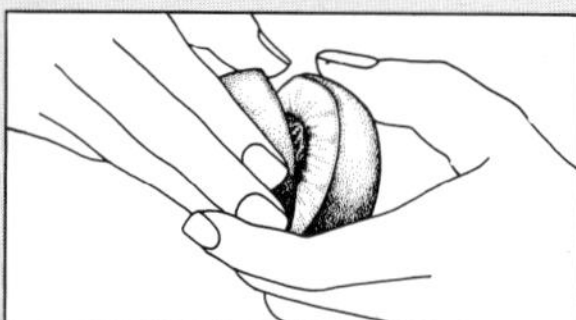

Separate the two halves

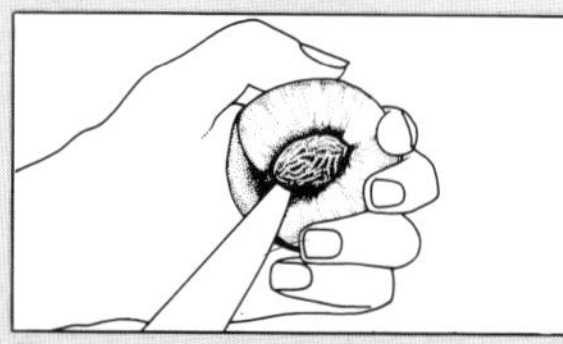

Remove pit with tip of knife

Cherries
Before cooking cherries, strip them of the stalks and ideally push out the pits with the tool known as a cherry pitter.

Currants
Before cooking, strip currants off the stalks by running a fork down the length of the stalk.

Gooseberries
Top and tail gooseberries with a knife or with scissors.

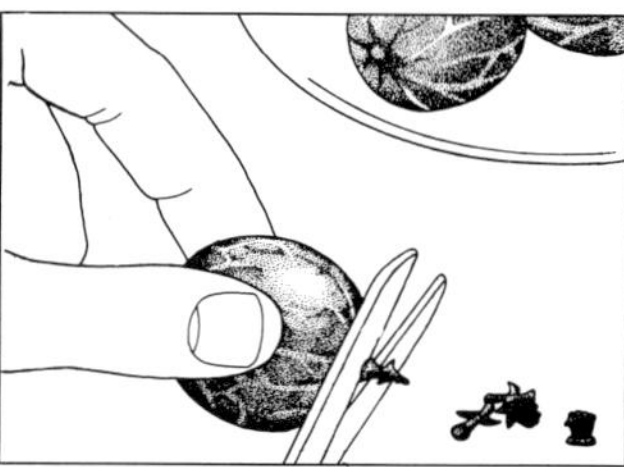

Top and tail gooseberries by snipping off stalk and flower ends

Grapefruit
To prepare a grapefruit, cut the fruit in half across and use ideally a curved saw-edged grapefruit knife to cut around inside the skin to loosen the flesh. Make deep cuts between the grapefruit pieces close to the membranes dividing them. Flip out any seeds with the point of the knife. The central core may be cut away, but this is not essential. Serve with or without sugar.

Empty half grapefruit shells look attractive used as serving 'dishes.' Use kitchen scissors to cut out a series of small V's around the edge of the half shells (known as vandyking). Florida cocktail – half orange and half grapefruit segments with a mint-leaf garnish – is usually served in this way.

To peel and segment a whole grapefruit, hold the fruit firmly with the tips of the fingers and cut a thin slice from the stem end of the fruit until the flesh just shows. Place the grapefruit, cut side down, on a plate and with a sawing action carefully cut the peel and pith off in strips to reveal the flesh.

Trim off any remaining pith. Carefully cut out each segment of fruit by placing the knife close to the membrane and cutting through to the center: work the knife under the segment and up against the next membrane to release the segment.

PREPARING GRAPEFRUIT

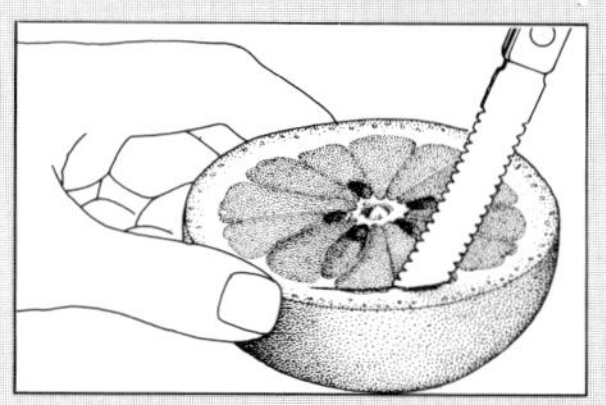

Loosen flesh from skin

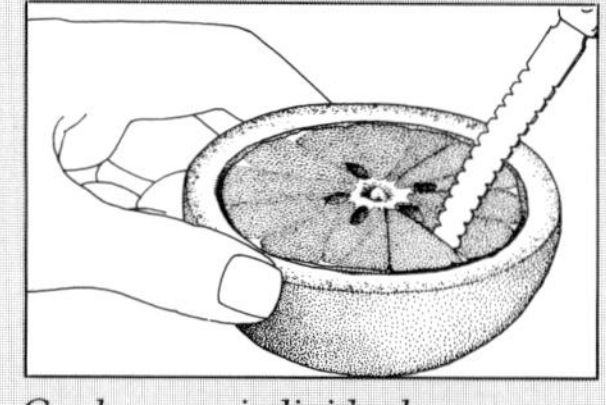

Cut between individual segments

PEELING WHOLE GRAPEFRUIT

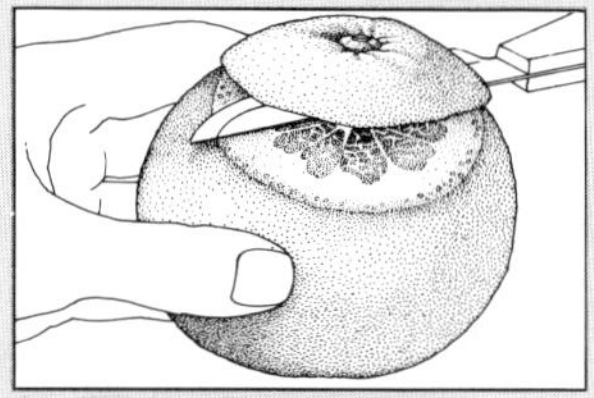

Cut off slice from stalk end

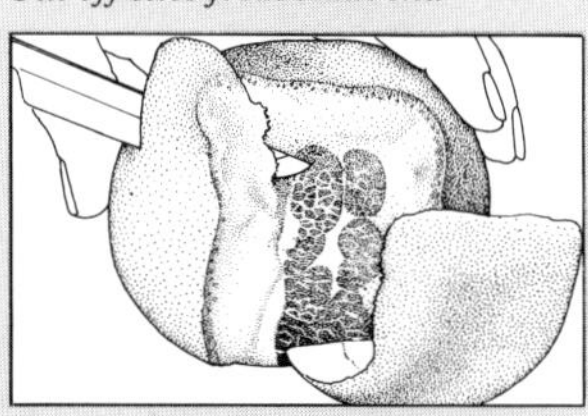

Remove strips of pith and peel

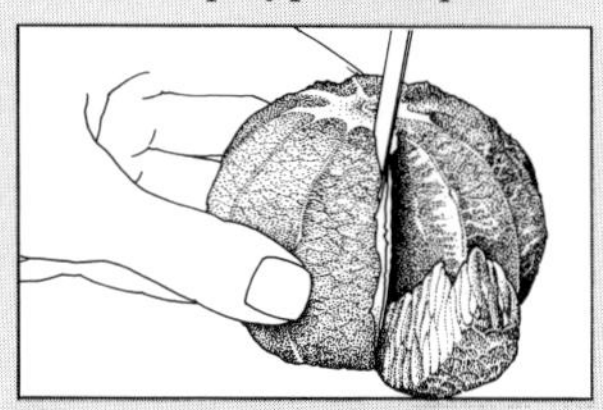

Cut out the segments

Grapes
Most grapes are easily peeled, away from the stem end using the fingernails. If the skins are difficult to remove dip a few grapes at a time in boiling water for 30 seconds, then plunge them immediately into cold water.

Remove the seeds from whole grapes by digging the rounded end of a clean bobby pin into the stem end of the grape; scoop out the seeds. Alternatively, make a shallow cut down the length of the grape, and ease out the seeds with the tip of the knife.

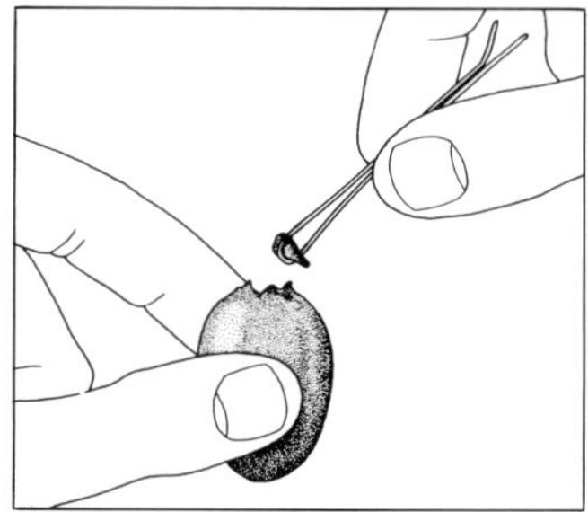

Remove seeds from grapes by inserting a bobby pin from the stalk end

Mangoes

These tropical fruits should not be cut until just before serving. Cut the fruit lengthwise, into three slices, above and below the seed. However, in this way the aroma escapes and ideally fresh mango should be served whole with only the skin cut. Peel the skin back with a knife and scoop out the pulp with a spoon.

SERVING MANGOES

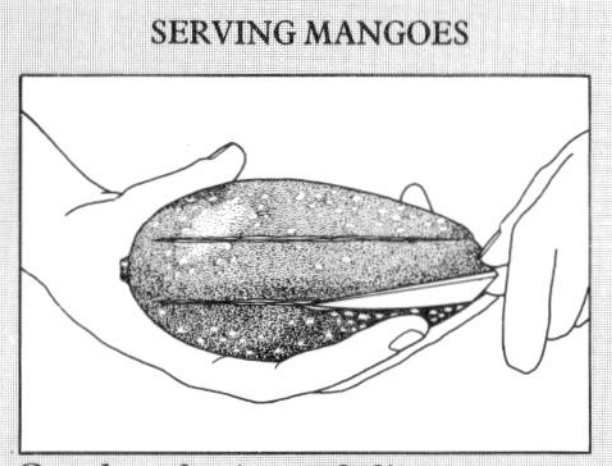

Cut three horizontal slices

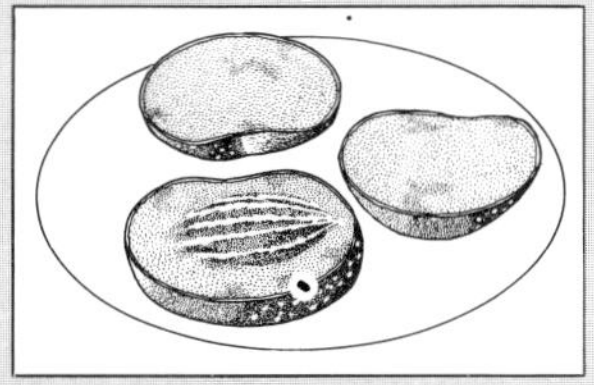

Serve the slices unpeeled

Melons

To prepare a large melon, such as honeydew, cut it in half lengthwise with a sharp knife. Cut each half lengthwise into segments and scoop out the seeds with a spoon or fork. A fully ripe melon segment may be served with the skin attached or the skin may be loosened by running the knife blade between flesh and skin. Leave the skin underneath the melon segment.

A small melon, such as a cantaloupe, usually only serves two people. Cut it in half across and scoop out the seeds with a teaspoon.

PREPARING MELON

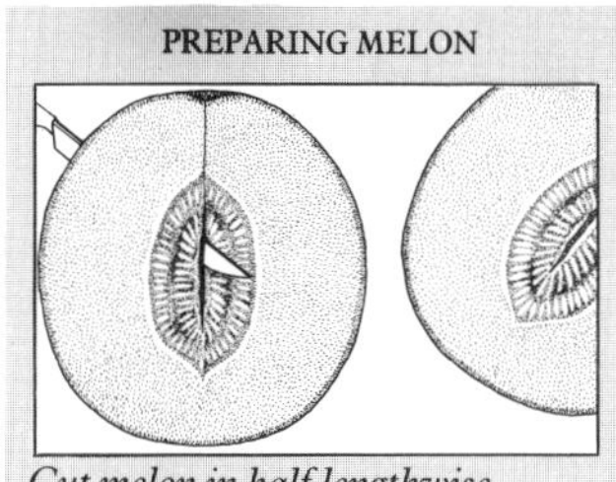

Cut melon in half lengthwise

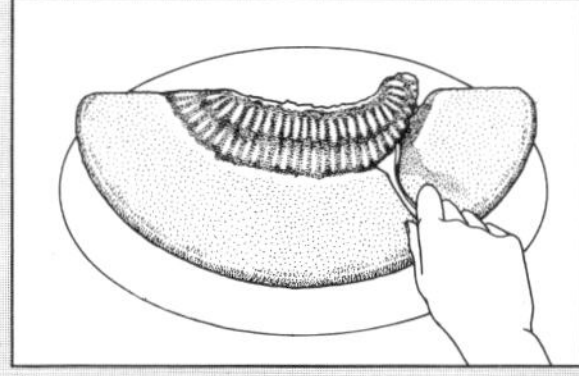

Remove seeds from melon segments

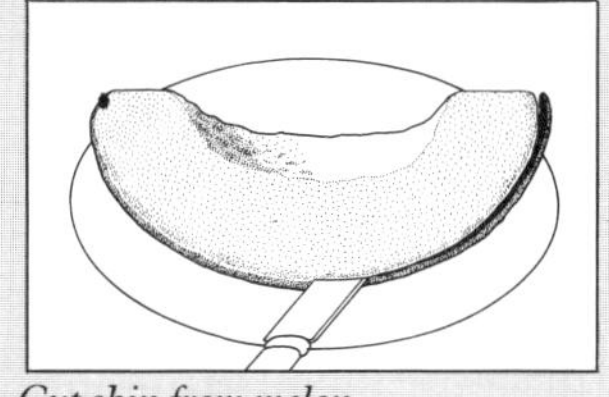

Cut skin from melon

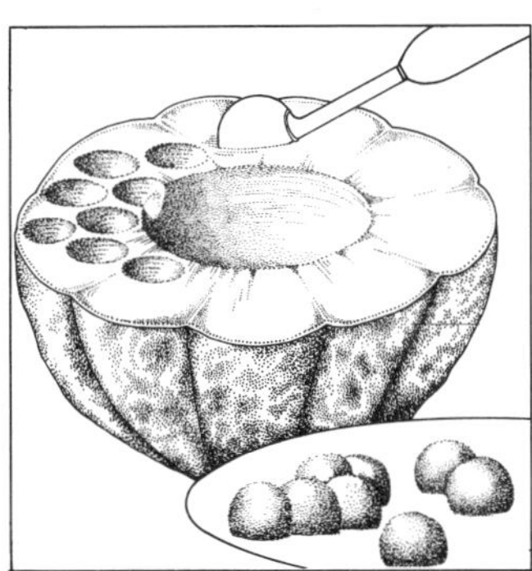

To make melon balls, use a small semi-circular scoop

Oranges

Peel and cut oranges as described under grapefruit. Alternatively, peel oranges in round strips, remove all pith and cut into slices across the grain. If oranges do not peel easily, chill them in the refrigerator for 1 hour or cover them with boiling water and leave for a few minutes.

Papayas

Prepare ripe fruits like melon, cutting them in half and removing the black seeds. Serve with lime (or lemon) juice as a dessert or breakfast fruit, or diced and mixed into a fruit salad.

Peaches

To peel fresh peaches, dip them in a bowl of boiling water, count up to ten, then drain and put the peaches at once in a bowl of cold water. Peel off the skin with a small knife.

Pineapple

A ripe pineapple is best served as a dessert fruit. Slice off the leaf and the stem ends, and cut the pineapple across into ½ in thick slices. Using a sharp knife cut off the skin and the woody 'eyes' in the flesh of each slice. Remove the tough center core with a small plain pastry cutter or an apple corer. Arrange the slices on a flat dish; sprinkle with sugar and 2 tablespoons of liqueur. Leave to marinate for about 2 hours before serving.

For a pretty party dessert, slice off the leaf end only and, without splitting the skin, cut around the edge of the pineapple between the flesh and skin, loosening it at the base as well. Extract the pineapple flesh, remove the core and cut the flesh into wedge-shaped pieces. Set the pineapple shell on a serving dish, replace the wedges and cover with the pineapple top. Pineapple shells also make attractive containers for fruit salads, pineapple sherbets, other ices and ice creams.

PREPARING PINEAPPLE

Slice off leaf top

Remove skin from pineapple slices

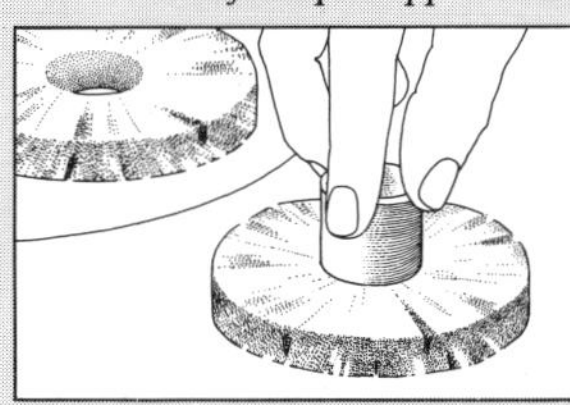

Stamp out woody cores

Strawberries

The calyxes at the stalk ends are sometimes left on the berries for decoration, but strawberries are usually hulled.

To hull strawberries, remove the green leaves and soft center stalk

Vegetables

Vegetables are at their best for food value and flavor when fresh. But if they have to be stored, keep them in a cool airy place, such as a larder or in the vegetable compartment of the refrigerator. However, certain fruits and vegetables should not be stored together. Carrots stored next to apples will take on a bitter taste; and potatoes will quickly spoil if they are stored with onions. Cut the leaves from root vegetables before storing, to prevent the sap rising from the roots.

Choose vegetables that are crisp and firm rather than hard. The size is sometimes an indication of age and quality. For example, very small vegetables may be flavorless because they are immature, whereas over-large vegetables may be old, and therefore coarse.

Prepare vegetables immediately before cooking by thorough washing and, if necessary, scrubbing with a brush. But do not soak vegetables at any stage during preparation because their mineral salts and vitamins are soluble in water. Because the most nutritious part of root vegetables and onions lies just under the skin, only a thin outer layer should be peeled away with a knife. If the vegetables are young, just scrape them lightly.

Vegetables can be used whole or can be cut up for quicker cooking. To cut vegetables, use a sharp kitchen knife. When slicing, do not lift the point of the knife from the chopping board but use it as a pivot. Keep the wrist flexible and raise the knife just above the vegetable before chopping down again. Guide the knife with a forefinger down the back of the blade.

Some vegetables – cabbages, for example – may be merely halved and quartered before cooking; but most can be prepared by the following methods:

Slicing
Cut the vegetables into narrow rounds or slices, and divide these into strips. Fine match-like sticks, known as julienne strips, are used to garnish soups.

Dicing
Slice the vegetables lengthwise into sticks; then cut these across into small cubes.

Shredding
Cut thin slivers from the sides of a vegetable, such as cabbage, which has been quartered. Slice evenly and rhythmically, always bringing the knife just above the vegetable before pressing down.

Rounds
Cut the vegetable crosswise to get thick, round slices.

Chopping
Cut the vegetables finely or roughly as required.

COOKING METHODS

After preparing vegetables, do not soak them. Only peeled potatoes need to be kept in water; otherwise they turn brown. Dried peas and beans are quicker to cook if soaked.

PREPARING VEGETABLES

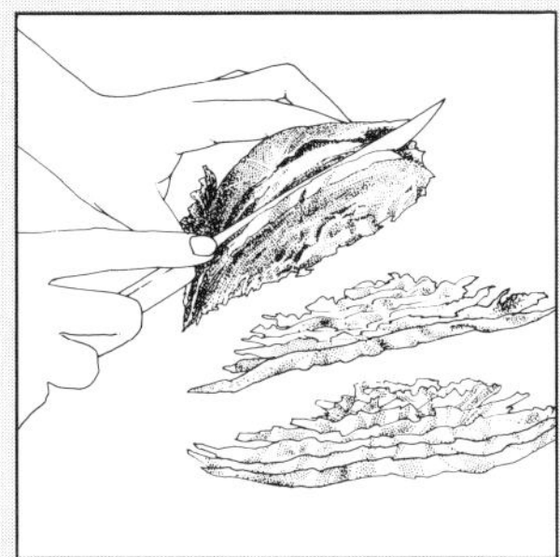

Removing stalk from cabbage

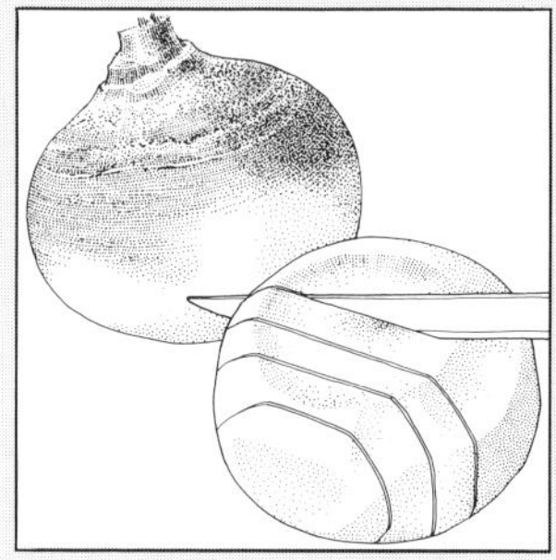

Shredding quartered cabbage

SLICING AND DICING

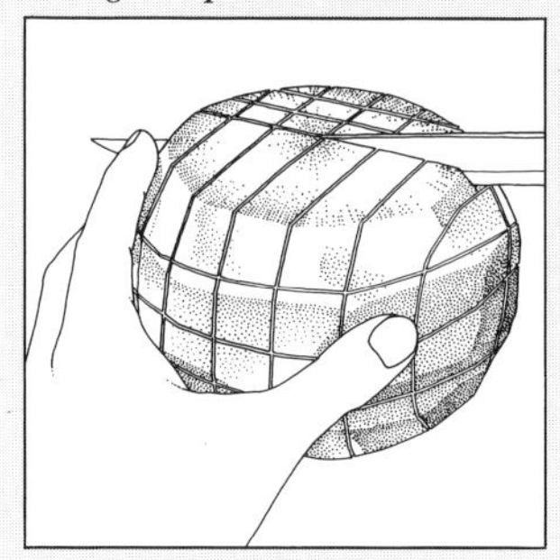

Slicing turnips into rounds

Cutting slices into dice

Boiling
Perhaps the most common mistake in boiling vegetables is to overcook them.

Use only a minimum of salted water, and for each cup of water add $\frac{1}{2}$ teaspoon of salt. Root vegetables are put into cold salted water, and all other vegetables into boiling water.

Bring the water to the boil. Add the prepared vegetables, cover the pan and quickly return to the boil. Reduce the heat and boil at moderate heat until the vegetables are tender but firm. The vegetable liquid can be used to make stock, sauce or gravy.

Steaming
Method 1 – Place the prepared vegetables in a steamer above rapidly boiling water. Sprinkle with salt, allowing 1 teaspoon to each pound of prepared vegetables. Cover the steamer with a tightly fitting lid, and steam until just tender, usually 3–5 minutes longer than the vegetables would take to boil.

Method 2 – Use a wide shallow pan. Melt 2–4 tablespoons butter in the pan, and add the prepared vegetables. Cover the pan with a tightly fitting lid, and heat over moderate heat until steam forms. Reduce the heat and cook until the vegetables are tender, shaking the pan occasionally.

Pressure cooking
Pressure cook older root vegetables and dried peas and beans. Follow the manufacturer's instructions, and time the cooking with care. Vegetables will quickly over-cook by this method.

Shallow frying (sauté)
This method is suitable for very

tender vegetables such as eggplant, zucchini and tomatoes, or for onion slices. Cook these vegetables in butter in an uncovered pan.

Most other vegetables must be pre-cooked or par-boiled before frying. Heat butter, oil or other fat in a heavy-based pan, add the prepared and thoroughly drained pre-cooked vegetables, and fry until tender and golden brown.

Braising
This method is suitable for root vegetables and onions. After preparing the vegetables, blanch them by plunging them into a pan of boiling water for 2–3 minutes.

Lightly fry the drained vegetables in butter in a pan. Then add ½–1 cup of stock to each pound of prepared vegetables. Season lightly, add a pat of butter, and cover with a tightly fitting lid. Cook until tender.

Lift the vegetables out of the pan and reduce the juices by rapid boiling, or thicken with cornstarch (see page 166).

Baking
Brush the prepared vegetables (cucumber, squash) with melted butter or oil and cook in an oven set at 400°F (200°C, mark 6) until tender.

Roasting
This method is applied to roots and tubers, usually cooked around a roast. Place the prepared vegetables in the hot fat and cook at 425°F (220°C, mark 7) for ¾–1 hour. Or par-boil the vegetables for 10 minutes, drain and then add to the hot fat. Roast for 20–30 minutes.

POTATOES

Potatoes fall into two main categories: waxy and mealy.

Waxy potatoes are best boiled, French-fried, roasted or used in salads. When buying waxy potatoes, check that any soil on them is damp and that the skin rubs off; these are signs of freshness.

Mealy potatoes can be baked, roasted, French-fried or used in potato salads.

PREPARATION OF POTATOES

New potatoes need only be washed, scraped lightly, and washed again. They may also be boiled in their skins and peeled before serving, to save scraping time. Mature potatoes should be washed well, peeled thinly, and then cut into even-sized pieces, and cooked as soon as possible.

A pound of mature potatoes gives about 3 portions; a pound of new ones about 4 portions.

COOKING METHODS

Boiled
Cut the potatoes into even-sized pieces and put into cold salted water; bring to the boil, cover with a lid and simmer about 15–20 minutes for new potatoes and about 20 minutes for mature potatoes.

Mashed
Boil mature potatoes. Drain well, and dry the potatoes in the pan over low heat. Using a potato masher or a fork, mash the potatoes in the pan until free of lumps. Alternatively, rub the potatoes through a sieve or a potato ricer.

Creamed
Put mashed potatoes in a clean pan. To each pound of potatoes add 2 tablespoons of butter, a little milk and seasoning, and put the pan over gentle heat; beat the mixture until light and fluffy. For a smoother mixture beat in 1 egg.

Duchesse potatoes
Prepare a portion of creamed potatoes with an egg and put the mixture in a pastry bag. Pipe into mounds, about 2 in high, on a lightly greased baking sheet, or into a border around a shallow ovenproof dish. Bake near the top of the oven at 400°F (200°C, mark 6) for about 25 minutes, or until golden.

Potato croquettes
Prepare creamed potatoes. Roll the mixture into cork shapes, and coat thickly with egg and breadcrumbs. In a frying pan heat the fat to 375°F (190°C) – at this temperature a cube of bread dropped into the fat should brown in 40–50 seconds. Fry the croquettes for 2–3 minutes, drain thoroughly and fry again, at the same temperature, for 2–3 minutes.

Fried (or sautéed)
Boil potatoes until they are almost cooked, and cut them into slices about ¼ in thick. Fry in hot fat, turning them until crisp and golden brown on both sides.

French-fries
Peel mature potatoes and cut them into ¼–½ in slices. Cut these slices into strips ¼–½ in wide. Soak in cold water. Drain well and dry thoroughly before using. Put some fat into a fryer (or a deep saucepan) and heat to 385°F (195°C). When a fry dropped in the fat rises to the surface, surrounded by bubbles, the fat is hot enough for frying. Place a layer of fries in a wire basket and lower into the fryer; cook for 4–6 minutes, or until golden. Drain well on absorbent paper towels. Just before serving, fry all the potatoes again for 1–2 minutes. Drain, sprinkle with a little salt, and serve.

Shoestring potatoes
Peel mature potatoes and cut them into very small fries, about the size of matchsticks. Cook as French fries, allowing a shorter cooking time – about 3 minutes for the first frying.

Saratoga chips
Peel and wash the potatoes. Cut into thin rounds. Soak in cold water, dry, and fry once only in hot fat for about 3 minutes.

Baked
Select good-sized baking potatoes, allowing one per person. Scrub, wash, dry and prick all over with a fork. Cut a small cross through the skin on the upper side of the potato. Bake near the top of an oven set at 400°F (200°C, mark 6) until tender in the center. Cut through the cross and open up the potato. Top with butter.

Roasted
Peel and cut the potatoes into even-sized pieces. Par-boil for 5 minutes, then drain well. Place in a roasting pan with melted lard or drippings, and roast near the top of the oven at 425°F (220°C, mark 7) for 40 minutes, turning once; or put the cut potatoes around a roast to cook for the last 50–60 minutes.

ARTICHOKES, GLOBE

PREPARATION:
Cut off stalk and, using scissors, trim off point from each outer leaf; rinse and drain. Rub cut surfaces with lemon. Chokes can be removed before or after cooking. Spread top leaves apart and pull inside leaves out to reveal hairy choke. Using a teaspoon, scrape away hairs to expose the heart or fond. Remaining leaves around the base can also be stripped away
COOKING METHODS:
Boiling Whole artichokes: 40–45 min, in salted water. Without chokes: for 15–20 min. Drain upside-down.
Braising Blanch for 5 min. Refresh in cold water. Place on a bed of sautéed vegetables, moistened with wine or stock and add a bouquet garni (page 183). Cover and cook for 1 hour.
Steaming Whole artichokes: Method 1, for 50–55 min. Without chokes: Method 1, for 20–25 min. Stuffed artichokes: Method 1, for 30–35 min.
SERVING SUGGESTIONS:
Hot: with melted butter or Hollandaise sauce (page 167). To eat, pull out one leaf at a time and dip edible base of leaf in sauce. Scrape off fleshy base of leaf between the teeth. When leaves are removed, eat heart with knife and fork. Cold: with mayonnaise, French dressing or tartare sauce (page 167).

ARTICHOKES, JERUSALEM

PREPARATION:
Scrub and thinly peel under running water; place in acidulated water.
COOKING METHODS:
Boiling For 25–30 min in acidulated salted water. Drain. Artichokes can be boiled in their skins and then peeled.
Steaming Whole artichokes: Method 1, for 35–40 min. Quartered: Method 2, for 30 min.
SERVING SUGGESTIONS:
Boiled or steamed with melted butter, Hollandaise or béchamel (pages 166 and 167) or cheese sauce.

ASPARAGUS

PREPARATION:
Cut off woody parts from base of stems. Using knife, scrape pale part of stems downwards. Tie asparagus in bundles, all heads together.
COOKING METHOD:
Boiling For 11–14 min, in salted water to just below the heads.
SERVING SUGGESTIONS:
Serve 8–10 stems per portion: an average bundle gives 3–4 portions.
Hot: with melted butter or Hollandaise sauce (page 167). Cold: with French dressing or mayonnaise (page 167).

AVOCADOS

PREPARATION:
Just before serving, slice in half lengthwise, around the seed, using a stainless steel or silver knife to prevent discoloration of the flesh. Leave the skins on if avocados are to be served as a first course with a filling or dressing. The flesh can also be carefully scooped out and mixed with salad vegetables or seafood.

If avocados are to be left for any length of time, toss the flesh in lemon juice to prevent discoloration.
COOKING METHODS:
Baking Peel off skin from halved avocados, slice thinly, place in buttered ovenproof dish, sprinkle with lemon juice and seasoning; cover with slices of chicken breast, white sauce, crumbs and butter. Bake at 375°F (190°C, mark 5) for 45 min.
SERVING SUGGESTIONS:
Usually served fresh with sauce vinaigrette (page 167), as a dip or a mousse.

BEANS, BROAD OR FAVA

PREPARATION:
Young and tender beans: wash, top and tail, and cook in their pods. Mature beans: remove from pods. Large beans: remove from their skin after cooking and make into a purée.
COOKING METHODS:
Boiling For 15–20 min, both in and out of their pods. Mature beans, up to 30 min.
Steaming Method 1, for 10–15 min.
SERVING SUGGESTIONS:
Serve small beans shelled or in their pods, tossed in butter, and sprinkled with finely chopped parsley or savory. Serve more mature beans with a white, parsley or cream sauce.

BEANS, GREEN

PREPARATION:
Young beans: wash, top and tail; leave whole or cut into 1½–2 in lengths. Mature beans: top, tail and string before slicing.
COOKING METHODS:
Boiling For 5–10 min in salted water. Refresh with cold water. Drain well, then re-heat with butter and herbs.
Steaming Method 1, for 10–15 min.
SERVING SUGGESTIONS:
Dress with garlic, anchovy or herb butters.

BEANS, LIMA

PREPARATION:
Wash the pods. Shell the beans just before cooking.
COOKING METHODS:
Boiling For 20–25 min, covered, in 1 in of salted water until just tender.
SERVING SUGGESTIONS:
Toss with butter.

BEETS

PREPARATION:
Cut off leaf stalks 1–2 in above the root, but do not trim off tapering root. Wash carefully to prevent the beet 'bleeding.'
COOKING METHODS:
Boiling Depending on the size, for 1–2 hours, in salted water. Slide off the skin when cooked.
Steaming Method 1, for about 2 hours.
Baking Wrap in buttered paper. Bake at 325°F (170°C, mark 3) for ½–1 hour.
SERVING SUGGESTIONS:
Cooked beets can be sliced or diced, and served cold in salads.

BROCCOLI

PREPARATION:
Wash thoroughly in cold water; drain well. Remove any coarse outer leaves and tough part of the stalk.
COOKING METHODS:
Boiling For 15–20 min in salted water.
Steaming Method 1, for 20–25 min
SERVING SUGGESTIONS:
With butter or Béarnaise sauce (page 167).

BRUSSELS SPROUTS

PREPARATION:
Wash, trim off damaged outer leaves. Make an 'X' cut in base of stems.
COOKING METHODS:
Boiling For about 10 min in minimum of salted water.
Braising Par-boil in salted water for 5 min. Drain and keep warm. Sauté thinly sliced onion rings. Add a little stock and seasoning. Simmer 5 min. Add sprouts; simmer for further 5 min, and baste occasionally.
Steaming Method 1, for about 15 min.
SERVING SUGGESTIONS:
Tossed with butter, sour cream and seasoning.

CABBAGES

PREPARATION:
Remove the coarse outer leaves; cut cabbage into quarters and remove hard center core. Wash thoroughly, drain and cook either in wedges or finely shredded.
COOKING METHODS:
Boiling Shredded cabbage: cook in salted water for 5–8 min. Cabbage wedges: for 10–15 min.
Braising Par-boil cabbage wedges in salted water for 10 min. Refresh in cold water. Place on a bed of sautéed vegetables. Add bouquet garni (page 183) and enough stock to cover. Bake for 1 hour at 350–375°F (180–190°C, mark 4–5). Red cabbage: braise shredded

cabbage in butter, add chopped apples, vinegar and sugar to taste. Simmer covered for 1 hour.
Steaming Shredded cabbage: Method 1, for 10 min. Cabbage wedges: Method 1, for 20 min.
SERVING SUGGESTIONS:
Toss boiled white and green cabbage with butter and seasoning.

CARROTS
PREPARATION:
Trim away root end and tip; remove any damaged areas and green patches. Scrub in cold water. Scrape young carrots; peel old ones with a potato peeler. Small carrots can be left whole; large ones can be cut into quarters, rings, sticks or cubes.
COOKING METHODS:
Boiling For 10–30 min in salted water or stock.
Steaming Method 1, for 15–40 min, depending on age and size.
SERVING SUGGESTIONS:
Toss boiled carrots with butter, chopped parsley or mint, or serve with a béchamel sauce (page 166).

CAULIFLOWERS
PREPARATION:
Cut off damaged outer leaves. If cauliflower is to be cooked whole, cut an 'X' in base of stalk. Alternatively, separate cauliflower into individual florets. Wash well in cold water.
COOKING METHODS:
Boiling For 12–15 min, in salted acidulated water, partially covered with saucepan lid.
Steaming Method 1, for 15–25 min.
SERVING SUGGESTIONS:
Serve the florets or whole cauliflower with white, cheese or parsley sauce.

CELERIAC
PREPARATION:
Wash, slice, then peel, dice or cut into matchstick strips.
COOKING METHODS:
Boiling For 25–30 min in salted, acidulated water with lid on. Drain.
Steaming Method 1, for 35 min.
Frying Sauté matchstick celeriac strips in butter for 30 min.
SERVING SUGGESTIONS:
Boiled celeriac with béchamel or Hollandaise sauce (pages 166 and 167). Celeriac can also be puréed, or grated fresh as a salad vegetable.

CELERY
PREPARATION:
Trim away root end and remove damaged outer stalks and green tops. Separate stalks and scrub clean in cold water. Remove any coarse fibers and cut stalks into even lengths: 2–2½ in for boiling; 3–4 in for braising or steaming.
COOKING METHODS:
Boiling For 15–20 min in salted water, covered with a lid.
Braising Blanch halved or whole heads of celery for 10 min. Sauté diced bacon, sliced onions and carrots in buttered casserole. Add celery and enough stock to cover. Bring to boil, cover and simmer 1½–1¾ hours.
Steaming Method 1, for 20–30 min.
Au gratin Sprinkle with grated cheese or breadcrumbs, and bake or broil.
SERVING SUGGESTIONS:
Boiled and steamed with cheese or parsley sauce, made from half the cooking liquid and the same quantity of milk. Fresh as a salad vegetable.

CHICORY
PREPARATION:
Discard damaged outer leaves. For salads, separate remaining leaves and wash thoroughly in cold water. Leave vegetable whole for braising.
COOKING METHOD:
Braising As for lettuce.
SERVING SUGGESTIONS:
Fresh as a salad vegetable, by itself or tossed in a French dressing; braised, with béchamel sauce (page 166).

CORN
PREPARATION:
Strip the husks off the ears and remove the silky threads.
COOKING METHODS:
Boiling Cook whole ears in water for 5–10 min. Add salt halfway through cooking time.
Steaming Method 1, for 10–15 min.
SERVING SUGGESTIONS:
With butter, salt and pepper.

CUCUMBERS
PREPARATION:
Peel cucumber, cut into strips, slice or dice. If cucumber is to be stuffed, cut in half lengthwise and scoop out seeds.
COOKING METHODS:
Boiling For about 10 min in salted water.
Steaming Method 1, for 20 min. Method 2, for 10–20 min.
Baking Peel, slice thickly, dot with butter and freshly chopped herbs. Bake at 375°F (190°C, mark 5) for 30 min.
SERVING SUGGESTIONS:
Boiled cucumber with a white or cream sauce flavored with dill, tarragon or celery seeds. Cucumber is also used as a raw salad vegetable or garnish.

EGGPLANT
PREPARATION:
Wipe, trim both ends and peel if necessary. Slice, dice or halve. Sprinkle cut surfaces with salt and leave for 30 min. Rinse and dry.
COOKING METHODS:
Frying Coat prepared slices in seasoned flour or leave plain. Fry in butter.
Broiling or baking Brush eggplant slices with melted butter or oil.
Stuffing and baking Cut eggplant in half lengthwise. Scoop out the pulp, leaving a shell. A savory mixture, including the pulp and other ingredients, is piled back into the shells then baked at 325°F (170°C, mark 3) for 20–30 min.
SERVING SUGGESTIONS:
Fried or broiled with meat; stuffed with Parmesan cheese topping, tomato or cheese sauce.

ENDIVE
PREPARATION:
Trim away outside leaves. Separate into spears or slice across. If endive is green, it should be blanched before cooking to reduce its bitterness.
COOKING METHODS:
Boiling For 15–20 min in salted, acidulated water.
Braising Scoop out the hard core at the base and leave endive whole. Blanch, if necessary, and drain. Butter casserole, arrange endive in bottom and dot with more butter. Add 2–3 tablespoons water and a little lemon juice and salt. Cover and bake for 1–1¼ hours at 350°F (180°C, mark 4).
SERVING SUGGESTIONS:
Serve boiled endive with cheese, béchamel (page 166) or tomato sauce.

FENNEL
PREPARATION:
Trim off top stems and slice off base. Scrub well in cold water.
COOKING METHOD:
Braising As for celery.
SERVING SUGGESTIONS:
Thinly sliced as a salad vegetable or as a garnish. Also used to flavor sauces and fish dishes.

KALE
PREPARATION:
Separate leaves from stems, remove mid-rib from leaves. Wash thoroughly in cold water. Cut leaves in pieces.
COOKING METHODS:
Braising In minimum salted water and a little butter for 8–10 min. Drain.
Steaming Method 1, for about 15 min.
SERVING SUGGESTIONS:
With butter or béchamel sauce (page 166).

KOHLRABI

PREPARATION:
Cut off leaves around bulb and trim off tapering roots. Scrub in cold water, then peel thickly. Small globes can be left whole. Slice or dice large ones.
COOKING METHODS:
Boiling Depending on size, for ½–1 hour in salted water. Drain.
Braising Par-boil in salted water for 5 min. Braise with a little chopped onion and bacon; moisten with white wine or stock. Cook for 1 hour or until tender, depending on size.
SERVING SUGGESTIONS:
Kohlrabi can be mashed, puréed, baked *au gratin* and used for fritters. Toss boiled kohlrabi in melted butter, or serve with a white sauce.

LEEKS

PREPARATION:
Cut off roots and green tops; remove coarse outer leaves if necessary. Cut down through the white part and wash carefully to remove dirt from leaves. Leeks can be left whole or halved, sliced into thick rings or 2 in lengths.
COOKING METHODS:
Boiling Boil 2 in pieces of leeks in salted water for 15 min. Sliced into rings, for 10 min. Whole, for 20 min.
Braising Blanch in boiling salted water for 5 min. Drain, sauté in butter for 5 min. Add stock or water to cover and a bouquet garni (page 183). Cover and cook for 1 hour.
Steaming Method 1, for about 25 min depending on the size of leeks. Leeks cut in rings: Method 2, for about 10–15 min.
Frying Prepared leeks may be blanched for 5 min, drained and marinated in lemon juice. Dip in a light batter before deep-frying.
SERVING SUGGESTIONS:
Boiled with a béchamel (page 166) or cheese sauce. Use young leeks as a salad vegetable.

LEGUMES (DRIED PEAS, BEANS, LENTILS)

PREPARATION:
Pick over and wash the legumes under running water. Place in a large bowl and cover with boiling water; soak for 2 hours.
COOKING METHODS:
Boiling Put in a saucepan and add salt – 1 teaspoon for ½ pound legumes. Bring to the boil and keep boiling rapidly for not less than 10 min (this is particularly important for dried beans in order to destroy the poisonous chemical lectin). Cover and simmer as follows: lima beans: 2½–3 hours; navy beans: 2–2½ hours; lentils: ½–¾ hour; peas 1–1½ hours; split peas: ¾–1 hour. Legumes can also be soaked overnight in cold water, drained and placed in a saucepan with fresh water and salt. Bring to the boil and simmer: lima beans 1 hour; navy beans ¾ hour; peas ½ hour; split peas ½ hour.
SERVING SUGGESTIONS
Hot: puréed with butter and seasoning. Cold: tossed in garlic-flavored French dressing. Also used in stews and casseroles. Dried, soaked beans must always be par-boiled for not less than 10 min and drained before being eaten.

LETTUCE

PREPARATION:
Trim off base and remove any damaged outer leaves. Separate the leaves and wash in cold water; drain well. Leave whole if lettuce is to be braised.
COOKING METHODS:
Boiling For 10 min in salted water. Drain thoroughly and chop finely. Heat butter in a pan and add a little chopped onion, garlic and cream. Stir in chopped lettuce and season.
Braising Blanch 5–6 min. Refresh under cold running water, and drain thoroughly. In a casserole, melt butter and fry a little chopped bacon, carrot and onion. Fold in tops of lettuce to make a neat shape and lay on fried vegetables. Add stock to a depth of ½ in, cover, bake 40–45 min at 325–350°F (170–180°C, mark 3–4). Pour over reduced pan juices.
SERVING SUGGESTIONS:
Boiled with Hollandaise (page 167) or cheese sauce. Fresh, shredded in green salads, tossed in dressings. Also used for garnish.

MUSHROOMS

PREPARATION:
Cultivated mushrooms: trim the base of the stalks, rinse mushrooms in cold water; dry well. Wild mushrooms: peel, and trim stems. Leave whole, quarter or slice thinly.
COOKING METHODS:
Steaming Cover and cook in the top of a double boiler with a little butter and salt for 20 min, or until tender.
Frying and broiling Wild mushrooms and flat cultivated mushrooms are suitable for frying and broiling. Fry sliced mushrooms in butter for 3–5 minutes, serve with juices. Brush whole mushrooms with butter or oil, broil under moderate heat for 6–8 minutes, turning once.
SERVING SUGGESTIONS:
Fried, with pan juices, cream and thyme. Button mushrooms as garnish or fresh in salads.

OKRA

PREPARATION:
Wash thoroughly but do not remove the stems.
COOKING METHODS:
Boiling For 7–15 min in salted water. Alternatively, par-boil for 5 min, then finish cooking in butter.
Braising Par-boil okra in boiling salted water for 5 min; braise for a further 30–45 min.
SERVING SUGGESTIONS:
Toss in melted butter or serve with Hollandaise sauce (page 167).

ONIONS

PREPARATION:
Trim roots and peel away papery skins. Onions can be left whole or chopped, sliced or diced. Scallions need the root removed and the tops trimmed.
COOKING METHODS:
Boiling Cook in salted water for 20–30 min, depending on size.
Braising Cook pearl onions in white stock or wine, butter and seasoning for 40 min.
Shallow-frying Cut onions in thin slices and fry gently in hot fat.
SERVING SUGGESTIONS:
Boiled with a white or cheese sauce; glazed pearl onions on their own, with chopped parsley or in béchamel sauce (page 166).

PARSNIPS

PREPARATION:
Cut off roots and tops, peel. If young, cut in thick slices; if mature, cut in quarters and remove the hard core.
COOKING METHODS:
Boiling For 30–40 min in salted water.
Roasting Par-boil for 5 min. Drain and roast with meat, or braise in butter with a little stock.
Steaming Method 1, for about 35 min; this should be applied only to young parsnips.
Purée Parsnips can be boiled with carrots and pumpkin, then puréed with a little butter and nutmeg.
SERVING SUGGESTIONS:
Tossed with butter and parsley.

PEAS

PREPARATION:
Shell fresh peas. (Snow or sugar peas are cooked, pods and all, in the same way as green beans.)
COOKING METHODS:
Boiling Gently for 15–20 min in salted water with a sprig of mint and 1 teaspoon of sugar. A little lemon juice helps to preserve the color.
Steaming Method 1, for about 25 min.

SERVING SUGGESTIONS:
Tossed with butter and chopped mint and walnuts.

PEPPERS, SWEET

PREPARATION:
Wash, cut in half lengthwise and remove the stalk, seeds and whitish membrane around the sides. Slice or dice as required. If peppers are to be filled with a savory mixture, cut around the stalk and lift away the core. Scoop out membrane and seeds.
COOKING METHOD:
Baking Par-boil in salted water for 10 min. Drain, fill with a savory meat or vegetable filling. Add a little stock and bake at 350°F (180°C, mark 4) for 25–30 min.
SERVING SUGGESTIONS:
Hot: with cheese or tomato sauce. Cold: with French dressing (page 167).
Diced or sliced fresh pepper is used in salads or as garnish.

PUMPKIN

PREPARATION:
Wash and cut pumpkin into bite-size pieces. Peel off skin, and remove pith and seeds.
COOKING METHODS:
Boiling For 20–30 min in salted water.
Steaming Method 1, for 35–40 min.
Roasting For 45–50 min around a roast of meat.
SERVING SUGGESTIONS:
With a cheese sauce.

RADISHES

PREPARATION:
If served whole cut off the tops, leaving ½ in of stalk, and remove tapering root; wash in cold water.
COOKING METHOD:
Boiling Cook large radishes whole in salted water for about 10 min.
SERVING SUGGESTIONS:
As a raw salad vegetable or as a garnish for savory dishes. Serve boiled radishes with a well-seasoned parsley sauce.

RUTABAGA

PREPARATION:
Trim stalk and root ends, peel thickly and cut in ½–1 in cubes.
COOKING METHOD:
Boiling For 30–40 min in salted water. Drain and dry out over gentle heat.
SERVING SUGGESTIONS:
Toss with melted butter and seasoning; Use in stews and casseroles.

SALSIFY

PREPARATION:
Scrub well in cold water, cut off top and tapering root end. Scrape off skin, cut into 1–2 in lengths. Plunge immediately into cold, acidulated water.
COOKING METHOD:
Boiling For 45 min in salted water.
SERVING SUGGESTIONS:
With a butter, white or Béarnaise sauce (page 167). Use leaves in salads or cooked as a green vegetable.

SHALLOTS

PREPARATION:
Prepare and cook as for onion.
SERVING SUGGESTIONS:
Used to flavor stocks and soups.

SPINACH

PREPARATION:
Wash spinach several times in cold water to remove dirt and grit. Do not dry, but place in a saucepan with no extra water.
COOKING METHOD:
Boiling Sprinkle leaves with a little salt; cover and cook gently, shaking the pan occasionally for about 10 min. Drain thoroughly.
SERVING SUGGESTIONS:
Re-heat with cream and seasoning, chop finely or make into a purée.

SQUASH, SUMMER

(Straightneck, crookneck and pattypan)
PREPARATION:
Wash but do not peel. Trim both ends. Slice, cube or leave whole.
COOKING METHODS:
Boiling For 10–15 min, or until just tender, in a small amount of salted water.
Steaming Whole squash: Method 1 for 15–20 min. Sliced: Method 2 for about 10 min.
SERVING SUGGESTIONS:
Toss in butter or serve with white or cheese sauce (page 167).

SQUASH, WINTER (Hubbard, acorn and butternut)

PREPARATION:
Scrub well. Cut Hubbard and butternut into serving pieces; cut acorn squash in half. Remove seeds and fibers.
COOKING METHODS:
Boiling Cook butternut for 25–30 min in salted water, then peel.
Baking Cook Hubbard at 400°F (200°C, mark 6) for 1 hour or until tender. Cook acorn squash, cut side down, for 25 min, then turn cut side up, add butter and seasoning, and cook for 30–35 min longer.

SWEET POTATOES

PREPARATION:
Scrub well and peel, if necessary.
COOKING METHOD:
Boiling Cook in skins in salted water, covered, for about 25 min. If peeled, cook uncovered for 15 min.
SERVING SUGGESTIONS:
As potatoes.

TOMATOES

PREPARATION:
Remove stalk if necessary. To skin: see illustrations on next page.
COOKING METHODS:
Broiling Cut tomato in half, top with a small pat of butter and season. Broil under moderate heat for 5–10 min.
Baking Prepare tomatoes as above or leave whole. Arrange in a shallow greased baking dish. Bake at 350°F (180°C, mark 4) for 15 min. Whole tomatoes should be placed stalk end down, cut crosswise on top and brushed with oil, before baking.
SERVING SUGGESTIONS:
Hot: as first course or accompaniment to savory dishes. Cold: sliced or quartered in salads and as garnish.

TURNIPS

PREPARATION:
Wash, trim stalk ends and tapering roots. Peel thickly. Small young turnips can be left whole; large ones should be quartered.
COOKING METHODS:
Boiling For 25–30 min in salted water.
Steaming Method 1, for 30–40 min.
SERVING SUGGESTIONS:
Toss in parsley and butter, or serve with a white sauce.

WATERCRESS

PREPARATION:
Wash thoroughly in cold water and drain well.
SERVING SUGGESTIONS:
Watercress is used in salads or as a garnish for savory dishes. Chopped watercress can be mixed with salad vegetables or mixed into sauces and mayonnaise.

ZUCCHINI

PREPARATION:
Wash the zucchini and trim both ends; cook without peeling, either whole, sliced in rounds, or halved with the centers scooped out, before filling with a savory mixture.
COOKING METHODS:
Boiling For 10–15 min in salted water.
Steaming Whole zucchini: Method 1, for 15–20 min. Sliced: Method 2, for about 10 min.
Baking Par-boil hollowed-out zucchini for 5 min. Drain, brush with butter and season. Bake at 375°F (190°C, mark 5) for 25 min.
SERVING SUGGESTIONS:
Sprinkled with tarragon or chopped parsley.

PREPARING GLOBE ARTICHOKES FOR COOKING

1. *Cut stalk off artichoke*

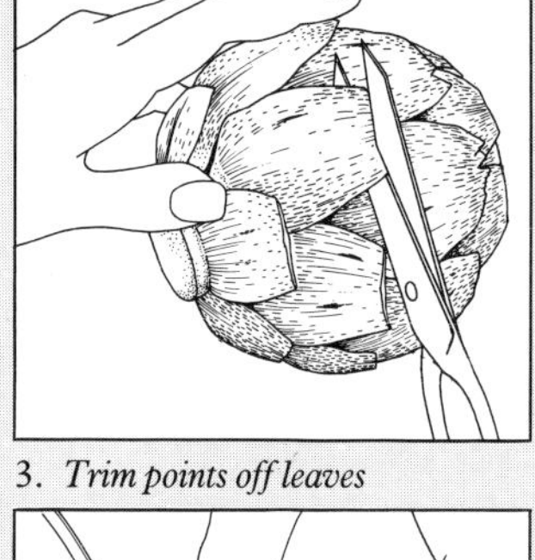

3. *Trim points off leaves*

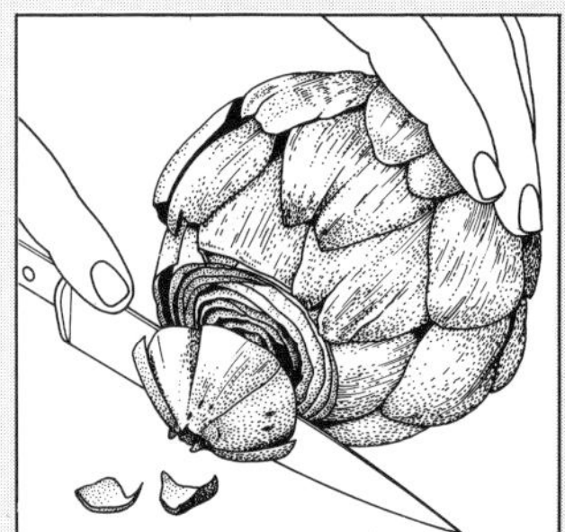

2. *Slice off top leaves*

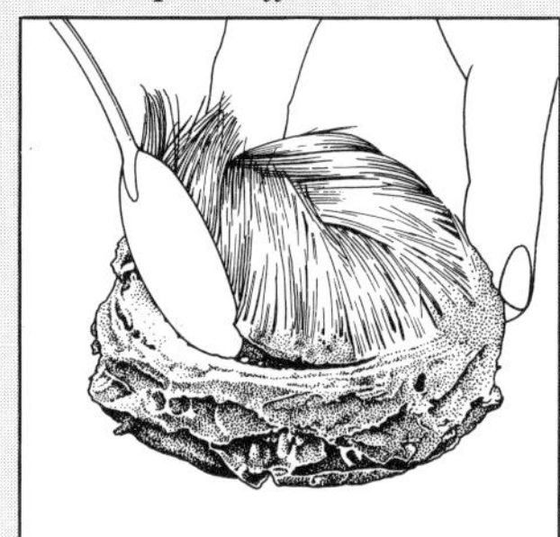

4. *Remove choke from fond*

ENDIVE

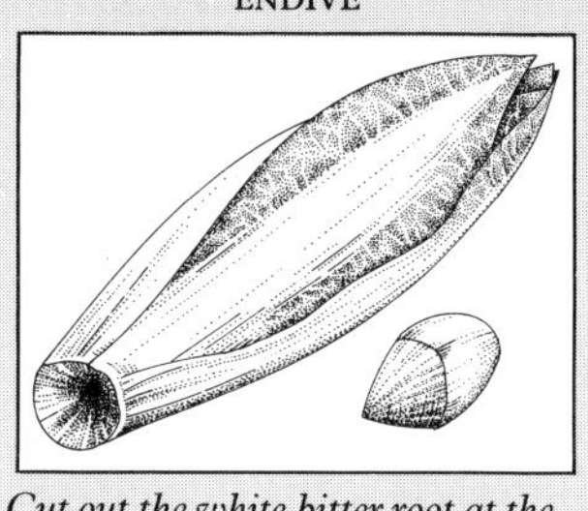

Cut out the white bitter root at the base of blanched endive

CORN ON THE COB

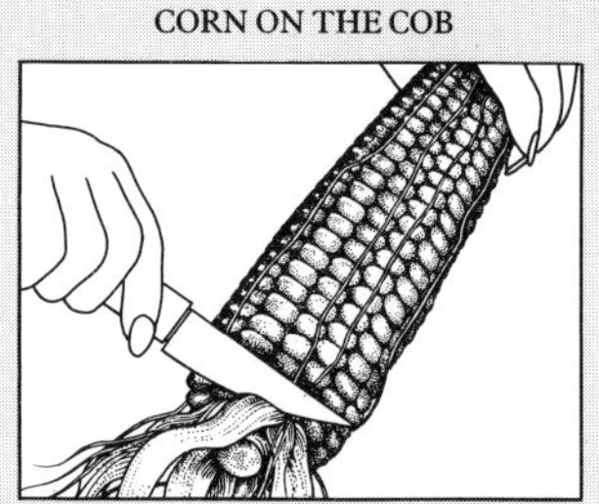

Strip the green husks and silky threads from corn on the cob

SKINNING FRESH TOMATOES

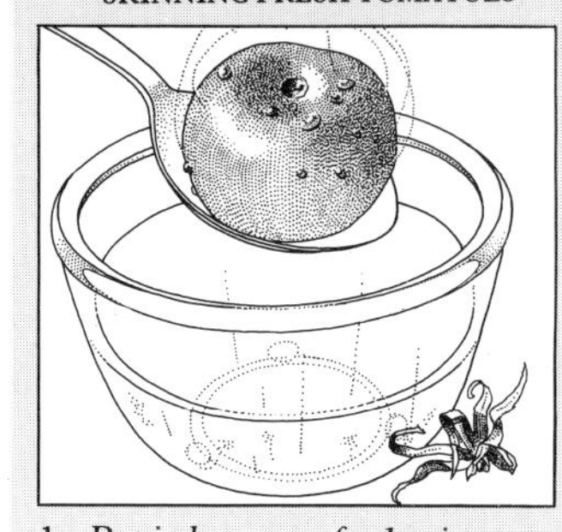

1. *Put in hot water for 1 min*

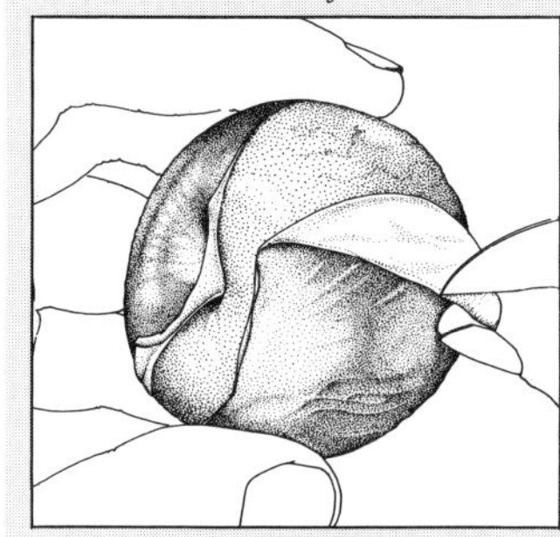

2. *Peel soft skin from wet tomato*

ASPARAGUS

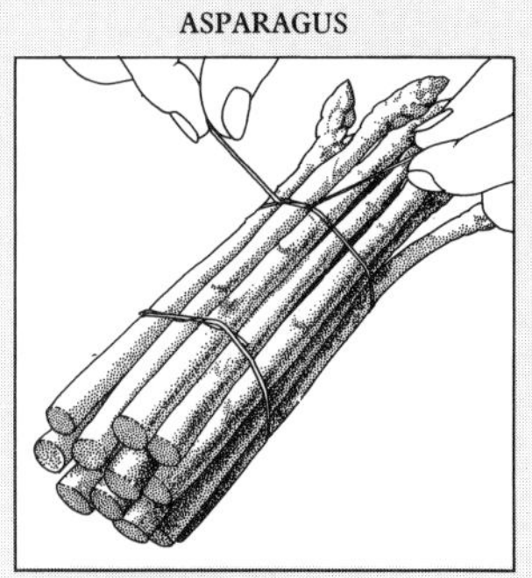

1. *Tie bundles with fine string*

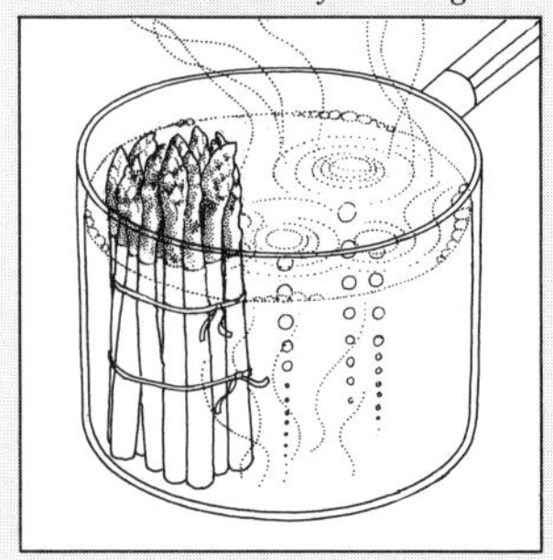

2. *Cook the bundles upright*

SQUASH

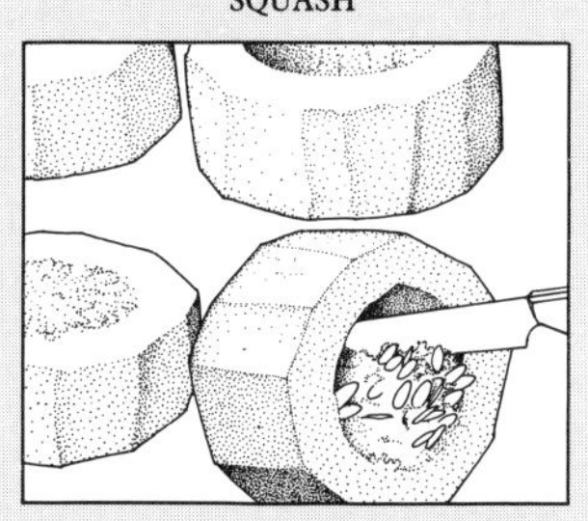

Scrape out the seeds from peeled squash slices

MUSHROOMS

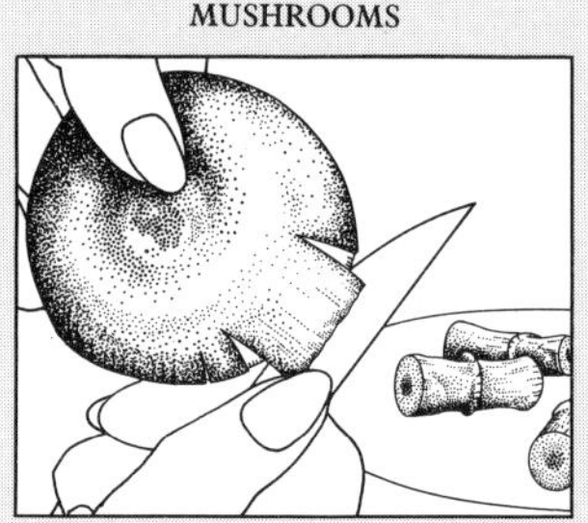

Trim by removing stalks, and peeling ragged skin

PEPPERS

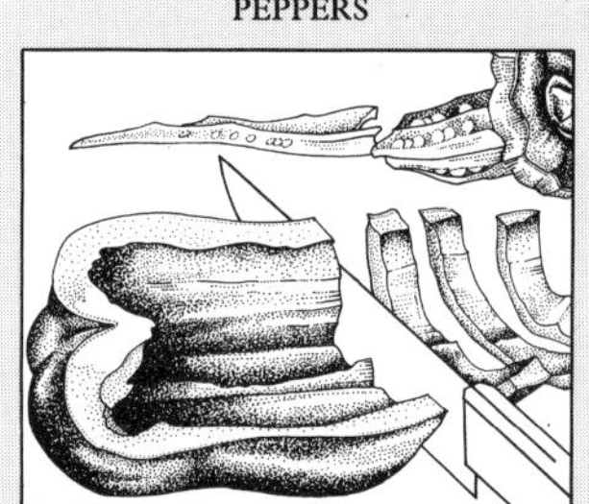

Slice peppers from which stalk and seeds have been removed

PEELING, SLICING AND CHOPPING ONION

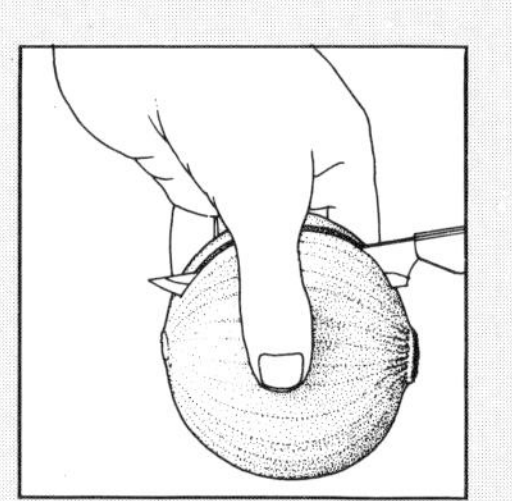

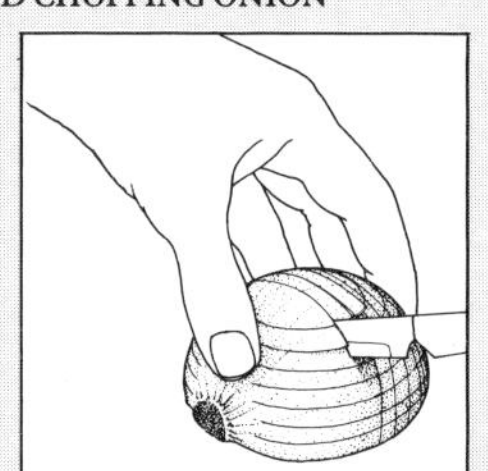

Peel off skin and trim root. Cut onion in half, through the root, then cut downwards in slices. To chop, turn the onion and slice across the first cuts. To dice, chop again across these cuts

Pasta, Rice and Legumes

All pasta is boiled, but cooking times vary according to the shape, size and freshness of the different kinds. Pasta should be cooked until it is just firm to the bite (*al dente*). Too long cooking turns pasta into a soft and soggy mass. Allow 4 ounces of pasta for each person. Rice, other cereals and dried peas, beans and lentils are also cooked by boiling.

Preparing pasta
Dried pasta swells in cooking, yielding about 3 times its uncooked weight. Cooking times are given below. Fresh pasta scarcely increases in bulk and needs no more than 4–5 minutes.

COOKING TIMES	
Cannelloni	20 min
Lasagne	10–15 min
Macaroni	15 min
Ravioli	15–20 min
Spaghetti	10–12 min
Tagliatelle	10 min
Vermicelli	5 min

For every 2 ounces of pasta, use $2\frac{1}{2}$ cups of water, and 1 teaspoon salt. Bring the salted water to the boil and add the pasta. The long strands of spaghetti should not be broken up. Hold the spaghetti at one end and lower the other into the boiling water; as the spaghetti softens and curls around in the water, push the rest of the spaghetti down.

Keep the pasta at a steady boil, uncovered, until just tender. Stir occasionally to prevent the pasta from sticking to the pan. To test, try a piece between the teeth; it should be just soft. Drain thoroughly in a colander. Return the pasta to the pan with a large pat of butter or a tablespoon of olive oil. Toss thoroughly, season with salt and pepper.

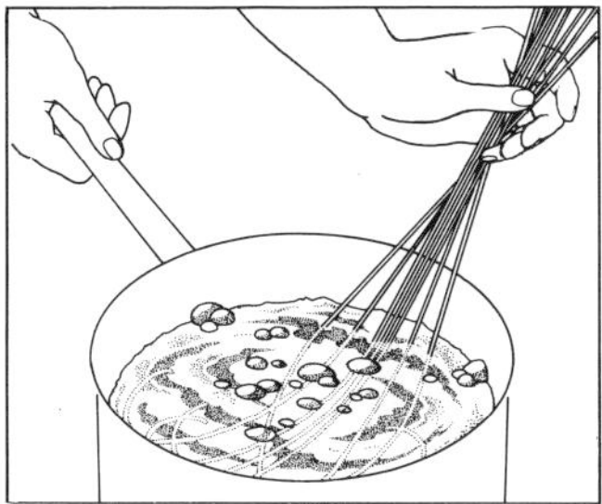

Do not break spaghetti, but curl the strands gradually into boiling water

In Italy pasta is invariably served as a first course; perhaps simply with butter and grated cheese, perhaps with oil and garlic and nothing else, perhaps with a more elaborate sauce. One of the most popular is pesto, a sauce made with basil, pine nuts, garlic and Parmesan. It can be made at home or bought ready to use. Grated cheese (Parmesan or Romano) is usually but by no means always served: never, for example, with sauces based on fish or shellfish.

In other countries pasta may be the main dish, perhaps for a light lunch or a family supper, especially if, like spaghetti bolognese, cannelloni or lasagne, it is served with a fairly robust sauce. In France buttered noodles are sometimes served as an accompaniment to meat.

RICE

Preparing white rice
Wash rice before cooking it by putting it in a strainer and rinsing it under cold running water. (This is not necessary with packaged American rice.) Allow 2 ounces uncooked rice per person. During cooking, rice almost trebles in bulk.

After cooking, rice should be dry and slightly fluffy, separated into individual grains. To obtain this result, cook rice by boiling or by absorption methods.

Boiling white rice
Use 8 cups of water and 1 teaspoon salt to each cup of rice. Measure the water into a large pan and bring to the boil; add the salt and rice. Boil the rice rapidly for 12–15 minutes, or until soft, but not mushy. To test the rice, squeeze a grain between thumb and forefinger – when cooked, the center will be just soft.

Drain the rice in a sieve and rinse it under hot water. Return it to the pan, with a pat of butter, and toss the rice.

Cover the pan with a lid and leave for 10 minutes to dry the rice. Shake the pan to prevent the grains sticking together.

Alternatively, put the drained rice in a shallow, buttered baking dish, cover it tightly and dry in the center of an oven pre-heated to 325°F (170°C, mark 3) for 10 minutes.

Absorption method 1
This is an easy cooking method which ensures tender separate grains. For each cup of rice (enough for three servings), use 2 cups of water or clear stock and $\frac{1}{2}$ teaspoon salt. Bring the water to the boil in a large pan, then add the salt and rice, stirring for a few minutes.

As soon as the water boils again, cover the pan with a tight-fitting lid.

Simmer for 15 minutes, when all the water should be absorbed and the rice dry and tender. Remove the pan from the heat and separate the grains with a fork. Serve immediately.

Alternatively, cook the tightly covered rice over low heat for 10 minutes, remove from the heat and leave the rice for 10 minutes before uncovering it.

Absorption method 2
Rice can also be cooked by absorption in the oven. Use the same measurements as in the first method, and put the rice in a casserole dish. Pour over boiling salted water, stir thoroughly and cover the dish tightly with foil and a lid. Cook the rice in the center of a pre-heated oven at 350°F (180°C, mark 4) for 30–45 minutes, or until all the liquid is absorbed and the grains are soft.

Cooking brown rice
Brown rice can be cooked in the same way as white rice, but needs a longer time. For boiled rice allow about 25 minutes, and with the absorption method, simmer the rice for 45 minutes. Brown rice cooked in the oven needs about 1 hour.

Cooking wild rice

This can be cooked in salted boiling water for about 25–30 minutes, then drained and dried in the same way as boiled rice.

Rice mold

Cold cooked rice can be made into an attractive hot or cold main course. Heat a garlic-flavored sauce vinaigrette (page 167) and toss the rice in this – cooked peas may also be added. Pack the dressed rice and peas loosely into a ring mold and smooth the top.

If the rice is to be served warm, set the ring mold in a roasting pan of boiling water. Cover the mold with foil and simmer on top of the stove for 10–15 minutes. Place a serving dish on top of the mold and turn it upside-down. The center of the mold can be filled with chopped chicken, flaked fish, or shrimp in a creamed sauce.

If the rice is to be served cold, put the mold in the refrigerator for about 1 hour or until firm. Turn out on to a serving dish and fill the center with seafood bound with a sharp mayonnaise.

RICE MOLD

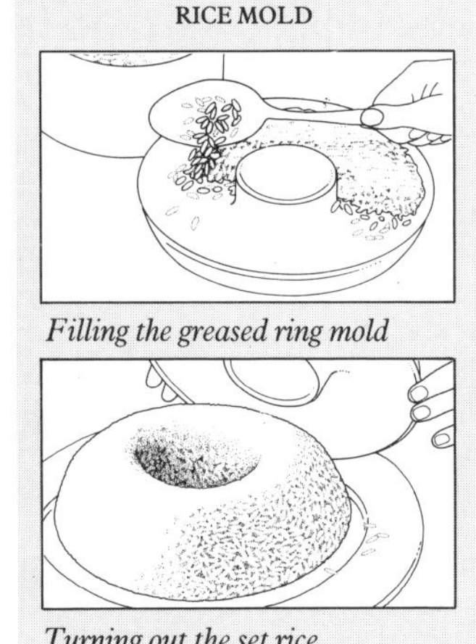

Filling the greased ring mold

Turning out the set rice

Rice salads

Cold left-over rice makes a good basis for a variety of salads. Toss the rice in a well-flavored sauce vinaigrette or a thinned-down mayonnaise (page 167), and serve with cold meat, fish or poultry.

For a more substantial course, mix the dressed rice with chopped ham or chicken, flaked fish and chopped pimientos, cooked peas or beans and corn kernels.

COOKING AND SERVING DRIED LEGUMES

Soak dried peas and beans (except for lentils, which need only two hours' soaking) overnight before cooking; alternatively, bring them slowly to the boil, simmer for two minutes, then leave for an hour before cooking.

To cook, put the legumes into a saucepan and cover with fresh cold water. Add salt to taste, bring to the boil and cook gently until soft.

Average cooking times are: lima beans, chick peas, 60 min; navy and soy beans, 45 min; split peas 30 min; lentils and dried peas 25 min. Stored beans may need more time.

Legumes, particularly lima beans and dried peas, are served as an accompanying vegetable. Navy and black beans and black-eyed peas, as well as dried whole or split peas, can be added to soups and stews.

Kidney beans are traditionally used in chili con carne, mixed with ground beef, onion and chili powder.

Lentils are cooked in soups and also in vegetable rissoles or in croquettes.

FRESH HERBS AND THEIR USE

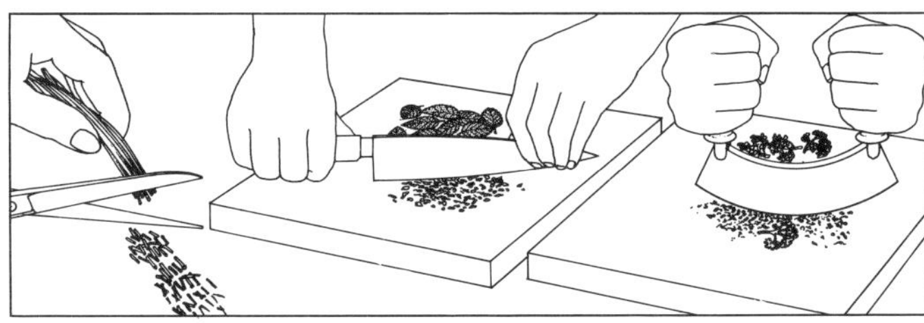

Fresh – or dried – herbs are much used in cooking to impart additional flavor to a dish. The choice of herb is entirely personal, but certain herbs go particularly well with certain foods.

Basil Use with oily fish, roast lamb, chicken, duck and goose. Also with tomato dishes.

Bay Use in bouquet garni; with oily fish, pork, veal, goose and in pâtés and terrines.

Chervil As garnish to soups, with delicate fish and shellfish. Also in salads and herb butters.

Dill Use to flavor sauces, salad dressings and mayonnaise. As garnish to fish soups, and to flavor lamb stews.

Fennel Use with roast lamb, oily fish and to flavor sauces. Fennel seeds are ideal with roast pork and chicken.

Garlic The traditional French flavoring, particularly with tomato and shellfish dishes. Much used in stews, dressings and herb butters.

Marjoram Ideal with strongly flavored oily fish, also with roast lamb, pork and veal, chicken, duck and partridge. A favorite herb with tomato dishes. Marjoram may be used as substitute for the Italian herb oregano, although marjoram has a much less powerful flavor.

Mint Fresh mint sauce is traditional with roast lamb. Use to flavor peas, new potatoes and carrots. Fresh leaves are used as a garnish with fresh fruit salads and iced tea.

Parsley The traditional garnish with fish and many soups. Used to flavor sauces and vegetable dishes. A necessary ingredient of bouquet garni and maître-d'hôtel butter.

Rosemary A favorite herb with oily broiled fish, and much used to flavor roast lamb, pork, duck and goose. May also be added to casseroled potatoes. Rosemary leaves are long and spiky, so they should be chopped with a sharp knife before being used.

Sage Mainly used in stuffings for pork, chicken and duck. Also used to flavor oily fish, especially eel.

Savory Summer savory has a more delicate mint flavor than winter savory. Both are used to flavor salads and soups, broiled fish and egg dishes. Especially good with green beans.

Tarragon Use to flavor white wine vinegar for pickling and in salad dressings and mayonnaise. Excellent with oily fish, in omelettes and for herb butters.

Thyme The traditional ingredient of a bouquet garni. Use to flavor oily fish, and roast pork, veal and poultry.

Stocks and Soups

The basis for all soups is good fresh stock usually made from the bones and flesh of fish, meat and poultry, with added vegetables, herbs and spices. The stock ingredients should harmonize with those of the finished soup. Chicken stock is most often used as a basis for vegetable soups, but stock based on a ham bone is very good with some vegetables, especially peas.

There are five basic stocks: brown (or household stock), white, fish, vegetable and game stock. Brown stock can be used for most soups, although fish, vegetables and game soups all gain in flavor when prepared with their own type of stock.

Fresh bones and meat are essential ingredients for brown and white stocks. Use marrow bone and beef shank for brown stock and veal shank for a white stock, and ask the butcher to chop the bones into manageable pieces. The chopped bones release gelatin while cooking, which gives body to the stock.

Vegetables give additional flavor, but avoid potatoes, which make the stock cloudy. Strong-flavored vegetables, such as turnips, rutabaga and parsnips should be used sparingly.

STOCKS

Brown Stock

PREPARATION TIME: *15 min*
COOKING TIME: *5 hours*
INGREDIENTS *(for 3½ quarts):*
1 pound marrow bones
2–3 pounds beef shank
3 tablespoons butter or drippings
1–2 leeks
1 large onion
1–2 celery stalks
½ pound carrots
2 bouquets garnis (page 183)
Salt and black peppercorns*

Blanch the bones for 10 minutes in boiling water, then put them, with the chopped meat and butter or drippings, in a roasting pan. Brown the bones in the center of the oven for 30–40 minutes, at a temperature of 425°F (220°C, mark 7). Turn them over occasionally to brown them evenly. Put the roasted bones in a large pan, add the cleaned and sliced vegetables, the bouquets garnis and peppercorns. Cover with cold water, to which ½ teaspoon of salt has been added.

Bring the contents slowly to boiling point, remove any scum from the surface and cover the pan with a tight-fitting lid. Simmer the stock over lowest possible heat for about 4 hours to extract all flavor from the bones. Top up with hot water if the level of the liquid should fall below the other ingredients.

Strain the stock through a fine sieve or cheesecloth, into a large bowl. Leave the stock to settle for a few minutes, then remove the fat from the surface by drawing paper towels over it. If the stock is not required immediately, leave the fat to settle in a surface layer which can then be easily lifted off.

Once the fat has been removed correct seasoning if necessary.

White Stock

This is made like brown stock, but the blanched veal bones are not browned. Place all the ingredients in a large pan of water and proceed in the same way as for brown stock.

Fish Stock

The basis for this stock is bones and trimmings, such as the head and the skin. White fish such as cod, haddock, halibut, whiting and flounder can all be used. Fish stock is less useful than other stocks as a basis for vegetable soups, but could be used for leek or celery soup.

PREPARATION TIME: *5–10 min*
COOKING TIME: *30 min*
INGREDIENTS *(for 1 pint):*
1 pound fish trimmings
*Salt**
1 onion
Bouquet garni (page 183) or 1 large leek and 1 celery stalk

Wash the trimmings thoroughly in cold water and put them in a large pan, with 2½ cups lightly salted water. Bring to the boil over low heat and remove any surface scum. Meanwhile, peel and finely chop the onion and add to the stock with the bouquet garni or the cleaned and chopped leek and celery. Cover the pan with a lid and simmer over low heat for 30 minutes. Strain the stock through a sieve or cheesecloth. Store, covered, in the refrigerator.

Fish stock does not keep well and should preferably be used on the day it is made.

SKIMMING STOCK

Lifting scum from boiling stock

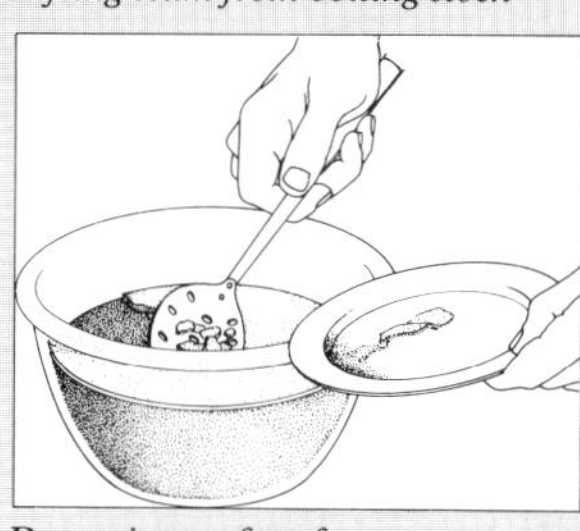

Removing surface fat

Poultry or Game Stock

The ingredients for this stock can be the carcass of a chicken, turkey or game bird, together with the feet of the bird, and the cleaned giblets. Cook as for white stock, simmering for 2–3 hours. Strain and remove the fat.

Vegetable Stock

This inexpensive but quick and tasty stock is made from uncooked vegetables. The ingredients may include the outer leaves of cabbage, lettuce and other greens, cauliflower stalks, and peelings from carrots, leeks and parsnips. Chop these trimmings roughly, put them in a pan and cover with lightly salted water. Put the lid on the pan, and simmer the stock over low heat. A bouquet garni (page 183) and 6–8 peppercorns may be added for extra flavor. Strain the stock through cheesecloth.

Cooking stock in a pressure cooker
Place the stock ingredients, with lightly salted water, in the pressure cooker – it must not be more than two-thirds full. Bring to the boil and remove the scum from the surface before fixing the lid. Lower the heat and bring to 15 pounds pressure. Reduce the heat quickly and cook steadily for 1 hour. Strain the stock and remove the fat.

Storing stock
If not required for immediate use, store prepared stocks in the refrigerator. After the fat has been removed, pour the cooled stock into a container and cover with a lid. It will keep for three or four days, but to ensure absolute freshness, boil up the stock every two days. Fish and vegetable stocks spoil quickly and should be made and used on the same day. If refrigerated they will keep for two days.

Freezing stocks
Stocks can be satisfactorily stored in the freezer, where they will keep for up to two months. Boil the prepared stock over high heat to reduce it by half. Pour the concentrated cooled stock into ice-cube trays, freeze quickly and transfer the stock cubes to plastic bags. Alternatively, pour the stock into freezing containers, leaving a 1 in space at the top.

To use frozen stock, leave it to thaw at room temperature, or simply turn it into a saucepan and heat over low heat, stirring occasionally. Add 2 tablespoons water to every cube of concentrated stock.

Ready-made stocks
Many ready-made stock preparations are available, usually in the form of canned broths, bouillon cubes, meat extracts, and meat-and-vegetable extracts. In an emergency, these preparations are acceptable replacements for home-made stocks, but they have a sameness of flavor and lack body and jelling qualities. As they are highly seasoned, be careful about extra flavorings until the soup has been tasted.

SOUPS

There are an enormous number of classic and international soups which all fall into two distinct categories, according to their consistency: thin soups and thick soups. Thin soups are again divided into consommés and broths; and thick soups into puréed and cream soups. Thick soups also include classic velouté soups, which are based on a velouté sauce, but these are seldom made today.

Thin Soups
(consommé and broth)
A consommé is a clear soup made from meat, poultry, fish or vegetables and clarified stock. The basic stock must be accentuated by the main ingredient, so that a beef consommé is made from brown stock and lean beef, a chicken consommé from chicken stock and chicken flesh. Consommés are particularly suitable for party menus and may be served piping hot or chilled as a jellied soup.

Broths
These semi-clear soups consist of uncleared stock with added meat, vegetables, rice or barley. Broths are often a by-product of the main course.

Thick Soups
This group includes puréed soups which are thickened with starchy ingredients, such as flour, cereals and potatoes. Cream soups are thickened with butter, cream and egg yolks.

The thickening agents, known as liaisons, also enrich the texture of a soup and change its color. Liaisons must be added in correct proportions to the liquid, otherwise the soup may curdle or become too starchy.

Liaison to liquids:

1–2 tablespoons flour...........
$2\frac{1}{2}$ cups liquid
(for purées rich in starch)

2–3 tablespoons flour...........
$2\frac{1}{2}$ cups liquid
(for purées with little starch)

1–2 egg yolks.....................
$2\frac{1}{2}$ cups liquid

$\frac{2}{3}$ cup cream.......................
$2\frac{1}{2}$ cups liquid

Puréed Soups
For these soups, the main ingredients are rubbed through a sieve or put through a liquidizer. The soup is further thickened with a starchy liaison. Puréed soups are usually made from vegetables, but can also be prepared from meat, poultry, game, fish and even fruit.

A purée made from starchy vegetables, such as dried peas, split peas, navy and lima beans, or potatoes, will produce a thick soup that needs little or no additional starch. It can be adjusted to soup consistency by adding stock or water. A thin purée from spinach or watercress will need thickening with flour. This also prevents the purée from sinking to the bottom. Mix the correct liaison of flour with a little hot soup, then stir it back into the soup, and bring to boiling point over gentle heat.

MAKING PURÉED SOUPS

Sieving cooked vegetables

Scraping purée off the sieve

Potato Soup
PREPARATION TIME: *15–20 min*
COOKING TIME: *20 min*
INGREDIENTS *(for 4–6):*
2 leeks
1 pound potatoes
3 tablespoons butter
5 cups white stock
Salt and black pepper*

Wash and finely chop the leeks and peel and roughly chop the potatoes. Cook the leeks in 2 tablespoons of butter in a large pan until soft, but not colored. Add the potatoes, and pour over the stock; season lightly with salt and freshly ground pepper. Bring the ingredients to the boil, cover with a lid and simmer until the potatoes are quite tender.

Remove the soup from the heat and leave it to cool slightly. Rub the soup through a sieve or put it through a liquidizer, a little at a time. Re-heat the soup over low heat, adjust seasoning and stir in the remaining butter.

Cream Soups

These thick soups are a combination of a puréed soup and béchamel sauce (page 166). They are thickened and enriched with cream, egg yolks or both. Cream soups take little time to prepare and are excellent for storing in a freezer.

Care is required when thickening with cream or egg yolks to prevent the soup curdling. Put the cream or yolks in a small bowl and beat in a little hot soup until the liaison has the same temperature as the soup. Blend the liaison slowly into the hot soup, stirring continuously, but do not let the soup reach boiling point. The soup can also be re-heated in the top of a double boiler.

Cream of Vegetable Soup

PREPARATION TIME: *20 min*
COOKING TIME: *15–20 min*
INGREDIENTS *(for 4)*:
1 pound mixed vegetables (carrots, celery, leeks, cabbage)
¼ cup butter
2½ cups béchamel sauce (page 166)
Salt and black pepper*
1¼–2 cups milk
½ cup cream

Peel or scrape and wash the vegetables before chopping them finely. Blanch the vegetables for 2 minutes in boiling water, then drain thoroughly.

Melt the butter in a heavy-based pan over low heat, and cook the vegetables, covered, for 5–10 minutes, until soft. Blend in the béchamel sauce and simmer gently for 15 minutes or until the vegetables are tender.

Rub the thick mixture through a sieve or put it through a liquidizer. Re-heat the soup without boiling, over low heat, thinning with milk to the desired consistency. Correct seasoning, and blend in the cream just prior to serving.

SOUP GARNISHES

Garnishes are added to soups either as an embellishment to improve the flavor or to provide a contrasting texture.

Consommé julienne, for example, is garnished with julienne (narrow) strips of carrot, celery, leek and turnip. These strips are boiled until soft in lightly salted water, then rinsed in cold water and added to hot consommé just before serving.

Consommé royale is a garnish of firm savory egg custard cut into tiny fancy shapes. Beat one egg with one tablespoon of cleared stock and pour into a small bowl or dariole molds. Bake the molds in a pan of water for 20 minutes or until firm, in the center of a pre-heated oven at 350°F (180°C, mark 4).

Pasta is used to garnish many thin soups. Macaroni, tagliatelle and spaghetti can be broken into short pieces and added to puréed soups for the last 20 minutes of cooking. For hot consommés, cook the pasta separately so that the starch will not cloud the soup.

Cheese makes a pleasant accompaniment to most vegetable soups. Choose a well flavored hard cheese, and serve it finely grated in a separate dish.

Bread croûtons are a classic garnish with thick soups. Remove the crusts from ½ in thick slices of bread; cut into cubes and toast or fry in a little butter until crisp and golden. Serve in a separate dish or sprinkled over the soup.

Dumplings are ideal for turning a meat or vegetable soup into a substantial family meal. Mix 1 cup self-rising flour with ¼ cup shredded suet and a sprinkling of salt and pepper. Bind the mixture with sufficient cold water to make a soft dough. Shape the dough into 16 balls and drop them into the soup for the last 15–20 minutes of cooking.

Melba toast is made by toasting thin slices of bread, splitting them through the middle, and toasting the uncooked surfaces under a hot broiler. Alternatively, cut stale bread into very thin slices, place them on a baking sheet and dry them off in the bottom of the oven until crisp and curling at the edges.

Vegetable and fruit garnishes add color to plain cream soups. Trim and wash celery leaves, watercress or parsley before floating them on the soup.

Cucumber may be cut into julienne strips as a garnish for chilled soups. For hot soups, sauté cucumber strips or thin rounds of leeks in a little butter.

Thin slices of lemon or orange make an attractive garnish for clear soups and tomato soup.

A mushroom garnish adds texture and flavor to cream soups. Fry the sliced mushrooms in a little butter until soft. Drain thoroughly before spooning them over the soup.

Thin onion rings add more flavor to soups. They can be sautéed like cucumber strips and leek rounds; alternatively, coat them in milk and flour, and deep fry them until crisp and golden.

SOUP GARNISHES

Julienne strips

Cut-outs for consommé royale

Cutting bread croûtons

Slicing Melba toast

Sauces and Dressings

Sauces first came into widespread use in the Middle Ages, to disguise the flavor of long-stored meat that had been inadequately cured. Today, they are used to add flavor to bland food, color to simple meals and moisture to otherwise dry foods.

BASIC WHITE SAUCE

This is prepared either by the roux or the blending method.

Roux method
A roux is usually composed of equal amounts of butter and flour which are then combined with liquid (usually milk) to the required consistency. Melt the butter in a heavy-based pan, blend in the flour, and cook over low heat for 2–3 minutes, stirring constantly with a wooden spoon.

Gradually add the warm or cold liquid to the roux, which will at first thicken to a near solid mass. Beat vigorously until the mixture leaves the sides of the pan clean, then add a little more milk. Allow the mixture to thicken and boil between each addition of milk. Continuous beating is essential to obtain a smooth sauce. When all the milk has been added, bring the sauce to the boil; let it simmer for about 5 minutes and add the seasoning.

A basic white sauce can also be made by the one-stage method. This consists of putting the basic ingredients (fat, flour and liquid) into a pan at the same time. Cook over low heat, beating until the sauce has thickened. Boil for 3 minutes and season.

MAKING A WHITE SAUCE

Blending butter with flour

Thickening the roux

Adding the remaining milk

Blending method
For this method the thickening agent is mixed to a paste with a little cold milk. Mix 2 tablespoons flour with a few tablespoons taken from 1¼ cups of cold milk. Blend to a smooth paste in a bowl, and bring the remaining milk to the boil.

Pour the hot milk over the paste and return the mixture to the pan. Bring to the boil over low heat, stirring continuously with a wooden spoon. Simmer the sauce for 2–3 minutes, until thick. Add a pat of butter and seasoning and cook for 5 minutes.

A basic white sauce can be made into other savory sauces, such as béchamel and velouté.

Béchamel Sauce
PREPARATION TIME: *20 min*
COOKING TIME: *5–10 min*
INGREDIENTS *(1 cup):*
1 cup milk
½ small bay leaf
Sprig of thyme
½ small onion
¼ teaspoon grated nutmeg
2 tablespoons butter
2 tablespoons flour
Salt and black pepper*

Put the milk with the bay leaf, thyme, onion and nutmeg in a pan, and bring slowly to the boil. Remove from the heat, cover with a lid and leave the milk to infuse for 15 minutes.

In a clean heavy-based pan, melt the butter, stir in the flour and cook the roux for 3 minutes.

Strain the milk through a fine sieve and gradually blend it into the roux. Bring to the boil, stirring continuously, then simmer for 2–3 minutes. Adjust the seasoning.

Velouté Sauce
PREPARATION TIME: *5–10 min*
COOKING TIME: *1 hour*
INGREDIENTS *(1 cup):*
2 tablespoons butter
2 tablespoons flour
2 cups white stock (page 163)
Salt and black pepper*

Make the roux with the butter and flour. Gradually stir in the hot stock until the sauce is quite smooth. Bring to boiling point, lower the heat, and let the sauce simmer for about 1 hour until reduced by half. Stir occasionally. Strain through a sieve.

Thickening agents for sauces
Basic white and brown sauces can be thickened or enriched with various other liaisons: cornstarch or arrowroot with water; beurre manié (kneaded butter and flour); egg yolks and cream.

Cornstarch and arrowroot
To thicken 1 cup of liquid to a sauce of coating consistency, stir 1 tablespoon cornstarch with 1½ tablespoons cold water, and mix into a smooth paste. Blend a little of the hot liquid into the liaison, then return this to the sauce. Bring the sauce to the boil, stirring constantly for 2–3 minutes to allow the starch to cook through.

Arrowroot is best used to thicken clear sauces that are to be served at once. To thicken 1 cup sauce use 2 teaspoons arrowroot mixed to a paste with water.

The sauce cannot be reheated and quickly loses its thickening qualities.

Beurre manié
This liaison is ideal for thickening sauces, casseroles and stews at the end of cooking. Knead an equal amount of butter and flour, about 2 tablespoons each, into a paste with a fork or the fingers. Add small pieces of the beurre manié to the hot liquid. Stir or whisk continuously to dissolve the butter and disperse the flour. Simmer the sauce until it is thick and smooth and has lost the starchy taste of raw flour. Do not let the sauce boil or the beurre manié will separate out.

EGG-BASED SAUCES

These rich sauces require care and practice to prevent them curdling. They are made from egg yolks and a high proportion of butter. Through continuous whisking, these two main ingredients are emulsified to the stage where they form a thick and creamy consistency.

Hollandaise Sauce

PREPARATION AND COOKING TIME: *20 min*
INGREDIENTS *(1 cup):*
3 tablespoons white wine vinegar
1 tablespoon water
6 black peppercorns
1 bay leaf
3 egg yolks
¾ cup soft butter, preferably unsalted
Salt and black pepper*

Boil the vinegar and water with the peppercorns and the bay leaf in a small pan, until reduced to 1 tablespoon. Leave to cool. Cream the egg yolks with 1 tablespoon butter and a pinch of salt. Strain the vinegar into the eggs, and set the bowl over a pan of boiling water. Turn off the heat. Whisk in the remaining butter, ½ tablespoon at a time, until the sauce is shiny and has the consistency of thick cream. Season with salt and freshly ground pepper.

Until the technique of egg-based sauces has been mastered, a Hollandaise sauce may sometimes curdle during preparation. This is generally because the heat is too sudden or too high, or because the butter has been added too quickly.

If the finished sauce separates, it can often be saved by taking it off the heat immediately and beating in 1 tablespoon of cold water.

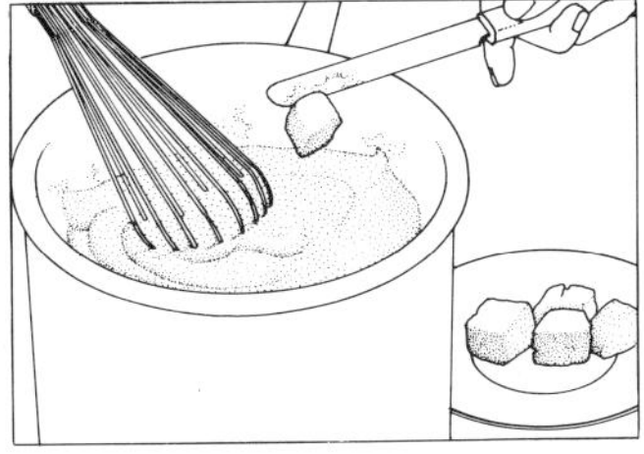

Whisking in pieces of butter to thicken Hollandaise sauce

Béarnaise Sauce

This sauce is similar to Hollandaise sauce, but has a sharper flavor. It is served with broiled meat and fish.

PREPARATION AND COOKING TIME: *20 min*
INGREDIENTS *(1 cup):*
2 tablespoons tarragon vinegar
2 tablespoons white wine vinegar
½ small onion
2 egg yolks
6–8 tablespoons butter, preferably unsalted
Salt and black pepper*

Put the vinegars and finely chopped onion in a small saucepan; boil steadily until reduced to 1 tablespoon. Strain and set aside to cool. Follow the method used for making Hollandaise sauce.

Mayonnaise

Mayonnaise and its variations are the most widely used of savory cold sauces. They are served with hors d'oeuvre, salads, cold meat, poultry and vegetable dishes. Mayonnaise, like Hollandaise and Béarnaise sauce, is based on eggs and fat, but oil is used instead of butter.

It is essential that all the ingredients and equipment are at room temperature. Assemble the bowl, egg and oil at least 1 hour before making a mayonnaise.

PREPARATION TIME: *20 min*
INGREDIENTS *(½ cup):*
1 egg yolk
¼ teaspoon salt
½ teaspoon dry mustard
Pinch sugar
Black pepper
½ cup olive oil
1 tablespoon white wine vinegar or lemon juice

Beat the egg yolk in a bowl until thick. Beat in the salt, mustard, sugar and a few twists of freshly ground pepper. Add the oil, drop by drop, whisking vigorously between each addition of oil so that it is absorbed completely before the next drop. As the mayonnaise thickens and becomes shiny, the oil may be added in a thin stream. Finally, blend in the vinegar.

A mayonnaise may curdle if the oil was cold or was added too quickly, or if the egg yolk was stale. To save a curdled mayonnaise, whisk a fresh yolk in a clean bowl, and gradually whisk in the curdled mayonnaise. Alternatively, whisk in a teaspoon of tepid water until the mayonnaise is thick and shiny.

SALAD DRESSINGS

A good dressing is essential to a salad, but it must be varied to accord with the salad ingredients. A sharp vinaigrette sauce is probably best for a green salad, but more substantial salads might need additional flavors.

Sauce Vinaigrette

PREPARATION TIME: *3 min*
INGREDIENTS *(½ cup):*
6 tablespoons oil
2 tablespoons vinegar
2 teaspoons finely chopped herbs
Salt and black pepper*

Put the oil and vinegar in a bowl or in a screw-top jar. Whisk with a fork or shake vigorously before seasoning to taste with herbs, salt and freshly ground pepper.

French Dressing

PREPARATION TIME: *3 min*
INGREDIENTS *(¾ cup):*
8 tablespoons oil
4 tablespoons vinegar
2 teaspoons Dijon-style mustard
½ teaspoon each salt and black pepper*
Sugar (optional)

Whisk or shake all the dressing ingredients together, seasoning with sugar (optional). Either of the following ingredients can be added to a basic French dressing: 1–2 crushed garlic cloves; 2 tablespoons chopped tarragon or chives; 1 tablespoon tomato paste and a pinch of paprika; 2 tablespoons each finely chopped parsley and onion; ¼ teaspoon anchovy paste (for cold fish).

Desserts

Desserts are often served before cheese, although gourmets maintain that desserts should follow the cheese. Family favorites include sweet pies and tarts (see pastry), as well as steamed puddings and custards. For party occasions, gelatins, mousses and home-made ice creams are ideal desserts.

STEAMED, BOILED AND BAKED PUDDINGS

Puddings can be steamed in a special decker steamer or in a large saucepan. Stand the pudding on a trivet or on skewers so as to raise it. Pour water into the pan until it reaches halfway up the mold. Keep at least a 1 in space around the mold.

Whichever steaming method is used, the water in the steamer or pan must be kept gently boiling throughout cooking. Top up with boiling water at intervals.

Preparing a steaming mold
Butter the mold lightly and cut and butter a disk of wax paper to fit the bottom; this prevents the pudding from sticking when it is turned out. Fill the mold no more than two-thirds with pudding mixture. Butter a piece of wax paper thoroughly and make a 1 in pleat in the center to allow for the pudding to rise. Lay the paper over the top of the mold and cover it with a piece of pleated foil. Tie the paper and foil covering securely with string below the lip of the mold. Make a string handle which will help to lift the pudding out.

Many traditional suet puddings are boiled rather than steamed. The steaming mold is covered tightly with a pudding cloth and immersed completely in a pan of boiling water. More usually, however, the pudding mixture is placed inside a scalded and flour-dusted pudding cloth. This is easiest done by laying the cloth over a colander, spooning in the pudding mixture and tying the corners tightly to shape the pudding. The two knots help to lift the pudding.

STEAMED PUDDINGS

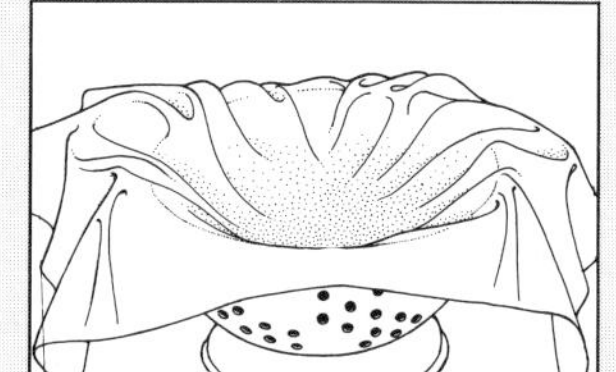

Place pudding cloth over colander

Spoon in mixture and tie up cloth

The pudding, ready for steaming

Turning out a pudding
Lift the pudding from the steamer or pan and remove the covering. Leave to cool and shrink slightly, then loosen the pudding at one side of the mold to let in the air. Place a dish over the mold, and turn it upside down.

Baked puddings
Apart from steaming and boiling, puddings can also be baked in the oven. The pudding mixture should be a little softer than for steamed puddings to give a crisp surface. To prevent jam-based puddings from caramelizing, set the dish in a shallow pan of water. Bake in the center of a pre-heated oven, at 350–375°F (180–190°C, mark 4–5).

GELATINS, MOLDS AND MOUSSES

These cold desserts are all made with gelatin, an extract from animal bones, tendons and skin. Unflavored gelatin is available in granular or sheet form. Fruit-flavored gelatins are also used; they come in granular form, in packages.

Some fresh fruit – pineapple, for example – contains enzymes which prevent the jelling action taking place. However, these enzymes will be destroyed if the fruit is bought canned or if it is cooked before being used for making the gelatins.

Setting gelatine
Jellied mixtures left to set in a refrigerator need less gelatin than those set at normal room temperature. In hot weather, and without refrigeration, increase the amount of gelatin by one-third, or reduce the amount of liquid. Desserts made in individual glasses need less gelatin than a dessert made in a mold for turning out later. Jellied mixtures tend to toughen if kept too long, especially in a refrigerator. They are best eaten on the day of making.

Directions for using granular gelatin are given on the package. In general, one envelope (1 tablespoon) will set 2 cups of liquid for molding in a refrigerator, and 2 teaspoons will set the same amount of liquid spooned into serving glasses. Fruit purées and ingredients of a similar consistency, such as molds and mousses, need 1 teaspoon gelatin to set 1 cup of mixture if it is to be served in dessert glasses or other small dishes.

For coating and glazing with aspic, for whisked gelatins and for setting fruit decorations, use the gelatin when it has set to the consistency of unbeaten egg white.

Sheet gelatin
Thin sheet gelatin must be washed in cold water and then soaked in a basin of cold water until soft, after 15–20 minutes. Squeeze the

softened gelatin lightly to extract surplus water, and place it in a bowl with the measured amount of liquid used in the recipe. Place the bowl in a pan of hot water and heat, without boiling, over low heat until dissolved. Six sheets of gelatin equal 1 ounce of granular gelatin.

SYLLABUBS AND TRIFLES

Syllabubs, which date back to Elizabethan times, were originally a drink, consisting of a bubbling wine, Sill or Sille, mixed with frothing cream. They later developed into a rich dessert with the addition of brandy and sherry, cream and sugar. The trifle, developed from the syllabub in the 18th century, became a little more substantial by the addition of sponge cake and jam.

Both syllabubs and trifles are ideal for dinner parties, as they can be made well in advance. The basis is still wine or liqueur or both, with eggs and cream.

EGG CUSTARDS

There are two types of custard: baked or steamed, and the softer pouring custard which is used as a sauce.

Egg whites set a baked custard, and the yolks give it the creamy consistency. However, as the yolks thicken at a higher temperature than the egg whites, it is important to cook custards at the correct heat. Too much heat, especially direct heat, will cause an egg custard to curdle. Use a double boiler for making a pouring custard and stand a set custard in a shallow container with a little cold water. If a double boiler is not available, use an ordinary saucepan over very gentle heat.

For baked custards, 2 whole eggs plus 2 egg yolks will set 2½ cups of milk. For a pouring custard use 4 egg yolks to every 2½ cups of milk.

MERINGUES

Meringue, with its crisp outer texture and aerated inside, forms the basis for many desserts: shells and baskets can be filled with cream or fresh fruit. Meringue is also a favorite topping for sweet pies and tarts.

Meringue is quite easy to make provided a few points are observed – the whisk and bowl must be absolutely clean and dry, and the eggs quite free from yolk. Ideally, use eggs that are 2–3 days old. The shapes of whisk and bowl also influence a good meringue; a balloon whisk gives greater volume but takes longer to whisk the whites than a rotary whisk. An electric mixer is the quickest, but gives the least volume. Choose a wide bowl when using a balloon whisk, and a narrow deep bowl for a rotary hand whisk.

The sugar for a meringue must be fine. Superfine sugar is generally used, but equal quantities of superfine and confectioners' sugar produce a meringue of pure white color and crisp melting texture. Do not use granulated sugar, as the coarse crystals break down the egg albumen, thus reducing the volume. If you use brown sugar, grind it finely first. A coffee grinder is excellent for grinding it to the consistency of superfine or confectioners' sugar; a food processor is useful if you are doing large quantities at a time.

Basic Meringue

INGREDIENTS:

2 egg whites
½ cup superfine sugar

Put the egg whites in a bowl and whisk them until they are fairly stiff and have the appearance of cottonwool. Tip in half the sugar and continue whisking the stiff whites until the texture is smooth and close, and stands in stiff peaks when the whisk is lifted. Lightly but evenly fold in the remaining sugar with a metal spoon.

ICE CREAM AND SHERBETS

Home-made cream ices and water ices (or sherbets) are quite different in both texture and flavor to the commercial varieties. It is as easy to make these at home as it is to make an egg custard or sugar syrup. Indeed, a basic ice cream is more often than not based on a custard enriched with heavy cream. The basis of a water ice is a sugar syrup flavored with fruit juice or purée.

Pointers to success

1. The amount of sugar in the mixture is important – if too much, the ice cream will not freeze, and if too little it will be hard and tasteless. Freezing does, however, take the edge off the sweetness and this must be borne in mind when tasting. In sherbets or water ices it is even more important to have the correct amount of sugar, as the soft yet firm consistency depends on the sugar content.
2. Some recipes recommend milk instead of cream, in which case the milk must be evaporated, not fresh dairy milk.
3. Use maximum freezing power. Whichever method is used for freezing the cream, it has a better texture if frozen quickly. Chill the equipment as well as the ingredients before starting.
4. Once the ice cream is frozen, it should be transferred to a shelf in the refrigerator for a little while before serving. Rock-hard ices are never pleasant and lose much of their flavor.
5. Ice cream may be stored in the freezer for up to 3 months.

Making ice cream in a refrigerator

If the refrigerator and freezer have the same temperature control, set the dial of the refrigerator at the coldest setting about 1 hour before the ice cream mixture is ready to freeze.

Make up the mixture according to the recipe. Remove the dividers and pour the mixture into ice cube trays or any other suitable freezing container, such as fancy molds, loaf pans, or strong plastic or stainless steel containers. Cover the trays or

Whisking the egg yolks
Breaking up ice crystals

containers with foil or lids and place in the freezing compartment.

To obtain a smooth texture, the ice crystals must be broken down as they form and the ice cream mixture whisked at intervals until part frozen and slushy. Remove the tray from the freezing compartment and scrape the ice crystals, which have formed on the sides and base, towards the center. Whisk the mixture with a fork until smooth, and return the tray, covered, to the freezing compartment. Thereafter, leave the ice cream undisturbed until it is firm, after 2–3 hours.

Freezing time varies with different refrigerators, but several hours are necessary in every case.

Making ice cream in a freezer

Set the dial to the coldest setting about 1 hour before the ice cream is ready to be frozen.

Prepare the ice cream mixture according to the recipe, place it in a mixing bowl in the freezer and leave it until mushy.

Remove the bowl from the freezer and whisk the mixture thoroughly with a rotary beater. Pour the ice cream into empty ice-cube trays or rigid plastic containers, and freeze until firm. Set the dial of the freezer to its normal temperature. If the ice cream is to be stored for any length of time the container should be sealed and labeled.

BATTERS

Batters provide the basis for a large number of dishes from simple lemon crêpes to Russian blini, French crêpes Suzette and our own waffles.

Batter is a mixture of flour, salt, egg and milk or other liquid. The proportions vary, depending on the consistency required. Crêpes, for instance, need a thin, cream-like batter, while fritters need a thick coating batter. For crisp coating batters, 1 tablespoon of oil may be used with $\frac{3}{4}$ cup of water, or the liquid may be half milk and half water.

Batters do not, as some people think, need to stand for a while before being cooked, although this may be done for practical reasons. Batter may be left, covered, at room temperature for any time up to 4 hours, or up to 24 hours in a refrigerator. It may be necessary to add a little more liquid to restore the batter to its original consistency.

Basic Crêpe Batter

PREPARATION TIME: *10 min*
INGREDIENTS *(for 8–10 crêpes):*
1 cup all-purpose or self-rising flour
*Pinch of salt**
1 egg
$1\frac{1}{2}$–$1\frac{3}{4}$ cups milk

Sift the flour and salt into a large bowl. Using a wooden spoon make a hollow in the center of the flour and drop in the lightly beaten egg. Slowly pour half the milk into the flour, gradually working the flour into the milk. When all the flour is incorporated, beat the mixture with a wooden spoon, whisk, or rotary beater, until it becomes smooth and free of lumps. Allow it to stand for a few minutes. Then add the remainder of the milk, beating continuously until the batter is bubbly and has the consistency of light cream.

To make crêpes, use a 7 in heavy-based shallow frying pan with sloping sides. Add just enough lard to gloss the pan to prevent the batter sticking. Fierce heat is necessary, and the pan should be really hot before the batter is poured in.

Pour in just enough batter to flow in a thin film over the bottom – tilting the pan to spread it. Use a jug or ladle for pouring in the batter. The heat is right if the underside of the crêpe becomes golden in 1 minute; adjust the heat to achieve this. Flip the crêpe over with a palette knife or spatula, or toss by flicking the wrist and lifting the pan away from the body. The other side of the crêpe should also be done in about 1 minute.

To store crêpes: if they are to be kept for a short time, stack them in a pile and cover with a clean dish towel. If they are to be stored for one or two days, put oiled wax paper between each crêpe, stack them and wrap the whole pile in kitchen foil and store in the refrigerator.

To re-heat crêpes: if crêpes are to be served with lemon and sugar, wrap three or four crêpes in foil and heat through in the oven at 300°F (160°C, mark 2). Alternatively, brush a flat pan with melted butter, arrange overlapping crêpes on it, brush with butter and put into a hot oven for 4–5 minutes, or heat the crêpes in a frying pan in an orange sauce as in the recipe for crêpes Suzette on pages 104–5.

COOKING CRÊPES

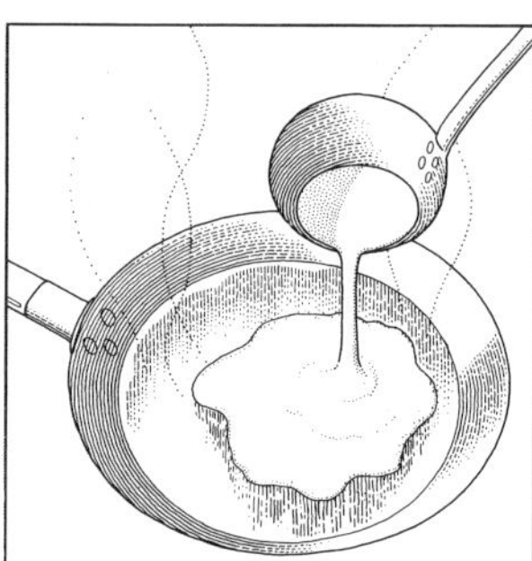

1. *Pour batter into greased pan*

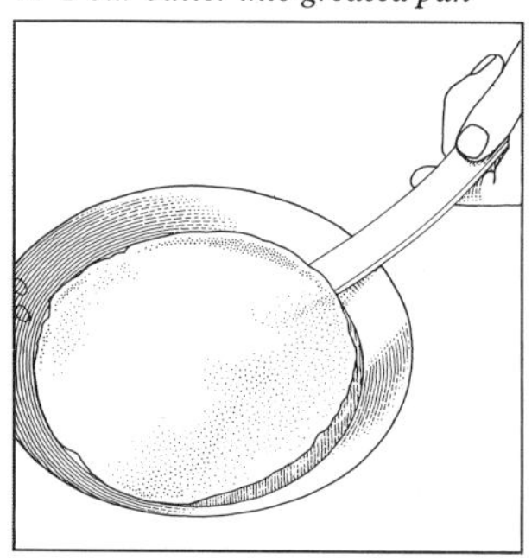

2. *Flip over the half-cooked crêpe*

3. *Straighten crêpe with knife*

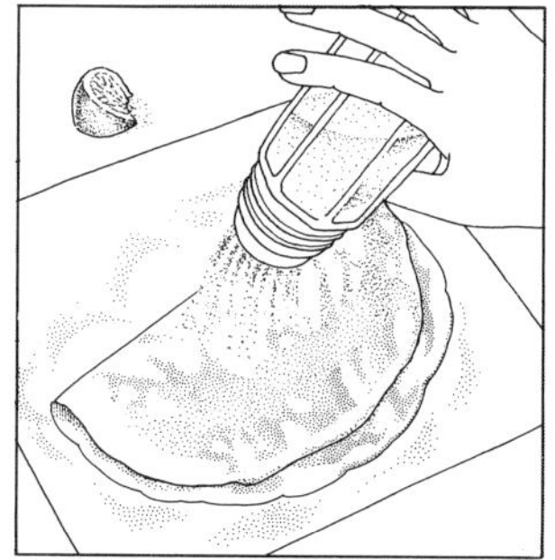

4. *Sprinkle with sugar and lemon*

Pastry

Although much mystique surrounds pastry-making, there are no great secrets to guarantee instant success, for pastry-making is an art which is mastered by care, patience and practice. There are, however, a few essentials which must be observed before good results can be achieved. The kitchen, working surface and utensils should be cool, and the recipe must always be strictly adhered to, especially in regard to measurements. Pastry should be made as quickly as possible, and handling kept to a minimum. Many pastries are best rested in a cool place before they are cooked.

PIE PASTRY

This popular and versatile pastry is used for savory and sweet pies, tarts, flans and tartlets. It is usually made by the 'rubbing-in' method, but there are several other ways of making pie pastry. All-purpose flour is recommended; self-rising flour may be used, but the pastry will be more crumbly. The fat should be lard or a white vegetable shortening; ideally, use equal amounts of lard and butter or firm margarine. Margarine alone produces a yellow, firm pastry.

The standard recipe is for 8 ounces pie pastry which always means 2 cups flour to $\frac{1}{2}$ cup fat. The amount of flour may be doubled or halved, but proportions of fat to flour should remain the same.

PREPARING TRADITIONAL PIE PASTRY

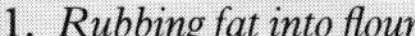

1. *Rubbing fat into flour*

3. *Kneading dough lightly*

2. *Mixing water into dough*

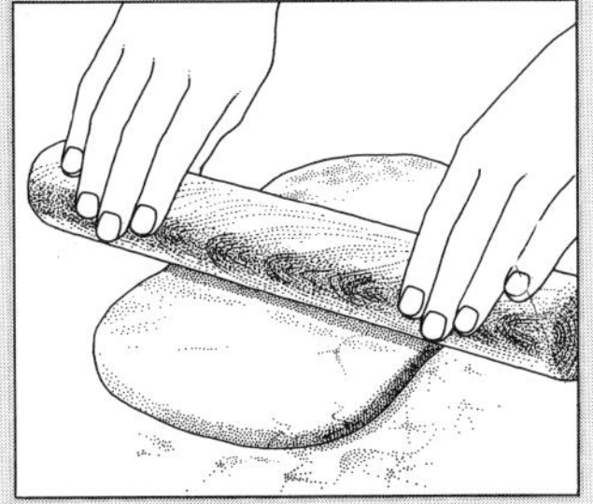

4. *Rolling out the pastry*

The standard recipe yields enough pastry to cover a 2 pint pie or baking dish, or a 9 in flan ring, or to line and cover a 7 in pie plate.

The following basic pie pastries may be used for both savory and sweet pies. Enriched pastry, however, is mainly used for lining flan rings. Pie pastries are usually baked in the center of a preheated oven, at 400°F (200°C, mark 6).

Standard Pastry

PREPARATION TIME: *15 min*
INGREDIENTS:
2 cups flour
*$\frac{1}{2}$ teaspoon salt**
$\frac{1}{4}$ cup lard
$\frac{1}{4}$ cup margarine or butter
5–7 tablespoons cold water

Sift the flour and salt into a wide bowl. Cut up the firm fats and rub them into the flour, using the tips of the fingers, until the mixture resembles fine breadcrumbs. Lift the dry mixture well out of the bowl and let it trickle back through the fingers to keep the pastry cool and light. Add the water, sprinkle it evenly over the surface (uneven addition of the water may cause blistering when the pastry is cooked). Mix the dough lightly with a round-bladed knife until it forms large lumps.

Gather the dough together with the fingers until it leaves the sides of the bowl clean. Form it into one piece and knead it lightly on a floured surface until firm and free from cracks. Chill for 30 minutes before use.

Roll out as required, using short, light strokes and rotating the pastry regularly to keep it an even shape.

Oil Pastry

This pastry produces a tender, flaky crumb. It must be mixed quickly and used at once – if left for any length of time, or chilled, it dries out and cannot be rolled.

PREPARATION TIME: *15 min*
INGREDIENTS:
5 tablespoons corn oil
7 tablespoons cold water
2 cups flour
*$\frac{1}{4}$ teaspoon salt**

Whisk the oil and water together in a large bowl, using a fork. Continue whisking until they are evenly blended. Sift the flour and salt together and gradually add it to the oil. Use two knives to incorporate the flour to a dough, then turn it on to a floured surface. Knead the pastry lightly and quickly until smooth and shiny. Roll out as above.

For oil pastry, use two knives to mix the flour and oil

Enriched Pastry
PREPARATION TIME: *10 min*
INGREDIENTS:
$1\frac{1}{4}$ cups flour
*Pinch salt**
6 tablespoons unsalted butter or margarine
1 egg yolk
$1\frac{1}{2}$ teaspoons sugar
2–3 tablespoons water

Sift the flour and salt into a wide bowl. Cut up the fat and rub it into the flour with the fingertips until the mixture resembles breadcrumbs. Beat the egg yolk, sugar and 2 teaspoons of water in a separate bowl and pour it into the flour mixture. Stir with a round-bladed knife, adding more water as necessary until the mixture begins to form a dough. Gather this into a ball and turn it on to a floured surface. Knead lightly.

PÂTE SUCRÉE

This pastry is the French equivalent of enriched pastry. It is thin and crisp, yet melting in texture, and neither shrinks nor spreads during baking. Pâte sucrée is usually baked blind (see next page).

PREPARATION TIME: *15 min*
RESTING TIME: *1 hour*
INGREDIENTS:
1 cup flour
*Pinch salt**
$\frac{1}{4}$ cup sugar
$\frac{1}{4}$ cup butter
2 egg yolks

Sift together the flour and salt on to a cool working surface. Make a well in the center of the flour and put in the sugar, soft butter and the egg yolks. Using the fingertips, pinch and work the sugar, butter and egg yolks together until well blended. Gradually work in all the flour from the sides and knead the pastry lightly until smooth. Leave the pastry in a cool place for at least 1 hour before rolling it out. Bake in the center of a pre-heated oven, at 350–400°F (180–200°C, mark 4–6).

STIRRED PASTRY

This rather sticky pastry is particularly suited to double crust fruit pies. The texture of the baked pastry is more like cookie dough than pastry.

PREPARATION TIME: *10–15 min*
INGREDIENTS:
10 tablespoons margarine
3 tablespoons butter
2 cups self-rising flour
*$\frac{1}{2}$ teaspoon salt**
3 tablespoons cold water

Beat the margarine and butter in a bowl until soft and well blended. Gradually add the sifted flour and salt, working it in with a wooden spoon. Finally add the water, blending well. The mixture will be sticky and difficult to work. Chill for at least 30 minutes.

Roll out on a well-floured surface or between sheets of non-stick paper, dredged with flour.

CRUMB CRUST

This is ideal for pie shells with fluffy chiffon-type fillings.

PREPARATION TIME: *15 min*
CHILLING TIME: *2 hours*
INGREDIENTS:
$\frac{1}{2}$ pound graham crackers, zweiback or gingersnaps
10 tablespoons butter
2–4 tablespoons sugar (optional)

COVERING A PIE DISH

Trim the pastry to fit the dish

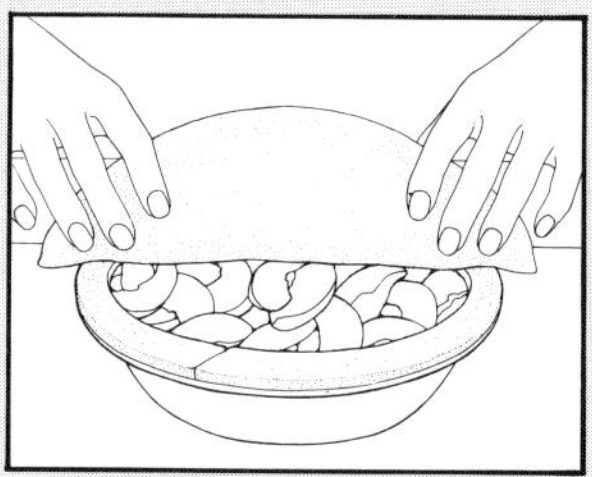

Cover the filled pie dish

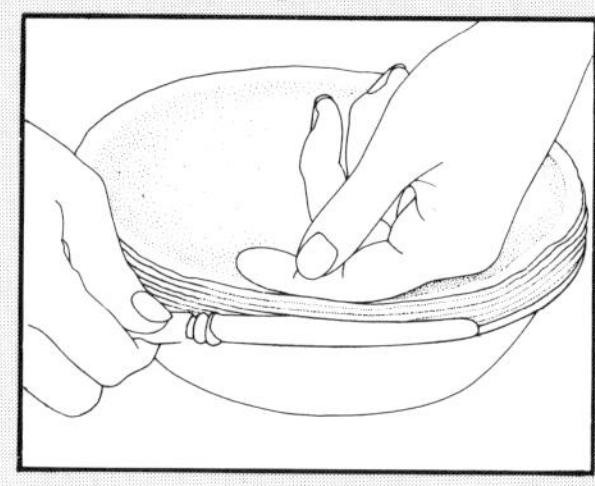

Seal pastry edges

MAKING A DOUBLE CRUST PIE

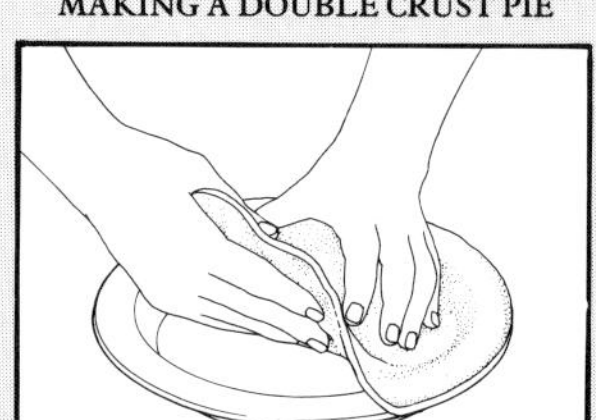

Lift pastry into pie plate

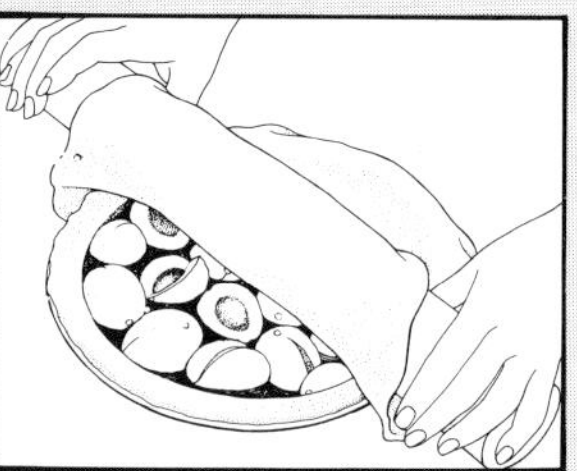

Place pastry lid in position

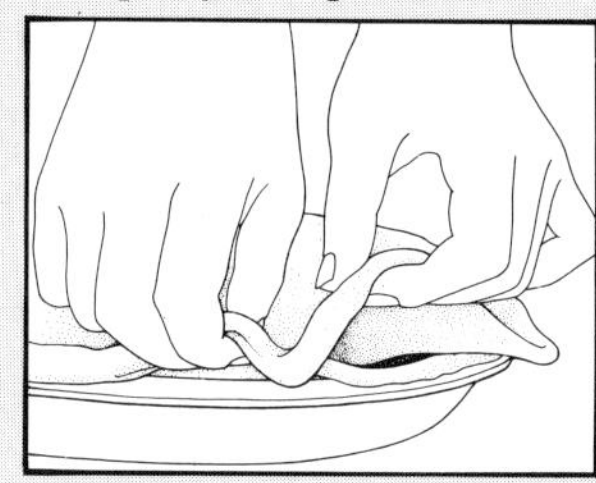

Fold surplus pastry under

Crush the crackers, a few at a time, with a rolling pin between two sheets of wax paper or in a plastic bag. For a fine crumb, break up the crackers roughly and put them in a liquidizer. Turn the crumbs into a deep bowl. Melt the butter in a small saucepan over low heat. Add the sugar, if used, to the crumbs and mix with the melted butter, stirring until evenly combined.

Spread the crumbly mixture into a 7–8 in wide shallow pie plate or tart pan; alternatively, use a flan ring placed on a flat serving dish or a loose-bottomed flan pan. With the back of a spoon, press the crumbs over the bottom and up the sides to form a shell. Chill the crumb crust in the refrigerator for 2 hours before filling it.

Covering a pie dish
Roll out the pastry to the required thickness (no more than $\frac{1}{4}$ in thick) and 2 in wider than the pie dish, using the inverted dish as a guide. Cut a 1 in wide strip from the outer edge of the pastry and place it on the moistened rim of the pie dish. Seal the strip with water where it

joins and brush the whole strip with water.

Fill the dish and set a pie funnel in the center; lift the remaining pastry on the rolling pin and lay it over the dish. Press the pastry strip and lid firmly together with the fingers. Trim excess pastry with a knife blade held at a slight angle to the dish.

To seal the pastry edges firmly so that they do not come apart during baking, hold the knife blade horizontally towards the pie dish and make a series of shallow cuts in the pastry edges.

Use the pastry trimmings to cut decorative shapes for the top of the pie. Cut a slit into the center of the pastry for the steam to escape, and decorate the edges by fluting or crimping.

Preparing a double crust pie
Divide the pastry into two portions, one slightly larger than the other. Shape the larger portion into a ball and roll it out on a lightly floured surface, to the thickness of a coin. Rotate the pastry between rolls to keep the edge round; if the edge begins to break pinch it together with the fingers. Roll out the pastry about 1 in wider than the inverted pie plate.

Fold the pastry in half and lift it on to the pie plate; unfold and loosely ease the pastry into position, being careful not to stretch the pastry. Put the cold filling over the pastry, keeping it slightly domed in the center. Roll out the remaining pastry for the lid, allowing about ½ in beyond the rim. Brush the edge of the pastry lining with water, then lift the lid on the rolling pin and place in position over the filling.

Seal the edges by either folding the surplus edge of the lid firmly over the rim of the lining, or by trimming the edges almost level with the plate and sealing them with a fork. Cut a slit in the center of the pastry lid for the steam to escape.

Lining a pie plate
For an open pie, roll out the pastry ⅙ in thick and about 1 in wider than the pie plate. Lift the pastry into the plate and ease it loosely over the bottom and sides. Trim the pastry with scissors to ½ in from the plate edge, then fold the pastry under the rim of the plate. Flute the edge so that the points protrude over the plate rim, thus allowing for any shrinkage that may occur during baking.

Lining a flan ring
Tarts are baked in plain or fluted rings set on baking sheets or in a French fluted flan pan with a removable bottom. Roll the pastry out as thinly as possible to a circle 2 in wider than the ring. With the rolling pin, lift the pastry and lower it into the flan ring. Lift the edges carefully and press the pastry gently into shape with the fingers, taking care that no air pockets are left between the ring and the pastry. Trim the pastry in a plain ring with a knife or scissors, just above the rim. On a fluted flan ring, press the pastry against the inner fluted ring edges then use the rolling pin to cut the pastry level with the rim.

Baking Blind
Sometimes pastry, especially tart cases and individual tartlets, has to be baked before the filling is put in. This is known as baking blind. Line the pastry case with

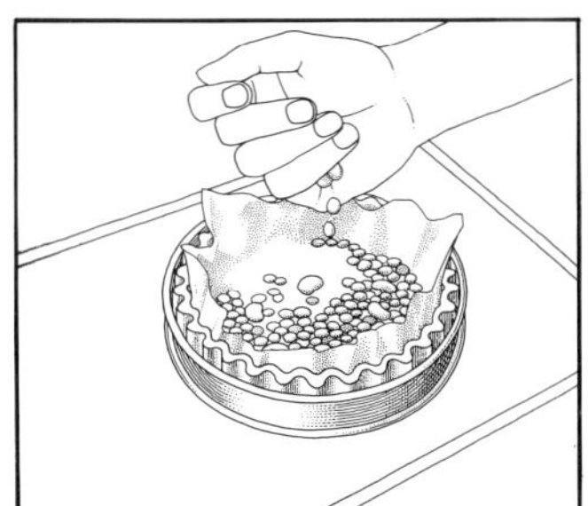

To bake blind, cover pastry with paper and weigh down with beans

foil or wax paper cut to shape and weigh it down with dried beans (if kept specially for this purpose, the beans can be used again and again). Bake the pastry case in the center of a pre-heated oven at 400°F (200°C, mark 6) for 15 minutes. Remove the beans and foil and bake for a further 5–10 minutes or until the pastry is dry and lightly browned.

Alternatively, and especially for tartlets, prick the bottom and sides of the pastry with a fork before lining it with foil. Dried beans are not necessary if the pastry is pricked.

Tart cases and tartlet molds should be left on a wire rack to cool and shrink slightly before being eased out of their molds.

Finishing and Decorations
The two edges of a covered pie can be finished in a number of decorative ways. To make a scalloped or fluted pattern, use the thumb or the back of a spoon handle to press the edges together. Alternatively, press the edges between your thumb and index finger, at intervals of ½–¾ in; draw a knife between the indentations towards the center of the pie.

Some pies can be finished with a twisted or ridged edge. Twist and slightly turn the edges together between thumb and index finger, at ½ in intervals. Alternatively, seal the edges with the tines of a fork.

DECORATING PIE EDGES

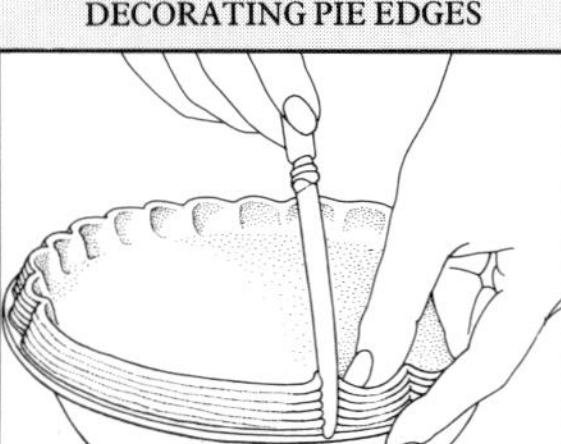

Making a scalloped pattern

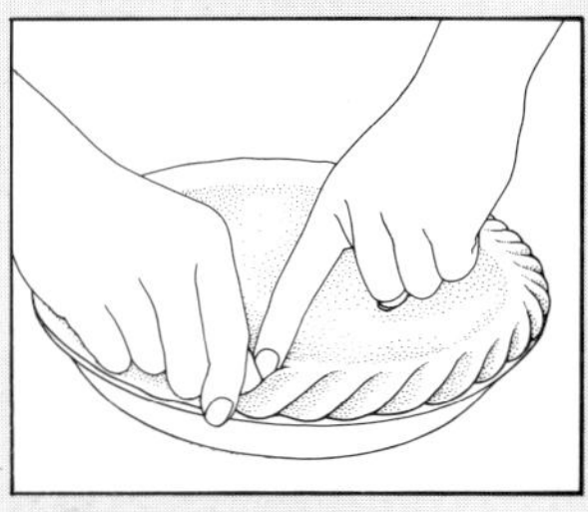

Making a twisted edge

The top of a covered pie may be decorated with the pastry trimmings. Roll the pastry out thinly and cut into small shapes.

To make leaves, cut the pastry into 1–1½ in wide strips and cut these into diamond shapes. With the back of a knife, trace the pattern of the ribs.

For a tassel, cut a 1 in wide pastry slice about 6 in long. Make cuts, ¾ in long, at intervals of ¼ in, then roll up the strip, place it on the pie and open out.

Finish the edges of open pies and tarts by fluting or crimping. A simple method, using a pair of scissors, is to make cuts just over ¼ in deep and a little over

PASTRY DECORATIONS

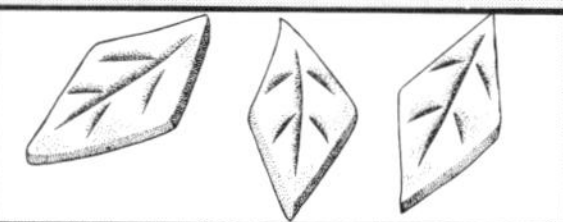
Pastry leaf shapes

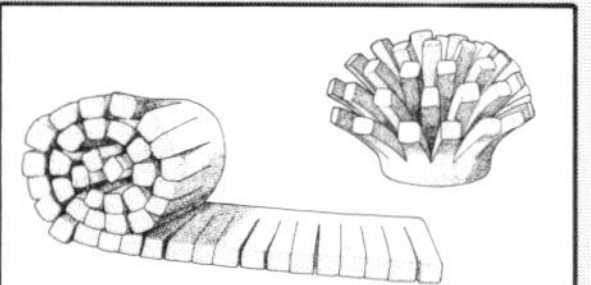
Pastry tassel

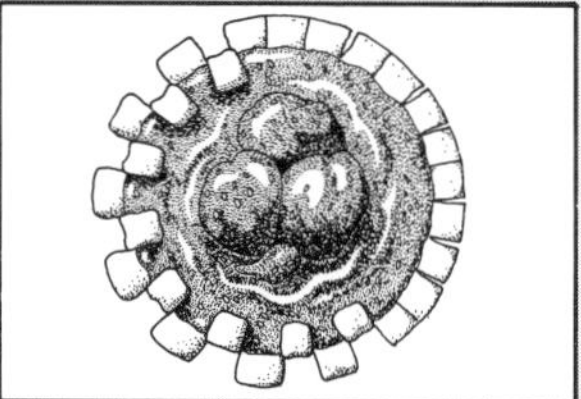
Cut edges on a tart

¼ in apart around the pastry edge. Fold alternate pieces of pastry inwards and bend the remaining pieces outwards. Or the edges can be decorated with thin pastry strips that have been twisted or braided. Moisten the pastry edge with water first.

A lattice pattern is a traditional decoration for many open tarts. Cut the rolled-out pastry trimmings into strips ½ in wide (a pastry wheel gives an attractive edge) and long enough to cover the tart. Moisten the tart edges, then lay half the strips over the filling, 1 in apart, and lay the remaining strips criss-crossing the first. Trim the strips to shape at the outer edge, or fold the pastry lining down over them for a neater finish. For a really professional touch, the pastry strips should be interwoven by laying them over the filling 1 in apart, and a strip of pastry at a right angle across the center. Lift alternate lengths of the first strips of pastry on one half of the tart and place a strip at right angles. Replace the top strips and repeat with the other side of the tart to complete the interwoven effect.

Lattice pattern: lay pastry strips over tart top; interweave crossing strips

Pies can be decorated with pastry flowers. Simple flowers are made by rolling a small piece of pastry to the size and shape of an acorn. Cut out two diamond shapes and pinch the edges to round them to a petal shape. Dampen the base of the petals and wrap around the wide base of the acorn shape. Pinch the pastry to seal the pieces together, then bend the tip of each petal slightly outwards.

More ornate flowers can be made by making a cross with a knife on a small, flattened round of pastry. Set the round on a square of dampened pastry; set this in turn on another square of dampened pastry, similar in size, to form a star pattern. Shape the corners of the squares to resemble petals. Pinch and shape each point of the central round of pastry into a petal to complete the flower.

Glazing

Brush the decorated pie or tart before baking to give a shiny golden look. Brush savory pies with beaten whole egg or with egg yolk diluted with a little water or milk, and a pinch of salt. Glaze sweet pies with milk or egg white and dust with sugar.

CHOUX PASTRY

This pastry is a French specialty and is used for cream puffs, chocolate éclairs and profiteroles. During cooking, the pastry should treble itself in size through the natural lift of air. The featherlight pastry surrounds a large cavity which can be filled with cream or confectioners' custard.

PREPARATION TIME: *20 min*
INGREDIENTS:
½ cup plus 2 tablespoons flour
¼ cup butter
*Pinch of salt**
¾–1 cup milk and water mixed (half of each)
2 beaten eggs

Sift the flour and salt on to a sheet of wax paper. Put the butter and the liquid in a heavy-based pan and cook over low heat until the butter melts, then raise the heat and rapidly bring the mixture to the boil. Draw the pan off the heat and pour in all the flour. Stir quickly with a wooden spoon until the flour has been absorbed by the liquid, then beat until the dough is smooth and glossy and comes away from the sides of the pan. Do not overbeat or the fat may leak out.

Cool pastry slightly, then beat in the beaten eggs, a little at a time. The pastry should be shiny and be thick enough to hold its shape, but not stiff. If the pastry is not going to be used immediately, cover the saucepan closely with wax paper and the lid to keep the dough pliable.

MAKING CHOUX PASTRY

1. *Heat butter and liquid*

2. *Pour flour into melted butter*

3. *Beat dough until smooth*

4. *Gradually add beaten egg*

PUFF PASTRY

This is regarded as the finest and most professional pastry. It is time-consuming but well worth making if a large quantity is required. Uncooked puff pastry may also be stored in the freezer for up to 3–4 months. When only small amounts of pastry are needed, commercially frozen pastry (available at some bakeries) is particularly useful. Puff pastry, which is used for savory pie crusts, as wrappings for meat and poultry, for vol-au-vents, cream horns, mille feuilles and palmiers, must be rolled out six times.

Vol-au-vents, patties and pastry crusts, which need the greatest rise and flakiness, should always be shaped from the first rolling of the finished dough. Second rolling, including trimmings from the first rolling, can be used for small items such as palmiers and crescents.

Prepared uncooked puff pastry can be stored for two or three days in the refrigerator.

PREPARATION TIME: *30–45 min*
RESTING TIME: *2½ hours*
INGREDIENTS:
4 cups flour
*2 teaspoons salt**
1 pound butter
1½–1¾ cups iced water
1 teaspoon lemon juice

Sift the flour and salt into a large bowl. Cut ½ cup of the butter into small pieces and rub it into the flour with the fingertips. Add the water and lemon juice and using a round-bladed knife, mix the ingredients to a firm but pliable dough. Turn the dough on to a lightly floured surface and lightly knead it until smooth. Shape the pastry into a thick round and cut down with a wet knife through half its depth in the form of a cross.

Open out the four flaps and roll them out until the center is four times as thick as the flaps. Shape the remaining firm butter to fit the center of the dough, leaving a clear ½ in all around. Fold the flaps over the butter, envelope style, and press the edges gently together with a rolling pin. Roll the dough into a rectangle 16 in × 8 in using quick short strokes. Roll lightly but firmly, back and forth, so as not to squeeze out the butter. Brush off any surplus flour between rollings.

Fold the dough into three and press the edges together with the edge of the little finger. Wrap the pastry in a cloth or wax paper, cover with plastic wrap and leave in a cool place (not the refrigerator) for 20 minutes.

Roll out the pastry, raw edge pointed to the left, to a rectangle as before. Fold and leave to rest for 20 minutes. Repeat rolling, folding and resting four times, giving the dough a half-turn every time. Leave the dough to rest for 30 minutes in the refrigerator before shaping it. Puff pastry, properly made, should rise about six times in height and should generally be baked in the center or just above, of a pre-heated oven, at 450°F (230°C, mark 8).

MAKING PUFF PASTRY

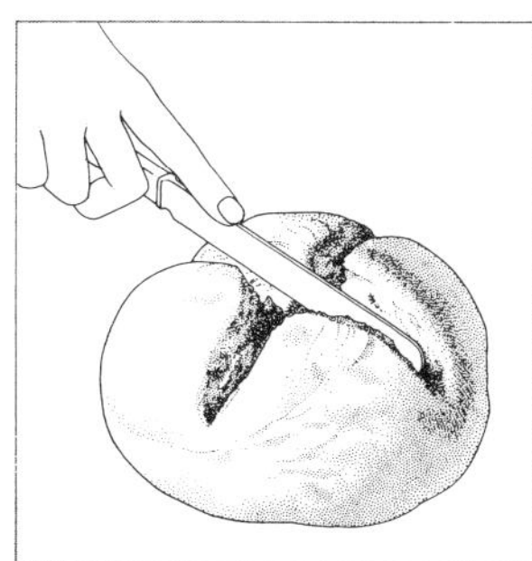

Cut a cross in rounded dough

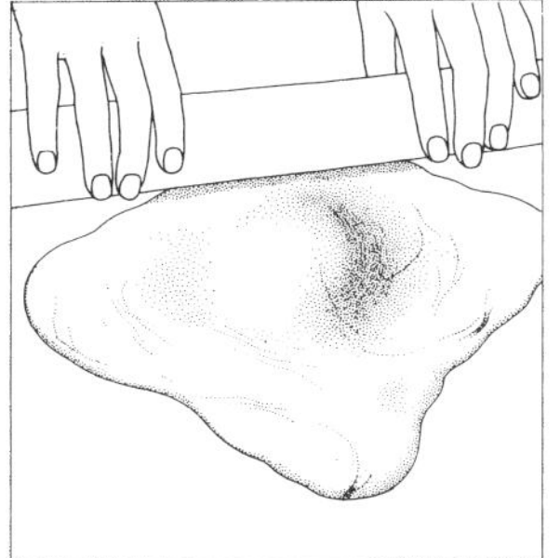

Roll out the flaps

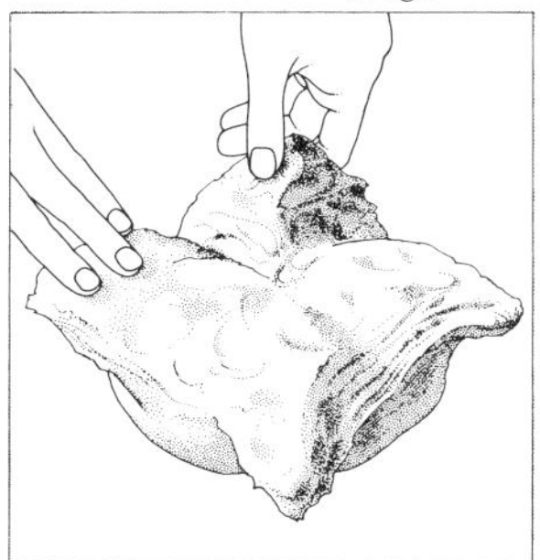

Fold out the four flaps

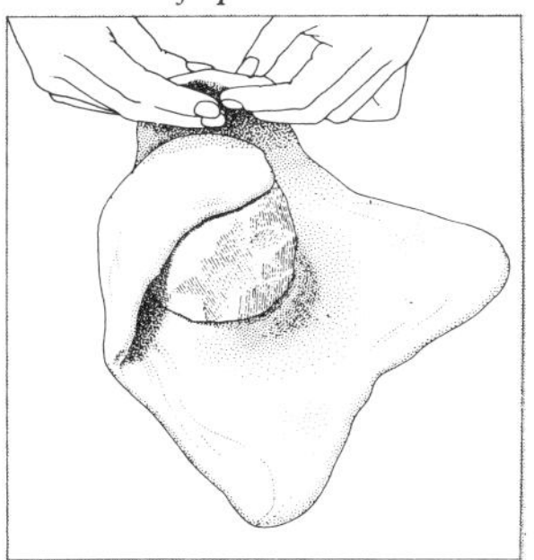

Place remaining butter in center

COMMON FAULTS IN PASTRY MAKING

PIE PASTRY

Hard and/or tough pastry: due to too much liquid, too little fat, over-handling or insufficient rubbing in.

Soft and crumbly pastry: too little water; too much fat, or self-rising flour used instead of all-purpose.

Shrunk pastry: excess stretching during rolling out.

Soggy pastry: filling too moist or sugar in a sweet pie in contact with pastry.

Sunken pie: oven temperature too low; cold pastry put over hot filling; too much liquid in filling, or too little filling.

Speckled pastry: undissolved sugar grains in enriched pastry crust.

CHOUX PASTRY

Mixture too soft: insufficient cooling of the flour before adding eggs; eggs added too quickly.

Pastry did not rise: self-rising flour used; oven too cold; too short baking time.

Sinking after removal from oven: insufficient baking; further period of baking sometimes remedies this defect.

PUFF PASTRY

Too few layers: insufficient resting and chilling; heavy rolling causing fat to break through and intermingle with the pastry; fat too soft.

Fat running out during baking: oven too cool.

Hard and tough pastry: too much water; over-kneading.

Shrinking pastry: insufficient resting; over-stretching during rolling.

Baking with Yeast

Home-baked bread has a strikingly different taste and texture from commercially baked loaves. Our daily bread is composed of such basic ingredients as flour, yeast, salt and liquid; enriched dough mixtures for buns and tea breads – such as babas and Sally Lunns – also include butter and spices, dried fruits and nuts.

Flour is the most important factor in bread-making, and the best loaves are made with hard-wheat flour or bread flour. Hard-wheat flour has a high gluten content (from which protein is formed) and aids rising in combination with yeast; it absorbs liquids easily and produces bread of light and open texture.

Flour
All-purpose flour is a mixture of hard-wheat and soft-wheat flours. For bread making, unbleached all-purpose flour is preferable. Wholewheat, or graham, flour produces yeast doughs of closer texture and with less rise than a white dough. As this flour contains the bran and germ of the wheat, it does not keep well and should be bought as needed. This flour gives bread its mealy taste.

Yeast
Fresh or compressed and active dry yeast may be used in bread-making. Many small private bakeries will supply fresh yeast, and some supermarkets and health stores also stock it. Active dry yeast is more concentrated than fresh yeast: ¼ ounce (1 package) of active dry yeast is the equivalent of a ⅔-ounce cake of fresh or compressed yeast.

Fresh yeast should have a creamy-beige color, and a firm consistency which crumbles easily when broken up. It can be stored in a loosely tied plastic bag in the refrigerator for up to 2 weeks, or in the freezer for up to 6 months.

Fresh yeast is added to flour in three different ways: it is rubbed in, blended with liquid or added as a batter. Rubbing in is suitable for soft doughs, quick-breads and sweet doughs. Blending with liquid is the basic way and is suitable for all bread recipes. The batter method is best suited for rich yeast doughs, and works equally well with fresh and dry yeast. It is not advisable to cream fresh yeast with sugar, as this results in the breakdown of some of the living yeast cells.

Rubbing-in method Crumble the yeast into the sifted flour and salt with the tips of the fingers. Add the specified amount of liquid to the flour and yeast mixture to make a soft dough. Work the dough with the fingertips to distribute the yeast evenly.

Blending with liquid Blend the yeast with part of the measured liquid; add this mixture to the flour and salt, together with the remaining liquid.

Batter method Mix one-third of the measured flour with the yeast, blended with all the liquid and 1 teaspoon of sugar. Leave in a warm place until frothy, about 20 minutes, then add the rest of the flour, the salt and any other ingredients that are specified.

Active dry yeast
This can be stored in a tightly lidded container for up to 6 months. Dry yeast is reconstituted in some warm water (110°F, 43°C). This water should be taken from the amount to be used in the recipe, first dissolved in the proportion of 1 teaspoon sugar to ½ cup water. Sprinkle the yeast over the water and leave in a warm place until frothy – after about 15 minutes.

Salt
Apart from improving the flavor of bread, salt also affects the gluten in the flour. If salt is omitted, the dough rises too quickly. If there is too much salt, this kills the yeast and gives the bread a heavy or uneven texture.

Liquid
This may be milk, water or a mixture of both. The amount varies from recipe to recipe, depending on the absorbency of the flour. Milk adds food value and strengthens doughs, improves the keeping quality and the color of the crust. For plain bread, however, water alone gives a better texture.

Fat
This is used in enriched yeast doughs for buns, croissants and tea breads which have a soft outer crust. Fat makes a dough soft and also slows down yeast action so that the dough rises less than plain bread dough.

Sugar
Too much sugar added to a dough mixture delays fermentation of the yeast cells; always follow the given quantities.

Although many recipes specify sugar, it is not at all necessary for fermenting yeast and may be omitted unless of course you want a sweet dough.

MAKING BREAD DOUGH

Pour the liquid into the flour

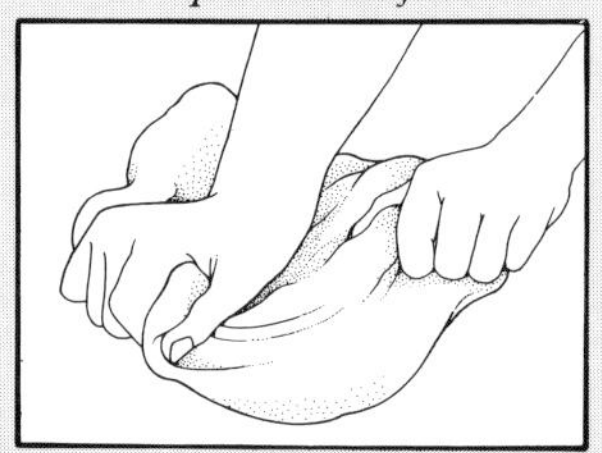

Knead until the dough is elastic

Leave to rise in plastic bag

Making the dough
Sift the flour and the salt into a mixing bowl, make a well in the center and add all the liquid at once. Mix it in with one hand until thoroughly incorporated. Add

more flour if necessary, and beat the dough against the sides of the bowl until it comes away cleanly. Knead the dough on a lightly floured surface.

Kneading is most important, as it strengthens and develops the dough and enables it to rise. Gather the dough into a ball with the tips of the fingers, then fold the dough towards the body. Press down on the dough and away from the body with the palm of the hand. Give the dough a quarter-turn and repeat the kneading.

Knead the dough for about 10 minutes until it feels firm and elastic and no longer sticks to the fingers – it is better to knead the dough too much rather than too little. Bread dough may be kneaded in an electric mixer.

Rising

After kneading, the dough must be set aside for rising until it has doubled in size. A large plastic bag is useful for the rising process. Pour a few drops of corn oil into the bag and swirl it around to distribute it evenly in a thin film. Put the dough in the bag, tie it loosely and leave the dough until it has doubled in size and springs back when lightly pressed with a finger. The time the dough takes to rise depends on the temperature. Ideally allow 12 hours in a cool room, and about 2 hours at normal room temperature. Dough left to rise in a refrigerator will need 24 hours.

If time is short, the dough can be made to rise in 45–60 minutes in a warm place, for example over a pan of warm water. Be careful, however, as too much heat may kill the yeast.

PREPARING LOAVES FOR BAKING

Shape or roll up risen dough to fit greased loaf pans

TRADITIONAL BREAD SHAPES

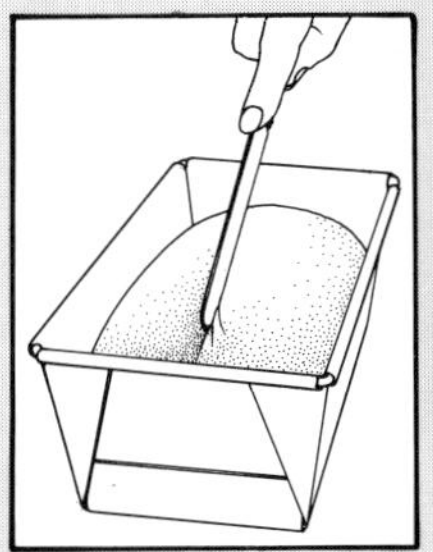

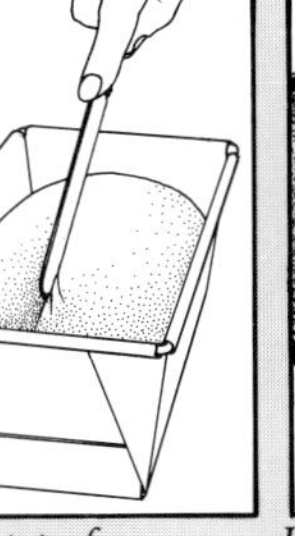

Score the top of a loaf with a knife

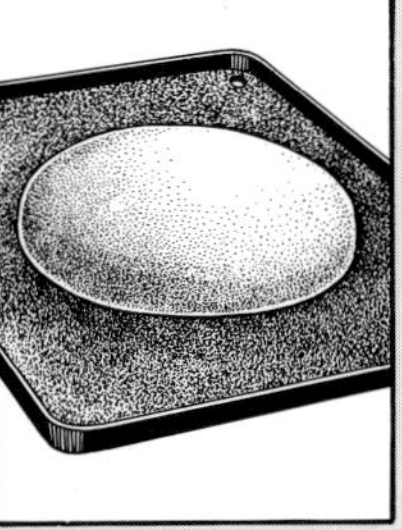

Round loaf is a lightly flattened ball of dough

Arrange dough in a round pan for a crown loaf

Punching down

After the initial rising the dough has to be punched down, or kneaded again, to knock out the air bubbles and to ensure a good rise and even texture. Shape the kneaded dough as required and put it into pans or on to baking sheets. Slip the pans or sheets into oiled plastic bags and leave the loaves to rise a second time at room temperature until double their size.

Baking

Remove the pans or baking sheets from the plastic bags and bake at 400–450°F (200–230°C, mark 6–8), according to the directions given in the individual recipes. A bowl of hot water placed in the bottom of the oven creates steam, which improves the texture of the bread.

Storing

Place the baked and cooled loaves in clean plastic bags, leaving the end open. To refresh a crusty loaf, wrap it in kitchen foil and put in the oven at 450°F (°230C, mark 8) for about 10 minutes. Leave it to cool in the foil.

Wholewheat Bread

PREPARATION TIME: *20 min (plus rising)*

COOKING TIME: *30–40 min*

INGREDIENTS *(for two 2 pounds or four 1 pound loaves):*

12 cups whole wheat flour
1 tablespoon sugar
*3–4 teaspoons salt**
2 tablespoons lard
4 packages active dry yeast
1 quart lukewarm water

Sift the flour, sugar and salt into a large bowl. Cut up the lard and rub it into the flour with the fingertips until the mixture resembles fine breadcrumbs. Blend the yeast, in a small bowl, with 1 cup of the measured water and pour it into a well in the center of the flour; add the remaining water. Using one hand, work the mixture together and beat it until the dough leaves the bowl clean. Knead the dough on a lightly floured surface for 10 minutes.

Shape the dough into a large ball and leave it to rise in a lightly oiled plastic bag until it has doubled in size. Turn the dough on to a lightly floured surface and knead again until firm. Divide the dough into two or four equal pieces and flatten each piece firmly with the knuckles to knock out any air bubbles. Stretch and roll each piece of dough into an oblong the same length as the pan; fold it into three or roll it up like a jelly roll. Lift the dough into the greased pans, brush the top with lightly salted water and place each pan inside an oiled plastic bag. Tie the bag loosely and leave to rise until the dough reaches the top of the pans.

Remove the pans from the bags, set them on baking sheets and bake in the center of a preheated oven at 450°F (230°C, mark 8) for about 30 minutes or until the loaves shrink from the sides of the pans. Cool the loaves on a wire rack and test by tapping them. If they sound hollow they are done.

For a fancy whole wheat loaf divide a quarter of the dough into four equal pieces; shape them into rolls the width of a greased 5 × 3 in loaf pan and fit them into the pan. Finish as before.

Quick Whole Wheat Loaves

PREPARATION TIME: *20 min (plus rising)*

COOKING TIME: *15–20 min*

INGREDIENTS *(for one 1 pound loaf and 8 rolls, or two 1 pound loaves):*

2 cups whole wheat flour
2 cups all-purpose flour
*2 teaspoons salt**
2 teaspoons sugar
1 tablespoons lard
1 package active dry yeast
1½–1¾ cups warm water
2–3 tablespoons cracked wheat or crushed cornflakes

Sift the two flours, the salt and sugar into a bowl. Cut up the lard and rub it into the flour with the fingertips. Blend the yeast with all the warm water until the yeast has dissolved. Make a well in the center of the flour and pour in the yeast liquid. Mix to a soft, biscuit-like dough, beating until it leaves the side of the bowl clean (if necessary, add a little more flour).

Divide the dough into two equal portions. Shape each piece to half fill a greased loaf pan and brush the top of the dough with lightly salted water; sprinkle with cracked wheat or crushed cornflakes. Place the pans on a baking sheet in a lightly oiled plastic bag, tie loosely and leave in a warm place until the dough has doubled in size. Remove the plastic and bake the loaves in the center of a pre-heated oven at 450°F (230°C, mark 8) for about 40 minutes. Test by tapping the loaves; if they sound hollow, they are baked. Cool on a wire rack.

Rolls Divide the whole, risen dough after re-kneading into 8 equal pieces. Roll each into a round on an unfloured surface, using the palm of one hand. Shake a little flour on to the palm of the hand, and press the dough down, hard at first, easing up until the rounds have the shape of a roll. Set the rolls well apart on floured baking sheets, put them into oiled plastic bags and leave in a warm place to double in size.

Remove the plastic and bake the rolls just above the center of the oven, pre-heated to 450°F (230°C, mark 8), for 15–20 minutes. Cool on a wire rack.

For soft rolls, set the shaped rolls ¾ in apart on the baking sheets and sprinkle generously with flour. The rolls will bake into contact with each other along the sides and the flour on top will give a soft surface.

Flowerpot Loaves Whole wheat bread may also be baked in flowerpots. Use clay pots – never plastic – grease them thoroughly inside and bake them empty in a hot oven several times to seal the inner surface and prevent the dough sticking. A clay flowerpot 4–5 in wide will hold half a portion of whole wheat dough. Finish and bake the loaf as already described.

Round Loaf Roll each piece of dough into a ball, flatten it and set on a floured baking sheet.

Crown Loaf Divide a quarter of the risen dough into five or six balls. Set these in a greased, 5 in diameter deep cake pan.

Poppy-seed Braid Divide the dough into three, and roll each into a 12 in long strand. Set the three strands side by side on a flat surface, and pass the left strand over the center strand, then the right strand over the center strand. Continue like this until the whole length is braided. Finally join the short ends neatly together and tuck them under.

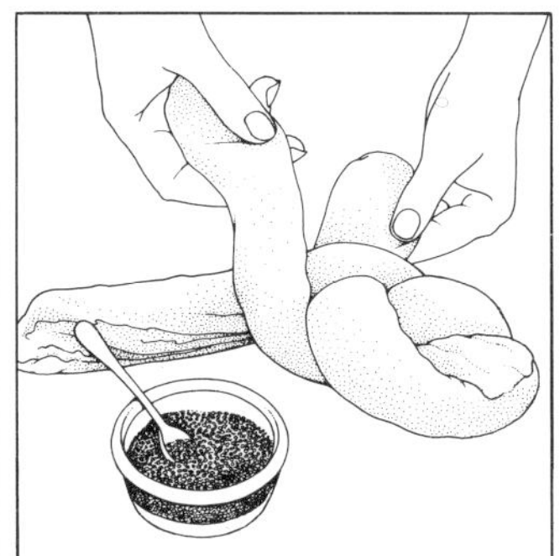

Braided loaf: for a three-strand braid, begin crossing the dough near the top

Place the braid on a lightly greased baking sheet. Beat an egg with a teaspoon of sugar and a tablespoon of water to make the glaze. Brush the braid evenly and sprinkle with poppy seeds. Put the braid on the sheet inside a lightly oiled plastic bag and set aside to rise again until the dough has doubled in size. Remove the plastic bag and bake the loaves in the center of a pre-heated oven at 375°F (190°C, mark 5) for 35–40 minutes. Tap the bottom of the loaves with the knuckles – if they sound hollow they are done. Cool the loaves on a wire rack.

Fancy Rolls Enriched white dough is ideal for light, dinner-type rolls which can be shaped in a variety of ways. Use about 2 ounces of risen dough for each roll. Roll a piece of dough out, about 4 in long, cut it in half lengthwise and, holding each strip at both ends, twist it three times. Alternatively, roll each strip into a strand and tie it into a knot in the center.

Shape 2 ounce pieces of dough into oblong miniature loaves and score the surface with five or six marks, at even intervals. With a scissor-point, make triangular cuts between the score marks, through the dough, so that the points are slightly raised.

FANCY ROLLS

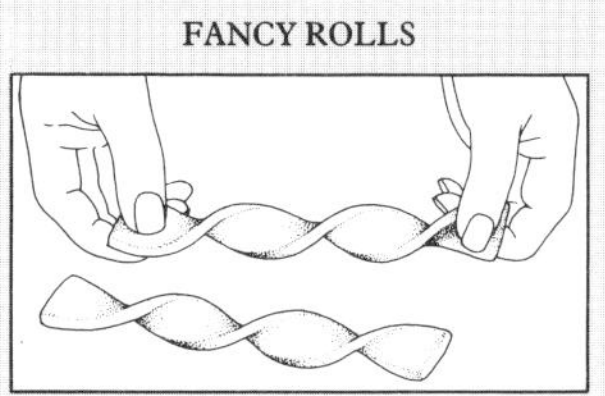

Twisting strips of dough

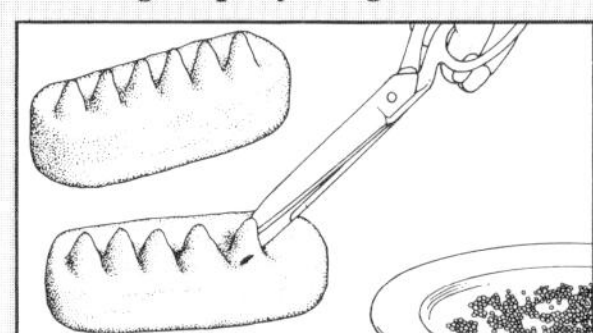

Snipping small cuts in rolls

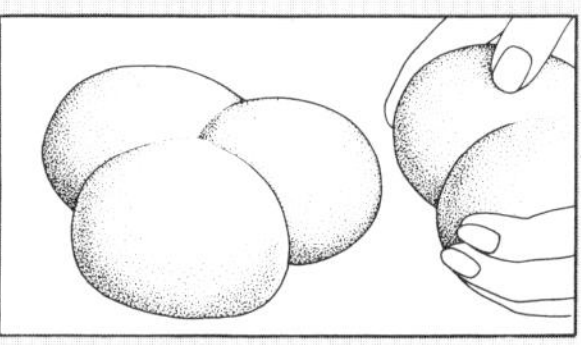

Setting rolls on baking sheet

Divide a 2 ounce piece of dough into three, shape into balls and set them on a baking sheet in such a way that all three balls touch each other.

Alternatively, roll a 2 in piece of dough into a thick strand and shape into a snail or 'S' form.

Brush the rolls with egg glaze and set them aside to rise until doubled in size. Bake the rolls just above the center of a pre-heated oven, at 375°F (190°C, mark 5), for 10–15 minutes or until golden.

Cake-making

The key to successful cake-making lies in following the recipe in detail, and in understanding the reaction of the various ingredients to each other. The basic ingredients are fat, flour, leavening agents, eggs, sugar and often fruit. Using the right size pans, correct oven position and temperature are also important factors.

Basically cakes fall into two categories: those made with fat, and the sponge types made without fat.

In fat-type cakes, the fat is either rubbed in, creamed or melted. Rubbed-in mixtures are generally used for plain, everyday cakes, such as Tyrol cake, while creamed cakes are rich and soft with a fairly close, even grain and soft crumb as in a layer cake.

In melted cakes, e.g. gingerbread, the fat, often with liquid, sugar, syrup or molasses added, is poured into the dry ingredients to give a batter-like consistency. Mix cakes by hand or use an electric mixer after incorporating the flour with fat and eggs.

Preparations

Always use the right size pan. Bigger, smaller or shallower pans than those called for can cause a cake to fail. If the pan is of incorrect size, fill to only half its depth so that the cake will rise to, but not above, the top. Test frequently to see if the cakes are cooked. Prepare the pan either by lining or by greasing with butter and sprinkling with flour. Set the oven to the correct temperature if the cake is to be baked at once after mixing, and assemble the necessary ingredients – eggs, butter and firm margarine should be at room temperature.

Fats

Butter, margarine, vegetable shortening, lard and corn oil are all used in cakes. However, they are not always interchangeable.

Butter gives the best flavor and improves the keeping quality of cakes, but firm margarine can be used in place of butter in most recipes, with only a slight difference in flavor. Soft margarine, sold in tubs, is composed of blended oils; it is particularly suitable for cakes where all the ingredients are mixed in one operation.

Vegetable shortening is light and easy to blend with other ingredients. Like lard, this fat contains little or no salt. Shortening and lard can be used interchangeably in recipes.

Corn oil is suitable for most recipes using melted fat, but it is advisable to follow the manufacturer's instructions, as the characteristics of oils vary. It is easy to mix in and gives a soft texture, but cakes made with it do not keep quite so well.

Flour

Cake flour is made from soft wheat and gives a lighter, crumblier texture. Self-rising flour is all-purpose flour to which baking powder and salt have been added in the proportions of $1\frac{1}{2}$ teaspoons baking powder and $\frac{1}{2}$ teaspoon salt for each cup of flour. All-purpose flour, cake flour and self-rising flour are all used for cakes. All-purpose and cake flour are usually sifted with a pinch of salt. Salt is added not only for flavor, but because of its chemical action which in effect toughens up the soft mixture of fat and sugar.

A mixture of all-purpose and self-rising flour is ideal for rich cakes which would rise too much if self-rising flour only were used. Other cakes, and in particular whisked cakes such as sponges, should be made only with all-purpose flour, as they have their own natural leavening agent – air.

In some melted cakes flour is mixed with baking soda. These cakes contain molasses, which on its own is slightly acid and must be offset by an alkali to act as a leavening agent.

Leavening agents

Baking powder is a ready-made blend of soda and cream of tartar, and these together form carbon dioxide. The rubbery substance in flour – known as gluten – is capable, when wet, of suspending carbon dioxide in the form of tiny bubbles.

Since all gases expand when heated, these bubbles become larger during baking, and thus cause a cake to rise.

However, cake mixtures can hold only a certain amount of gas, and if too much leavening agent is used the cake will rise well at first, but later collapse, and this results in a heavy, close texture. A combination of cream of tartar and baking soda is sometimes used as an alternative to baking powder, in the proportion of $\frac{1}{2}$ teaspoon cream of tartar to $\frac{1}{3}$ teaspoon baking soda.

Eggs

These give lightness to cake mixtures, as they expand on heating and trap the air beaten into the mixture. When whisked egg is used in a cake mixture, air instead of carbon dioxide causes it to rise.

Cakes with a high proportion of egg, such as sponge cakes, need little if any leavening agent.

In creamed mixtures, the eggs are beaten in, not whisked, and a little additional leavening agent is required. In plain cakes, where beaten egg is added with the liquid, the egg helps to bind the mixture but does not act as the main leavening agent.

Sugar

Granulated sugar is the most commonly used sweetener for cakes, although the finer superfine sugar is sometimes used.

Brown sugar, dark or light brown in color, is good for rubbed-in, melted and fruit cakes. The color and flavor add richness and the soft, moist quality helps to keep certain cakes in good condition longer.

You can easily grind your own granulated sugar, whether white or brown, to the desired degree of fineness.

Syrup, honey and molasses, often combined with sugar, are used to sweeten, color and flavor cakes such as gingerbread. They give a close, moist texture.

Fruit and peel
Always choose good-quality dried fruit. Stored golden raisins sometimes become hard, but they can be plumped up in hot water, and thoroughly drained and dried. Wash any syrup from candied cherries and dry them thoroughly.

Candied fruit peel can be bought ready-chopped, but make sure that it looks soft and moist. Coarsely chopped, thin cut peel sometimes needs more chopping to make it finer. Large pieces of candied orange, lemon, grapefruit and citron peel should be stripped of sugar before being shredded, grated or chopped.

Preparing cake pans
All cakes should be baked in pans that have been greased, greased and floured, sugared or lined with paper. The final appearance of a cake depends largely on the expert preparation of the cake pan.

Layer cake pans and deep cake pans for rubbed-in mixtures are often greased only by brushing melted shortening evenly over the inside. But as an extra precaution against sticking and for ease of turning out, a paper liner of greased wax paper fitted into the bottom is a good idea. The paper does not necessarily have to reach the edge of the pan but the center must be covered.

For fatless sponges, flour the greased pan to give an extra crisp crust, or dust it with flour, blended with an equal amount of sugar. Shake the dusting mixture around the pan until evenly coated, and remove excess by gently tapping the inverted pan.

For baking small cupcakes, fluted paper baking cups set in muffin or cupcake pans are by far the easiest to use; otherwise grease the pans thoroughly.

Cooking parchment paper can be used instead of wax paper to line both round and rectangular pans. Pans with a non-stick surface need no greasing or lining, but a paper lining helps to protect against a solid crust, especially during long baking. If the cakes are to be baked in non-stick pans, reduce the baking time by a few minutes as these pans brown the contents more quickly.

Lining a round cake pan
Cut a strip of wax paper as long as the circumference of the pan and 2 in wider than the depth of the pan. Make a fold about 1 in deep along one of the long edges, and cut this at ½ in intervals up to the fold, at a slight angle. Curve the strip and slip it around the sides of the greased pan, nicked fold downwards so that this lies flat against the bottom of the pan.

Cut a circle of paper slightly smaller than the bottom of the pan and drop it in over the nicked paper. Then brush the paper with melted fat. For rich cakes with long cooking times, line the pan with a double thickness of paper.

Lining a rectangular pan
Measure the length and width of the pan and add twice the pan's depth to each of these measurements. Cut a rectangle of wax paper to this size and place the pan squarely in the center. At each corner, make a cut from the angle of the paper as far as the corner of the pan.

Grease the inside of the pan and put in the paper so that it fits, closely overlapping at the corners. Brush the paper with melted fat.

LINING CAKE PANS

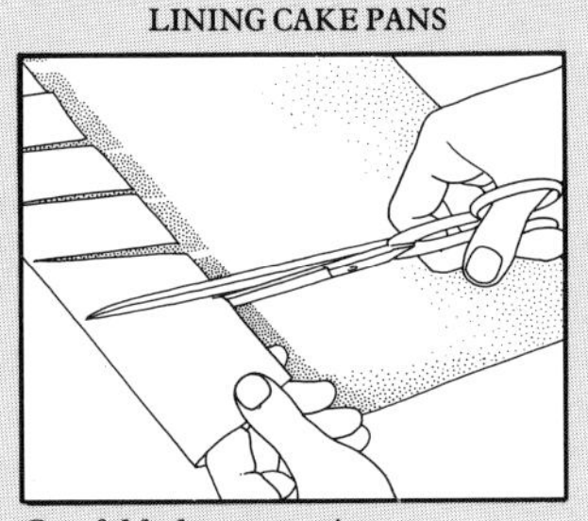
Cut folded paper strip

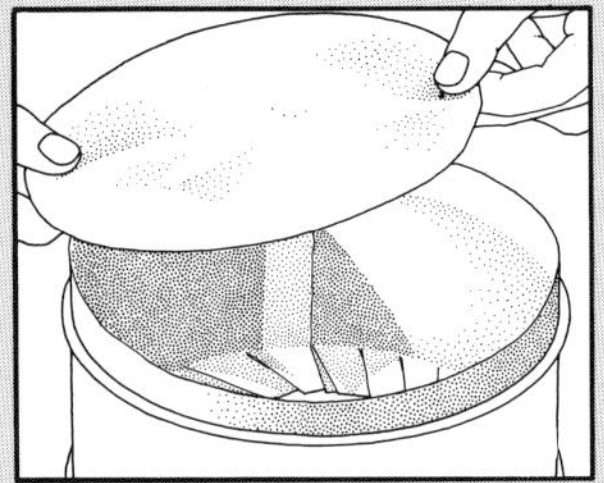
Cut a circle to fit bottom of pan

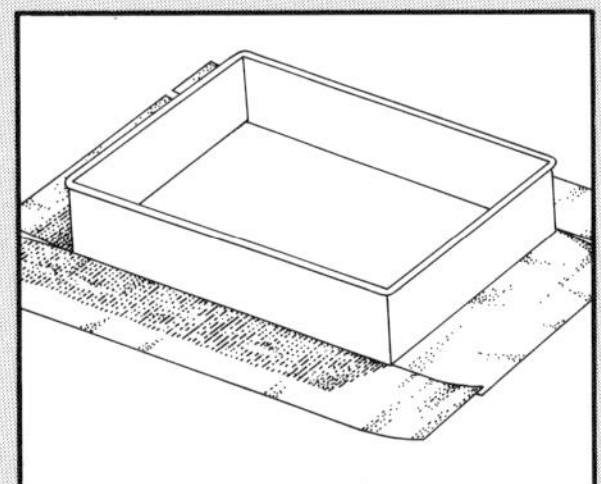
Center rectangular pan over paper

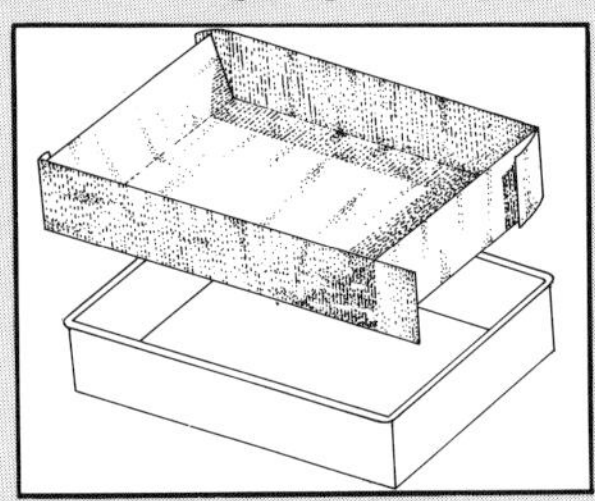
Cut and fold paper to fit pan

Oven positions
In gas ovens, the hottest shelf is at the top, but in electric ovens the heat is more evenly distributed. A cake is generally baked in the center of the oven.

When baking two cakes, place them side by side but do not let them touch the side of the oven or each other. If the pans are too large, bake the cakes on two oven shelves but avoid placing the pans directly over each other, and switch the pans around when the cake mixture has set.

Small cakes are usually baked above the center, but not at the top of the oven. Place the pans or patty pans on baking sheets before putting them in the oven.

Cooling cakes
With only a few exceptions, all cakes should be thoroughly cooled before being cut, frosted or stored. After baking, most cakes are best left to settle in their pans for 5–10 minutes before being turned out. Large cakes and rich fruit cakes are often left to get lukewarm before turning them out.

Run a spatula, small palette knife or round-bladed knife around the edge of the cake (do not use metal tools on non-stick pans). Place a wire rack over the cake and invert both the cake and rack, then lift the pan carefully. The lining paper may be peeled off or left on. Turn the cake with the aid of a second rack or the hand so that the top is uppermost. Leave the cake to cool completely on the wire rack. To prevent the wire mesh marking the surface of a soft-textured cake, first place a dish towel over the rack.

Storing cakes
Storage time depends on the type of cake. Generally, frosted cakes stay fresh longer than unfrosted cakes, and the more fat in the cake mixture the longer it keeps. Fatless sponges should

TURNING OUT CAKES

Run knife along inner edge of pan

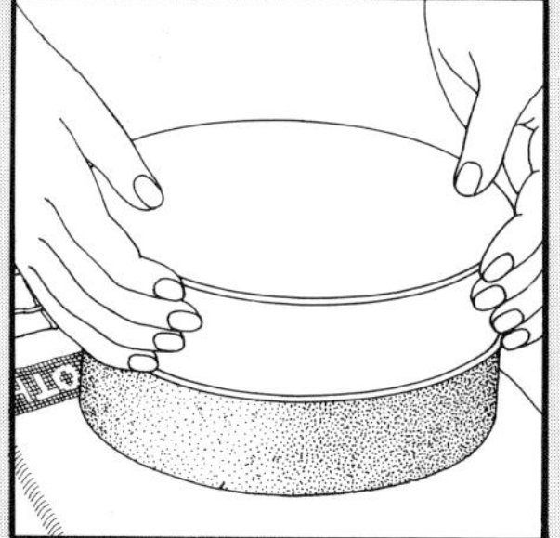

Invert cake onto covered rack

preferably be eaten on the day of baking.

Store both plain and frosted cakes in airtight cake tins or similar containers. Cream-filled cakes are best kept in the refrigerator. Wrap fruit cakes with the lining paper left on in kitchen foil before storing. If slightly warm when wrapped they retain the moisture better. Most cakes freeze well.

RUBBED-IN CAKES

These plain cakes are the easiest of all to make. As the proportion of fat to flour is half or less, rubbed-in mixtures are best eaten when fresh or within 2–3 days of baking. Rubbing in consists of blending flour and fat to a crumb-like mixture, using the fingertips.

To keep the mixture cool, raise the hands high when letting the crumbs drop back into the bowl. Shake the bowl occasionally to bring bigger crumbs to the surface. Make sure the texture is even, but do not handle more than necessary, or the crumbs will toughen and the fat become soft and oily.

The amount of liquid added can be critical: too much results in a doughy texture, whereas too little gives a crumbly cake which quickly dries out. For a large cake, the mixture should only just drop off the spoon when gently tapped. An example is the Tyrol cake on page 136.

CREAMED CAKES

These are all made from the basic method of blending fat with sugar. Put the cut up butter or margarine into a bowl large enough to allow the fat–and sugar–to be beaten vigorously without overflowing. With a wooden spoon, beat the fat against the sides of the bowl until soft; add the sugar and beat or cream the mixture until fluffy and pale yellow. After 7–10 minutes the volume should have increased greatly and the mixture should drop easily from the spoon. Eggs may be added whole or beaten.

If an electric mixer is used, set the dial at the speed suggested in the manufacturer's instructions, and allow 3–4 minutes for beating. Switch off the mixer from time to time and scrape the cake mixture down into the bowl. An example is the layer cake on page 133, or the farmhouse fruit cake on page 136.

CREAMED CAKE MIXTURE

Beat butter and sugar until fluffy

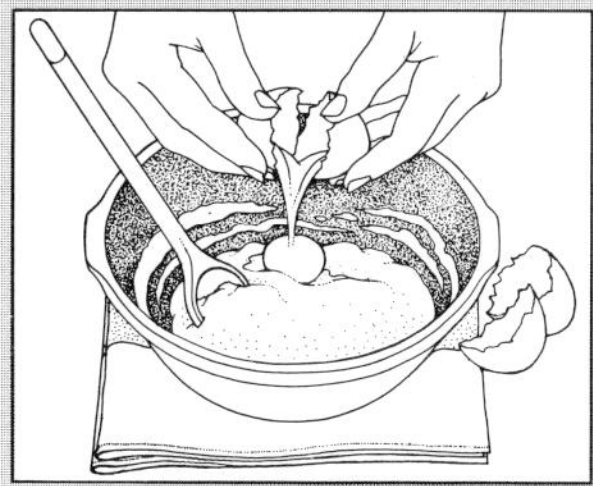

Break egg into mixture and stir

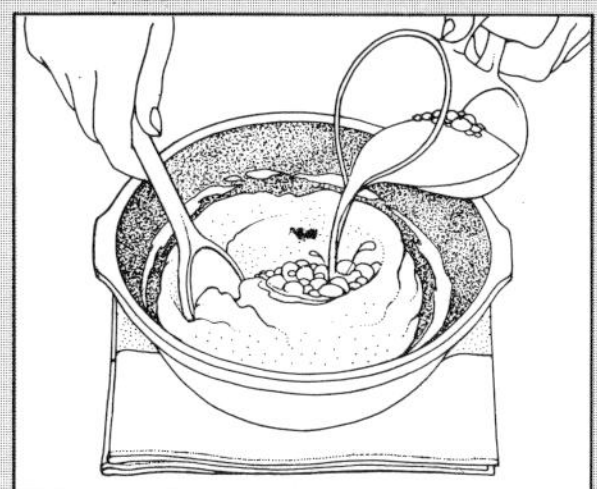

Alternatively, add beaten egg

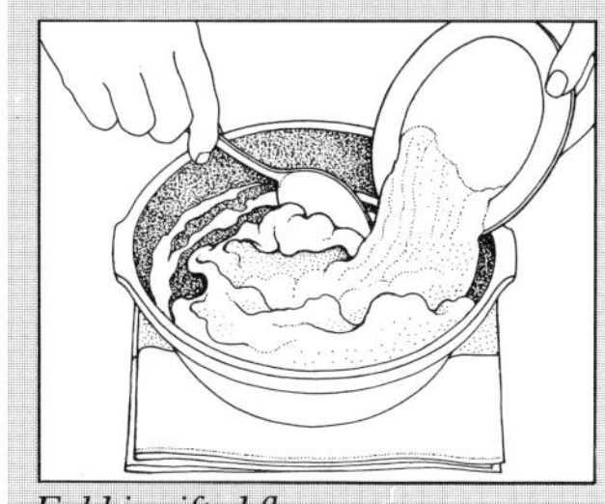

Fold in sifted flour

WHISKED CAKES

These are the lightest of all cake mixtures, their texture depending entirely on the incorporated eggs. The fatless cake mixture is used for sponges, which should be baked as soon as mixed.

Use a hand-operated, rotary or balloon whisk and to stabilize the mixture, place the deep bowl of eggs and sugar over hot, not boiling, water. Do not let the mixture become too hot or the sponge will have a tough texture. For a maximum rise, the mixture should be thick enough to leave a trail when the whisk is lifted. If an electric mixer is used, it is unnecessary to heat the bowl.

Blending in the flour is another important step. Sift the flour two or three times, the last time over the whisked egg mixture, then fold it carefully into the mixture without flattening the bulk. Use a metal spoon or rubber spatula in a figure-of-eight movement. An example is the strawberry cream sponge on page 134.

ENRICHED BUTTER SPONGE CAKES

When butter is added to a whisked sponge mixture, it is known as Genoese sponge, a richer variety than fatless sponges and one which needs slightly longer baking, but keeps better. Genoese sponge mixtures are used for gâteaux, layered with cream and fruit, or baked and cut into small individual cakes before being iced and decorated.

MELTED CAKES

These have a dense, slightly tacky texture and a consistency similar to a thick batter. Molasses or syrup is a major ingredient, with baking powder as the main leavening agent together with baking soda. An example is the gingerbread on page 133.

Fats and Oils

Fats and oils play an important part in cooking, as they contribute to or sometimes alter the flavor of food, especially when frying. The term "fat" can be taken generally to include all fatty substances, but it can also mean those which are solid at room temperature, those which are liquid being called "oils." Conveniently, this division more or less coincides with the division into saturated and unsaturated fats.

FATS

These are mainly derived from animal foods, such as meat and dairy products, but can also be produced from oily fish, nuts and vegetables.

Butter
Butter is made from the fatty substances skimmed from full cream milk. It is churned and then pressed to squeeze out water, and sometimes salt is added. It is used as the cooking medium for egg dishes and for sautéing and shallow frying over moderate heat. It is not suitable for frying at high temperatures as it burns easily, but a mixture of oil and butter will withstand quite a high heat without turning black.

Clarified butter
This can be heated to a much higher temperature than ordinary butter without burning, and is therefore more suitable for frying and also for brushing food, for example fish, that is to be broiled. It is an expensive cooking medium, as 1 pound of butter produces only about 10 ounces of clarified butter. To make it, melt the butter in a small pan over gentle heat and cook without stirring until the butter begins to foam. Continue to cook without letting it brown until the foaming stops. Remove the pan from the heat and let it stand until the milky deposits have sunk to the bottom, leaving a clear yellow liquid. Pour this carefully through cheesecloth into a bowl. Clarified butter can be used in liquid or solid form and will keep for several weeks in the refrigerator.

Maître d'hôtel butter
A popular garnish for broiled meat or fish. Blend a tablespoon of finely chopped parsley with ½ cup of softened butter and season to taste with salt, freshly ground pepper and a few drops of lemon juice. Other herbs, such as tarragon, chervil or chives, can also be used.

Drippings
This is the rendered fat from beef, bacon, pork or poultry. A roast or bird will usually yield quite a lot, or it can be bought already rendered down. As it has a fairly high water content, it tends to splatter and is better used for roasting and shallow-frying than for deep-frying.

Lard
This is processed from pure pork fat and is excellent for frying. It is also used in baking some pastries and cakes.

Margarine
Made from vegetable oils blended with milk and vitamins, and sometimes with butter, margarine is interchangeable with butter for baking purposes and for sautéing.

Shortening
That sold under various brand names in cans is usually composed of oils, such as soybean, corn or peanut, made solid by incorporating hydrogen into them, which also improves the keeping qualities. Some shortening is a combination of vegetable and animal or dairy fats. Use for sautéing, deep-frying and for baking.

Suet
Suet is the fat deposit from the loins and around the kidneys of beef or sheep. It is sold fresh for grating or already shredded and packed; it can be used in pastries, puddings and stuffings.

OILS

Edible oils are derived from fish, vegetables, cereals, fruit, nuts and seeds. They vary in color and flavor, and choice is a matter of individual taste. Cold-pressed oil is the most natural (and most expensive) form, smelling and tasting strongly of its origin. Refined oil (often misleadingly called "pure") has had most of the vitamins and virtue bleached out or otherwise chemically removed, although some vitamins may be added back.

Corn oil
Fairly inexpensive and a good all-purpose oil with a mild taste.

Olive oil
Valued for its distinctive fruity taste and its affinity with certain foods. Suitable for frying and also for salad dressings: for these the best, but alas expensive, is the first pressing, also known as virgin oil.

Peanut oil
Also known as groundnut or arachide oil, this is a pleasant-tasting oil which will withstand quite high heat without burning.

Safflower oil
Expensive, but often recommended for a cholesterol-lowering diet as it is extremely high in polyunsaturated fats and in particular linoleic acid, the one essential fatty acid which cannot be manufactured by the body.

Sesame oil
Made from sesame seeds, this has a distinctive taste. It is much used in the Middle East for baking and also makes a good salad dressing.

Soy oil
A neutral-tasting oil, this is high in polyunsaturates and not too expensive.

Sunflower oil
An excellent all-round oil: can be used for frying and for salad dressings, high in polyunsaturates but cheaper than safflower oil.

Walnut oil
Very expensive; its strong nutty taste is much appreciated in salad dressings.

A to Z of Cooking Terms

A

acidulated water Cold water with a little lemon juice or vinegar added: this prevents discoloration of some fruits and vegetables
al dente Of pasta; cooked – but firm to the bite
antipasti Cold or hot Italian hors-d'oeuvre
arrowroot Starch made by grinding the root of a plant of the same name. Used for thickening sauces
au gratin Cooked food, covered with a sauce, sprinkled with crumbs or grated cheese, dotted with butter and browned under the broiler

B

bain marie 1. A large pan of hot water, or 'bath,' in which a smaller pan is placed for cooking contents or to keep foods warm. 2. A double boiler
beating Mixing food to introduce air, to make it lighter and fluffier, using a wooden spoon, hand whisk or electric mixer
binding Adding eggs, cream or fat to a dry mixture to hold it together
blanching Boiling briefly 1. To loosen the skin from nuts, fruit and vegetables. 2. To set the color of food and to kill enzymes prior to freezing. 3. To remove strong or bitter flavors
blending Combining ingredients with a spoon, beater or liquidizer to achieve a uniform mixture
boiling Cooking in liquid at a temperature of 212°F (100°C)
bouquet garni A bunch of herbs, including parsley, thyme, marjoram, bay, etc., tied with string; or a ready-made mixture of herbs in cheesecloth
braising Browning in hot fat and then cooking slowly, in a covered pot, with vegetables and a little liquid
brine Salt and water solution used for pickling and preserving
brioche Soft bread made of rich yeast dough, slightly sweetened
brûlé(e) Applied to dishes such as cream custards finished with caramelized sugar glaze

C

cannelloni Large macaroni tubes, stuffed with savory fillings
capers Pickled flower buds of the Mediterranean caper bush
casserole 1. Cooking pot, complete with lid, made of ovenproof or flameproof earthenware, glass or metal. 2. Also, a slow-cooked stew of meat, fish or vegetables
champignon Mushroom; champignon de Paris, cultivated button mushroom
charlotte 1. Hot, molded fruit pudding made of buttered slices of bread and filled with fruit cooked with apricot jam. 2. Cold, molded dessert consisting of ladyfingers and filled with cream and fruit, or a cream custard set with gelatin
charlotte mold A plain mold for charlottes and other desserts, sometimes used for molded salads
chilling Cooling food, without freezing it, in the refrigerator
clarified butter Butter cleared of water and impurities by slow melting and filtering
cocotte Small ovenproof, earthenware, porcelain or metal dish, used for baking individual egg dishes, mousses or soufflés
colander Perforated metal or plastic basket used for draining away liquids
compôte Dessert of fresh or dried fruit, cooked in syrup and served cold
concassé Roughly chopped. Applied to vegetables, such as tomatoes
conserve Whole fruit preserved by boiling with sugar and used like jam
cornstarch Finely ground flour from corn, which is used for thickening sauces, puddings, etc.
crème Applied to fresh cream, butter and custard creams, and thick soup
crème brûlée Cream custard with caramelized topping
crème caramel Cold molded egg custard with caramel topping
crème fraîche Cream that has been allowed to mature but not to go sour
creole Of Caribbean cooking; prepared with pimientos, tomatoes, okra, rice and spicy sauces
crêpe Large, thin pancake
crêpes Suzette Crêpes cooked in orange sauce and flamed in liqueur
crimping Making a decorative border to pie crusts
croûtes 1. Pastry covering meat, fish and vegetables. 2. Slices of bread or brioche, spread with butter or sauce, and baked until crisp
curd Semi-solid part of milk, produced by souring
curdle 1. To cause fresh milk or a sauce to separate into solids and liquids by overheating or by adding acid. 2. To cause creamed butter and sugar in a cake recipe to separate by adding the eggs too rapidly

D

dariole Small, cup-shaped mold used for making puddings, sweet and savory gelatins, and creams
dice Cut into small cubes
dough Mixture of flour, water, milk and/or egg, sometimes enriched with fat, which is firm enough to knead, roll and shape
dredging Sprinkling food with flour or sugar
dusting Sprinkling lightly with flour, sugar, spice or seasoning

E

éclair Light, oblong choux pastry split and filled with cream, usually topped with chocolate icing
en croûte Encased in pastry
entremets Sweet or pudding

F

fines herbes Mixture of finely chopped fresh parsley, chervil, tarragon and chives
flambé Flamed; e.g. food tossed in a pan to which burning brandy or other alcohol has been added
folding in Enveloping one ingredient or mixture in another, using a large metal spoon or spatula
fool Cold dessert consisting of fruit purée and whipped cream
freezing Solidifying or preserving food by chilling and storing it at 32°F (0°C) or lower

G

garnishing Enhancing a dish with edible decorations
gelatin Transparent protein, made from animal bones and tissue, which melts in hot liquid and forms a jelly when cold.
génoise A rich sponge cake consisting of eggs, sugar, flour and melted butter; baked in a flat pan
ghee Clarified butter made from the milk of the water buffalo
glacé Glazed, frozen or iced
glaze A glossy finish given to food by brushing with beaten egg, milk, sugar syrup or jelly after cooking
gnocchi Small dumplings made from semolina or potatoes
granita Water ice
griddle Flat metal plate used to bake breads and cakes on top of the stove

H

hard sauce Sweet butter sauce flavored with brandy, rum or whiskey, which is chilled until hard, and melts when served on hot puddings
herbs Plants without a woody stem, used for their aromatic properties
hors-d'oeuvre Hot or cold appetizers served at the start of a meal
hulling Removing green calyx from strawberries and raspberries, etc.

I

icing Sweet coating for cakes
infusing Steeping herbs, tea leaves or coffee in water or other liquid to extract the flavor

L

langue de chat Flat, finger-shaped cookie served with cold desserts
lasagne Wide ribbon noodles, sometimes colored green
leaven Substance, such as yeast, which causes dough or batter to rise
legumes Plants with seed pods, such as peas and beans
lentils Seeds of a legume, soaked and used in soups, stews and purées

A to Z of Cooking Terms

M

macaroni Tubular-shaped pasta of varying lengths and shapes
macédoine Mixture of prepared fruit or vegetables
macerate To soften food by soaking it in liquid
meringue Whisked egg white blended with sugar
mirabelle 1. Small yellow plum, used as tart filling. 2. A liqueur made from this fruit
mousse Light sweet or savory cold dish made with cream, whipped egg white and gelatin

N

niçoise In the Nice style, e.g. cooked with tomatoes, onion, garlic and black olives
noodles Flat ribbon pasta made from flour, water and egg
nouilles Noodles

P

paella Dish of saffron rice, chicken and shellfish
paprika Ground, sweet red pepper
par-boiling Boiling for a short time to cook food partially
parfait Frozen dessert made of whipped cream and fruit purée
pasta Paste made with flour and water, sometimes enriched with egg and oil
pastry Dough made with flour, butter and water and baked or deep-fried
pastry wheel Small, serrated wooden or metal wheel for cutting and fluting pastry
pearl barley De-husked barley grains, used in soup
pectin Substance extracted from fruit and vegetables. Used to set jellies and jams
petits pois Tiny young green peas
pilaf, pilau Near-eastern dish of cooked rice mixed with spiced, cooked meat, chicken or fish
pimiento Green or red sweet pepper
pipe To force meringue icing, savory butter, potato purée, etc., through a pastry bag fitted with a tube, to decorate various dishes
pizza Open-faced pie consisting of a yeast dough topped with tomatoes, cheese, anchovies and olives
poaching Cooking food in simmering liquid, just below boiling point
polenta Corn meal, or flour made from maize, dried and ground
potage Thick soup
pot barley Whole barley grains, containing the bran and germ
praline Sweet consisting of unblanched almonds caramelized in boiling sugar
preserving Keeping food in good condition by treating with chemicals, heat, refrigeration, pickling in salt or boiling in sugar
pudding Baked or boiled sweet dessert
purée 1. Sieved raw or cooked food. 2. Thick vegetable soup which is passed through a sieve or an electric liquidizer

Q

quiche Open-faced pastry case filled with a savory or sweet mixture

R

ratafia 1. Flavoring made from bitter almonds. 2. Liqueur made from fruit kernels. 3. Tiny macaroon
ratatouille Stew of eggplants, onions, peppers and tomatoes cooked in olive oil
ravioli Small savory-filled pasta envelopes
reducing Concentrating a liquid by boiling and evaporation
rennet Substance extracted from the stomach lining of calves. Used to coagulate milk for junket and for making cheese curd
rigatoni Ribbed macaroni
risotto Savory rice, fried and then cooked in stock; often finished with cheese

S

sauté To fry food rapidly in shallow, hot fat, tossing and turning it until evenly browned
savarin Rich yeast cake, which is baked in a ring mold and soaked in liqueur-flavored syrup
scald 1. To heat milk or cream to just below boiling point. 2. To plunge fruit or vegetables in boiling water to remove the skins
scallion Young onion with an undeveloped bulb
seasoned flour Flour flavored with salt and pepper
seasoning Salt, pepper, spices or herbs which are added to food to improve flavor
sherbet Water ice made with fruit juice or purée
sifting Passing flour or sugar through a sieve to remove lumps
simmering Cooking in liquid which is heated to just below boiling point
skimming Removing cream from the surface of milk, or fat or scum from broth or jam
soufflé Baked dish consisting of a sauce or purée, which is thickened with egg yolks into which stiffly beaten egg whites are folded
soufflé dish Straight-sided circular dish used for cooking and serving soufflés
spaghetti Solid strands of pasta
spring-form mold Baking pan with hinged sides, held together by a metal clamp or pin, which is opened to release the cake or pie
starch Carbohydrate obtained from cereal and potatoes
steaming Cooking food in the steam rising from boiling water
sterilizing Destroying germs by exposing food to heat
stewing Simmering food slowly in a covered pan or casserole
straining Separating liquids from solids by passing them through a sieve or through cheesecloth
strudel Thin leaves of pastry, filled with sweet or savory mixtures, which are rolled up and baked
syllabub Cold dessert of sweetened thick cream, white wine, sherry or fruit juice
syrup A thick sweet liquid made by boiling sugar with water and/or fruit juice

T

tagliatelle Thin flat egg noodles
timbale 1. Cup-shaped earthenware or metal mold. 2. Dish prepared in such a mold
truffles Rare mushroom-like fungus, black or white in color, with a firm texture and delicate taste. Expensive delicacies, truffles are mainly used for garnishing
tube pan Ring-shaped pan for baking cakes
tutti frutti Dried or candied mixed fruits, added to ice cream

U

unleavened bread Bread made without a leavening agent which, when baked, is thin, flat and round

V

vanilla sugar Sugar flavored with vanilla by enclosing it with a vanilla bean in a closed jar
velouté 1. Basic white sauce made with chicken, veal or fish stock. 2. Soup of creamy consistency
vermicelli Very fine strands of pasta
vinaigrette Mixture of oil, vinegar, salt and pepper, which is sometimes flavored with herbs

W

wafer Thin cookie made with rice flour; served with ice cream
waffle Batter cooked on a hot greased waffle iron
whey Liquid which separates from the curd when milk curdles. Used in cheese-making
whipping Beating eggs until frothy or cream until thick
whisk Looped wire utensil used to beat air into eggs, cream or batters

Y

yeast Fungus cells used to produce alcoholic fermentation, or to cause dough to rise
yogurt Curdled milk which has been treated with bacteria.

Z

zest Colored oily outer skin of citrus fruit which, when grated or peeled, is used to flavor foods and liquids
zester Small tool for scraping off zest

Index

Q

R

The Good Health Cookbooks

The Publishers wish to express their gratitude for major contributions by the following people:

Editor: URSULA WHYTE
Art Director: MICHAEL McGUINNESS
Designer: SANDRA DEON-CARDYN
Diet Consultant: MIRIAM POLUNIN
Home Economist: VALERIE BARRETT
Additional Photography: PHILIP DOWELL
Editorial Adviser: NORMA MACMILLAN

The Publishers also wish to acknowledge the help of the following:

Gilly Abrahams for editorial help; Fred and Kathie Gill for proof reading; Mary-Anne Joy for help with calorie counting; Terri Lamb and Carole Perks for design assistance; Vicki Robinson for indexing; and Michelle Thompson for food preparation. Additional photographic props were supplied by Graham and Green. The recipe for gluten-free pastry on page 10 is based on one from Rita Greer's Gluten-free Cooking (Thorsons Publishers Ltd, 1983). The recipe for low-fat pastry on page 95 comes from Miriam Polunin's The New Cookbook (Barrons Educational Series Inc).

The Good Health Cookbooks are based on CREATIVE COOKING, **to which the following made major contributions:**

Chief Editorial Advisers: JAMES A. BEARD, ELIZABETH POMEROY, JOSÉ WILSON
Photographers: PHILIP DOWELL, ALBERT GOMMI
Home Economists: HELEN FEINGOLD, JOY MACHELL
Stylist: KATHY IMMERMAN

Writers:

Ena Bruinsma
Margaret Coombes
Derek Cooper
Margaret Costa
Denis Curtis
Theodora FitzGibbon
Nina Froud
Jane Grigson
Nesta Hollis
Kenneth H. C. Lo
Elizabeth Pomeroy
Zena Skinner
Katie Stewart
Marika Hanbury Tenison
Silvino S. Trompetto, MBE
Suzanne Wakelin
Kathie Webber
Harold Wilshaw

Artists:

Color:
Roy Coombs
Pauline Ellison
Hargrave Hands
Denys Ovenden
Charles Pickard
Josephine Ranken
Charles Raymond
Rodney Shackell
Faith Shannon, MBE
John Wilson

Black and white:
David Baird
Brian Delf
Gary Hincks
Richard Jacobs
Rodney Shackell
Michael Woods
Sidney Woods

Black and white photography:
Michael Newton

Typesetting: Tradespools Ltd, Frome **Printing and Binding:** William Collins Ltd, Glasgow